México's Nobodies

México's Nobodies

SUNY series, Genders in the Global South

Debra A. Castillo and Shelley Feldman, editors

México's Nobodies

The Cultural Legacy of the Soldadera and Afro-Mexican Women

B. Christine Arce

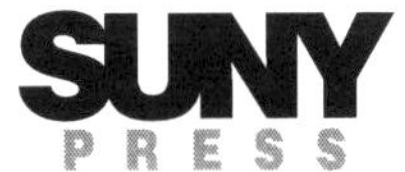

Published by State University of New York Press, Albany

For information, contact State University of New York Press, Albany, NY
www.sunypress.edu

Production, Diane Ganeles
Marketing, Michael Campochiaro

Library of Congress Cataloging-in-Publication Data

Names: Arce, B. Christine, 1974– author.
Title: México's nobodies : the cultural legacy of the soldadera and
  Afro-Mexican women / B. Christine Arce.
Description: Albany : State University of New York Press, 2017. | Series:
  SUNY series, Genders in the global South | Includes bibliographical
  references and index.
Identifiers: LCCN 2016021650 (print) | LCCN 2016053183 (ebook) | ISBN
  9781438463575 (hardcover : alkaline paper) | ISBN 9781438463582 (pbk. :
  alk. paper) | ISBN 9781438463599 (e-book)
Subjects: LCSH: Women—Mexico—History. | Women, Black—Mexico—History. |
  Racially mixed women—Mexico—History. | Women soldiers—Mexico—History.
  | Women revolutionaries—Mexico—History. | Sex role—Mexico—History. |
  Mexico—Race relations. | Women in art. | Blacks in art. | Art and
  society—Mexico—History.
Classification: LCC HQ1462.A63 2017 (print) | LCC HQ1462 (ebook) | DDC
  305.40972—dc23

I dedicate this book to the spirit and living memory of my father, Simeón Arce González, who did not make it to the end, but tried his best; to my grandmother Carmen González Razo, who is now reunited with her son, and was as strong and resilient as the soldaderas; and to my best friend, grandma Christine Dow Retelsdorf.

Contents

List of Illustrations ix

Acknowledgments xv

Introduction: The Paradox of Invisibility 1

**Part One: *Entre Adelitas y Cucarachas*:
The Soldadera as Trope in the Mexican Revolution**

Chapter 1
Soldaderas and the Making of Revolutionary Spaces 37

Chapter 2
The Many Faces of the Soldadera and the Adelita Complex 79

Chapter 3
Beyond the "Custom of Her Sex and Country" 115

Part Two: The Blacks in the Closet

Chapter 4
Black Magic and the Inquisition: The Legend of La Mulata
de Córdoba and the Case of Antonia de Soto 147

Chapter 5
"Dios pinta como quiere": Blackness and Redress in Mexican
Golden Age Film 185

Chapter 6
The Music of the Afro-Mexican Universe and the
Dialectics of *Son*   225

Conclusion: To Be Expressed Otherwise   273

Notes   283

Bibliography   301

Index   317

Illustrations

Fig. 1.1 "Soldaderas on the platform at the Buenavista train station," México City, D.F., April 1912; Gerónimo Hernández. © #5670 CONACULTA. INAH.SINAFO. FN.MÉXICO, Archivo Casasola. Dry gelatin plate. 38

Fig. 1.2 "Soldier and soldaderas on the roof of railcar," México City, D.F., 1914. © #474156, CONACULTA. INAH. SINAFO.FN.MÉXICO, Archivo Casasola. Silver impression over gelatin. 42

Fig. 1.3 "Soldaderas prepare food on the roof of a railcar," México City, D.F., 1914. © #6388 CONACULTA. INAH. SINAFO.FN.MÉXICO, Archivo Casasola. Nitrate film negative. 44

Fig. 1.4 "Federal soldiers and their families on the roof of the railcars," México City, D.F., 1914. © #5600 CONACULTA. INAH.SINAFO.FN.MÉXICO, Archivo Casasola. Dry gelatin plate. 46

Fig. 1.5 "Soldier and soldaderas in a train car," México, 1914. © #474156 CONACULTA. INAH.SINAFO.FN. MÉXICO, Archivo Casasola. Silver impression over gelatin. 48

Fig. 1.6 "Federal soldiers, soldaderas and the railway administrator on the platform of the train," México City, D.F., April 1913. © #6293 CONACULTA. INAH.SINAFO.FN.MÉXICO, Archivo Casasola. Dry gelatin plate. 49

Fig. 1.7   "Madero's troops in the patios of Buenavista train
             station," México City, D.F., 1910. © #5774
             CONACULTA. INAH.SINAFO.FN.MÉXICO,
             Archivo Casasola. Dry gelatin plate.   51

Fig. 1.8   "Troops and their families watching an opera
             presented to the Army troops," México City, D.F.,
             October 10, 1921. © #6399 CONACULTA. INAH.
             SINAFO.FN.MÉXICO, Archivo Casasola. Nitrate film
             negative.   52

Fig. 1.9   "Soldaderas at a military camp," México City, D.F.,
             1914. © #5886 CONACULTA. INAH.SINAFO.FN.
             MÉXICO, Archivo Casasola. Nitrate film negative.   53

Fig. 1.10   "Soldaderas departing from the 'Piedad' Barracks of
             the 180th Batallion with carts and artillery," México
             City, D.F., 1914. © #6234 CONACULTA. INAH.
             SINAFO.FN.MÉXICO, Archivo Casasola. Dry gelatin
             plate.   55

Fig. 1.11   "Portrait of a revolutionary girl holding a rifle,"
             México City, D.F., 1913. © #33348 CONACULTA.
             INAH. SINAFO.FN.MÉXICO, Archivo Casasola.
             Negative of security film.   57

Fig. 1.12   "Zapatista soldaderas in Xochimilco," August 1914,
             México City, D.F. © #451107 CONACULTA. INAH.
             SINAFO.FN.MÉXICO, Archivo Casasola. Silver
             impression over gelatin.   60

Fig. 1.13   "Soldaderas in firing position against the men of
             José Inés Chávez García," Michoacán, México, 1917.
             © #63945 CONACULTA. INAH. SINAFO.FN.MÉXICO,
             Archivo Casasola. Negative of security film. In
             Photographing the Mexican Revolution, John Mraz identifies
             original image as follows: "Soldaderas learning how to
             defend themselves," Ario, Michocán, February 1914;
             J. Guerrero, *La Ilustración Semanal*, March 3, 1914.   61

Fig. 1.14   "Portrait of the revolutionary Coronela Amelio Robles,
             smoking in a room," México City, D.F., 1914. © #33492

CONACULTA. INAH. SINAFO.FN.MÉXICO, Archivo
Casasola. Gelatin over nitrate film. 63

Fig. 1.15 "Soldadera kisses a soldier," México City, D.F., 1913.
© #6212 CONACULTA. INAH. SINAFO.FN.MÉXICO,
Archivo Casasola. Dry gelatin plate. Agustín and Gustavo
Casasola caption this image as "Soldadera congratulates
her 'Juan' for returning unscathed after the Battle of
Rellano" in *Historia Gráfica de la Revolución* (447). 67

Fig. 1.16 "Soldadera with flag and sword in a train station,"
México 1914. © #287639 CONACULTA. INAH.
SINAFO.FN.MÉXICO, Archivo Casasola. Security film. 69

Fig. 1.17 "Soldaderas on the platform at the Buenavista train
station," México City, D.F., April 1912; Gerónimo
Hernández. © #5670 CONACULTA. INAH.SINAFO.
FN.MÉXICO, Archivo Casasola. Dry gelatin plate. 72

Fig. 1.18 "Revolutionaries and soldaderas," México, 1915.
© #186449 CONACULTA. INAH. SINAFO.FN.MÉXICO,
Archivo Casasola. Series: Emiliano Zapata. Security film. 75

Fig. 2.1 "A soldier says goodbye to his wife at the Buenavista
train station," México City, D.F., 1913. © #6094
CONACULTA. INAH. SINAFO.FN.MÉXICO,
Archivo Casasola. Dry gelatin plate. 86

Fig. 2.2 "Valentina Ramírez, soldadera," Sinaloa, México, 1911.
© #68115 CONACULTA. INAH. SINAFO.FN.MÉXICO,
Archivo Casasola. Nitrate film negative. 88

Fig. 2.3 "Federal soldier says goodbye to a woman," México City,
D.F., 1914. © #6342 CONACULTA. INAH. SINAFO.
FN.MÉXICO, Archivo Casasola. Dry gelatin plate. 102

Fig. 3.1 "Federal Soldier and his family," México City, D.F.,
1915. © #5015 CONACULTA. INAH. SINAFO.
FN.MÉXICO, Archivo Casasola. Dry gelatin plate. 115

Fig. 3.2 "Carmen Robles, soldadera," México 1913. © #186387
CONACULTA. INAH.SINAFO.FN.MÉXICO, Archivo
Casasola. Dry gelatin plate. While the Fototeca has
identified this image as Carmen Robles, the name of this

woman is still under debate. For example, the Casasola
brothers and the Chicago Museum of Mexican Art
identify this image as, "Portrait of a Female Soldier from
Michoacán, 1910" (242).   138

Fig. 5.1   "Revolutionaries and soldadera in front of a home,"
              México, 1914. © #33833 CONACULTA. INAH. SINAFO.
              FN.MÉXICO, Archivo Casasola. Nitrate film negative. In
              Photographing the Mexican Revolution John Mraz identifies
              this image as "Zapatista colonel Carmen Robles, Guerrero,
              ca. 1913." Likewise, Agustín and Gustavo Casasola identify
              her as revolutionary leader Carmen Robles with her
              chief officers after the battle of Iguala, Guerrero (750).   188

Fig. 6.1   "Toña la Negra in publicity poster for her first tour of
              Cuba at the beginning of the 1940s." Courtesy of the
              Fototeca of Veracruz/IVEC, n.d.   226

Fig. 6.2   "Toña la Negra next to the carnival court of the 'ugly'
              King." Courtesy of the Fototeca of Veracruz/IVEC, n.d.   250

Fig. 6.3   "Toña la Negra and Celia Cruz." Courtesy of the
              Fototeca of Veracruz/IVEC and Rafael Figueroa, n.d.   253

Fig. 6.4   "Toña la Negra in publicity photo from her early
              period." Courtesy of the Fototeca of Veracruz/IVEC, n.d.   254

Fig. 6.5   "Toña la Negra and Agustín Lara enjoying the applause
              after a performance in Veracruz." Courtesy of the
              Fototeca of Veracruz/IVEC, n.d.   255

Fig. 6.6   "Toña la Negra playing Marta la mulata alongside
              Antonieta Pons, one of the famous Cuban rumberas
              in the film *Konga Roja*," 1943. Courtesy of Filmoteca
              of the UNAM #1061-10.   258

Fig. 6.7   "Toña la Negra at the piano." Courtesy of the Fototeca
              of Veracruz/IVEC, n.d.   261

Fig. 6.8   "Toña la Negra between Pedro Vargas (left) and
              Agustín Lara (right), in the film dedicated to Lara's
              love life, *Mujeres en mi vida*," 1949. Courtesy of the
              Filmoteca of the UNAM #1364-38.   264

Fig. 6.9   "Toña la Negra singing with Agustín Lara in the film, *La mujer que yo amé*," 1950. Courtesy of the Filmoteca of the UNAM #3193-8.   266

Fig. 6.10   "Toña la Negra accompanied by Son Clave de Oro in another landmark *rumbera* film, *Humo en los ojos*," 1946. Her face is visibly whitened for this performance despite wearing traditional *jarocha* dress. Courtesy of the Filmoteca of the UNAM #2467-8.   269

Fig. C.1   Foreground: Installation of "Kevlar Fighting Costumes." Left Background: "Soldadera" film installation. Right background: "Kevlar rebozo," Vincent Price Art Museum, Los Angeles California, May 16–August 1, 2015. Courtesy of artist Nao Bustamante. Photo by Dale Griner.   000

Fig. C.2   "Installation piece 'Chac-Mool.' Video still of Leandra Becerra Lumbreras drumming." Vincent Price Art Museum, Los Angeles California, May 16–August 1, 2015. Courtesy of artist Nao Bustamante.   000

Fig. C.3   "Chac-Mool contraption." The viewfinder exhibits video loop of Leandra Becerra Lumbreras drumming. Vincent Price Art Museum, Los Angeles California, May 16–August 1, 2015. Courtesy of artist Nao Bustamante. Photo by Dale Griner.   000

Acknowledgments

This book would have been impossible without the stalwart support of my family, my incredible mother Bridget, father Simeón, sister Lisa Carmen, grandmother Christine, partner Carlos, and son Santiago. My mother and Lisa rearranged their lives in order to take turns watching my son so that I could work, a sacrifice I will never forget, and without which the book in its present form would have been impossible. I am proud, indeed honored, by how many people contributed to this project and whose influence and acuity helped me to formulate the ideas presented here, and I apologize to anyone who is not mentioned by name. First and foremost, Francine Masiello and José Rabasa both saw this project evolve from a dissertation into the book you now hold. Francine's love of poetry wove its way into my readings, as did her keen perspective and ability to pull apart incomplete ideas, and equally amazing talent to help you build them back up again. She is the epitome of what it means to be a mentor, guide, interlocutor, and friend. I continue to learn from her grace, robust humor, and creativity. José's intellectual generosity and passion, his theories of knowledge and subalternity were seminal to the shape my work would take and some of the core ideas I put forth in this book. I am forever in their debt.

This book passed through the hands of many brilliant people and in the course of its itinerancy improved it in innumerable ways. I'd like to thank George Yúdice for his careful and painstaking reading of every chapter, providing rigorous insights and necessary criticisms; he too was an exemplary mentor, colleague, and amazing friend whose dedication and support has been a source of admiration. All of my colleagues at the University of Miami deserve special mention; but in particular, Subha Xavier, Lillian Manzor, Elena Grau-Lleveria, Gema Pérez Sánchez, Cristina Civantos, Andrew Lynch, Yvonne Gavela, Eduardo Negueruela, Joel Nickels, Donette Francis, and Tracy Devine Guzmán. I am indebted to Doris Careaga and Sara Gusky for their fine work, which, in turn, kept me inspired. Infinite thanks to my friend, comadre, and interlocutor Anna Deeny Morales for reading many iterations of the introduction and providing her creative, poetic, and unrelenting eye. My gratitude to the fierce women of SWAG who helped me recover my voice and situate myself in the process—Dania Abreu-Torres, Michelle Nasser, and the unstoppable Zeli Rivas. All inspiring women of color whose scholarship and insights were critical for the development of this book over the course of many years of lucha y comadraje.

A heartfelt thanks to John Sullivan of IDIEZ, whose sociolinguistic insights on Náhuatl and indigenous thought in general provided the armature for many of the ideas present in this book. Many programs and institutions deserve special mention for supporting the research that went into this project: the UC Berkeley Department of Spanish and Portuguese, the UC Berkeley Center for Race and Gender for a fellowship that allowed me to conduct the initial research for the second part of the book, the University of Miami Center for the Humanities faculty fellowship that allowed me to streamline the manuscript, and the members of the group who read early versions of the first part of the book. Thanks to John Funchion for turning me on to Rancière and to Tim Watson for his careful comments. In addition, the University of Miami Max Orovitz and Provost research fellowship allowed me to travel on two separate occasions to conduct research in México at the Archivo General de la Nación.

Infinite gratitude to Rafael Figueroa who made all of the images of Toña la Negra available to me in addition to helping me locate obscure material; he is a wonderful collaborator and friend. Many thanks to Julio Ramos for his generous, thorough, and invaluable readings of chapters 4 and 6, which he finished in record time. A debt of gratitude to José Salgado, whose support of this project was critical and whose brilliant insights are unmatched. There are countless people who have contributed to my project along the way by engaging in vital and enriching dialogues that helped me formulate and solidify my arguments: Sonia Montes, José Amador, Damon Scott, Constanza Svidler, Heather McMichael, Nadia Celis, Kristen Block, Rakhel Villamil-Acera, Arturo Motta, Ifeona Fulani, and Gabriela Erandi Rico-Spears. To my soldaderas in arms, Sonia Barrios Tinoco, whose intellectual support and friendship has been unwielding, to Sarah Schoellkopf, whose vitality and emotional support pushed me forward, and to Beatriz Castro-Ferrer, I owe my renewed spirit. Thanks to Vivianne Mahieux, whose readings were incisive and whose enthusiasm was a personal and professional source of energy. I thank all the other anonymous readers who helped tighten what was at times unwieldy and whose superb insights have enriched the book beyond measure. A special debt of gratitude to my editor Beth Bouloukos for her support, brilliance, and patience, and to the series editors of Genders in the Global South, Debra A. Castillo and Shelley Feldman, whose scholarship I have admired greatly for many years; it is an honor for me to be included in their series. Warm thanks to my friends Jessica Munoz and Lee Davis for reading early versions of the first chapters and for their personal support during this process. For the encouragement of all my friends, who either sent me messages or provided childcare so I could squeeze in a few more hours, your help will never be forgotten: Karina Xavier, Claudia Pozo, Marina Crouse, Megan Garber, Carla and Tom, Joy Regueira, Vicki Woods, Sweetjoy Hachuela, Caroline Faria, Mitzi Carter, and Jason and Leilani Pearl. I thank my grandmother and tocaya Christine, who never stopped believing in me even when she thought I was too wordy; my grandmother Carmen, whose spirit I felt in my research; and my father, whose love, commitment, and knowledge inspired everything I did in this book, even if he didn't realize it. He was unable to see it finished, but I know he loved helping me through it—accompanying me on research trips to Veracruz, and listening to several of my conference talks with my dedicated mother. And I thank Carlos, who has been there from the beginning and seen it through to the end—his insights are in every chapter and his care of our son made it possible. Finally, I thank the light of my life, my son Santiago Emiliano, who has patiently waited through the first four years of his life to see this finished and finally get my full attention.

Acknowledgments are due to the SINAFO-INAH (Fototeca of the National Institute of Anthropology and History of México), the Fototeca of Veracruz and IVEC (Institute of Culture of Veracruz) and the Filmoteca of the National Autonomous University of México (UNAM) for their permission to reproduce images from their respective collections. Images from the *Soldadera* Exhibition held at the Vincent Price Museum are courtesy of the artist, Nao Bustamante. A section of chapter 5 was first published as "La Negra Angustias: The Mulata in Mexican Literature and Film" in *Callaloo* 35.4 (2012), 1085–1102, copyright © 2013, and is reprinted with the permission of Johns Hopkins University Press. Parts of an early version of chapter 6 were first published as "Entre la Habana y Veracruz: Toña la Negra and the Transnational Circuits of *Música Tropical*" in *Archipelagos of Sound: Transnational Caribbeanities, Women and Music* (2012) and is reprinted with the permission of University of West Indies Press.

The Paradox of Invisibility

La cucaracha, la cucaracha / ya no puede patalear
porque del viento una racha / de patas la hizo voltear.

[The cockroach, the cockroach / Can no longer crawl
Because a strong gale / has flipped her onto her backside] (357)[1]

> —"La vida y muerte de la cucaracha"
> [The Life and Death of the Cockroach],
> Corrido Zapatista, 1917

Negrita de mis pesares / ojos de papel volando
Negrita de mis pesares / ojos de papel volando.
A todos diles que sí / pero no les digas cuando
Así me dijiste a mí / ¡por eso vivo penando!

[Little black woman of my sorrow / with flickering paper eyes,
Say yes to them all / but don't say when,
Just like you said to me / which is why I live in grief!]

> —"El son de la negra"
> [The *Son* of the Black Woman],
> Blas Galindo, 1940[2]

Metaphor consists in giving the thing a name that belongs to something else.

> —Aristotle, *Poetics* 1457b

Some might argue that nobody worships their mothers and virgins more than Mexicans, and there is no doubt that for the last five hundred years no saint has been more revered than the Virgin of Guadalupe. On the other hand, "La Cucaracha" [The Cockroach] is a Mexican folk song inspired by a raucous camp follower that can be heard in everything from children's toys to the horn of a lowrider. But these maligned women were more than just bawdy camp tramps doped up on weed. While the ring of the cucaracha melody resonates in ears across the globe and the image of the Virgin is ubiquitous, Mexican women, in their capacity as warriors, as *soldaderas*,[3] have been lamentably ignored. I first read about these women in a few paragraphs from a textbook on Mexican history that exceeded more than five hundred entries. As my research continued, I realized that these women had many names, roles, and avatars. More importantly, however, they were influential actors in both the Independence Movement of 1810 and the Mexican Revolution of 1910. Their images, as cucarachas or seductresses, reverberated throughout the Mexican cultural imaginary despite their general invisibility in official history. Likewise, blacks have been in México since the Spanish invasion. One of the first conquistadors, Juan Garrido, was black and yet, until recently, he and other Afro-Mexicans have been dismissed as culturally irrelevant, if considered at all despite the burgeoning historiography recuperating their contributions to Mexican culture. Indians, on the other hand, have been romantically included in their metonymic capacity as exotic icons of the past. They are relevant as small parts of a mestizo whole in which their infantilized "noble passivity" constitutes the acceptable part of a "cosmic race" that celebrates Indian history only in its glorious antiquity.

Inspired by these elisions and contradictions, this book aims to link these anonymous people who have become figures in Mexican culture and that, paradoxically, have overwhelmed the country's social and aesthetic imaginary: the soldadera (female camp followers of the Mexican Revolution), the mulatas (women of African and Spanish ancestry),[4] and the Afro-Caribbean rhythms performed by artists such as Toña la Negra. Though different, all share one undeniable attribute: they have been relegated to the margins of México's official memory and history despite the fact that their figures flood the arts. Corridos, novels, murals, photography, films, theater, and music refer to them without respite. The arts incessantly breathe their presence into culture, especially at moments of fracture in the hegemony of the national narrative, and in this way the bodies of these marginal subjects are *figured* and *disfigured* by the tropological forms their representations have taken by means of metonymy, mythification, or caricature. The fractures in the national narrative occasioned by large-scale revolution, regional insurrection, or racial panic conversely allow each of these figures, in different ways, to slip through. Such a process leads to a tension that allows for their presence to be felt while simultaneously impoverishing it through flat character portrayals and stereotype. This book unravels the striking paradox constituted by the concomitant erasure (in official circles) and ongoing fascination (in the popular imagination) with those nameless people who both define and fall outside of traditional norms of Mexicanness. As such, this study seeks to reveal the ways in which cultural production has contoured what it means to be a woman, black, indigenous, mixed-race, or a peasant in México as well as examine how these figurations contribute to the construction of the social, political, and cultural world. Like the ballad in the epigraph, which is a Zapatista version of the traditional "Cucaracha" corrido (a song that is now universally representative of Mexican folklore), or the "Son de la Negra," the *son jaliciense* cited about a seductive black woman (one of the most popular in the mariachi repertoire), the stunning paradox that constitutes their simultaneous presence and absence is what inspires the chapters in this book. People who abound as nameless figures in diverse forms of Mexican cultural production—from novels, film, music, photography, murals, theatre to popular balladry—elucidate how the aesthetic realm, in all of its forms and manifestations, exercises a singularly decisive role in creating history and imagining selfhood, both individual and communal.

The national narrative that is fed to school children in the elementary primers, that monumentalizes a few heroes at the expense of others, neglects the anonymous many who helped create this problematic sense of "nation." There is an inherent movement, a fundamental rhythm and counter-rhythm, or "discurrere,"[5] that moves itself in and out of the variegated fabrics and forms we call culture. This movement is sensorial: it moves through the visual, auditory, and physical domains that define human activity. Above all, it moves through the diverse domains of the aesthetic realm; it is manifested in the visual scenarios created by the physical presence of soldaderas in the public sphere, the legends of mulata witches that whisper the presence of Africans despite the nation's historical amnesia regarding slavery. All of these people embody a movement of ideas, sounds, scenarios, life forms, histories, legends, myths, and images by disrupting the inviolability of a national narrative in the grip of what was once (and may be again) an authoritarian one-party regime.

In the chapters that follow we encounter many individuals and study different renditions of the same story. She is a beautiful mulata, possessor of an intense gaze that renders those men who look at her impotent to her charms. She lives on the edge of town and mysteriously prepares potions that have miraculous effects on her patients. This is México's colonial legend of the Mulata de Córdoba. Her dangerous beauty became the inspiration for poetry, film, and even an opera produced by some of México's most illustrious artists. Alongside the enchanting Mulata existed "wretched" soldaderas (some mulatas themselves) who many called *cucarachas* or *adelitas*, trudging stolidly behind (but also next to) their male counterparts in one of the most important revolutions of the twentieth century. These women collected water, cured the wounded, gave birth under the stars or, engulfed in gun smoke, picked up the rifles of their dead mates to continue firing where their soldiers left off. They abound as the supernumerary background in any film or novel about the Mexican Revolution of 1910. All of these folklorized figures are ironically unremarkable in the annals of history—or perhaps they are, as theorized by José Rabasa, "without history."[6] And yet, they are fixtures of the Mexican aesthetic and cultural imaginary. Moreover, these figures represent real people who traveled and dwelled in multiple worlds, willingly or not, and contributed to new and also old ways of knowing, where the practice of daily life created ruptures that transformed familiar places.

In the wake of Octavio Paz's *Labyrinth of Solitude* (1950), excellent scholarship has theorized the hypermasculinity that has come to define Mexican attitudes toward women, the construction of womanhood in mariological terms—as either surplus or violent loss—and the displacement of the blame of conquest onto the Mexican Eve: *la Malinche*.[7] However, the Malinche and her "damned sons" did not monopolize the markers of womanhood. Jocelyn Olcott and many others argue that before and especially after the Revolution, "*Abnegación*—selfless, martyrdom, self-sacrifice, an erasure of self and the negation of one's outward existence—became nearly synonymous with idealized Mexican femininity and motherhood" (15–16). In *The Cage of Melancholy* (1987), Roger Bartra coins the term "Chingadalupe" as a way to contend with the inevitable crisis caused by extraordinary female figures caught in the trap of the virgin (Guadalupe)/whore (Malinche) dichotomy. Texts such as Jean Franco's *Plotting Women* (1989), Debra Castillo's *Easy Women* (1998), Robert Irwin's *Mexican Masculinities* (2003), Jocelyn Olcott's *Revolutionary Women* (2006), Sergio de la Mora's, *Cinemachismo* (2006), Laura Gutierrez's *Performing Mexicanidad* (2010), and Rita Urquijo Ruiz's *Wild Tongues: Transnational Mexican Popular Culture* (2013)[8] in addition to many others have paved the way for appreciating how gender has determined citizenship, and consequently, the ways in which both female and male artists have negotiated striated gender divisions in diverse forms of cultural production.

Mexican blackness, in turn, was dressed in tropical fanfare and woven into the national aural fabric through an acoustics of otherness. By the first half of the twentieth century, the mulata, both as a singular figure and a recognizable diva, becomes emblematic of this exoticized otherness while the mulato fades from view, visible only in base caricature, as testified by the controversy over Memín Pinguín, a popular comic book character of a black boy with simian-like features. His image became memorialized in a special edition of the Mexican stamp in 2005, causing an uproar by activists and politicians in the United States. Curiously, he is so beloved that many prominent Mexican intellectuals (including Carlos Monsiváis) refused to acknowledge the racism inscribed in a figure such as his, looking instead to the nobility of Memín's character as evidence to the contrary. The irony, of course, is that his character is not based on the experience of Afro-Mexicans, but rather on the creator's (Yolanda Vargas Dulché) favorable impression of Afro-Cuban children while on a trip to Havana. Why the trials and tribulations of an Afro-Cuban child raised in the capital of México is zealously defended as Mexican cultural patrimony but Afro-Mexicans today still have not convinced the Mexican state to recognize them as autochthonous communities or as an ethnic category for the census speaks to the power of the national discourse that violently excludes them.

Irwin argues that nationhood in México was constructed as a "virile institution": a brotherhood of men who had to define and redefine what it meant to be male and masculine. While Irwin (quoting Matthew Gutmann) reminds us that by the time of the Mexican Revolution, "Mexico came to mean machismo and machismo came to mean Mexico (24)," the evolving notions of Mexican masculinity—both before the Revolution and ever since—have been tenuous and contingent (Irwin xvii). Indeed, the nineteenth-century Porfirian penchant for Europeanizing, effete art and dandyism was countermanded (Irwin states almost hyperbolically) with the obsession over the man of action after the Revolution of 1910. This masculinist tension climaxes in the racializing gestures that at once glorify and deplore the "brute" force and "savage" sexuality identified with the *campesino* (Indian, mestizo, and black) while simultaneously emasculating them due to their subordination in the social and racial hierarchy. This conundrum becomes manifest in debates about "virile" or "effeminate" literature as the "gendered rhetoric of race and class shifts and twists, sometimes within the same text, to suit the goals of the author" (xxix). However, Irwin claims contradictions tend to go unnoticed precisely because "[g]ender as a main element of the Mexican national *habitus*, goes unquestioned even as it becomes entangled in blatantly racist stereotypes" (xxix). Laura Lewis, in *Hall of Mirrors*, similarly informs us how discourses surrounding gender and race were forged early on in the colonial enterprise, intersecting in vital ways that still inflect, and conflate, the meaning of race and gender for subaltern subjects today. Indians were feminized, rendered childlike as wards of the colonial power while blacks were positioned as the "henchmen" of the Spanish, the intermediaries who would victimize and "contaminate" them with degenerate morals and brutish violence. Thus, she astutely underscores how Spaniards situated themselves as both the colonial oppressor and protector of the vulnerable, feminized Indian (97). By the nineteenth century and well into the twentieth, "Real Mexican men are at first white *criollos*, and later *mestizos*" (Irwin xxxv).

In contrast to Irwin's argument, Ignacio Sánchez Prado explains that the debates emerging in 1925 around "virile" and "feminine" literature became the tropological axis through which intellectuals sought to define, in contradictory ways, the urgent desire for a national culture by deploying these terms as metaphors for "domestic" and "foreign" (*Naciones intelectuales* 37). Even in the absence of a unified national literary project, the revolutionary man of action constituted the raw material for this nationalist zeitgeist, and novels such as *Los de abajo* by Mariano Azuela, were identified as "virile" precisely because of their autochthonous subject matter and crude realistic form. The protagonists in such novels were admired for their masculine vigor even when they were considered brutish "hordes" and, paradoxically, consolidated the revolutionary spirit into an aesthetic mode that would herald the onset of a national consciousness. The recourse to a tropological language of gender difference points to the anxiety of intellectuals and elites who would conjoin—even in abstraction—the foreignizing elements of culture with a constructed femininity that reads as weakness, both in intellect and in form. Moreover, this gender difference is inflected with a necessary racializing discourse that excludes not only Indian and mulato men, but mestizo *campesinos* from access to the lettered city through their positioning as the unlettered "hordes." Inscribed in this national discourse, then, is the feminizing of the brutish man of action (through intellectual weakness and racialized inferiority) and the exaltation of the abnegating, sacrificing mother. Consequently, women, peasants, blacks, and Indians become associative metaphors that signal a folkloric, exotic otherness that will be controlled by the strong man of letters. We can thus appreciate how the anxious project of creating a national culture was firmly entrenched in this racialized and gendered language.

However, Irwin reminds us that the performative nature of masculinity de-links biology and masculinity in significant, intricate ways. Women who performed heroically did so in their capacity as *mujeres abnegadas*, forsaking themselves for love of *pater* and *patria*, or as transvested men, dressing themselves in "masculine" valor in order to fight as soldadaderas and *soldadas*. Valiance and vigor are not only available to biological men, but were coded as male attributes available to women who could perform them convincingly. Jocelyn Olcott has informed us that in the post-revolutionary milieu "[w]omen who had served as armed combatants made claims as *veteranas* [but] women also demanded benefits as the wives, widows, and orphans of revolutionary veterans, highlighting the fluidity between roles of combatants and noncombatants during the revolutions armed phase" (21). Olcott further argues that in the post-revolutionary era, "The common language of abnegación reflected not the stability of gender identities but, rather, mounting anxiety about fragmenting conceptions of femininity" (16–17). The discourse of women's *abnegación* was used to advocate both for and against women's activism and citizenship, allowing those on opposing sides to appreciate that "Mexico stood at the threshold of dramatic changes" (17). Indeed, even after engaging in armed combat and appropriating the language of *abnegación* to quell gender anxieties, suffrage campaigns following the Revolution were unsuccessful and women (while nonetheless inching forward), were rewarded for neither their "macho" valiance nor self-sacrificing abnegation. Rather, in the provinces and rural towns "women's intrusion into activities normally construed as masculine, such as wage labor, military engagement, and political machinations, provoked attacks against the instability of gender roles" (17). Vesting oneself in a masculine-coded honor or acting heroically as a *mujer abnegada* did not ultimately translate into any meaningful recognition of the work performed by women before, during, or after the Revolution. Tabea Linhard, in her study on the soldadera and female militants in the Spanish civil war, similarly confirms that even in female-authored "representations of fearless women, preexisting discursive conventions silence and erase the complexities that women's participation in these struggles implies" (*Fearless Women* 18). In turn, mulata women, when not figured as seductive witches or tropical divas, were likewise represented as abnegating mothers or Mexican mammy figures.

In her book *American Anatomies*, Robyn Wiegman traces the state and social mechanisms in the United States that exclude blacks and women from equal citizenship through the asymmetrical and analogical relationship "between race and gender that would come to underlie comparative anatomy in the nineteenth century" (43). These twin categories are the product of an optic logic that undergirds the "articulation of racial essence" where the "body as the inevitable locus of 'being,' depends on a series of bodily fictions assumed to unproblematically reflect the natural meaning of flesh" (21). This complex examination of the analogical relationship between the gendered and racialized body helps to illuminate the othering process in México despite the very different history of racializing bodies in Latin America, the more fluid (but no less problematic) conceptions of race, and the state-sponsored rhetoric of inclusion through the insistence on the narrative of mestizaje— understood as both biological and cultural.

Wiegman's argument unpacks the racializing process that operates in tandem with a gendering otherness in the United States, shedding light on the evolution of race as a construct since the late eighteenth and nineteenth centuries, the effects of which continue to manifest themselves in contemporary social problems. For blacks in the U.S., the "ability to be gendered marked the entrance to the human, public community, providing both civic roles (such as the reproduction of mothering) while simultaneously fragmenting citizenship according to a deeply exclusive masculine universalism" (68). Wiegman's analysis hinges on three points that help shed light on these twin mechanisms I will explore that have to do with the othering of blacks, Indians, and women in México. First, white womanhood is revered, even necessary for the propagation and "civilizing" of the nation-state. The civic duties incumbent on the white woman are key to catapulting the nation forward despite her infantilizing sub-mission, which, unlike the black man, does not dehumanize her. The second is that a universal, decorporealized manhood becomes the marker for citizenship and for participation in the nation-state, thus excluding white women but not black males due to the privileges afforded by a patronymic. Even when a "universally particular body" exists in an "epidermal prison house," men enjoyed the benefits of a *name* as well as the "symbolic possibilities that accrued to the masculine as the precondition for the patronymic, as the name that guaranteed legitimate lineage" (68). Finally, the pairing of these two work together in contradictory, politically pernicious ways because "[b]y figuring blackness as a feminine racial formation, the possibility of the African (American) male assuming an equal position with the crusader for advanced civilization, the white male, was thwarted and racial hierarchies became further entrenched according to the corporeal inequalities inscribed by sexual difference" (55).

Even though whiteness is not so straightforward in México (elites were often called *peninsulares* or *españoles* in the colonial racial hierarchy, with *calidad* and lineage playing important roles), womanhood was predicated on a notion of "decency" based on codes of conduct proper to middle- and upper-class women who are interpreted as white (read civilized or European) even if they are not. In this way, Wiegman's consideration of the processes through which marginal subjects are othered adds density to my development of the term "nobodies." I understand "nobodies" as an alternative form of addressing this fundamental marginalization and its simultaneous figuration in the arts. Gender and race cannot be engaged independently because Mexican nationalist discourse and art grapple with the entangled strands of both. Moreover, through the denial of a name "one can extend the discussion of the patronymic's domestic organization to the realm of the public as well, where the patronymic has served as the framework for defining the very possibility of citizenship" (67). Through the pluralization of particular qualities attributed to soldaderas, such as promiscuity and degeneracy (cucarachas/mitoteras), sweetness and motherliness (adelitas/juanas), or alternatively, the singularization of blackness (*la* Negra Angustias, *la* mulata de Cordoba, Toña *la* Negra), proper names are disappeared and their identities become abstracted into a play of trope. In contrast to this nominal abstraction, the *body* in "nobody" directly points to the very real and concrete place they have in the background, the spaces they occupy, the contributions they make, and the violence inflicted on their flesh. Their *nobodiness* is clearly a product of their *othering* but also the practical and strategic disappearing of them by Mexican national discourse through the denial of a proper name (soldadera and mulata) as well as the regulation of their bodies. This disappearing, however, happened in different ways: on the one hand the overrepresentation of the soldadera in the crafting of a post-revolutionary identity blinds the spectator/reader through excess;

while on the other, the absolute elision of blacks from Mexican historical consciousness makes the striking figure of the mulata exotic and foreign.

In line with Wiegman's arguments regarding the appropriation of identity politics in the United States, the Mexican state has deftly managed the language of the underdog in order to institutionalize a revolution that would maintain and legitimate an authoritarian state party for over 71 years (and counting).[9] By proselytizing a political ideology of otherness, the Mexican state has kept the same people in power and simultaneously blocked access to its nobodies, creating what Claudio Lomnitz would refer to as a "Silent México." By abstracting the violence inflicted onto their real bodies, and with no names and no real voices, they are no-bodies; paradoxically folklorized while summarily eliminated.

What I seek to understand is how such gendered and racialized constructs are belied or even undone through the very art forms that perform such gendering and racializing. While womanhood and race are invariably defined in concrete terms, the tremors that unsettle these constructs are manifested by the fascination with which both elites and peasants beheld, and represented, these extraordinary people: black, mulata, white, mestizo, and indigenous women. That they lack proper names—the properties of art allow these contradictions—provides a window into popular sentiment and elite fetish along with the concomitant prejudices of each. The cultural texts examined in this book witness the complex ways in which traditional womanhood is defined by masculinist gestures and disrupted by racializing ones. Indeed, the anxieties regarding a hegemonic notion of race and gender are brought to task with the figure of the soldadera; her simultaneous masculine and maternal heroism was an embarrassment to military officials. At the same time the mulata triangulates native blackness with a foreign intrusion and exotic sexuality, providing a way to negotiate and explain unraveling sexual mores rooted in the countryside and the corruption of white-male desire.

All the prominent female figures I study—Adelitas, Cucarachas, Angustias, Antonia de Soto, La Mulata de Córdoba—derive their strength from the traditional markers of female *abnegación*, transgressive cross-dressing, or both. We will consider stunning examples such as Agustín Casasola's portrait of the Afro-Mexican soldadera, featured on the cover of this book and discussed in chapter 3, who pairs her long earrings and soldier pants with a gun in her pocket, or Antonia de Soto in chapter 4, who travels, works, and marauds as a male even while she is courted for her female beauty by the devil and her indigenous accomplice, or Toña la Negra in chapter 6, whose legendary lurid mouth is disguised by her sultry yet maternal voice, and whose Mexicanness is dressed in a Caribbean tropicality.

Although cultural production can create and perpetuate stereotypes that often impoverish images of social subjects, it also reflects a popular desire to represent what exists "in reality": women on the battlefield, blacks in the fields and mines, the mulata as mother, the Indian as a relevant purveyor of knowledge. Rather than atavistic icons of a bygone era, these figures are brought to life, although figuratively, and in an often diminished form. Inspired by the work of Hayden White, Diana Taylor, Michel de Certeau, Jacques Rancière, José Rabasa, and others, I argue that the figures who populate the literary, visual, and musical imaginary constitute much more than base entertainment for the masses or a curious motif in cultural production by patronizing elites; they reflect an almost latent communal will to narrate that which the official history often ignores. In the aesthetic resides something more than artifice: possibility. The insistent will to reproduce these figures in the aesthetic realm, and the concomitant desire by members of diverse classes to consume these products signals how history can be narrated differently. To understand the paradox created by this (dis)figured cultural visibility and historical absence, I employ something similar to what James Maffie has called a "polycentric epistemology"; an approach that allows us to occupy multiple epistemological positions to interpret diverse cultural forms. By destabilizing Western epistemes, we can engage both Western and non-Western interpretative modes to analyze cultural production generated by communities that are both of, and not of, the "West." Moreover, we recognize that the aesthetic realm is of paramount importance in the production of knowledge and the crafting of history.

I introduce the terms *tlacuepa*, *olin*, and *tlalticpac*[10] in order to explain a concept I call the "slippery word." This idea is a mechanism by which we can understand the paradox of the supposed rigidity of the aesthetic realm and its simultaneous plasticity. It permits us—the spectators and community who interpret—to ascribe to these figures an agency, or at least an "other" identity or set of possibilities that can be read against the flat stereotype. Tropological discourse, as formulated by Hayden White in *Tropics of Discourse*, informs my readings of the movement of these figures and complements the indigenous concepts I invoke regarding movement, rupture, metaphor, language, knowledge, and the arts. Finally, I propose that an engaged spectatorship is part of the relationship that exists between affect and the aesthetic realm, which in turn, produces a kind of disruptive knowledge. This aspect of my polycentric and decolonial approach is unorthodox, and I understand that some readers might react with distrust to this performative exercise; however, using notions of movement, metaphor, paradox, translation, rupture, twisting, and turning allows me to bring together a broad array of peoples, characters, tropes, and spaces forgotten, neglected, or censored in official memory and history of México, permitting us to appreciate what the arts and popular culture accomplish, and what they do not.

These indigenous concepts can be used as interpretative clues that illuminate how mestiza, indigenous, and mulata women could leave the home and take up arms in battle, or abandon the "legitimacy" of marriage to become an unofficial "wife" for a week, month, or year; or how black Mexicans could at once be present and absent, an integral component of the emerging colonial polis, registered as delinquents in the Inquisition archive yet invisible in the national imaginary; how indigenous people can be emblematized as icons and tourist curiosities yet be considered politically irrelevant. The domain of the aesthetic allows for nuance: for words and images to point to and move while generating new, disruptive yet often ephemeral life forms as exoticized *mulata* revolutionaries or ambulant wartime indigenous "mistresses" acting in the "custom of their sex and country." Although cultural production, in both its high and popular forms, maintains a proclivity to metonymically freeze these people into a static identity, these figures, despite (or perhaps because) of their proliferation in all forms of cultural production, are conspicuously slippery. This permits the disfiguring nature of cultural production to simultaneously reveal other possibilities beyond *cucarachas* or beguiling *adelitas*; to imagine the flesh-and-blood individuals who flitted in the background as playing an integral role in what today is Mexican culture, history, and politics.

The Turning and Twisting of Words

In the Náhuatl spoken in the Huasteca region of México, there is no single word for "translation," but rather, a phrase—*tlacuepa*—that means "the turning, or twisting of words." In Fray Alonso de Molina's dictionary,[11] the same root is also employed to describe someone who makes an excuse or does not do what is asked of him, or when the word is compounded, it means to contort or twist a material, such as wood. The word "translation" in English or Spanish means to carry a word from one language to another (*pasar algo de un lado a otro*),[12] thus operating under a substitutional logic that presupposes the possibility for a word or idea to be wholly transferred. In contrast, in Náhuatl this "transference" or substitution is already compromised by its "twisted" nature.[13] Although I am not suggesting that there is a foreclosure of the prospects for translation in Náhuatl, it is intriguing that the very possibility of translation, at least according to this definition, is compromised by the questioning of philological, cultural, and historical commensurability. I believe this concept to be fundamental toward understanding Nahua and indigenous thought in general, especially in counterpoint to the English and Spanish definitions of translation, as language is likened to a malleable material that is turned or twisted.

James Maffie, in his ambitious tome *Aztec Philosophy*, further supports this idea by explaining that "[t]wisting involves ordering and arranging [. . .] It gives its object a shape conducive to the transmission of energy; a shape that allows energy to flow freely" (268). This twisting movement, *malinalli*, is an aspect of *teotl*: an immanent, vital energy that vivifies the cosmos and is in a constant state of becoming as a deified movement (261). *Malinalli*, which translates to twisted grass, herb, or thing, is one of three kinds of "motion-change" that manifests *teotl* and "involves transformation *between* different kinds of things (cotton into thread), *between* different conditions of the same thing (disorderly into orderly), and [. . .] *between* vertical layers of the cosmos" (266). Akin to the term *tlacuepa*, *malinalli* as a metaphysical concept refers to the twisting, turning movement that is not "disheveled," "entangled," "dangerous," "impure" or "polluted," but rather a process, a movement and ordering that twists one thing into another (263).

In turn, Hayden White explains the etymology of the word "trope" in order to illuminate the function it plays in discourse: "The word *tropic* derives from *tropikos*, *tropos*, which in Classical Greek meant 'turn' and in Koiné 'way' or 'manner.' It comes into modern Indo-European languages by way of *tropus*, which in Classical Latin meant metaphor or 'figure of speech' and in Late Latin, especially as applied to music theory, 'mood' or 'measure'" (*Tropics of Discourse* 2). In a gesture reminiscent of the meaning and usage of *tlacuepa*, White claims that "troping is both a movement *from* one notion of the way things are related *to* another notion, and a connection between things so that they can be expressed in a language that takes account of the possibility of their being expressed otherwise" (2). White's theory of tropo-logical discourse is likewise fundamental to my understanding of the figures under consideration because movement is critical for discourse's "mediation" between supposed oppositions of error and truth, ignorance and understand-ing, imagination and thought, because it provides continuity between them. Tropes allow for the mobility inherent in apprehending change, and cog-nitively registering it into language. Furthermore, in discourse it comes to constitute a manner, way, or mood, or what White says in modern English would be "style." The musicality inherent in the very word registers the idea of it embodying an implicit movement or rhythm. For example, a helio-trope is a flower that turns with the rotation of the sun, thus moving toward the life force that sustains it. Trope, as a figure of speech, likewise "turns a phrase," creating a relationship between two unlike things, or abstracting from the literal in order to render a second figural meaning. Like the flower, this movement—this turning—sustains it; that which it turns toward constitutes its "life force." This movement contains within it an inherent rhythm and counter-rhythm, not to mention that rhythm partakes of different moods; it can maintain a faster or slower measure, and in language, can render second-ary, tertiary, and perhaps infinite possibilities. So to "turn a phrase" is com-monly used to describe the use of trope in figurative and literary language, bearing a striking similarity to how the "turning of words" describes the act of translation in Huastecan Náhuatl.

Cultural producers and consumers participate in a shared, if not always even, tropological imagination. In this imagination metaphors undergird the symbolic system in which we operate, from the most quotidian, mundane actions to the most complex philosophical ruminations. George Lakoff and Mark Johnson explore how even the most commonplace phrases describing everyday actions and understandings, such as the signification of space through vertical and horizontal analogies as well as trite expressions such as "love is a journey" or "time is money," form part of a profound metaphorical system that regulates our epistemological and ideological regimes. As an instrument for understanding experience, Lakoff and Johnson consider metaphor as primordial as the senses: "It is as though the ability to comprehend experience through metaphor were a sense, like seeing or touching or hearing, with metaphors providing the only ways to perceive and experience much of the world. Metaphor is as much a part of our functioning as our sense of touch, and as precious" (239). Not only do Lakoff and Johnson contend that metaphors are conceptual in nature, they also conclude that as a vehicle for understanding "they play a central role in the construction of social and political reality" (159).

These conceptual metaphors thus come to constitute the places held by people in the telling of a nation's history. The notion that a relationship can be drawn between two unlike things that are known, in order to explain something that is unknown, is useful for understanding the way in which a particular event or people are remembered and narrated. In this book I explore how individual people come to embody larger conceptual metaphors in México, such as how the soldadera as an occupation came to represent the overwhelming cultural panic provoked by women bursting out of the home and into the public sphere. Indeed, to relate the traditional female domestic sphere to the scripted domain of male activity produced what Debra Castillo calls an unwritten catachresis. This catachresis is the product of the mixing of two metaphorical domains that led to the soldaderas' identification within the only conceptual fields that were available to society at that time: mothers, sweethearts, or whores. Hence they were villainized or idealized, but their significance was marked by the uneasy tension that the larger society felt by observing these women living out in the open, occupying public spaces in traditionally male spheres. They created new *places* by domesticating these public domains, and ultimately, by establishing a *habitus* in the midst of war.

Hayden White proposes that tropes embody visions of, or attitudes toward the world; George Lakoff, in turn, finds in metaphor—an instance of trope—crystallized explanations of the world. Tropes and metaphors guide us in our expectations of our realities—both experienced and imagined. This project is concerned with defining those expectations within the confines of the nation-state, and explaining how these roles are either constituted or disrupted through the aesthetic realm. I understand the aesthetic realm as constitutive of forces that unsettle what Lakoff and Johnson have called the myth of objectivism: "In a culture where the myth of objectivism is very much alive and truth is always absolute truth, the people who get to impose their metaphors on the culture get to define what we consider to be true—absolutely and objectively true" (160). By interrogating how these personages based on real people are rendered discursively, this book untangles the tropological way figuration stands in for certain notions of what it means to be a woman, indigenous, or black in México. Chantal Mouffe and Ernesto Laclau reiterate this idea when they conclude that "[s]ynonymy, metonymy, metaphor are not forms of thought that add a second sense to a primary, constitutive literality of social relations; instead, they are part of the primary terrain itself in which the social is constituted" (*Hegemony and Socialist Strategy* 110). My approach engages the power of trope and figurative language as more than a literary phenomenon that adds style or beautifies language, but as argued by Laclau, Mouffe, and White, acts as an integral part of the socialization process that blurs the boundaries between literal and figural, "truth" and "fiction."

As metaphors, these figures exist in relation to another object; they are "given the name that belongs to something else," perhaps unintelligible in their own right. As catachresis, there is no metaphor that even approximates their representation, no language that explains who or what they are. Consequently, in an ill-suited mixed metaphor, they are reduced to the sloppy tropic diction of unofficial narratives. As metonymies they operate merely as parts, as fractures or flickers that eclipse the totality in favor of the fragment, and in this reductionism, deny the variability and diversity that comprises the whole. In *Routes*, James Clifford reflects on Arjun Appadurai's theory of the metonymic freezing of non-Western people noting that "one part or aspect of peoples' lives come to epitomize them as a whole, constituting their theoretical niche in an anthropological taxonomy" (24). This "metonymic freezing" describes the problem I grapple with in this work. By freezing these figures in different forms that are amenable to the exclusionary narrative proposed by the nation-state, European colonizers and their progeny, Catholic tradition and patriarchy, the protean energies of these people as human beings are violated. For example, mulatas have been elided in the national memory, and yet rendered exceptional as metaphors of excess, desire, and racial contamination; and the corridos, films, novels, and photographs do not fully encompass the complexity of the soldaderas' participation in the Revolution. That soldaderas could also be black is hardly considered, yet there is a prize-winning novel (and later film) about this very figure. The multifarious ways in which they as individuals and communities participated in the construction of Mexican society is denied, and thus, they paradoxically constitute an invisible but indelible component of its history, politics, spirituality, and culture. For this reason, I contend that the domain of the aesthetic acts, both positively and negatively, as a primary agent that sounds where official histories are silent, that shows where they are invisible, that pulses where movement has stopped.

Indeed, thinking about the *turns* in tropological language helps to appreciate how the phrase *tlacuepa* in Náhuatl underscores that there is already a figural rendering of language that requires a movement, a *turning* toward a mode of understanding that will necessarily relate to what White calls other "encodations of experience"—and the possibility of *being* otherwise (5). Moreover, for the ancient Nahuas, *olin*,[14] or movement, is what generates life; it is what keeps the world moving and prevents entropy. Similarly, tropism as a biological phenomenon indicates growth or a turning movement in response to environmental stimuli. Through movement, the organism maintains life and all the life forms that depend on it. Tropological language is always rendered in relationship to something else; it is through this relationship, this turn toward another meaning that discourse, and by extension narrative, is created. Alfredo López Austin explains that in Nahua thought, relational taxonomies are created in association with each other, not as mutually exclusive categories or substitutions, but as different things that can all instantiate the same force in a different form. In this way, a heart of a cactus can instantiate a human heart, or a heart shaped out of amaranth dough. They are all manifestations of the same primordial notion through difference; they all are and are not the same. The cultural figures I study all point toward "another" meaning; say one thing in order to express another, move "to and fro" between how they are figured in cultural production and how their real-life experience "refuses incorporation into conventionalized notions of truth" (White 5). In her exemplary study of Nahua thought, *The Slippery Earth*, Louise Burkhart examines the literal meaning of the word *tlalticpac*, which conveys a place not "on earth" but "on the point or summit of the earth," and indicates being caught or tangled in a tight place or space that is "in-between" dangers, away from the center (58). The idea of the turning or twisting of words, in conjunction with the notion of the *tlacticpac* tropologized as the "slippery earth" inspire what I call the "slippery word": an interpretative mode that ascribes a slippery knowledge or way of comprehending social change and rupture to the arts. This riff of Burkhart's explanation of the *tlacticpac* as part of the Nahua moral universe proposes that the "word" is also "slippery"; its turning and twisting, its tangled strands, its woven metaphors, move simultaneously toward knowledge and away from it, revealing glimpses of everyday reality while obscuring it. Although this metaphor privileges the primacy of language, the aesthetic realm in all its forms provides the slippery material that constitutes a kind of disruptive "knowledge."

Rather than constitute hard contradictions or discrete meanings, the word in language as an instrument of the aesthetic realm, slips among oppositional modes, moves between the "center" and the "periphery." Using the

Nahua trope of the "slippery earth" as a way to understand the role of language, but truly, the role of the aesthetic in Latin *América*, provides us with a way to comprehend and attend to the divergent "identities" within it. It sheds light on the multiplicity of life ways and diverse temporalities that constitute a place that has been marked by a strikingly violent periodicity: a radicalized version where the "before" exists as a primordial or prehistoric past, where the "now" exists as a romanticized mestizo present, and the future is an aspiration to an undefined "Western" sameness. It provides us with a way to understand the need to hear about soldaderas rendered as debauched *cucarachas* in corridos, to see caricatured noble Indians in films, or hear about mesmerizing mulatas in legends and songs. These figures are held hostage by a kind of metonymic freezing that nonetheless provide hints of knowledge, of ontological difference. It also helps us to understand why the aesthetic realms turn to them time and again as reproducible models of gendered and racialized otherness in Mexican culture.

The slippery word or the "twisted" translation never defines anything absolutely and positively. Corridos are never the same with each iteration, even when they are recorded. All the images of these real people constitute an aesthetic intervention, a flicker of knowledge that makes itself present through their staging as what Jacques Rancière calls the "supernumerary." Through art we witness scenes from everyday life, such as revolutionary women building a campfire in the dining room of an abandoned mansion or giving birth on top of a train. We see mulata women as tragic mothers, seductive witches, and revolutionary heroes. Black Mexicans are remembered as curious "visitors" despite making vital contributions to indigenous and mestizo cultural forms, while also incorporating Spanish and indigenous spiritual practices into their own. The images of these people slip in and out of diverse semiotic regimes that contradict each other, but yet, reveal at that same time that they obscure.

The "twisting and turning" of words that organizes the notion of *tlacuepa* in Náhuatl resonates in the language used by both Gilles Deleuze and Jacques Rancière and the rhythmic movement of trope described by White. However, the substitutional impulse of metaphor becomes lost, and the movement inherent in Western tropes is taken one step further. In the form of a slippery word, image, or sound, the aesthetic realm in its manifold forms can reveal what is oftentimes beyond historical language; it conceals at the same time it exposes, confuses as it illuminates. This book is moved by anonymous individuals—women we know exist[ed] and who find their way as figures into the aesthetic realm. They are not always portrayed favorably, but the flickers of these people reveal a desire, both on behalf of the symbolic producer and the audience, to see and feel them in a shared tropological imaginary. Our cultural and creative sensibilities are what distinguish humankind; they are what help us understand our place in the world, but also what can often stultify our notions of identity. Art moves to and fro between creating static stereotypes and opening up stunning possibilities, new forms of enunciation by those whom Jacques Rancière has claimed are not visible, audible and are nameless within hegemonic narratives (*The Politics of Aesthetics* 92). The aesthetic domain recognizes these ruptures; it is inspired as much by slippages as by static forms and thus moves between the center and the *tlalticpac*.

Possibility and the Aesthetic

In a move he imagines will upset historians, Jacques Rancière inveighs against the science of history and locates it in the same narrative mode as literature by claiming that "[w]riting history and writing stories come under the same regime of truth" (38). He strategically steers away from discourses that claim everything is a "narrative" as this leads to an unproductive dialectic between "real" and "artifice," but rather, proposes that models of fictionality in the arts were appropriated as models for the "presentation of facts and forms of intelligibility" (38). He does not claim that "History" is merely composed of stories we tell ourselves, but that "the 'logic of stories' and the ability to act as historical agents go together. Politics and art, like forms of knowledge, construct 'fictions,' that is to say *material* rearrangements of signs and images, relationships between what is seen and what is said, between what is done and what can be done" (39).

The agency implicit in creating art (in all of its modalities) but also interpreting it generates multiple possibilities for re-thinking history, but more importantly, ascribing a radical potential to the aesthetic realm to not only intervene in the telling of "history," but also, to make it. Destabilizing this epistemological regime is part and parcel of these claims to the politics of aesthetics. Rancière maintains that the task of fiction is not to compare reality with its images or appearances but to create "different realities, different forms of common sense [. . .] different spatiotemporal systems, different communities of words and things, forms and meanings" (*The Emancipated Spectator* 102). Thus he ascribes the power to create different realities to art, where the subaltern will disrupt hegemonic notions of common sense.

The significance of the aesthetic, in all of its forms, is relevant for a broad range of people: its impact is not only felt by the artist or an elite group of aesthetes in the "know," but is also important for communities that are nameless and disenfranchised, but who nonetheless spectate, observe, and interpret. Rancière argues for the agency of the spectator by maintaining that observation is not merely a passive enterprise, but rather, an active one. Simply by spectating we create meaning, which in turn begets a political act: the interpretative act generates meaning likened to the act of composing a poem because the spectator's interpretation constitutes its own brand of poetry. Moreover, one of the arguments he makes for defending the politics of aesthetics is that the "proletarian," or worker, is separate from her occupation and all the prescribed social functions that are a part of this identification: "an emancipated proletarian is a dis-identified worker" (73). Although speaking from a specifically European, post-industrial context where he identifies the proletarian (and not the indigenous *campesina*) as the subject who is emancipated, or rather, who will be "dis-identified" from their work (ignoring the complexities produced by uneven temporalities woven into the violence of coloniality), the larger point regarding the power of the interpretive act remains; the emancipated spectator (whether the dis-identified worker or *campesina*) will create aesthetic regimes of consciousness through her consumption—and production—of art.[15] However, this "emancipation" neglects what I suggest is the possibility that the spectator and the artist/participant may already be one and the same. For example, in oral balladry those who perform the corridos are likewise spectators in addition to members of the community for, and with whom, they perform.

With this idea of an aesthetic reciprocity in mind, one of the most compelling contributions Rancière makes to political and aesthetic theory is his notion of being "apart together" which itself is a riff on Mallarmé's verse, "Apart, we are together" from the prose poem, "The White Water Lily" (1885). In a striking metaphor inspired by Mallarmé's poem in addition to Gilles Deleuze and Felix Guatarri's reflections on the role of the artist and the political valency of art, Rancière contemplates the artist's work as a "new sensory fabric" that is torn, wrested, and woven from the "fabric of ordinary experience." The "distribution of the sensible" is what unites mankind; part and parcel of this human experience is the ability to feel, and thus, "[w]eaving this new fabric means creating a form of common expression or a form of expression of the community—namely, 'the earth's song and the cry of humanity'" (56). By using a metaphor involving the production of textiles, he claims that the solitude of the artist is false and that the paradox of being "apart together," or rather, alone within a collectivity, is disavowed, as both the artwork and the human collective is the product of "intertwining and twisting together of sensations" (56). Thus, Rancière claims that not only is the dis-identified proletarian a cultural consumer, but the "aesthetic experience" has a political effect to the extent that it wields the power to disrupt normative roles for the individual as well as the community, and in this way contributes to the constitution of a collective's breath (72). He finds relevance in the aesthetic realm that unsettles the exhausted dialectic between the didactic possibilities inherent to art or utilizing the arts as a politicizing force on the one hand, and art for art's sake on the other. We might consider this position as an opportunity to unbind the rigidity in which many of these popular subjects have been figured by both middle-class and elite producers, but also by themselves in the corridos, and reevaluate the ambivalence that undergirds their representational surplus. Furthermore, the spectator herself—as either an invisible supernumerary subaltern or a member of the dominant classes—can appreciate this ambivalence and propose a different interpretation. The act of inhabiting particular spaces (such as the soldaderas in chapter 1, or the runaway mulata slave in chapter 4), operates in concert with a diverse community that consumes and interprets these acts. The experience of the aesthetic reflects the tousled strands of daily life, art, and possibility.

To be sure, there have been many valuable objections to Rancière's "distribution of the sensible," due in part to the celebratory uptake of his work. For example, Peter Hallward contends that Rancière's definition of the democratic community as intermittent, a fracture or interruption overemphasizes the "isolated process of intellectual *self*—emancipation" (154). Others have found the relationship he draws between the power of aesthetic communities and politics casuistic at best. With regard to its application to Latin America, and México in particular, Ignacio Sánchez Prado has critiqued the limitations of Rancière's framework, even when "[i]t is also true, however, that Mexico has been the site of some of the most clear real-world illustrations of what Rancière calls 'the distribution of the sensible' and the 'presupposition of equality' [. . .] a moment 'when equals declare themselves as such, though aware that they have no fundamental right to do so' " (374). Aside from the general complaints that center around Rancière's Eurocentrism, heralding high art as examples of the void and supplement, and the silence regarding practical suggestions, Sánchez Prado's argument against Rancière's distribution of the sensible speaks to the paradox that emerges in its application to México: the "persistent absorption of the politics into a 'police' embodied in a hegemony that refuses to go away" (379). What's more, Rancière's insights cannot speak to the point made earlier regarding the multilayered processes of subalternization in a country marked by a violent coloniality. Consequently, in México "consensus and dissensus, politics and police: all coexist paradoxically within the same temporality, the same culture(s), the same social performativities," leading to the "invisibility of the intertwined relationship between power and emancipation" that constitute these "uncomfortable" paradoxes (379). Regarding the relationship between the arts and dissensus in México, critics such as Gareth Williams, in contrast, understand the imagistic impact of the famous photograph of peasant leader Francisco Villa (at the Aguascalientes Convention) sitting in the presidential seat as a "trace of freedom [that] suggests the possibility of a life *other than* that defined by the historical terrain of sovereign command, pointing instead to the possibility of thinking the political in a relation of *withdrawal* from historically defined vicissitudes and horizons of the law" (*The Mexican Exception* 63). In turn, Sánchez

Prado avers that interpretations drawn from Rancière (such as Williams's reading) fetishize moments "of resistance and interregna." Instead, Sánchez Prado advises to recognize the limits of Rancière's distribution of the sensible so that we might begin to engage "a durable politic, one that does dissolve into the memory of a hope that withers after an ephemeral explosion" (381).

On the other hand, Graciela Montaldo contends that Rancière's reception in Latin America can be regarded as an "ideological empathy" that has "offered Latin Americans a way to exchange voices and discourses, while allowing for the articulation of a specific theory about their own political participation," in this way permitting them to use his "ideas as instruments" but also, to *disagree* (335). Acknowledging that there is not a prescription for effecting emancipation, Montaldo underscores that Rancière's aesthetics operate as a "specific regime of perception that shares forms of social behavior with politics" (337). Moreover, she argues that in "Rancière's philosophical and political theory, emancipation is linked to the need for a notion of equality that does not presuppose homogenization, but rather accounts for diversity [. . .] emancipation allows social logic to be seen as a change of the limits that separate subjects and make them unequal" (338). Far from perfect, this is precisely the virtue of a framework such as that offered by Rancière: to open up dialogue and acknowledge both the possibilities and limits of the arts.

That México is now, more than ever, an authoritarian state and that the road toward any semblance of democracy is still long has been evidenced in multiple ways throughout the last eight decades. It began with the promulgation of a vacuous revolutionary rhetoric that serves only the authoritarian elites in the names of murdered peasant icons such as Villa and Zapata. It is manifest in local movements celebrated on the world stage that have not, in the case of Zapatismo, put la "ley indígena" into place, nor in the case of Ayotzinapa, brought justice to the families of the forty-three disappeared students. This authoritarianism is strident when it denies Afro-Mexicans the right to be constitutionally recognized as viable communities. Only in December 2015 were they allowed to include a box in the midterm census that would identify them as black. As Sánchez Prado observes: in México "politics" and the "police" are enraptured in a tight embrace. However, as argued by Williams and Montaldo, art registers the profound, necessary and inevitable moments that allow us to think—and be—otherwise. Rupture and dissensus as imagined through the aesthetic realm recall another kind of history (for those whom José Rabasa has said are without history), allow "the people" in all of their diverse configurations to both create and consume art for themselves, independently of whether it is absorbed by hegemonic forces. To face, indeed, inhabit these paradoxes is not necessarily to fetishize rupture or ephemeral democracy, but to recognize past and imagine future disruptions: the continual becoming, movement, and power of daily life, one that is both static and dynamic. Art, while not a political antidote to inequality and oppression, is also not just a product of it, or against it; it is a way.

Why discount the longitudinal effects, the broader warp and weft of these infinitesimal moments, such as Villa seated with a lopsided grin in the presidential chair next to a dour Zapata, or in our case, of a transvested once nameless Afro-Mexican soldadera staring intently into the camera with her gun in her pocket, military pins, peasant Zapatista hat, and earrings dangling? Indeed, her name and title has changed several times: this portrait was until recently thought to be taken by Agustín Casasola in 1910 and was captioned as a nameless "soldadera from Michoacán," and is now identified by the Fototeca of the Mexican Institute of Anthropology and History as Carmen Robles, a Zapatista Colonel from Guerrero with a date of 1914. She is, notwithstanding her newfound identity, an historical figure about whom very little is known. The imagistic effect of this one portrait defies the static post-revolutionary narrative of abnegated womanhood and melancholic mestizaje. This woman alone, through the multiple ambivalences communicated in the portrait and its contradictory captions, speaks of all the different ways of being and becoming a post-revolutionary woman: black and mestiza, masculine, feminine, anonymous (soldadera) and official (Coronela), improvised and yet posed. Even if "absorbed in to the police," circulated in postcards and on exhibition covers, does this annul the potential effects of dissensus, reduce the impact of being *otherwise* to mere fetish? Even if the state, or "hegemonic forces" say one thing, do not the spectators interpret and subsequently create something else? These eruptions, these moments of dissensus cannot be brushed aside because, unlike Emiliano Zapata and Francisco Villa, the people in this book were not even granted the dignity of a first name and patronymic. They were appropriated only in the political abstraction of the official art promoted by an authoritarian regime, or in the popular culture through base caricature.

The popular sensorium, although manipulable and shot through with its own contradictions, is precisely that: a work in process, constantly revising itself even when it stubbornly insists on upholding tradition. The corrido bears witness to this; heralding war heroes and manly valor, it also did not ignore its women, even if only to present them as *cucarachas* or *adelitas*. Alas, soldaderas were brown in the eyes and imaginations of the upper classes but were almost always white in the films where they played leading ladies. However, in the only novel about a female revolutionary hero she is powerfully black. This novel was good enough, by the way, to win the Mexican national literature prize although seldom taught in literature courses. And in the widely circulated image that graces the cover of this book, the soldadera is unequivocally black; in a portrait bereft of military heraldry, her right hand's proximity to the gun utters an undeniable threat, paradoxically complying with stereotypes of black female deviance and disavowing this trope as she stares back at the camera in a knowing gaze.

To reduce the profoundly disruptive power of these moments in the arts to fetish further impoverishes, and even violates, the legacy of people who expressed their dissent in voiceless gestures and awkward glances, appropriating official places for unofficial use, creating new spaces and attitudes out of traditional places and norms. While things appeared to "return to normal" for the soldadera, and the mulata is still not recognized as racially significant, these cultural forms, images, and distortions constitute a kind of emancipatory act that questions the normativity of Mexican womanhood—not only in the midst of the Revolutionary tumult—but also before and afterward. These twisted and tangled metaphors point precisely to our imperfection, to the morbid embrace of hegemony, consent and dissent, but more importantly, to an ever present possibility.

The fact that soldaderas were kicked out of the army, that blacks are considered negligible at best despite the explosion in Afro-Mexican historiography, and Indians are treated paternalistically and are politically disenfranchised, speaks to the important role that the arts have held in witnessing these people in brief vignettes and deformed cameos. It is not only the seasoned cultural critic who can recuperate these stories, and through a critical interpretative lens, appreciate the irony behind the disfigured image or base caricature. The affective reception on behalf of the spectator, the experience of viewing/listening/reading/dancing/singing also constitutes a form of knowledge, challenging or unsettling the possibility of truth. I do not claim to recuperate the voice of the "real" subaltern; I suggest that the iterative nature of these figures in the arts in conjunction with artists who reproduce their images time and again, and the audience who consumes them, constitutes a kind of knowledge and inserts these people, however negatively, back into the historical imaginary.

In a metaphor highlighting the importance of weaving, Rancière concludes the section titled "Aesthetic Separation, Aesthetic Community" from *The Emancipated Spectator* in a poetic, albeit grandiose language that proposes "[t]he operations of twisting, seizing and rending that define the way in which art weaves a community together are made *en vue de*—with a view to and in the hope of—a people which is still lacking" (57). While his gesture is purely metaphorical, I turn toward the concrete example of weaving as an art form in Wixárika (Huichol) communities. Stacy Schaefer observes that Wixárika women associate weaving and creating textiles with "thinking with a good heart." The heart, or *iyari*, acts as a part of the "soul" and memory. There is an intimate link—that is not metaphoric—between art, crafting textiles, spirituality, community, and knowledge. Moreover, mastering the art of weaving is a highly respected profession that opens the mind and heart to Wixárika knowledge and facilitates "curing patients, communicating with gods [. . .] creating textiles and living an upright life" (85). Thus, we see a clear example of how the artist participates in the creation of art and knowledge while simultaneously belonging to a specific community. Although the mastery of this art is not something all participate in, the weavers/artists do not exist outside of or in opposition to the community; they are vital members of it. Moreover, weaving is the master trope of Aztec-Mexica-Nahua metaphysics whereby the "cosmos is a grand weaving-in-progress" and *teotl*, as a cosmic vital energy, "is the weaver, the weaving, and the woven" (Maffie 14). Inspired in part by Cecilia Klein's notion of a "weavers paradigm" and work by Schaefer on the Wixárika, Maffie claims weaving functions as an organizing principle of Aztec metaphysics through the concept of "agonistic inamic unity," which pairs the Western notion of *agon* with the Náhuatl word *inamic* (referring to complementary opposites) to describe how the Aztec world functions through conflict, revision, movement, generation, and degeneration. Weaving, then, "concretely instantiates agonistic inamic unity" (140) by treating "warp and weft fibers as inamic partners to be united into a single fabric" (142).

As noted by Thelma Sullivan and Maffie, weaving, and in particular spinning and spinning instruments, are invested with a highly sexualized symbolism: through the twists of *malinalli*, the "thread moves up and down the vertical spindle rod in the course of its transformation from fiber into thread" (265–66). Although performed by both sexes (such as the Zapotec weavers or Tzetzal loom pedalers), weaving is often gendered as a feminine activity[16] and as such, is an under-appreciated art form that nonetheless produces knowledge: a perfect metaphor for appreciating the contributions of México's nobodies to its culture and history. Part of the fabric, yet indistinguishable, Mexican women as soldaderas, transgender soldiers, as activists, as tragic mothers, as mulata voices, or as runaway slaves are part and parcel of what holds Mexican culture together, in nameless fragments and singular threads. Folklorized, tokenized, exchanged, and circulated as cheap cultural artifacts, these women (not unlike Zapotec tapestries) are at once powerful and powerless, invisible, nameless and yet omnipresent.

In sum, the Rancièrian subject, although a fracture or interruption, is not positioned antagonistically to the world around it, but forms an intimate part of it through what he calls a "chaosmatic breath." Inspired by this notion and the idea of an emancipated spectator, the art of the Wixárika weavers and the general notion of a an indigenous (Mesoamerican) and African participatory universe, I suggest that the symbolic producer and community are mutually constituted, that knowledge is produced through the creation and consumption of the aesthetic, and that this invokes a generative space of multiple possibilities. Even middle-class and elite cultural producers, in spite of their defamation of the popular and marginalized classes, turn to the figures I examine time and again. While Paz focuses on the tear, the *rajada*, we neglect the mending performed by women. Even in their capacity as debauched cucarachas or violent mulata witches, their place in the social and cultural imaginary belies the silent abjection of the literary and cultural spaces they occupy. Mexican culture is riddled by a profoundly gendered nationalism where the very figure of the mestizo, supposed to undo the originary violent rape of the indigenous and African woman, conquest of the indigenous man and enslavement of the African, is rendered ineffectual by the master trope that validates him in his approximation to whiteness and reproduction of Eurocentric epistemes. Mestizo consciousness claims to incorporate all the disparate parts, but the emancipatory project in this "impure imagination," as Joshua Lund describes it, necessarily fails.

Que me maten de una vez: Melancholic Mestizaje

Bundled into the cult of mestizaje is the "cult" of death and the notion of a specific brand of Mexican melancholia, such as that theorized in the famous treatise by Paz. This notion of melancholy creates a distressed, antiquarian veneer through which we can appreciate the idiosyncrasy of Mexican "national character," where "the idea of death" (as elegantly studied by Claudio Lomnitz) is primordial. This cult of death and fatal melancholy, witnessed in the well-worn verses from the corrido dedicated to the soldadera "La Valentina," romanticizes the futility of the powerless masses, creates a cult out of desperation and waxes romance over poverty: "Si me han de matar mañana que me maten de una vez" [If they're going to kill me tomorrow, they may as well kill me now]. Furthermore, the notion of a "melancholic *mexicanidad*," as described by Roger Bartra in *La sangre y la tinta* is tied to two figures, the iconic "sad and unknowable" Indian, who has been captured in the photography taken of Mexico's indigenous populations as well as in the arts, and more importantly, to the fraught figure of the mestizo, who, being uniquely "sensitive" to the liminality of a biological and cultural inconstancy, is endowed with a supposed "emotionality" that "is proper to situations of transitions and borders" (145). Many important scholarly books have debated the problems of mestizaje as a hegemonic, pervasive discourse that has been developed and nurtured in multiple iterations across Latin America. Marilyn Miller, in *Rise and Fall of the Cosmic Race*, contends that the "slipperiness of *mestizaje* as a somatic or semiotic category of signification" is a product of many centuries where race was an indelible ontological category, even if it was contested and not uniformly applied (7). Within the diverse and contradicting taxonomies that were created, "the mestizo was frequently converted into an essential racial type who possessed specific traits that were alternately positive or negative, thus casting him and his counterparts (the mestiza, the mulatto, the mulatta, etc.) as either villains or heroes in the drama of identity" (7). In the end, she attests that "*mestizaje* and its variants have been claimed in a vast array of political and cultural projects in the Americas in attempts to solve the riddle of identity for the diverse inhabitants of the area" (25).

Furthermore, in *The Inner Life of Mestizo Nationalism*, Estelle Tarica describes mestizo nationalism as the offspring of *indigenismo* (a state and cultural project designed to vindicate indigenous people through paternalistic political policies and the arts), which would become "the ideological glue transforming revolutionary nationalisms into populist hegemonies in Mexico and the Andes" (187). These state projects, anchored in an imagined (and uneven) racial identity, operated as "a mechanism for the state to accrue power through listening to small voices, voices whose virtue resides precisely in their smallness vis-à-vis the powerful" (187). Tarica contends that these political and cultural movements worked against themselves, because in "the process of strengthening the icon of Indian authority, indigenismo disempowers Indians politically: that irony is part and parcel of indigenista normalization" (199). Therefore, this new mestizo "proclaims an intimate affinity with Indians" (xxii) and converts him "fetishistically, into a norm" (184). The "normalization" of the (fetishized) icon reflects many of the issues at stake in this book; creating icons out of the disempowered further evacuates them of a political voice, power, and future potential. It continues to subordinate indigenous knowledge to Western epistemes because, as expressed by Tarica, it subscribes to "a notion of citizenship understood as the exercise of reason over nature," where the Indian "inside" constitutes a kind of noble, primordial instinct (199). The 1994 Zapatista uprising spoke precisely to this conundrum, simultaneously foregrounding indigenous knowledge while decrying the manipulation of the Indian icon, because not only do Mayas continue to live in poverty and "outside" of history, they are actively persecuted by wealthy landowners and the state.

In contrast to the "normalization" of the Indian as a melancholic and mute icon, Peter Wade contends that it "has often been argued that 'black' is a racial identification, while 'indian' is an ethnic one," which further leads to the misguided idea that there exists a kind of "superficial" or soft racism in Latin America compared to the "deep" racism of the United States (*Race and Ethnicity in Latin America* 23). For Mexican nationalists, discussing Indianness in terms of ethnic identity and blackness in terms of race buttresses the idea that there is "no" racism in México. Christina Sue's ethnography of the Port of Veracruz, *Land of the Cosmic Race*, is revealing in this respect because Veracruz, located on the Gulf coast of México, is regarded as one of the centers of Afro-Mexican culture. According to Sue, racial discourse in Veracruz is Janus-faced. On the one hand, there exists a discourse of racial inclusion that celebrates blackness, but on the other, an active practice of exclusion. The contradiction between the discourse and reality is a product, she claims, of the three pillars of post-revolutionary ideology in México: (1) mestizaje (2) non-racism and (3) non-blackness (14). Her research uncovers that for many residents of the Port, their understanding of race as a category and racism as a practice is intimately linked to blackness. Moreover, their understanding of blackness as it relates to them is situational and mutable. Even those who would in private call themselves *morenos* (a euphemism for blacks), in public do not understand themselves as "true blacks" because of imported notions of race from the United States or their projection of "real" blackness onto the Caribbean (28). Despite the fact that Sue's evidence is taken only from one city, and includes neither the rural countryside where many Afro-Mexicans reside, nor other important coastal communities who are seeking to be recognized by the Mexican state as Afro-Mexican, her evidence underscores that mestizo nationalism, even in areas where there is significant variation in phenotype and race-color identity, is interpreted as monolithic. Furthermore, it accommodates heroic Indian figures such as Cuauhtémoc, but excises the figure of the black hero, even from his own story. As various ethnographic accounts have attested, Gaspar Yanga, who established the first free black town in the Americas, today is ignored and almost irrelevant, even to the inhabitants of the city that bears his name and history: "and yet their lack of a formal or informal education that identifies and acknowledges the importance of Gaspar Yanga, and other blacks in the making of Mexico, robs our informants of that legacy and its implications" (Charles Rowell, "The First Liberator of the Americas," 9).

Despite the insistence on a race-blind mestizaje as a resolution to a diverse population, the complexities of racial identification in México are difficult and profound, as the preference for whitening and whiteness remains intact. Thus, we observe that even where the Afro-Mexican presence is prominent, the discourse of mestizaje has operated successfully to keep Afro-Mexicans subordinate, and worse, invisible and (almost) inaudible. Mexican "melancholy," as we will see in the second half of the book, will compound its tragic tenor when negotiating the unwanted Afro-Mexican presence through the tense language of melodrama that simultaneously acknowledges and dismisses. For example, Laura Gutiérrez signals the complex role of film melodrama in the construction of gender and self-identification because "[f]or the first time mass audiences were also 'recognizing' themselves as they were being socialized into Mexican manhood and womanhood, in the mirrored cinematic screen held up before them" (*Performing Mexicanidad* 103). Likewise, the silver screen will consequently become one of the privileged cultural mediums that will socialize Mexicans into prescribed roles that tangle gender and race, ironically "recognizing" the complexities of these very constructions in the Afro-Mexican voice that will emerge surreptitiously in Afro-Caribbean rhythms.

The tentacular reach of mestizaje and its concomitant contradictions to other parts of Latin America, where blackness is also deflected onto an imagined and romanticized Indianness is powerful. What's more, the impact of Mexican melancholia and negotiations of race, gender, and class in film melodrama will move beyond the borders of Mexican spectatorship and acquire a transnational dimension, a phenomena evidenced in the work of Ricardo Chica in his riveting ethnography of black neighborhoods in Cartagena, *Cuando las negras de Chambacú se querían parecer a María Félix* (2015). According to Chica, Mexican melodrama and melancholia was sold, distributed, and appropriated by means of film spectatorship in subaltern neighborhoods in Cartagena, neighborhoods which were not only marginalized and poor, but predominantly black. Chica reveals how Mexican Golden Age cinema was translated into a pedagogical mode for emergent Colombian citizenship, one that was recognizable by poor blacks and interpreted as a way to occupy public spaces, to assume blackness, and to accept the miserable conditions of daily life by at once romanticizing and deploring their abjection. In the end, the intimate nexus crafted between melancholy, Mexicanness, and mestizaje through Golden Age film and other cultural forms exceeded the boundaries of even the nation-state and would have important repercussions throughout Latin America: the crafting of an abnegated womanhood, disappearing blacks, romanticizing mestizos, and tokenizing Indians.

To conclude, the figures I study are portrayed in rigid ontological terms while they simultaneously turn toward something much more complex and mutable. They slip in and out of static representations and disfigured social identities; however, films, books, songs, photographs, and legends do not congeal their subjects, the "supernumerary" participants, in art. The concepts of *tlacuepa, tlalticpac,* and *olin* help us to understand the complex troping of the figures presented in cultural production as more than mere stock characters that entertain the masses, but rather, as manifestations of new, or rather, torn identities and bent collectivities. The apparent petrification of the material form belies a slippery nature; like a piece of cloth, it can be twisted into another form, or even torn apart. The turning of words (*tlacuepa*) and the preeminence of movement (*olin*) are dynamic concepts that help to comprehend the irony of what are at once rigid and yet disruptive historical, literary, and cultural figures; these are people who cohabitate within the contradictory realms of a permeable periodicity that encompasses art and history, ubiquity and anonymity, tradition and revolution.

Traditional historical writing relies on empirical fact, an archival document that *proves* someone or something existed, said something, or did something. In contrast, these scenarios, novels, plays, short stories, corridos, photographs, murals, communiqués, festivities, poems, films, lithographs, performances, chores, music, activities, and occupations become aesthetic places, spaces, and forms that constitute a singularly open forum where the "invisible," or what the Zapatistas have called "nameless and faceless," can convene. The domain of the aesthetic does not *prove* or identify, but rather points to; words do not define but are "twisted and turned." These aural, visual and linguistic movements constitute an intervention in their own right, twisting the corpus of official History and turning it toward the realm of unofficial Knowledge. Both language and art slip from one meaning, or form, into another.

The notion of *olin* helps to understand the movement in visual, oral, and performative language that creates these fissures, these moments of fracture and lapse, at the same time that the substitutional language of metaphor may congeal. Nevertheless, trope creates a movement of language; its inability to define reflects the very slippery moments when no name is possible, when new possibilities and ambivalent names emerge. The notion of *olin* conjures new and distinct forms of being in its implicit movement: the actual physical movement of the soldaderas, the rhythm and circuitry of the folk ballads and Afro-Mexican music, the racial and cultural ambivalence of the mulata. Cultural production in all its forms intervenes not only to tell the stories of those who remain officially invisible, but actually contributes positively to the re-imagining of what might be considered static or "traditional" identities and ways of life. Like a hologram holds simultaneously contradictory images, the reality of *Nuestra América* as a place where multiple life forms coexist, where periodicity is rendered porous, where art and aesthetic sensibility is both of and not of the West, is the place where the slippery word, the plasticity of the image and the reverberations of sound make present what has remained ambivalent in the history books and absent in official discourses. It is where language and the aesthetic is twisted and turned in simultaneously incongruous yet illuminating forms. It is the place *nobodies* become *somebodies*, are given the name that belongs to something else, if only fleetingly, awkwardly, and unevenly.

The first part of this book, "*Entre Adelitas y Cucarachas*: The Soldadera as Trope in the Mexican Revolution" explores the movement of the soldaderas and their peripatetic migrations outside of the domestic domain and into the public sphere, creating a veritable motile *habitus*, or as James Clifford has theorized, a "dwelling-in-travel." The soldadera, who had a fundamental role in the making of the Revolution, was left unrecognized and unremunerated, yet she filled the pages, screens, and imaginations of Mexicans of the revolutionary and post-revolutionary era. How Mexicans would interpret their revolutionary behavior however, is another matter. By exploring films, popular poetry, photography, and prose, I discuss the tension between how they appropriate traditional spaces and the way this gets interpreted by Mexican society, between what the soldaderas are called and how they are represented in the arts, and its divergence with the roles they actually performed, constituting the basis of a new ontological mode, one that explodes the strict virgin/whore binaries and begins to carve out new ways to be a woman in México.

Chapter 1, "Soldaderas and the Making of Revolutionary Spaces," argues that by breaking from traditional notions of female behavior, soldaderas created what Diana Taylor would call a performative "scenario." It examines their appropriation of the revolutionary train by creating new "places" that resulted in the undoing of traditional public and private spaces and the prevailing middle-class notions of common sense. The infinite number of versions this scenario could produce underscores the multivalence of this scene both for those who participate in it, and for those who view it: the soldaderas around the campfire, dutifully trudging behind their men, on top of the trains, cooking, cleaning and fornicating in the open air covered only by gun-smoke and the stars. These scenarios, which are repeatable, prosaic, and yet multivalent, would brand their place in the imaginary of Mexicans for generations to come. This chapter further examines how these scenarios were captured on film and the impact of the circulation of these images on the Mexican imagination.

Chapter 2, "The Many Faces of the Soldadera and the Adelita Complex," explores the representation of these women in literary, visual, and oral cultural production by unpacking the prevailing tropes that originated in the corridos "La Adelita" and "La Cucuaracha." I consider how the overwhelming visibility and shocking presence of the soldadera forced popular balladeers to change the conventions naturalized by narrative balladry. Female soldiers had a delimited space that they could occupy in the narrative corridos, and the bards did not ignore the historical reality that was not knocking on their door, so to speak, but literally breaking it down. The resurgence of the Mexican corrido was catalyzed by the Revolution of 1910, and three of the most recognizable songs to emerge from this renaissance of popular balladry were about women: "La Adelita," "La Cucaracha," and "La Valentina." Unfortunately, because they do not adhere to traditional conventions of corrido balladry, folklorists do not consider them "real" corridos, but rather, catchy songs, lyrical renditions that, despite their popularity, do not correspond to the hearty ballads of the time-old tradition that have their origins in medieval Spain. In effect, they are given names that belong to someone else; although Adelita and Valentina were real-life women, their names became abstracted from the reality of battle, from the specificity of time, and are immortalized as love-objects. La Cucaracha (a corrido about a drunken soldadera), already divorced from the world of man and plunged into an animal-like state, constitutes any harlot who entertained the troops. Still, these three are not only recognized nationally, but also internationally as emblems of Mexican folk music, operating as unofficial anthems of the Revolution. Through metonymy, these abstractions come to represent the whole of female participation in the Revolution.

Chapter 3, "Beyond the Custom of Her Sex and Country," ends the first part of the book by examining some of the more ambivalent renditions of the soldadera figure in the works of John Reed, Elena Poniawtoska, and Nellie Campobello. By reflecting on how the trope of death is woven in as cohering metaphor, I consider how these figures, in addition to the image of an Afro-Mexican soldadera thought to be taken by Casasola, twist the rigidity of the Cucaracha/Adelita stereotype into unheard of forms that will constitute new, albeit ephemeral, practices of Mexican womanhood.

The second part of the book, "The Blacks in the Closet," unearths the legacy of the African presence in the Mexican cultural imaginary, focusing on the figure of the mulata and Mexican music in the form of *son jarocho* and the prevalence of *música tropical*. The mulata, like the soldadera, lacks a proper name and place in legitimate society, identified only through the sexual congress of an anonymous black slave woman and a Spanish father who will deny her his name. Whereas indigenous people are considered part of an obscure bygone era, forever rendered in the preterite tense, blacks do not even figure into this romanticized past, appearing almost *ex nihilo*. Unlike the muddled masses that define the image of the soldadera, mulatas mark their presence through the emergence of singular, exceptional figures that are easily brushed aside by the populace as curious anomalies. However, blacks had a formidable role in the forging of early colonial history and culture. In 1640, New Spain contained the second largest population of enslaved Africans and the greatest number of free blacks in the Americas. In 1646, according to Gonzalo Aguirre Beltrán, Europeans totaled 13,780, Africans 35,089, Indians 1,269,607, Indomestizos 109,042, Euromestizos 168,568, and Afromestizos came in at 116,529. By 1810, free blacks comprised about 10 percent of the total population, constituting a significant minority while Africans constituted .1 percent, and Europeans .2 percent (234).[17] The combined total of Africans and their descendants is striking considering that at times they actually outnumbered the Europeans, and the majority of the population never stopped being comprised of indigenous people (falling to 60 percent in 1810). Such figures counter the notion that blacks constituted an insignificant minority in New Spain. As Herman Bennett reminds us, in 1646 at least half of the black population lived in México City, the vice-regal center, cultivating a decidedly urban cultural expression that solidified the black community (*Colonial Blackness* 5).

The fourth chapter, "Black Magic and the Inquisition: The Legend of La Mulata de Córdoba and the Case of Antonia de Soto," examines how blacks were part and parcel of the nascent colonial regime and culture, as many were considered more culturally assimilable than the indigenous populations. The General Archives of the Nation in México City houses an astounding number of trials by slaves litigating against their masters within the confines of their rights as Christian subjects. There are also a considerable number of court cases involving mulatos and free blacks defending themselves against the Inquisition for a variety of charges, including heresy, bigamy, and witchcraft. Thus, by critically examining the legend of La Mulata de Córdoba and the Inquisition case of the runaway slave Antonia de Soto, we see how this colonial legend begets a whole mythology regarding black women in México. They are associated with witchcraft, magic, unknown origins, or a "tropicalized" elsewhere that infected the local populace with its hyper-sexualized presence, and then, disappeared. These disappearing acts will mark the legacy of all blacks in México; there are glimmers, hints, traces, and insinuations, but never claims about their contributions to Mexican history and culture.

Chapter 5, " 'Dios pinta como quiere': Blackness and Redress in Mexican Golden Age Film" examines the figuring of the mulata in the novel and film, *La negra Angustias* and the films, *La Mulata de Córdoba*, *Angelitos negros*, and *Negro es mi color*. In all of these films produced at the height of Mexican's Golden Era, we see the destiny of the mulato children end in tragic negligence. Together these films make an incipient attempt to contend with the problem of racism against blacks in México, but also gesture toward an ambivalence regarding the significant contributions of blacks to Mexican culture. By representing blackness as exceptional, displacing it onto the Caribbean or abstracting the position of blacks in México into a universal dilemma of racism as part of the legacy of slavery, these films reproduce the very racism that they attempt to rectify. In several of the films, the mulata protagonist is portrayed as phenotypically white and represents a sort of Mexican version of the "tragic mulatta" as they openly reject their blackness while the films attempt rather weakly to reconcile the protagonists to their "past." Undoubtedly, blackness is represented in atavistic terms, a curious throwback that is destined, through the ambiguous position of the abandoned mulato progeny, to disappear. In contrast, Angustias, the protagonist in the novel by Francisco Rojas González, makes a strong claim to her blackness; however, this claim becomes repudiated by the inability of white, *criollo* society to incorporate her black body and female desire. The acceptance of her black body ultimately condemns her to social invisibility.

The sixth chapter, "The Music of the Afro-Mexican Universe and the Dialectics of Son," begins with a reflection on the potentialities of popular music to respond to a social reality and history, but also to configure it. Musical culture is one of the most obvious ways blacks in New Spain, who arrived since at least the Conquest if not before, have reminded their fellow compatriots that they too have had a hand in the forging of what is considered contemporary Mexican culture. The ardent acceptance and appropriation of "tropical" music and dance—such as the *danzón* and *son cubano* that form an integral part of the carnival festivities in Veracruz—points to the Gulf Coast as a part of the greater Caribbean, and by extension, part of the diasporic community of Africans. For example, *danzón* has been enjoyed in Veracruz since its introduction over a hundred years ago, and is part of the regional culture of the Gulf Coast. However, as is demonstrated by Cuba's homage to México City, Guadalajara, and the Yucatán in their annual festivals reclaiming the *danzón* as part of Cuban cultural heritage, *danzón* is not exclusive to the tropical Port of Veracruz; it is central to Mexican culture.

Originating in the state of Veracruz, *son jarocho* is one of México's most traditional musical genres that is a product of the Afro-Mestizo universe that has been fashioning itself since the sixteenth century. *Son jarocho*, an example of what sociologist Ángel Quintero calls "música mulata," insinuates itself into the fabric of the national narrative through its most popular songs: "El Chuchumbé" and "La Bamba." These songs are some of the oldest *sones* that were a product of Afro-Mexican popular culture and the traditions of the people "de color quebrado" [of broken color]. "La Bamba," made internationally famous by Chicano artist Richie Valens, alongside "La Adelita" and "La Cucaracha," is one of the most well-known tunes in Mexican culture. Such songs, in particular "La Bamba" and "La Cucaracha," are startling examples of how México's nobodies are the subjects and originators of musical traditions that would come to constitute the culture of a globalized Mexicanness. Their circulation is part of the power of movement, of *olin* as an epistemological construct, and music as a social force.

This chapter also considers the impact of Cuban music and culture on Mexican cultural production and identity by focusing on Toña la Negra, the matriarchal mulata figure who is a national icon and performer of boleros as well as Cuban *son* from the Gulf Coast of Veracruz, México. Toña la Negra paradoxically constitutes the quintessence of Mexicanness through her status as the model *jarocha* (a term used to refer to inhabitants of Veracruz which means person of "mixed blood") despite her claim to blackness. Finally, the triangulation of a racialized Caribbean identity with the strong African presence in Veracruz is the larger subject of this chapter.

In conclusion, cultural production, although insistent on maintaining rigid caricatures of these figures, in its circuitry, rhythm, and movement reveals fundamental elisions, and it is in these aesthetic possibilities that glimpses of other "truths" may be ascertained by those who choose to look. Each of these figures circulates in the national imaginary in all the forms that figural speech and acts may take. But as tropes, figuration does violence to the individuals who these forms pretend to represent. These individuals are the women who took up arms alongside men in order to revolt against tyranny in

1910. They are the Africans and their descendants who helped construct this emerging Spanish colony by becoming Christians and an integral component of the nascent colonial culture only to be summarily eliminated as a presence hundreds of years later, emerging in triangulation with the Caribbean, or as curious "guests." These chapters turn toward the past in order to re-imagine the present by revealing how art has manipulated the representation of these individuals into a language that can only be expressed otherwise.

Part One

Entre Adelitas y Cucarachas

The Soldadera as Trope in the Mexican Revolution

1

Soldaderas and the Making of Revolutionary Spaces

Junto a las grandes tropas de Francisco Villa, Emiliano Zapata y Venustiano Carranza, más de mil novecientos líderes lucharon en bandas rebeldes. Las soldaderas pululan en las fotografías. Multitud anónima, comparsas, al parecer telón de fondo, sólo hacen bulto, pero sin ellas los soldados no hubieran comido ni dormido ni peleado.

[Together with the great troops of Francisco Villa, Emiliano Zapata and Venustiano Carranza, more than one thousand nine hundred leaders fought in rebel bands. The soldaderas hovered in the photographs. An anonymous multitude, groups in the background, they only form a blurry shape, but without these women the soldiers would not have eaten, slept or fought].

—Elena Poniatowska, Las soldaderas

Elena Poniatowska chose this photograph (see Fig 1.1) as the cover of her important book on the participation of soldaderas, the thousands of women who accompanied troops of male soldiers and acted in a wide range of capacities, during the Mexican Revolution. Originally thought to have been taken between 1910 and 1914 by Agustín Casasola, it is one of the most widely disseminated portrayals of the soldaderas. Indeed, the image contains all the elements Roland Barthes might consider relevant for both a journalistic and posed photograph. In his book, *Camera Lucida*, Barthes suggests that for the photographer, the best picture would be taken when that subject is not aware of the camera, thus capturing the original and unaffected state of the subject (32).

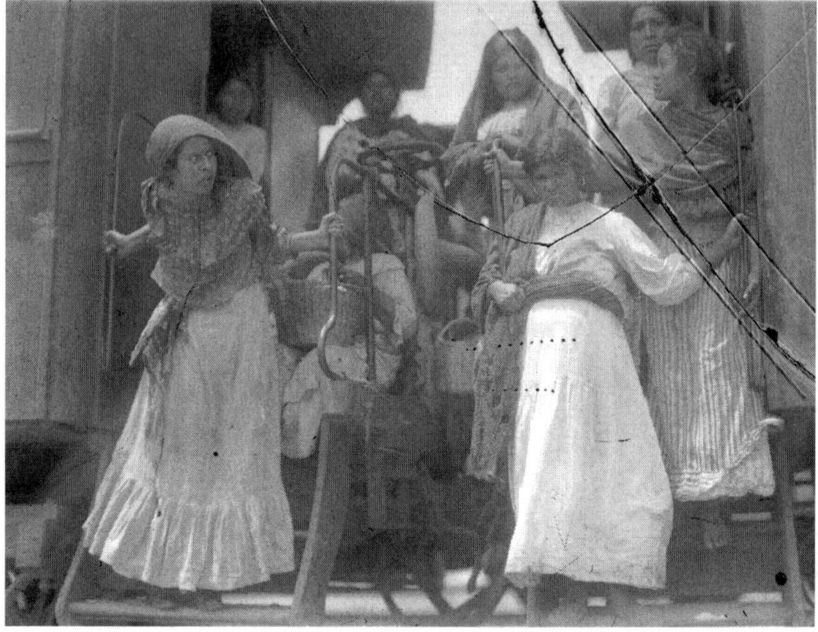

FIGURE 1.1. "Soldaderas on the platform at the Buenavista train station," México City, D.F., April 1912.

It is clear that certain figures in this photograph are caught unaware, while other women are very much conscious that they are being photographed, and are in fact posing, or looking directly into the camera. The woman to the left, whose image alone has been cropped and reproduced innumerable times, is hanging from the train and wears a rather desperate expression on her face. Is she looking for her *soldado*? Is she simply a vendor looking to sell her wares, or is she looking for trouble? Her ambiguous expression, one that is simultaneously worried and reminiscent of the mischievous stereotype we see of the soldadera in so many texts, is emblematic of the very ambiguous nature of the soldadera herself. Unlike this random shot, the young pregnant woman to the right is very much aware of the photographer capturing her image. Barthes describes the process of posing and becoming an image as a self-constitutive act, claiming that "once I feel myself observed by the lens, everything changes: I constitute myself Nin the process of 'posing,' I instantaneously make another body for myself, I transform myself in advance into an image" (10). Although her head is slightly bent, she is looking directly at us, squinting as if the sun were in her eyes, or as if she were uncomfortable with being photographed. Is this timidity, like Poniatowska describes below, or annoyance? Behind her a woman with a *rebozo*[1] covering her head is slightly out of focus, but likewise looks demurely into the camera, posing for what might be her single moment of anonymous immortality. The whole scene, though typical of those we have come to associate with the Mexican Revolution of 1910, is nonetheless missing some of the vital elements: soldiers, rifles, and horses.

Poniatowska describes these photographs as a contradiction to the kind of story told by the canonical authors of the Mexican Revolution. In the following passage from her book *Las soldaderas*, she remarks on the vision projected by Casasola's images and how they undermine archetypal figures like "La Pintada" provided by Mariano Azuela's classic revolutionary novel *Los de abajo* (1915), the model on which México's premier film diva María Félix's[2] character "La Cucaracha" (1959) was based:

> En las fotografías de Agustín Casasola, las mujeres con sus enaguas de percal, sus blusas blancas, sus caritas lavadas, su mirada baja, para que no se les vea la vergüenza en los ojos, su candor [. . .] sus manos morenas deteniendo la bolsa del mandado o aprestándose para entregarle el máuser al compañero, no parecen las fieras malhabladas y vulgares que pintan los autores de la Revolución mexicana.

> [In the photography by Agustín Casasola, the women with their percale petticoats, their white blouses, scrubbed faces, lowered gaze hiding the shame in their eyes, their candor [. . .] their brown hands holding the money pouch or rushing to pass their partner his Mauser, do not seem like the foul-mouthed, vulgar beasts the authors of the Mexican Revolution would make them out to be]. (13)

This photograph reveals a fundamental ambiguity: we see the "caritas lavadas," "blusas blancas," "enaguas de percal," "mirada baja" and "candor" while we simultaneously observe what might be either the weariness of their dress or the deterioration of the image. We also notice that women are caught unaware as pieces of the revolutionary background, and in the foreground, as protagonists and subjects "becoming" images before the click of the camera shutter is completed.

Soldaderas constituted the "anonymous multitude" and "blurry shapes" that helped to make the Mexican Revolution of 1910 (which preceded both the Russian and Cuban Revolutions) a reality. Poniatowska lauds the role of photography in preserving the legacy of the soldaderas and laments that were it not for the work of Agustín Casasola, Jorge Guerra, and the "kilometers" of film shot by Salvador Toscano, the presence of these women would be lost because history has only denigrated them (21). She compiled many of these photographs into a book which functions as a cultural and historical memoir, poetically splicing together bits and pieces from novels, corridos, history, and revolutionary chronicles in a disjointed and almost miscellaneous fashion, not unlike the haphazard way in which the soldadera traveled and has been remembered. She, like myself and many others, laments both the historical and cultural representation of these women as miserable camp followers who were not much more than prostitutes, troublemaking and vulgar "cucarachas," or sweet-faced "adelitas" patiently waiting for their men to come home. These photographs, however, reveal something more than the histories related to us through revolutionary novels, chronicles, and films; they reveal a presence that has been effaced, misunderstood, maligned, and distorted, but that nevertheless *existed*.

Both Susan Sontag and Roland Barthes suggest one axiomatic truth: photography provides proof of what at one point existed at a moment in time. Barthes states that "[e]very photograph is a certificate of presence" (87) and Sontag claims that "[p]hotographs furnish evidence" (5). These blunt aphorisms become undeniably true in the case of the soldadera as they are almost the sole empirical testament to their existence; but more important, they are the closest approximations to what might have constituted their reality. This photograph is in fact witness to their multiple stories, to their roles in the background as what Poniatowska calls "bultitos de miseria" [bundles of misery] as well as in the foreground: as nurses, generals, warriors, spies, cooks, wives, mothers, daughters, lovers, prostitutes, and companions. It also speaks to the forced, improvised, or even arbitrary nature of their participation in addition to their willed and conscious involvement. By posing for photographs, they created images and constituted their subjectivity; by deflecting their gaze from the intrusiveness of the camera, they constituted themselves as part of the background.

This one image single-handedly emblematizes and obscures the legacy of the soldadera. As it turns out, this photograph has traveled through historical memory and was not even taken by Agustín Víctor Casasola at all, but, as John Mraz affirms in his book on the Casasola legacy in Mexican photography, by Gerónimo Hernández (*Photographing the Mexican Revolution* 240). It has been interpreted and misinterpreted as an icon of revolutionary womanhood in what Mraz calls a "condensed comedy of errors" (240). It first appeared on the cover of the newspaper *Nueva Era* on April 8, 1912, where the "cutline proclaimed, 'I will defend my Juan'" (240). It subsequently disappeared only to reappear thirty years later in Gustavo Casasola's (Agustín's brother) compilation published in 1942, *Historia gráfica de la Revolución*, labeled as "Adelita-la-soldadera" accompanied by the following information: "The soldadera has seen all of Mexico, crossing from border to border" (240). Indeed, the conflicting hypotheses regarding the origin of this image abound. Mraz confirms that it couldn't have been taken in 1910 because there were very few troop movements that year, but rather, was shot in 1912, at the Buena Vista Station in México City where troops were preparing to travel north in order to quell the rebellion of Pasqual Orozco (240).

Now that we know the historical "truth," the empirical fact that situates this photograph in a specific time and place, does it tell us anything more about what it was like to be a soldadera, or if indeed these women, whose image has traveled "throughout the Americas, Europe and Asia," actually were soldaderas at all (240)? Like the crack in the original glass negative, this broken image, often cropped to leave the other women out, constitutes an historical fragment, a flicker of knowledge, an alternative *saber*[3] that allows us to meet these women and surmise their history. "I will defend my Juan" sounds like a romantic line from a film we would all like to see, but hardly constitutes any historical truth because these women occupied the slippery spaces in between the cavalry and the *retaguardia* [rearguard], the immobile home and the ambulant hearth, the abnegating wife and the loose woman. With this image in mind, this chapter will argue that the mobile presence of the soldaderas affected women's *place* in Mexican history, but also created, through the aleatory nature of a popular uprising, revolutionary *spaces* that led to a split from previous models of female behavior. I claim that this particular military intervention by the soldaderas, more than in previous wars, constituted a radically different ontological state marked by movement and the creation of a *habitus* in motion. That is, the oppositional tensions implicit in stasis and movement coincide with the mode in which the soldaderas *travel*.

Art, in all its forms and figurations, has been instrumental to remembering these women at the same time it has deformed their legacy. The first part of this book will examine the way the female body becomes the site of a powerful tropological discourse in revolutionary and post-revolutionary México, leading to my theoretical queries: why does her body constitute the site of such discursive tension? Why is the image of this figure, bandoliers across her chest, carrying both child and *molcajete*[4] in her *rebozo*, braids flowing, synonymous with the Mexican Revolution, yet discursively and hence historically erased in the same gesture? How does this figure point to the fissures in the nation's historical memory with regard to its public women? Soldaderas mark the limits of the rhetoric of the nation-state and their very nomenclature debases the real worth of female participation in war. The contradictions in the photographic images foreground the very paradoxical nature of the soldaderas' historical invisibility, and yet, figural ubiquity. I will first explore the movement of the soldaderas and the importance of the train in their peripatetic migrations outside of the domestic domain into the public sphere as a concrete example of how they created a veritable motile *habitus*, or as James Clifford has theorized, a "dwelling-in-travel." By breaking from traditional notions of female behavior, they created what Diana Taylor would call a performative "scenario." This scenario—which is repeatable, prosaic yet multivalent—would brand their place in the imaginary of Mexicans for generations to come. The following section will unpack some of the concepts that the example of inhabiting the train makes manifest: the creation of a scenario, "dwelling-in-travel" through revolutionary practices and tactics, and divergent occupations of place and space. I will then present a brief herstory that will outline what little is known about the soldaderas, and conclude by returning to the image examined at the beginning. The contemplation of this image will allow us to reconsider the role of photography in preserving their memory vis-à-vis the cultural products that showcase them in the following chapter.

Y se les fue el tren . . .[5]

Throughout the Revolution all the rail workers contributed to the cause, because the Mexican Revolution was made on the train-tracks.[6]

—Guillermo Treviño in Documentary by John Mraz,
Hechos sobre los rieles [Made on Rails] (1987)

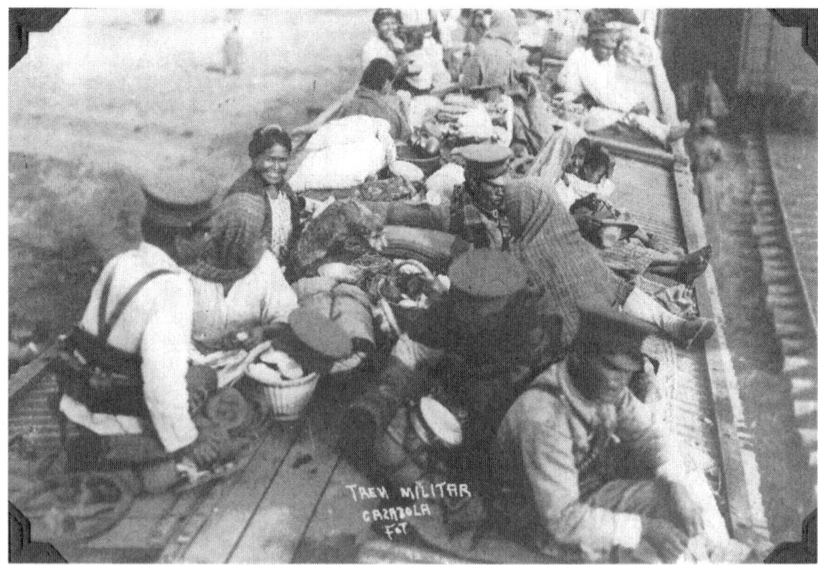

FIGURE 1.2. "Soldier and soldaderas on the roof of railcar," México, 1914.

One of the most important instruments of the Mexican Revolution was the locomotive, and many believe, as emphasized by railroad union leader Guillermo Treviño in John Mraz's documentary about the trains in México, that the Revolution was literally "made on the rails." That is to say, that it revolutionized war practices by transporting the arms, cavalry and of course the soldaderas on its rooftops; any of a dozen films featuring the soldadera during the Revolution will showcase the train as practically a character in the revolutionary drama. The soldaderas had no official texts: the trains were one of their texts, their "practiced places," whose image now resonates as the icon of one of most important revolutions of the twentieth century. They certainly "got on" the trains (albeit in unconventional fashions) by climbing onto the rooftops; but they also got in the cars with the animals, and some even tied planks below, hanging perilously in the lurch if the train hit a sharp curve.

Regarding the risks of the train's mobility, Michel De Certeau, in *The Practice of Everyday Life*, pronounces the following dictum which we could use to consider the ways in which the soldadera occupied the locomotive: "[t]o get in [the train], as always, there was a price to be paid. The historical threshold of beatitude: history exists where there is a price to be paid" (113). The soldaderas inhabited the trains, made a space out of a transient, marginalized place, lived through movement, not stasis; they blurred and even obliterated the frontiers between private and public spheres, creating a humble home out of a what for De Certeau is a bourgeois vehicle. However, the making of a space for De Certeau is also the unmaking of stasis, of a "proper" (what De Certeau calls a place) and is actualized as a vortex of conflicting variables of time and energy:

> A space exists when one takes into consideration vectors of direction, velocities, and time variables [. . .] It is in a sense actuated by the ensemble of movements deployed within it. Space occurs as the effect produced by the operations that orient it, situate it, temporalize it, and make it function in a polyvalent unity of conflictual programs or contractual proximities [. . .] In contradistinction to the place, it has thus none of the univocity or stability of a "proper." (117)

Somehow, the soldaderas paradoxically accomplished both. They made and unmade the train as a place by defying its "proper" function but also by simultaneously domesticating it; the train operates as multiple "phatic topoi." By claiming it as a place, they created their own "proper" and embodied space, undoing the "proper" grounded by hegemonic groups.

The train in motion creates a dynamic relationship between the inside and the outside, the relative stasis of the railroad car, closed in by the windows, and the constantly changing field of vision: "The machine is the *primum mobile*, the solitary god from which all the action proceeds. It not only divides spectators and beings, but also connects them; it is a mobile sym-bol [sic] between them, a tireless shifter, producing changes in the relationships between immobile elements" (113). The train paradoxically divides and connects simultaneously. This relationship, for De Certeau, is negotiated through the chiasm of the windowpane or the rail because it inverts the immobility of the inside with the mobility of the outside (112). However, in our case this division is rendered ambivalent, as it is not always clear who the spectators are. For De Certeau, the spectator is located within, gazing out and observing the countryside from a privileged position of speed and isolation. But this neglects that beyond the windowpane people are gazing back *onto* the train; the visual image of the revolutionary train in México with its troops cooking on the roof or hanging perilously below must have been impressive, carving out a place, and new revolutionary space in the national imaginary. De Certeau reminds us that the railroad combines dreams with technology and is haunted by the speculative, constituting "[a] strange moment in which a society fabricates spectators and transgressors of spaces, with saints and blessed souls placed in the halos-holes (*aureoles-alvéoles*) of its railway cars" (113). The train in México and Latin America in general did

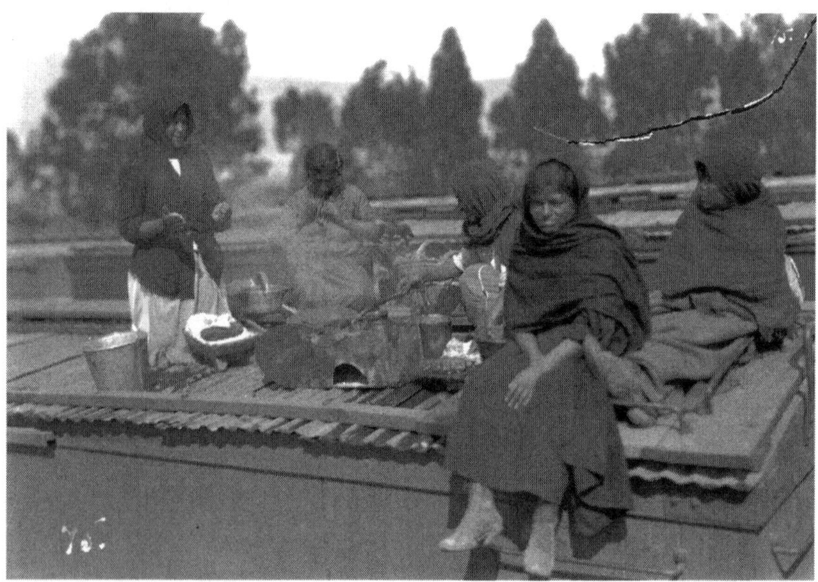

FIGURE 1.3. "Soldaderas prepare food on the roof of a railcar," México City, D.F., 1914.

invoke the speculative; it combined dreams with technology by symbolizing, in nationalist discourse, progress and change. It also allowed for movement, initially just of goods, but during the Revolution it provided for the movement of people who had hitherto remained secluded by poverty to their villages. It provoked the movement of ideas—and hope.

Like the Nahua notion of *olin* (a deified movement), the soldadera also creates relationships between oppositional elements, between life and death, between home and elsewhere, between patriarchy and female subjectivity, between stasis and movement. However compelling De Certeau's notion of "space" is, in addition to his vision of the train as a vehicle of modernity, this vision is limited in scope. Although the train functions as an object of mobility and travel, as a transgressor of space and of a proper place, its articulation in De Certeau is marked by a profoundly bourgeois notion of travel. Falling within the purview of James Clifford's objections to traditional Western conceptions of "travel" and "travelers," De Certeau's idea of train travel invokes a specific form of travel and a specific kind of traveler. While the image of the train has been troped in Latin America as a symbol of modernity and progress, the separation between spectator and object put forth by De Certeau becomes problematic when we consider the ways in which soldaderas and the *soldados* occupied the spaces within the body of the train, its "halos" and "holes": the windowpane and the rail become obsolete partitions. For De Certeau it is the bourgeois machine par excellence, where the people interred are surrounded by glass and iron: "The incarceration–vacation is over [. . .] There comes to an end the Robinson Crusoe adventure of the traveling noble soul that could believe itself intact because it was surrounded by glass and iron" (114). This bourgeois vision is severely problematized by the soldaderas (and soldiers) riding, living, and reproducing on the train's rooftop. It did not occur to him that the spectator would be *outside* of the train traveling on its roof, or in a windowless car with the livestock, or underneath its bowels perilously tied to a plank. This is how the soldaderas embodied this moving place. He does not imagine that the "noble soul" would still be intact when surrounded by, rather than steel and glass, the rudeness of nature, by the velocity of the wind. Her "nobility" is constituted by her emancipation from the metal and glass cage, she is incarcerated only by the elements. Soldaderas simultaneously turned the *primmum mobile* into a home, a proper place, but also one of the most important spaces of the early twentieth century; they revolutionized the *primmum mobile* by transforming it into a living organism.

The train, like the soldaderas, was utilized as a critical vehicle for making the Revolution a reality; she buckled under the weight of all her bundles, was at once a weapon, a way to move around and a home—or she was blown to bits. Indeed, by redefining and re-purposing the top of the train, they moved beyond the weight of a modernity that never came, and closer to an undefined,

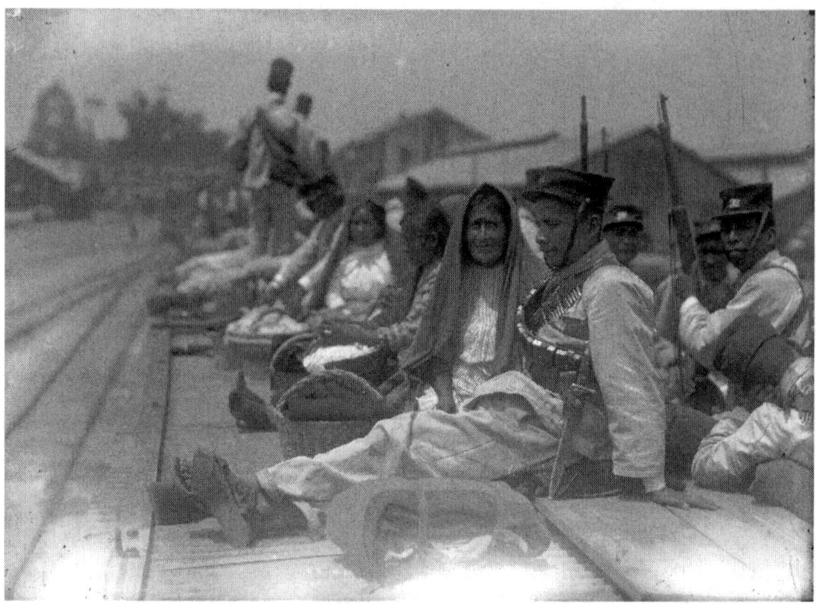

FIGURE 1.4. "Federal soldiers and their families on the roof of the railcars," México City, D.F., 1914.

unimagined postmodernity. In a superbly written passage, Poniatowska utilizes the trope of the soldadera as a metaphor for understanding and appreciating the importance of the train as an icon in revolutionary México:

> La locomotora es la gran heroína de la Revolución Mexicana. Soldadera ella misma, va confiada y resoplando, llega tarde, sí, pero es que viene muy cargada. Suelta todo el vapor y se asienta frente a los andenes para que vuelvan a penetrarla los hombres con el fusil en alto. Allí sube la tropa a sentársele encima. Ella aguanta todo, por eso las huestes enemigas quieren volarla por los aires

> [The locomotive is the great heroine of the Mexican Revolution. A soldadera herself, she travels huffing and puffing but is confidant; she arrives late, that is true, but she is quite burdened. She blows off steam and sits in front of the station when the men, with their rifles upright, penetrate her again. The troops climb up to sit themselves on top of her. She can support it all, even when the enemy army tries to blow her to smithereens]. (20)

In an interesting tropological triangulation, the train becomes figured as a soldadera, turning the sexualized trope of the train as phallic on its head by making it feminine. The train for Poniatowksa becomes another instantiation of the soldadera. Although the war took its toll, blew her to smithereens ("volarla por los aires"), she continued on, served as cover while her inhabitants patched her up, waited patiently while they laid more track in front of her.

Unlike De Certeau's phallic notion of the train as a *primmum mobile*, the train is more like a womb. As a vehicle of modernity, it returns to the most basic of functions. Denying the vanguard obsession with speed and technological progress, it is more like Poniwatoska's trope: she straggles overburdened, moves slowly—*eppur si muove*—is monumental but mute, except when she screams her arrival or departure producing a frantic hysteria in her wake. For De Certeau, the train bears an almost god-like resemblance, huge and monumental; but it is a god undone when it is housed in the station and is "almost incongruous in its mute, idol-like inertia" (114). The train in revolutionary México is not undone by its temporary stasis; it respires, recovers, provides shade, and marks the landscape like a beautiful animal. The inertia of the idol does not undo her; it creates her. Like the soldadera who is incarcerated by her place in the cultural order, the train incarcerates its passengers, but then expels them like newborn children; each time the train stops its passengers are somewhere "else," somewhere "new." Like the soldadera, the train adapts itself to travel, to movement and change. Indeed, it domesticates this movement, becoming a place and space (what Guillermo Delgado L. would call a sp/l/ace) where the most quotidian actions take place: both the train and the soldadera revolutionized the Revolution. The train is a moving paradox: ancient and modern, dynamic and static. Like *olin*, it moves in and out of human, political and social dramas; like *olin*, its movement is necessary for the perseverance of human kind within an aleatory social revolution. This movement provides the precarious balance within the order of the cosmos.

My reading of the impact of the train in revolutionary México is manifest, for example, in the raw, documentary-style cinematic language of the film *La soldadera* (1967) by Mexican filmmaker José Bolaños. The film, which was inspired by John Reed's chapter titled "Elizabetta" from his book *Insurgent Mexico* (which I will discuss at length in chapter 3), uses a neo-realist technique that purported to represent the "reality" of the Revolution with the train serving as a character alongside the soldadera. In multiple scenes when the train pulls into a station, we hear the diegetic sound of the steam engine as the only relevant sonic backdrop: the heavy breath of the train resembles the fatigued respiration of an animal, a beast of burden, and by this token vivifies, and even humanizes, what was at one moment a symbol of man's technological progress. At another point in the film we witness the protagonist, the soldadera Lázara, give birth on top of the moving train, bringing new life into a home in flux. In yet another even more poignant moment, the soldaderas pray beneath a parked railcar, lighting candles for their soldiers who are engaged in battle. All the recognizable referents of daily life, which includes giving birth, praying, resting, and waiting, take place en route to somewhere else.

The way in which the soldaderas occupied the train provides us with a very concrete example of how they transformed the revolutionary landscape, and through revolutionary tactics and practices, dwelled and traveled simultaneously, unbinding traditional notions of domesticity and travel. This vibrant living in motion was not lost on the arts; as witnessed in Bolaños's movie, it is in all the films, novels and even corridos. The *mise-en-scène* presented to us in diverse forms of cultural production captures, however briefly, the radical nature of the new life forms that were in the midst of creating themselves. The trope of the soldadera slips in and out of focus, but its presence in the arts allows us as spectators, readers, and critics to appreciate what became

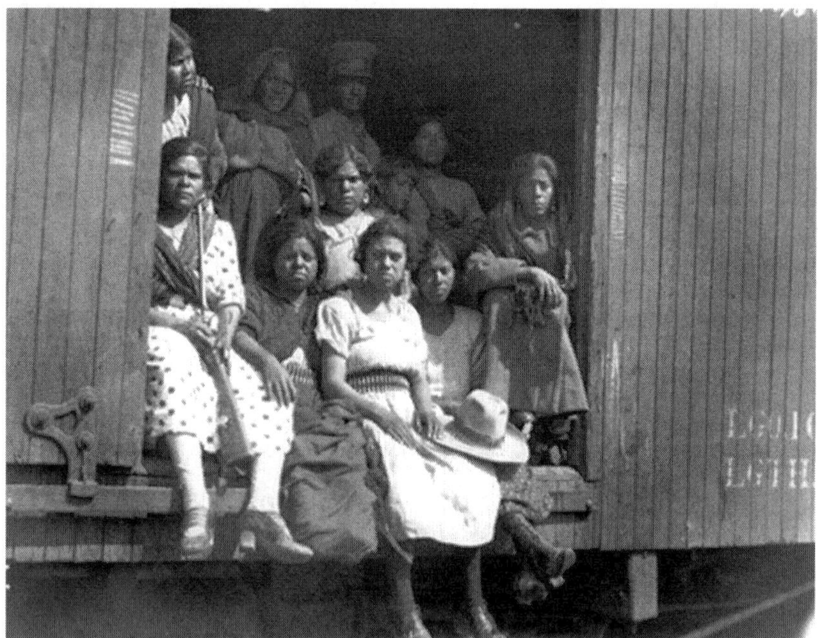

Figure 1.5. "Soldier and soldaderas in a train car," México, 1914.

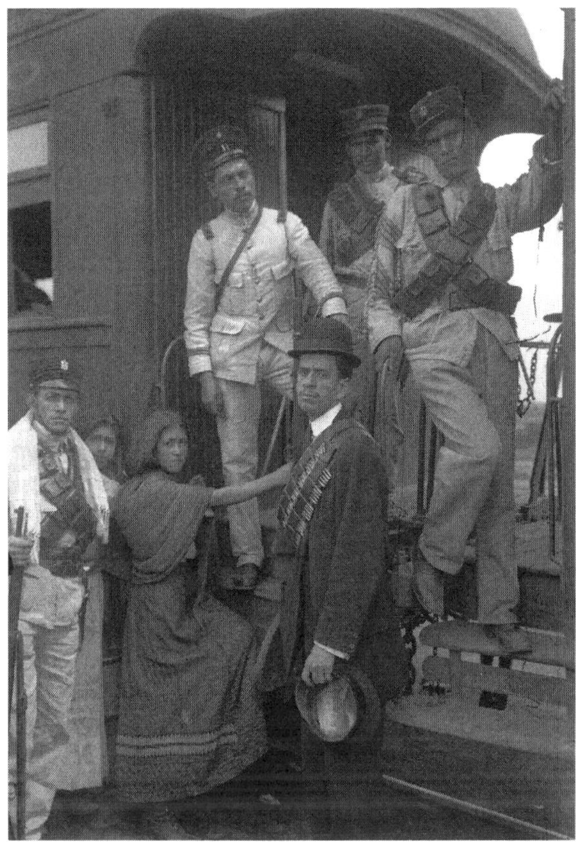

FIGURE 1.6. "Federal soldiers, soldaderas and the railway administrator on the platform of the train," México City, D.F., April 1913.

a profound, albeit ephemeral, moment of social change that took place on the road.

Revolutionary Practices on the Road

From the migrations of the Chichimecas and their encounters with the Toltecas as narrated in the *Historia Tolteca-Chichimeca* in the sixteenth century, to the founding of Tenochtitlan in the mythical spot where the eagle was seen devouring a snake on a cactus, travel in México has been a primordial part of its chorographic, social, historical, and ritual imaginary. The idea of travel, however, has been generally envisaged within a very specific set of terms ranging from adventure and proselytization to conquest. In his book *Routes,* James Clifford challenges traditional notions of travel within Western epistemological frameworks by addressing our perceptions as well as its effects in the construction of culture and knowledge. Clifford suggests travel "denotes a range of material, spatial practices that produce knowledges, stories, traditions, comportments, musics, books, diaries, and other cultural expressions," and that even the most exploitative and impoverished conditions of travel do "not entirely quell resistance or the emergence of diasporic and migrant cultures" (35). The appearance of peasant and middle-class women in Mexican public spheres discussed by Elena Poniatowska, Carlos Monsiváis, and Debra Castillo is conditioned by this notion of travel. They broke out of their homes and native communities and into the national imaginary. They traveled the countryside, coming into contact (many for the first time) with other communities throughout México. Clifford not only nuances the notion of travel by revealing its ideologically constructed nature, he also expands who can be considered a traveler:

> And in this perspective the notion that certain classes of people are cosmopolitan (travelers) while the rest are local (natives) appears as the ideology of one (very powerful) cultural localization, the making of 'natives,' which I criticized at the outset [. . .] Rather what is at stake is a comparative cultural studies approach to specific histories, tactics, everyday practices of dwelling and traveling: traveling-in-dwelling, dwelling-in-traveling. (36)

Traditionally, these movements by military troops have not been considered travel because travel was defined by a specific class-consciousness: poor people and women did not travel in the way conquistadors, explorers, anthropologists, diplomats, and upper-class bourgeoisie did. The soldaderas' task was itinerant in nature: when the troops moved, so did the women who supported them. Unlike traditional notions of domesticity, they traveled and dwelled simultaneously, creating images and practices that mutually constitute and disavow each other. Clifford's notion of "traveling-in-dwelling" is nowhere more applicable than to the soldadera. Her specific yet anonymous history, her "tactics" and "practices" of dwelling through travel all contributed the forging of a new language.

As implied by this notion of simultaneous dwelling and travel, meaning is not just discursively constructed; the body and its interaction with space are extremely important in determining the nature of social structures and environments. In *The Archive and the Repertoire,* Diana Taylor points to the limits of discourse by highlighting the importance of the body and the material in the production of meaning: "Instead of privileging texts and narratives, we could also look at scenarios as meaning-making paradigms that structure social environments, behaviors, and potential outcomes" (28). Taylor contributes to my understanding of the impact of the soldadera through her contention that performance moves beyond the linguistic/discursive realm because metaphors do not operate solely on the level of language: they are also embodied performances. Furthermore, Taylor underscores the importance of place because *scenarios* become encoded, transient places that are reproduced in order to create meaning: "In other words, scenarios exist as culturally specific imaginaries—sets of possibilities, ways of conceiving conflict, crisis, or resolution—activated with more or less theatricality. Unlike trope, which is a figure of speech, theatricality does not rely on language to transmit a set pattern of behavior or action" (13). By dwelling and traveling simultaneously, the soldaderas created very specific and recognizable *scenarios*.

The notions of "place" and "space" are highly contested issues that have contributed to a vibrant debate regarding dwelling, belonging and displacement. De Certeau defines place as an "instantaneous configuration of

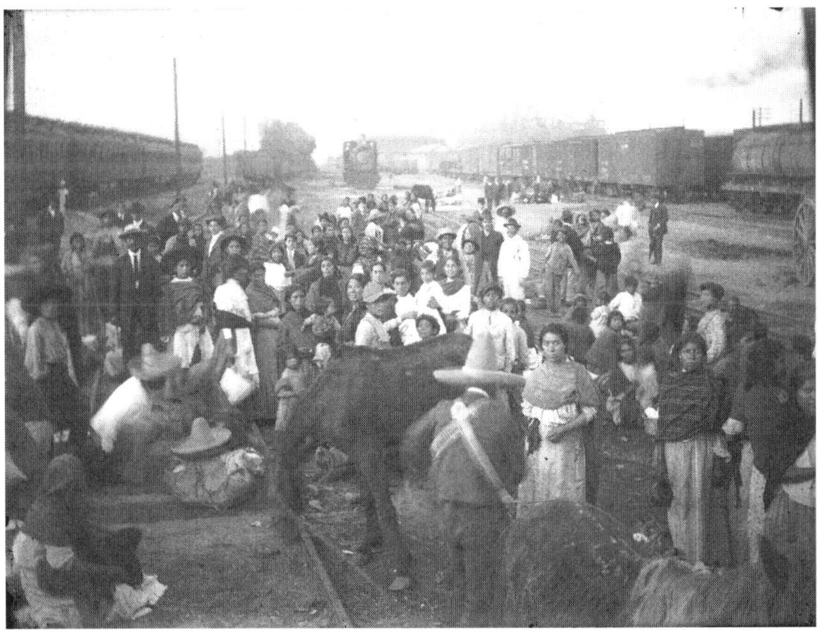

FIGURE 1.7. "Madero's troops in the patio of Buenavista train station," México City, D.F., 1910.

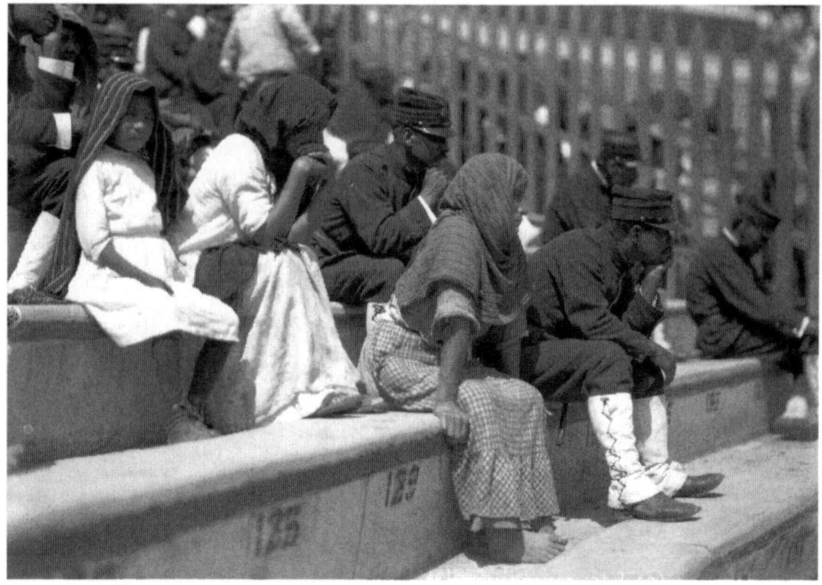

FIGURE 1.8. "Soldiers and their families watching an opera," México City, D.F., October 10, 1921.

positions," which "implies an indication of stability" (117). No two things can be in the same location, or place (117). Conversely, when considering the traditional notion of place as "static," John Agnew refers us to a more radical understanding that unbinds the reified notions of place, defining it instead in terms of a mobility that is "disruptive of place" and that "does not necessarily require long histories of sedentary habitation"—such as the case of migrant itineraries and commuting paths (327).[7] Place, likewise, can be conceived of as a "locale," such as a shopping mall or a vehicle (326). Agnew further questions traditional notions of "place" by pointing to humanist theorists who consider human agency as primary in the constitution of place and space: "places are woven together through space by movement and the network ties that produce places as changing constellations of human commitments, capacities, and strategies" (325). Furthermore, David Harvey claims that the strength of the classic Lefebvrian notion of place construction is that it "refuses to see materiality, representation and imagination as separate worlds [. . .] while simultaneously insisting that it is only in the social practices of daily life that the ultimate significance of all forms of activity is registered" ("From space to place and back again" 23). However, feminists de-emphasize human agency as central because "[p]lace is seen as constituted out of space-spanning relationships, place-specific social forms, and a sense of place associated with the relative well-being, disruption, and experience of living somewhere" (Agnew 325). Finally, Guillermo Delgado L. makes a provocative suggestion that might circle this impasse, seeking to invoke indigeneity as a way in which Native people imagine space and place. He claims place and space, in the indigenous imaginary, do not lie in discrete opposition. He uses Andean languages as an example, and in particular focuses on the word "pacha"—a term that constitutes "one fused concept amidst several similar expressions, sp/l/ace" (1). That is, both place and space become mutually constitutive terms that are part of an effort to re-member the land, belonging, history, and knowledge.

Indeed, there has been much debate regarding the importance of place and space, but we can appreciate that both human agency and movement in the more radical considerations of place have blurred the boundaries between the two. Delgado's neologism, sp/l/ace, pushes it one step forward (and back) through an incursion in indigeneity as a way to destabilize the place/space dialectic in order to consider other ways of conceiving of land, home, occupation and identity. Both Delgado and José Rabasa have pointed to indigenous cartography—where ritual migrations, important human occupations and sacred locations (both real and mythical) are part of identifying the land—as a way to unfetter Western notions of place and space as well as appreciate alternatives.

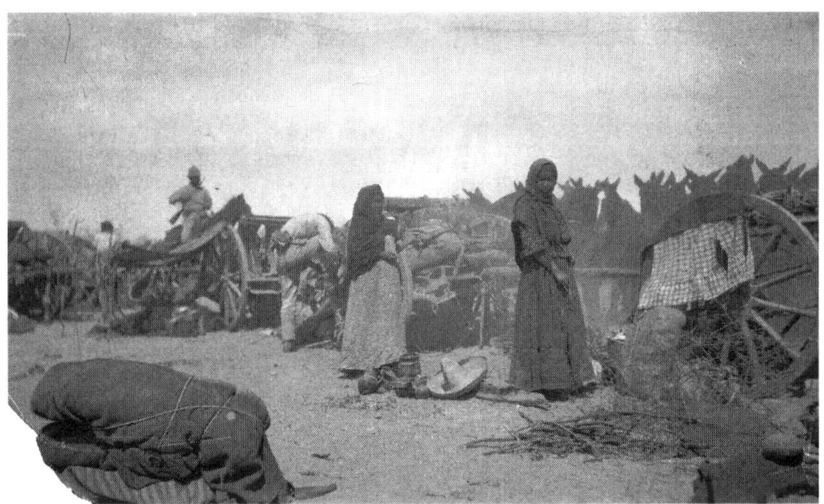

FIGURE 1.9. "Soldaderas at a military camp," México City, D.F., 1914.

These debates about place and space make evident that *where* the "scenario" unfolds becomes critical, because despite the itinerancy of the actors, and the inconstant nature of the place (on top of a train, around a campfire, in the barracks, in a burnt-out hacienda, on the side of the road, in a ditch, under a tree), the scenario is recognizable. For this reason Taylor describes her notion of scenario as an "act of transfer, as a paradigm that is formulaic [. . .] and often banal because it leaves out complexity, reduces conflict to its stock elements, and encourages fantasies of participation" (54). However, this lack of complexity does not mean that the scenario will not "conjure up multiple deep-seated fears and fantasies" (54). What makes these scenarios so commanding is that they require embodiment, yet, "[t]he body in the scenario, however, has space to maneuver because it is not scripted [. . .] the scenario more fully allows us to keep both the social actor and the role in view simultaneously and thus recognize the uneasy fits and areas of tension" (55). It is these "uneasy fits" that create the possibilities for the soldaderas to inseminate change into the cultural economy that regulates their behavior and interprets their acts. We can appreciate, then, the way in which the *scenario* created by the soldadera is both formulaic and recognizable, yet open to changes. As we will see in the following chapters, soldaderas actively practiced an alternative language through the embodied reproduction of these scenarios, but also through the small changes inherent to each iteration of these new sp/l/aces.

In a similar gesture, De Certeau illumines the importance of occupying space by using the structures of trope in rhetoric, denominating these practices a "residing rhetoric" that must be, in Clifford's words "discursively mapped and corporeally practiced [. . .] It must be worked, turned into a discrete social space, by embodied practices of interactive travel" (54). While for Hayden White "troping is the soul of discourse"—the mechanism which makes discursive expression and meaning possible—De Certeau employs the rhetoric of language in order to understand the syntax of daily life (*Tropics of Discourse* 2). Metaphors can be embodied and De Certeau uses the rhetorical operations of language as a hermeneutic for interpreting the quotidian. He links the performative with the tropological in a way that makes the praxis of daily life its own self-constitutive language, which like discourse, is full of its own metaphors. For this reason De Certeau claims that the practice of cooking or walking, for example, can be understood rhetorically because "[t]he art of 'turning phrases' finds an equivalent in an art of composing a path (*tourner un parcours*)" (100). Although his theorization of walking as a spatial practice is located within the context of the city (and not the countryside or the battleground as is the case with the soldaderas), I find it particularly enlightening with respect to the consumptive practices that, as with language, function tropologically. He claims that walking can be understood through synecdoche and asyndeton: "Synecdoche expands a spatial element in order to make it play the role of a 'more' [. . .] and take its place [. . .] Asyndeton, by elision, creates a 'less,' opens gaps in the spatial continuum and retains only selected parts of it that amount almost to relics" (101). In this sense, the soldaderas "trudge" behind their juanes and the cavalry, carrying children on their backs, cooking beans over the fires, dragging along their bundles with things they often picked off the dead. These movements synecdochally become the dense details that replace the totality, transforming the singular bodies into one ambulant mass that "[w]alk[s], which alternately follows a path and has followers, creates a mobile organicity in the environment, a sequence of phatic topoi" (99).

Asyndeton cuts out the other aspects—joy, heroism, ferocity, dignity—and consequently it "undoes continuity and undercuts its plausibility" (101). In diverse cultural products we witness them trudging, suffering nobly, whining, cowering, skulking, and scheming, but we do not see them walking firmly to the *paredón* (firing wall), holding the rifle high, gently nursing a newborn child or wounded soldier. We are missing the "conjunctive loci" and consequently, "the figures of pedestrian rhetoric substitute trajectories

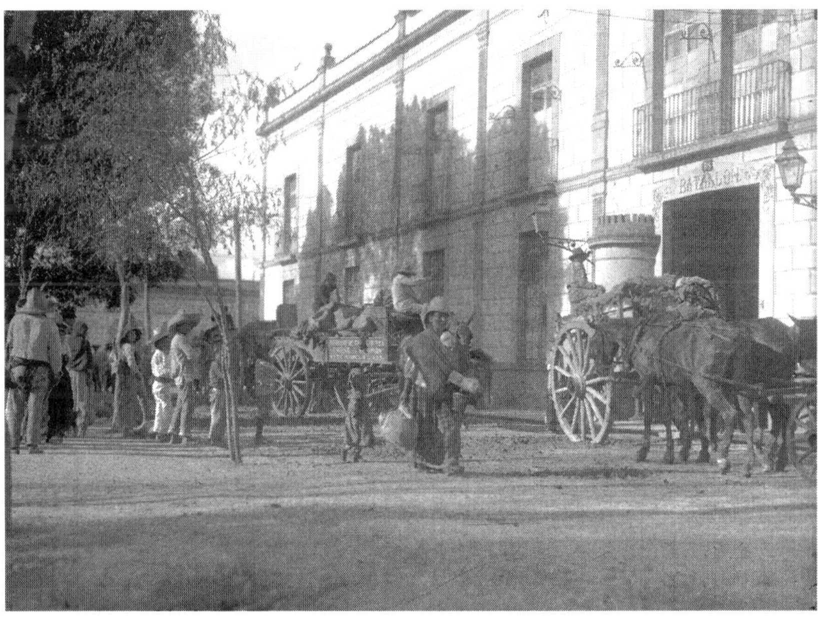

Figure 1.10. "Soldaderas departing from the 'Piedad' Barracks of the 180th Batallion with carts and artillery," México City, D.F., 1914.

that have a mythical structure, at least if one understands by 'myth' [. . .]
an allusive and fragmentary story whose gaps mesh with the social practices
it symbolizes" (102). The ellipses in the gait of the soldaderas and the dust
that billowed from their heavy footsteps shrouded them in myth, a reality
which has been harshly inveighed by some scholars and cultural critics. These
ellipses became the basis of a social injustice that not only misrepresented
them; it marginalized them within the very social revolution they helped to
effect. Deprived of political rights and military remuneration, they were also
denied their place in the making of the Revolution and were not included in
what is considered one of the most progressive (but unpracticed) constitu-
tions of the twentieth century.

De Certeau maintains that "to walk is to lack a place" (103). Although
it appears he privileges space-making over place, he underscores the very
important act of embodiment, of occupying "static" places (cities, buildings,
streets) through the dynamic practices of movement, walking, and inhabiting.
While they walked, the soldaderas scavenged for food, cooked, cleaned, and
reproduced. But they also sang, danced, nursed, spied, and fought valiantly.
They left their "proper" homes and walked the countryside, the battlegrounds,
the provincial villages, and the big cities. Lacking a "place" they were paradoxically omnipresent, consequently creating new "places" through movement,
such as the tops of trains, burnt-out haciendas and itinerant campgrounds.
They also forged new spaces, both figurative and real, by revising traditional
female behavior (and the concomitant places which they traditionally occupied). The aesthetic realm, in its reproduction of this ambulant phenomenon,
hints at this agency, highlights its urgency in the midst of wartime imperatives, delights in female valor and subsequent abjection, but only permits
glimmers of alternative sp/l/aces while not naming them as such. In the end,
unrecognized and unsung, the soldaderas "trudged" their way into history,
and sadly right out of it, living and dying on the road.

Women and the Revolution—A Brief Herstory

Who was the soldadera? What was her actual role in the Revolution of 1910?
The truth is we don't know much. Many are familiar with her *image* in a
rebozo, bandoliers crisscrossing her chest, trudging along in the dust; this
is the image that has been figured time and again in all forms of cultural
production. Many would say they were wives, others servants, lovers, or prostitutes, but most commonly they are referred to as camp followers. Regardless
of their official title, their participation in the Revolution became a means for
them to travel, work independently as well as have different sexual partners.
As their soldiers, or "juanes," perished, they were free to find new mates

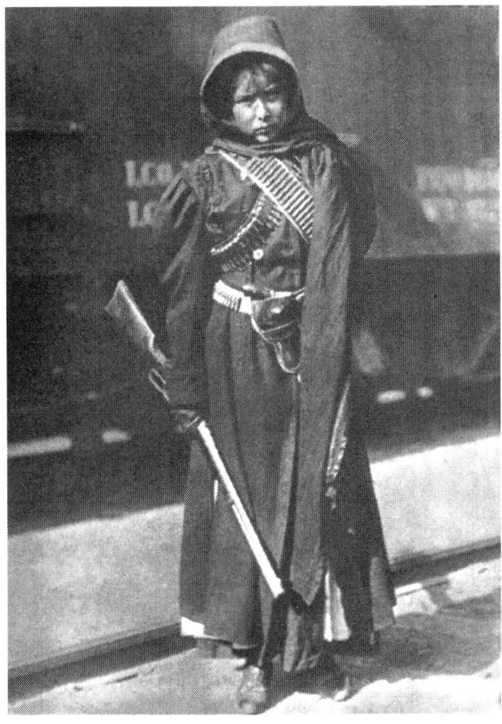

FIGURE 1.11. "Portrait of a revolutionary girl holding a rifle," México City, D.F., 1913.

or clients. These denigrated women were not simply prostitutes or servants but integral parts of the military units. They worked to feed and nurse the troops, bore children but also took up arms when their soldiers fell. Many held military rank, heading their own battalions. Poniatowska remarks on the nominal erasure of their participation by pointing to fear of female agency as a motive for the historical suppression of their diverse roles: "El que nunca hayan tenido un nombre específico o una participación clara en la milicia se debe al tradicional ninguneo de la mujer en México y al temor de los jefes militares que ascendieran y llegaran a ocupar cargos de relevancia dentro de las fuerzas armadas" [The fact that they never had a specific name or a clear role in the military is due to the traditional marginalization (or "nobodiness") of women in México and the military chiefs' fear that they would ascend to power and occupy important jobs in the armed forces] (22). But in order to appreciate the figure of the soldadera in the arts, we should review briefly what little we know about the appearance of the soldadera in the historical context of the Mexican Revolution.

Cultural critic Carlos Monsiváis invokes a powerful scene when summing up the interventions of México's lost female soldiers:

> "Y una moza que valiente los seguía . . ." Al terminar la batalla, la mujer permanece. La del vientre fecundo (la esclava ideal) se incorpora y, de pronto, aprovechándose de los movimientos de Carmen Serdán o de las vacilaciones del instante, se echa a andar. No con demasiada suerte: al cabo de las caminatas prodigiosas, la mujer revolucionaria se deja mitificar y el mito, al estipular carácter y condiciones, confirma y garantiza la esclavitud y transforma amargamente virtudes naturales en peso muerto para sus descendientes. ¿No hubiese podido la mujer en la revolución elaborar una herencia más alivianada? Ni modo, a ella le hicieron arrojar sobre sus descendientes una carga fatal de abnegación, sufrimiento callado, estoicismo y obstinada veneración por el hombre.

> ["And a valiant girl followed them . . ." When the battle is over, the woman remains. The one with the fertile womb (the ideal slave) gets up, and all of a sudden, taking advantage of the movements begun by Carmen Serdán or the vacillations of the moment, begins to walk. Not with a lot of luck, mind you: at the end of the prodigious marches, the revolutionary woman allows herself to be mythified, and the myth, by stipulating the conditions of her character, confirms and guarantees her slavery and bitterly transforms her natural virtues into dead weight for her descendants. Could not the women of the Revolution have crafted a lighter legacy for themselves? No way! They had her throw upon her descendants the fatal weight of abnegation, silent suffering, stoicism and an obstinate veneration for their men]. (*Amor perdido* 23)

At the end of the battle, the woman remains. Walking wombs, enslaved both by their obstinate abnegation and their ignorant fealty to their men, Carlos Monisváis inveighs the harsh legacy these women left in their wake. They trudge in the dust, which serves both as dead weight and legacy: an unwritten text that blows away with the winds of time. However, despite the weight of their legacy as particulate matter, the glimmers revealed in art produced during and after the Revolution by both the lettered and popular classes exemplifies not just the varied ways that women participated, but the diverse nature of the women themselves. The daily practice of war in the Mexican Revolution of 1910, and their different aesthetic representations collapses the one-dimensional perception of women as mere victims in war, deconstructing the definition of their roles in relation to men. As the intensity of the revolutionary violence escalated, women of all classes were driven in far greater numbers toward various forms of participation. Although the soldadera joined the Independence Movement of 1810 and became renowned in the Revolution of 1910, scholars such as Elizabeth Salas, in one of the only monographs ever written about these women, trace her origins to the Mexica *auianimes*, *mociuaquetzques* and camp followers of the latter part of the Mexica Empire.[8] Unlike other female participants in the Revolution who have vanished into obscurity, the demonized or romanticized figure of the soldadera has become famous while most of the real soldaderas have remained anonymous.

Daily life, history, and art produce different orders of reality; the women who participated and the discourse that captured their participation as soldaderas, the official discourse that reengineered their name(s) and hence the quality of their participation, the capture of some or all of this by aesthetic realm. Many artists created images—both stifling and ambivalent—that continue to circulate in all forms of cultural production to this day. Claudia Schaefer underscores the strict division and mythification of the soldadera types by claiming that women fell into three archetypes: "the doll-like beauty, the subjugated wife and mother, and the prostitute" (*Textured Lives* 6–7). The actual "work" of the soldadera can be identified from its etymological derivation. We owe the origins of the title to the Spanish conquistadors who imported the name from women of the same profession in Spain. The derivation of the name soldadera comes from the word *soldada*, which means "soldier's pay."[9] The soldadera was given the soldier's *soldada* and was thus entrusted to purchase food and provisions for her soldier. Hence, she worked as a contracted employee, and as such she exercised the same rights that an employee would. She was free to leave her employer if a better one came along. She was also free to take on more soldiers if she wished, and oftentimes marketed her culinary or economizing expertise in order to attract better-paid officers. Salas avers that "[w]orking for soldiers became a way for poor, lower-class women to eke out a meager living for themselves and their children" as they were not bound by traditional marriage practices and could even supplement their income as laundresses, food-sellers, and prostitutes (xii). The contractual nature of her office conflicts with long-standing perceptions of her as either the wife or the lover of the soldier. It also contrasts with her deification as the sweet, subservient and self-abnegating "Adelita" or "Valentina."

Certainly many soldaderas were loving, considerate wives and lovers, but not all willingly followed their husbands/lovers or family members into war. In her book, *Against All Odds: The Feminist Movement in Mexico to 1940*, Anna Macías quotes Julio Guerrero in order to illustrate this predominant perception about the soldaderas:

> [They are the women] who accompany the husband or lover on his military marches, carrying a child, a basket filled with clothing, and working utensils. In the abandoned battlefield they carry

the water to their wounded masters and despoil the dead of their
clothing . . . They are jealous and courageous . . . and their moral
code has two precepts . . . absolute fidelity to and unconditional
abnegation for the husband or lover, and respect for the officers
of the battalion or regiment. (41)

This description, although illustrative of some of the women who became
soldaderas, erroneously portrays all soldaderas as "self-abnegating creatures,"
not unlike loyal canines, who left none but themselves unattended (41). This
representation commends the soldadera for her work ethic but ignores the
different aspects of her job. In the line of Western Christian female idealization, it makes the heroine the one who suffers stoically, not the one who
takes up arms, whether through the artillery of bullets or words. To be sure,
this is obviously more favorable than her classic portrayal as the camp prostitute or parasite who represents the dregs of society, but it misrepresents
her through a patriarchal idealization. By paying homage to her fealty and
nurturing support, Guerrero, like Mexican society, created a myth that ignores
the important roles she played within the ranks of the army—as a soldier,
spy, arms smuggler, intermediary, or organizer.[10]

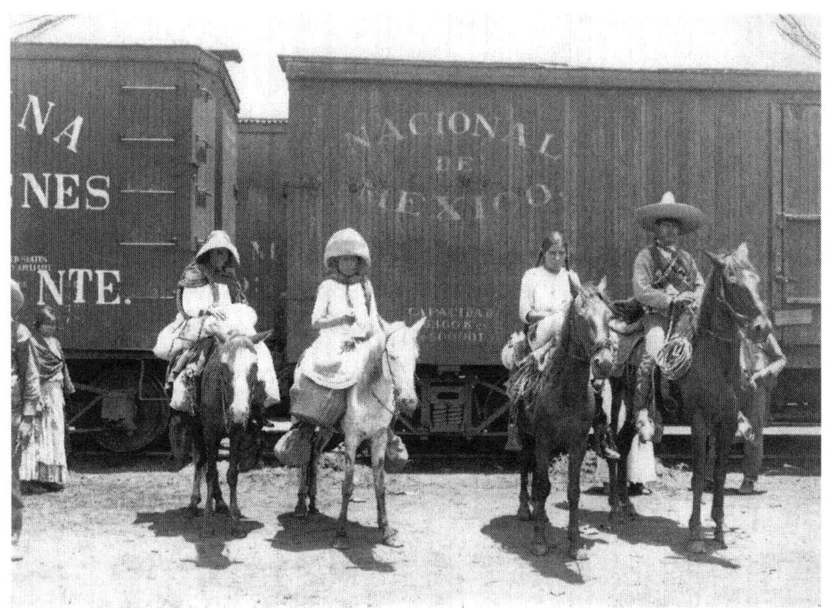

FIGURE 1.12. "Zapatista soldaderas in Xochimilco," August 1914, México, D.F.

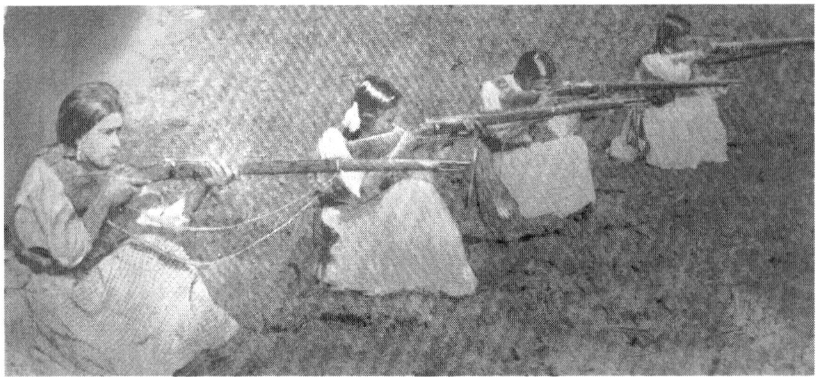

FIGURE 1.13. "Soldaderas in firing position against the men of José Inés Chávez García," Michoacán, México, 1917.

The soldadera has been mythified in this idealistic way through various artistic media. Although a fair number of "Coronelas" and "Generalas" have made appearances in the corridos, literature, and cinema, cultural production has nevertheless favored the Adelita, Valentina, and Galleta. Many corridos idealized (and sexualized) her as the beautiful woman who the soldier longs to take as his wife, the angel who cured his wounds, or the muse he has lost. Julia Tuñón Pablos underscores this proclivity when she laments, "this stereotyping, like a stiff handmade doll, threatens to rob us of the warmth and complexity inherent to all social actors" (86). All forms of cultural production romanticized the soldadera, and although much was based on the lives of real people (whose histories are all subject to contention), it does not represent the soldadera movement in general. In this way it fails to recognize those women who participated in what was considered the more "masculine" realm of active war. Anna Macías distinguishes between the soldadera who cooked, nursed, and remained relatively uninvolved in the actual fighting, and the coronela who took up arms, organized troops, and rose up in the military ranks. Although this distinction is useful, it neglects that many soldaderas did take up arms, and when their soldier perished, picked up his rifle and continued for him. It also suppresses the role they played as intermediaries, smuggling arms and various other military activities in addition to ignoring that many women became soldaderas because they were abducted or raped. Salas informs us that María Villasana López was abducted, along with her sister, at fourteen years of age by a Villista general. She recollected that "her mother wept and pleaded for them to leave us with her, but not our tears, our panic, or our screams helped us at all" (72).[11] Similarly, Guadalupe Vélez became a soldadera because her father forced her to marry a thirty-two-year-old man who raped her when she was thirteen. When he decided to join the Villistas she was obligated to go with him (72). Indeed, not all of the soldaderas were loving wives, daughters, or lovers; many were forced to join against their will as they were subject to the vagaries of war.

Nor were soldaderas always romantically idealized. Pancho Villa was rumored to particularly despise them as they slowed down the troops (especially his famous cavalry charges) and were troublemakers. He even executed ninety women and children that he had taken prisoner. In general, they were disdained as irredeemable concubines who were vulgar, shameless and foul-mouthed (35). They were also thought to be mindless because they "gave their absolute fidelity and unconditional servitude to their soldier mates" (36).

Finally, many women from the middle and upper classes also contributed to the rebel cause. Soto categorizes the participation by class: the lower classes were the soldaderas, the middle classes served in all capacities, and the upper classes lent their time to the health organizations such as the Red or White Cross. Yet again this division seems to be somewhat misleading. Many women from the middle and upper classes fought, organized networks, smuggled arms, printed and disseminated newspapers, crafted revolutionary ideologies, and were soldaderas. Many women of the *Porfiriato* actively fought against the Díaz regime prior to the Revolution. The female family members as well as friends of Madero were particularly instrumental to his movement. The Plan de San Luís Potosí was actually transported over the border by the American-born wife of Madero's friend. Many, such as Carmen Serdán, participated in fomenting the revolutionary zeal in order to meet the date set by Madero; the first battle actually occurred at her house. Although her home was besieged and most of her family killed, she still held up her rifle and rallied the people to continue the revolutionary fervor.

The papers *La Corregidora*, *El Vésper*, *La Reforma*, *El Desmonte*, and *La Guillotina* were all financed and disseminated by women who were instrumental in these ideological efforts and groups such as Hijas de Cuauhtémoc, Amigas del Pueblo, Regeneración y Concordancia were organizations that sought to advance women's rights through the Revolution. Women such as Estela Ramírez, Teresa Villarreal, Elisa Acuña y Rossetti, Dolores Jiménez y Muro, and Juana Gutiérrez de Mendoza were all important figures who collaborated with the Zapatistas. Dolores Jiménez made an important contribution to the revolutionary ideology through her collaboration on the Plan de Ayala. Her introduction to the Plan delineated the famous Zapatista formula for agrarian reform for which his movement is best known. She also served with the PLM and Madero prior to her work with Zapata. Middle-class Hermila Galindo also contributed to ideology as she worked closely with Carranza, delivering many speeches that defended the constitutionalist

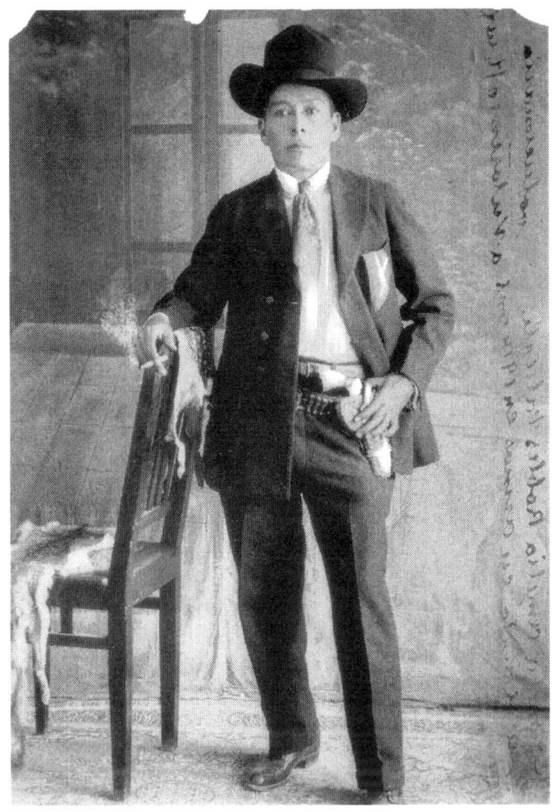

FIGURE 1.14. "Portrait of the revolutionary Coronela Amelio Robles, smoking in a room," México, 1914.

revolution. She stressed a robust nationalism and made various attempts to promulgate women's rights. Although her views on women were radical to some, her oratorical skills earned her great acclaim in the formation of the revolutionary rhetoric. In *Emergence of the Modern Mexican Woman*, Shirlene Soto reports that she was quite prolific in her writings: *La doctrina Carranza y el acercamiento indolatino* (1919) was one of five different books she published on the Mexican Revolution (52).

Although most soldaderas have remained anonymous, there are a few soldaderas who became famous by rejecting traditional roles of subservience and participating militarily. Carmen Robles, Margarita Neri, Margarita Mata, María Aguirre, Juana Lucio, and María Luisa Escobar were all prominent soldaderas who fought as rebel leaders and commanders during the Revolution.

Margarita Neri can be distinguished as one of the most famous, both for her military prowess and for her dancing. In 1910 she led a troop of a thousand men through Tabasco and Chiapas, vowing to decapitate Díaz with her own hands. It is said that as she neared the state of Guerrero, the governor, out of fear, had himself shipped away in a crate. As her story has been shrouded in myth, there is much contention about the actual details of her life. Soto states that contradictory reports portray her as both "commanding Zapatistas in Morelos and as cutting off the ears of Zapatistas sent to recruit her" (45). In any case, she was reputed to be a respected guerrilla commander. Transgender Amelio Robles is another remarkable figure, in part because he began cross-dressing during the Revolution and retained a traditional masculine body image and identity afterward; "in pose, gesture, and wardrobe" he was both a dandy, violent "macho," and philanderer (Gabriela Cano "Unconcealable Realities of Desire" 41). He was rewarded for his military service in the Zapatista army and was recognized as a revolutionary veteran. In 1989 they turned his house into a museum five years after his death in an effort to restore " 'women to the Mexican Revolution." In a tragic irony, in order to revise military history and celebrate the role of women in the Revolution, they censored his sexuality and masculinity by naming it the "Amelia Robles Museum-House," very much against his will to be recognized as a male (49).

Although primarily "camp followers," soldaderas have played many different roles, all of which have not been fully appreciated. Salas particularly illustrates this when she states that these women have had no common label due to the fact that the military chooses to marginalize them in male domains, utilizing them only when necessary: "For this reason, the heroic camp follower or fighter of one war might be condemned as a prostitute or unnatural woman in another era" (xi). Women who became soldaderas did so for many different reasons: some followed the troops in order to improve their lives through work, while others were given no choice; some wanted heroic recognition (like we see in the novel *La Negra Angustias* by Francisco Rojas González studied in chapter 5), while others stayed behind the battle lines to cook and care for their soldiers (such as Jesusa Palancares discussed in chapter 3). Others took on more "male qualities" such as domination and decisiveness, while many were submissive. Many stood up to the military commanders, although generally under the guise of patriotic rhetoric, or made their own tactical decisions (such as we see in the play *Soldadera* by Josefina Niggli examined in the following chapter). But the stereotype of the sweet, submissive Adelita or the dark peasant scavenger with a "look that was inexpressive, like that of an idiot" is grossly insufficient (Soto 27). They were crucial to military success in México, regardless of whose side they were on or what role they adopted.

I contend that the term soldadera becomes a word to describe what was socially unacceptable; it is a way to debase the real worth of a militarily active female participant of war. While the word itself is etymologically ambiguous, it operates as a way to describe women living outside of the confines of the home in forms not conducive to traditional family life. Rather than describe them as soldiers (although some women did hold high military rank), they are instead reduced to a degenerate military status, one that does not actually exist and cannot expect any remuneration or even recognition. Salas decries their official eradication from the military as policymakers for both Carranza and Obregón did not want them to continue in the Mexican Army, and General Joaquín Amaro, the minister of war, banned them from the barracks in 1925 because "he considered them to be 'the chief cause of vice, illness, crime and disorder' [. . .] The fact that thousands of soldaderas had been killed during the Revolution had no bearing on the decision to eliminate them from the army" (49). Even after their sacrifices, which were unrecognized and not remunerated by the state, this official interdiction summarily erased their contributions and hard work. We see that their degenerate military status is also a product of the inferiority complex the Mexican army felt relative to more developed nations, particularly the United States. Many military officials complained that the presence of the soldaderas subjected them to undue ridicule by the U.S. military, and was not becoming of a modern army. Not until 2007 did México begin allowing women to train in elite military schools to become engineers, pilots, and other specialists who can rise to the rank of general, although they still were not allowed to participate in direct combat (*USA Today*, Sept. 28, 2007).

The soldadera remains nameless, but entertains the public by the campfire, on the page, and on the screen. Middle-class transgressions of place and title through diverse forms of active intervention in the Revolution become displaced onto the vilified yet culturally commemorated soldadera. The middle- and upper-class bourgeois woman, who also contributed significantly to all aspects of the revolutionary campaign, not only remains unremunerated and unrecognized, she has been left out of the focal point of cultural production entirely.[12] Movies have not been made about Leonor Villegas de Magnón, who started the White Cross and was a key supporter of Carranza (she could not find anyone to publish her autobiography in her lifetime) or Sara Madero. But through its pejorative connotations, "soldadera" became a word with a multiple and contradictory metaphoric code; by evading a concrete definition the usage of this term is able to escape its own negation and debasement.

As mentioned, although the Mexican Revolution has produced an infinite historiography, very few historical texts include the soldaderas. Indeed, there are many faces to the soldaderas, and their legacy is not reducible to one sexually provocative story as these women ranged in race and age, had different family backgrounds as well as regional and class identifications. Debra Castillo, in her book *Easy Women*, comments on the representation of the Mexican woman offered by corridos and literature written during the Revolution, the violent period and for decades after:

> Yet, here too, in the revolutionary songs and legends, an attentive reader/listener will still find hints of how the cultural emergencies provoked slippages in gender conventions [. . .] Up to one half of all Mexican women had shaken loose from their traditional roles. The enormity of this phenomenon marks modern Mexican society and literature with a deeply felt, if largely unwritten, catachresis [. . .] This historical ellipsis conditions modern and contemporary Mexican literature, in which the loose woman is remembered and put under erasure in the same gesture. (5)

Castillo astutely makes a few striking points: "loose" women are not absent in the literature and cultural production that was created in the wake of the Revolution, quite the contrary, their images reverberate throughout popular folk music, novels, theatre, and of course cinema. Nonetheless, these representations of the Mexican woman mask a salient yet unspoken cultural panic that was a result of what she calls slippages in gender conventions. The fact that up to half the women in México were either roaming the country or engaged in nontraditional activities provoked an historical ellipsis that conditions our notion of women's participation in the Revolution. This ellipsis in official history is a product of a paternalistic state and chauvinistic society that prefers not to recognize, or remember, women at the forefront and in the background of one of the most important peasant uprisings of the hemisphere, consequently disappearing their memory.

Carlos Monsiváis quite candidly illuminates the nature of this "cultural emergency" when he states "[i]n the chapter on prostitution, México inaugurates the century, if not with the world record, definitely in an advantageous position (120 of every one thousand women between the ages of 15 and 30 were registered prostitutes)"[13] (66). Monsiváis takes these records from the end of the Porfirian reign, however during the Revolution, as noted by Castillo, these numbers only intensify given that according to some scholars (such as Anna Macías) up to half of the women in México turned to prostitution: "Whatever the exact number of female soldiers, *soldaderas*, and actual prostitutes [. . .] there is general agreement that, in that period of tremendous social upset, women were on the loose and on their own in Mexico" (4–5). Moreover, these numbers do not include unregistered prostitutes, servants, and women from the countryside. Whether or not these numbers are accurate, what is important is the sheer volume of women transgressing the domains of main-stream respectable society. The soldadera was known to move from soldier to soldier, either because her husband or *juan* died, or maybe because someone offered her a better deal. This liberty, although very negatively portrayed in cultural production as fickle capriciousness or the stereotypical *ingrata* [ungrateful woman], was in fact very beneficial for these women because they were free to find someone else if they were mistreated. In the case of death, which unfortunately was widespread and inevitable, they were not simply left at the mercy of the community as a traditional widow might have been. Instead, they picked up and moved on—and quite often that meant to another man. This harsh reality led to a tightening of middle-class social mores dictating what constituted a "mujer decente" [upright woman], and of course to a paradoxical loosening of traditional female spheres and activities occasioned by wartime realities, for example, by making the train a domestic place.

¿Dónde están las mujeres decentes?

Mexican cinema and literature abound with loyal wives, protective mothers and innocent daughters who are all inscribed within a very specific notion of idealized womanhood undergirded by the notion of "decency." But the

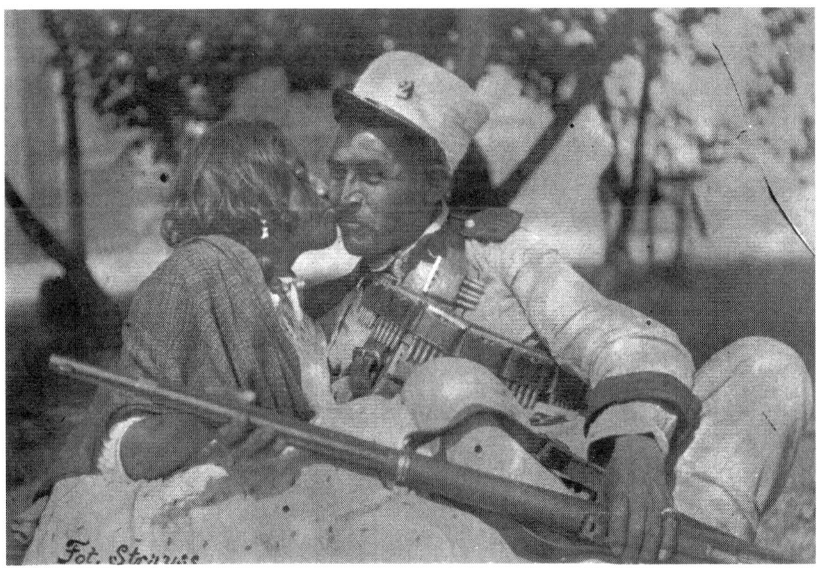

FIGURE 1.15. "Soldadera kisses a soldier," México City, D.F., 1913.

reality is that women were "on the loose" in revolutionary México. Although Castillo's book is mainly about the figure of the prostitute, she does qualify that by labeling prostitutes "easy" women, identifying what she considers a national obsession with the fallen woman in Mexican literature, beginning with Gamboa's *Santa* (1903) and ending with Irma Serrano's *A calzón amarrado* (1978). Her point is nonetheless relevant for the case of the soldadera given that she discusses how Mexican women—both indigenous and (afro) mestiza—shook "loose" of tradition, breaking outside of the home and community to join the Revolution. Although this is nothing new, as women since pre-Conquest times have participated in war, in this particular context it takes on a new valence because women seemed to join in record-shattering numbers. Moreover, there is a radical difference that distinguishes women's public participation in the Revolution of 1910 from others eras: visibility. As noted by Poniatowska, they were recorded "hovering" in the background. The Revolution was filmed and photographed, and women's participation after at least five hundred years of European cultural and political colonization, although not officially recognized, was unofficially overwhelming. As Barthes observes, "Each photograph is read as the private appearance of its referent: the age of Photography corresponds precisely to the explosion of the private into the public, or rather into the creation of a new social value, which is the publicity of the private: the private is consumed as such, publicly" (98). Thus photography becomes the testament and instrument of this "explosion;" an explosion that was social, political, and aesthetic and that was occasioned by the participation of women in the Revolution. Tuñon Pablos criticizes the "temptation to see the women of the Revolution, perhaps more than those of other historical moments, through a heroic lens that delights in the photographs in which they appear with rifles and bandoliers" (86). She claims that, while "[s]ome women dressed as men so they could take part in the struggle; some were troop commanders [and] most had a less prominent, although not necessarily less important, role" (86). Tuñon Pablos makes an excellent point: the image of the few women photographed in military regalia or with bandoliers lends itself to a falsely celebratory gesture that does not reflect the reality of their military status, thus participating in the mythification of this figure. Notwithstanding this contention, to dismiss the photographs would be to neglect that they nevertheless reveal a presence, a reality that existed, and which permits these women to constitute themselves in the many roles they incarnated. Gareth Williams pushes this point even further when he assesses the role of technology as both an index and agent of socialization:

> In twentieth-century Mexico the historical spectacle of the revolution—the convergence between the advent of technological reproducibility and the forcible entry of the masses into the

domain of sovereignty—moved the image out of the realm of aesthetic distinction into that of social function and ushered in a fundamental shift in collective perception. The vast photographic and filmic production of the revolutionary decade is an inventory of human action, an imagistic arrest of the concrete conditions of life in its (often cruel) immediacy, and the exposure of a new political optic that revolutionized the social function of art in Mexico and beyond. (*The Mexican Exception* 41)

While some of the photographs featuring soldaderas were indeed stylized and posed, others caught them in the background, underscoring the diverse ways in which they participated, and in which their presence was to be interpreted by those who observed them—both in real life and as a photographic image. It also highlights the different ways these women presented *themselves* to the photographer.

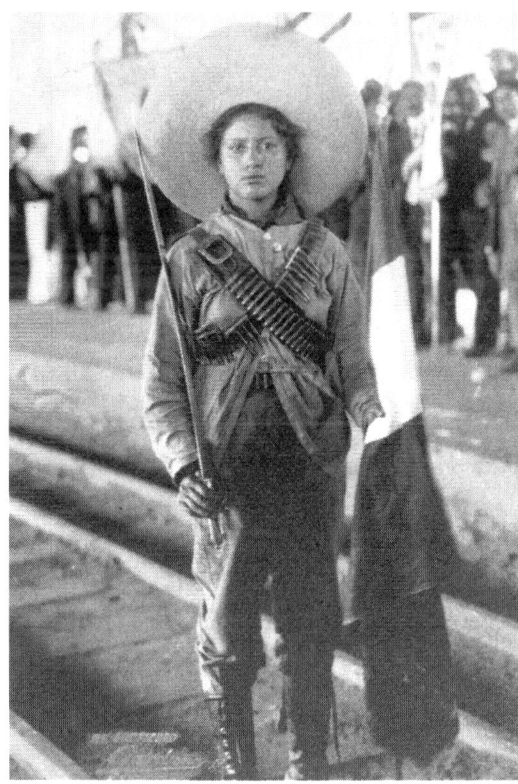

Figure 1.16. "Soldadera with flag and sword in a train station," México 1914.

The overwhelming participation of women in the Revolution created
an emergency of sorts, as the traditionally bound and gendered spheres
began to bleed, and within that bloody confusion women who crossed the
boundaries became socially marked and consequently stigmatized, because
"[w]omen who infringe upon the public space remain scandalous, and this
continuing scandal [. . .] resides initially in the impact of a female-gendered
human being in an unexpected public space, quite apart from assumptions
about her sexual availability" (Castillo 4). Castillo describes interviews with
middle-class women recorded in a book by Roberto Martínez Baños, Patricia
Trejo de Zepeda, and Edilberto Soto Angli where it was found, not surprisingly, that when women engaged in public activity made comments involving
freedom of sexual expression, this talk was "immediately translated by the
middle-class women interviewed into a de facto definition of prostitution,
one that presupposes that sexual freedom is incompatible with womanhood
itself" (6). Moreover, Castillo makes a compelling argument for placing these
middle-class values within the context of the Revolution. This Revolution,
in which perhaps up to half of its women participated, permanently marked
and changed the constitutive nature of gender identity by blurring categories of public and private, tradition and change, catapulting women to the
fore, but also contradictorily, to the back of the social agenda heralded by
the revolutionary ideals. The "phantasm of prostitution" buttresses Castillo's
claim regarding the panic invoked by middle-class women who wish to define
themselves outside of the domestic realm. That is, the trauma for the middle
classes lies in the desire for women to loosen the economic bonds their husbands impose on them.

For this reason, I claim that the soldadera is one of the many avatars of
the prostitute because in traditional, patriarchal and mestizo Mexican society,
to be outside of the home is to be public, and to be public is not constitutive
of a middle-class *mujer decente*. Ever since the vilification of la Malinche,
the phantasmatic presence of prostitution in relation to public or powerful
women is always hovering in the background. The negative portrayals of the
soldadera overlap with this phantasm of prostitution, testifying to the application of middle-class values to a group of women who, although largely lower
class, were nevertheless economically and racially diverse. Therefore, we can
begin to imagine the ways in which art figures the tension between the desire
to impose a middle-class sobriety on a wartime reality that exhibited women
of all classes and colors out on the field. It is the aesthetic realm that intervenes, despite itself, to tell the story that history does not. Castillo states that
"[t]he sexualized woman's body is at the same time insistently present and disturbingly abstracted into a play of trope, which is also an unconscious social
commentary" (18). The contradiction that Castillo illuminates when she states
"insistently present" and yet "disturbingly abstracted" is indeed a paradoxical

product of Mexican society's inability to negotiate the multiple meanings as well as the social, historical, and sexual implications of the soldadera. The threat of falling into disrepute is a recurrent trope (Castillo claims obsession) in Mexican cultural production. In light of this, it is no coincidence that the soldadera, and not the nurse for example, has been at the center of cultural production. Middle-class Mexican society needed the soldadera to be dark, indigenous, and from the lower classes, whether or not she actually was. By abstracting an ever-present sexualized body, both cultural producers and the Mexican public/spectator reveal their uneasy fascination with these audacious women, penalizing while secretly admiring them and taking a perverse pleasure in their sexualized figures. As Castillo cleverly signals, the historical ellipses are also reflective of the sexualized ellipses in the literary texts. Despite the historical omissions and lack of official title, these women paradoxically titillated and aroused their public at the same time that they were deplored by them. Consequently, a specific brand of soldadera emerged: "adelitas." La Adelita would become the camp sweetheart, beautiful and noble but profoundly marked by the imminent threat of disrepute, although her cute name would attenuate the negativity associated with soldaderas as members of the lower classes. The derided *cucaracha* represented the inevitable destiny of the fallen woman; she constituted the other, ugly side of the beguiling Adelita.

Arriving or About to Leave?

I would like to return to the photograph we examined at the beginning, in part because its ambivalence both communicates, and disavows, the multiple stories that get lost in the trope of the soldadera that we will study closely in the following chapters. Barthes's notion of *punctum*, of an element that opens up, or expands the photograph and produces a startle, or trauma, is useful for interpreting this image. He muses, "for *punctum* is also: sting, speck, cut, little hole—and also a cast of the dice. A photograph's *punctum* is that accident which pricks me (but also bruises me, is poignant to me)" (27). This notion of *punctum* as a cut, or hole is compelling to me in this photograph, because although it is intended to be read metaphorically, this image is literally riddled with specks, holes, and tears; it is conspicuously torn in the corner and there are multiple black spots or stains. However, the idea of *punctum* is almost overwhelming in my reading, as there are simply too many: the starched whiteness of the dress which covers what appears to be a protruding belly of the girl to the right, and the apparent disheveled state of the woman to the left. Is her dress stained, or is this a product of the photo's deterioration? Another "point" of *punctum*: the girl to the right, although her head is slightly bent, is nonetheless gazing directly into the camera, and at her

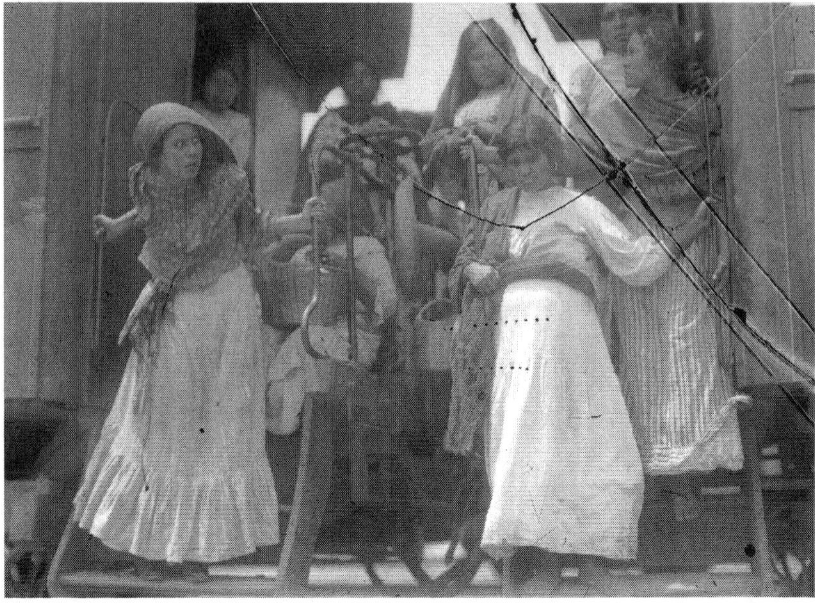

FIGURE 1.17. "Soldaderas on the platform at the Buenavista train station," México City, D.F., April 1912.

future spectators. The apparent rip in the upper right corner (as mentioned, the original glass negative of this image is cracked) would actually tear this women's head off. The other woman's gaze is directed outside of the photograph searching for something we cannot see, or do not know exists. In this way, the photograph is simultaneously random and posed.

Furthermore, the ambiguity of place becomes another point of *punctum*: is this scene before or after a battle? Mraz now affirms that they are at a station in México City traveling northward, but, despite this new information and the effort taken to locate it in a particular time and place, the image begs certain questions of anyone who gazes upon it: is the distressed form of the photograph occulting something we cannot see? The train is anticipating movement, but is it arriving or about to leave? The photograph is damaged, but are the women dirty from travel, or is the battered state of the photograph disguising their "caritas lavadas"? It is this utter lack of knowledge, of certainty, that I find compelling and that constitute these multiple points of Barthian *punctum* in my reading. The manifold points of *punctum* that "pricked" my gaze were also constituted by the pricks in the image, making this worn photograph the perfect metonym for the diverse women who participated in, and created, this Revolution. Their distressed historical representation mirrors the distressed state of this photograph as it reached me: the pregnant woman who looks into the eyes of the photographer and her spectator is literally and symbolically being threatened by the imminent beheading constituted by the "tear" in the corner of the photograph. To be sure, other prints made from the original negative may not reflect the wear and tear present in the one I first contemplated. Or, perhaps the crack in the glass negative produced the effect of the torn photograph, and in the end, a flawed reading. Nonetheless, the "version" of the photograph I first observed bore the marks of this distress. But it is precisely this circulation (now digital, cropped, and amplified in myriad ways), the ways in which this image traveled, and its subsequent disfigurement as a result of years of traveling and being handled, that forces me to consider the parallel wear and tear on the image of the soldaderas. This photograph reminds us that who they were, what they did, and why they did it can only be reconstructed through the vignettes, disfigured and torn, we are afforded in the cultural imaginary. Why are these women so insistently re-*membered* in the arts when in the official history they are hardly considered? Photographs like these recuperate the embodiments of the soldaderas that get elided, despite being posed, formulaic, or distressed.

Indeed, Mraz at first hypothesized that these women were prostitutes because they were in the main cabin and the soldaderas usually traveled on top or below, while the federal officer's women traveled in the cars along with the prostitutes. He was chided by Miguel Ángel Morales as being "reckless and erroneous" and elegantly acceded to his mistake, deciding instead that they were probably food-vendors and not soldaderas or prostitutes at all (242). In the end, what changes Mraz's opinion about who these women were is determined by the particular place they were standing when the photograph was taken. What is fascinating is that these women are just as easily labeled prostitutes as they are food-vendors or the "privileged followers of federal officers." Surprisingly (or perhaps not), these vastly different women (prostitutes, food-vendors, privileged federal officers "wives") are confused, conflated as an indistinguishable human mass at the same time they are assigned different names. In Maria Luisa Ocampo's play examined in chapter 2, soldaderas are called "mujeres" [women] or "muchachas" [girls], while Josefina Niggli titles her play *Soldadera* in honor of them. In chapter 3 John Reed is not sure if Elizabetta, the woman to whom he dedicates a whole chapter in his chronicle on the Revolution, is a "vieja" (another term for soldadera) or a displaced peon. In turn, Nellie Campobello (also considered in chapter 3) generally does not mention them, but does however include a prominent story about a coronela named "Nacha Ceniceros." Unlike other pieces that include soldaderas, she gives her protagonist a first and last name along with a military rank but, in her revisions of the story in a later edition, curiously turns the "old soldadera" who counsels Ceniceros into an "old lady" instead. It is evident then, that the term "soldadera" was profoundly fraught and was born of a class bias.

While Poniatowska does not enter into a reflection on what any particular photograph narrates in her book on the soldadera, she does comment on them as a whole, and on their metonymic power as a discourse that counters the official narrative. Barthes likewise comments on the power of metonymy in photography as he claims "[h]owever lightening-like it may be, the *punctum* has, more or less potentially, a power of expansion" (45). Metonymy functions as a series of parts constituting a whole through relationships of origin, causality, or contiguity. Nowhere more than in these photographs and in particular this photograph, do we see this metonymic function at work. The soldaderas embody the parts of a revolutionary landscape in flux; their multifarious and contradictory roles constitute them as the effects of a tumultuous ideological cause.

Such as the metonymic relationship between a creator and its product (as when one calls a painting by the name of its painter), we can understand the soldadera as a product of a chaotic revolution, but simultaneously the originary source of a cultural aesthetic or image. The multiple points of *punctum* in my constructed reading reflect the multiplicity of their narratives, and of the women themselves. This complicates what we have come to know about soldaderas; they not only followed the camps, they led them (as well as twentieth-century Mexican society) into a new world where women broke free from the strictures of their private lives and erupted onto the public scene as almost complete individuals, as simultaneously mothers and whores, lovers and warriors. They became the creators of a *culture* of revolution while they were simultaneously its victims; they turned revolution, which is marked by quotidian danger and tumultuous travel into a *habitus*.

Their *rebozos*, which they sometimes wore crisscrossed in front like bandoliers, also operated as metaphorical weapons and symbols of resistance. In what would appear to be a substitutional gesture, they replaced a weapon (the bandoliers) with a humble, indigenous article of clothing that serves various functions: the *rebozo* is a shawl, but also the carryall or sack in which they transport their children and cooking utensils. However, this is not just a mere metaphorical or symbolic gesture. Diana Taylor helps us interpret this act:

> [T]he pre-Conquest worldview was governed by a system of equivalences rather than one based on representation and mimeticism. An image, for example, was not a representation of the god, but one more actualization of the god. The human heart, offered in sacrifice, nourished the deities, but in fact, it was only one of many offerings. The heart-shaped fruit from the cactus

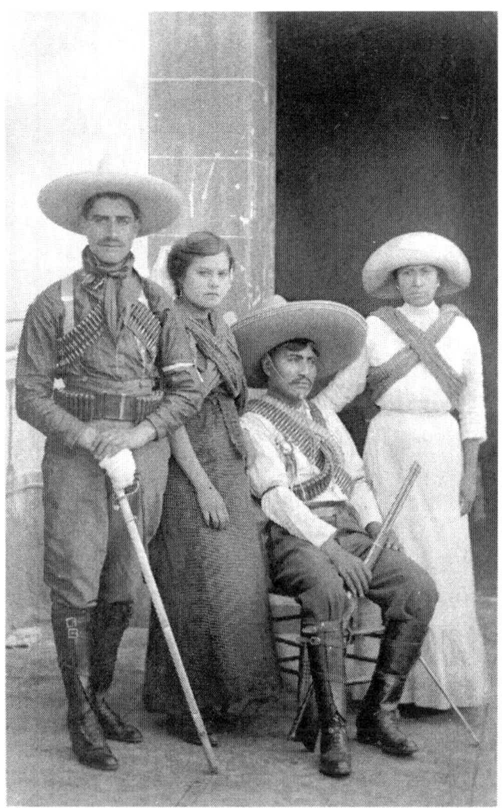

FIGURE 1.18. "Revolutionaries and soldaderas," México, 1915.

also served in sacrifice, not because it stood for, or replaced, the human heart but because it was equivalent, one more manifestation of nourishing food. *Thus, the Mesoamericans established a whole system of equivalences in which the heart, like the rose, shared a deep correspondence. 'Like' refers to this system of multifaceted correspondence rather than a metaphoric substitution or approximation.* (Emphasis added, 106–7)

This humble article of clothing cum domestic tool is transformed into a weapon, and not just as a symbol of resistance in the metaphoric sense, but rather as another manifestation of resistance, an actualization of struggle and war. The *rebozo* carries that which will nourish the soldiers, that which transforms agricultural products into sustenance, and the progeny who represent both the soldadera and the soldier's immortality, as they in turn, will continue the fight. The *rebozo* speaks to their indigeneity, refuting the historically subordinated status of Native people in México, making visible and present what for many belongs to a remote past. In fact, the photographs reveal that even middle-class and *criolla* women wore their more elegant *rebozos* crossed in front like bandoliers, and despite the fact that these photographs were stylized, this act was one of solidarity and war. Nonetheless, the *rebozo*, like the soldadera, became multivalent and multifarious; it paradoxically transcended class and culture. It was at once an article of clothing that almost timidly conceals while it was an instrument of movement; it was appropriated for utilitarian needs while it provided warmth as a garment; it became the flag of the soldaderas while it was constituted as a quintessentially *Mexican* article of clothing. The rebozo operated as an instrument of death (crossed in front like bandoliers) as well as in the preservation of life (transporter of food and children); it belongs to both war and peace, the feminine domestic sphere and the masculine public sphere. In fact, in the summer of 2014 the London Museum of Textiles held a special exhibit dedicated to the *rebozo* titled, "Made in Mexico: The Rebozo in Art, Culture and Fashion." The headline from the article that covered it read as follows: "Fashion for Revolutionaries! The incredible story of how the colourful rebozo scarf changed the course of Mexican history" (Ruth Styles, *Mail Online*, May 28, 2014). Indeed, a fascinating tribute to this unassuming, and yet powerful, article of clothing.

The impact of this garment was not lost on Nao Bustamante, a video and performance artist who would a year later feature the *rebozo* in her 2015 exhibition, "Soldadera" by crafting a special *rebozo* made of Kevlar, a bulletproof shawl that never existed, but that speaks volumes to the multivalence of this intimate, domestic, traditional, and yet revolutionary feminine accessory. Bustamante's *rebozo* accompanies the frilly late-Edwardian war dress, also made of Kevlar, that she would craft in honor of a battalion of revolutionary women she observed in a photograph donning similar attire, reminding us that the *rebozo* also was an article of feminine "decency"; it obscured their faces in so many photographs, protected the women from the sadistic gaze of the public eye and the photographer's lens at the same time it made their presence in the public sphere *known*. Sometimes all we see in the images is the shadow of a *rebozo*, indicating that a woman (and probably her child) was *there*.

In these photographs, these women are captured both arbitrarily as well as intentionally posed; they appear looking demure and dainty as well as disheveled and troublesome; they are in the background as well as in the foreground; standing still while in movement. We see the space created by revolution: the train, the baskets of food, the "shadowy" peasant background, and the singular heroic figures in the foreground. In sum, the photographs perform a discursive counterpoint to the official narratives surrounding women's participation in the Revolution. The multivalence present in this one image will make manifest the conflictive nature of the tropes that proliferate about these women and the way in which their bodies, both real and figural, travel. The aesthetic realm and the popular imagination has allowed us to reflect on how these women contributed to the war, and what the effects of this visible presence in the public sphere were on the women who came after. Tragically, everything went back to normal once the political regime stabilized, but the image of the soldadera remained, disfigured yes, but alive. This image of the soldaderas boarding, or perhaps getting off the train—both in its cropped and amplified form—is testament to the rupture, the flickers of possibility that the soldadera posed to Mexican womanhood.

Literature, films, and popular poetry all select the renditions of the stories they want to tell about the soldaderas, choosing between the inevitable mother/whore binary. Despite the penchant for romanticizing singular images over the muddled masses, the photographs tell a different story, one that remains vague, and which ironically constitutes a kind of evidentiary source from which our history of these women is drawn. The following chapter will closely study the diverse appearances made by the soldadera in various forms of cultural production by exploring the dueling tropes of "la Adelita" and "la Cucaracha" as well as the derivations that have constituted the basis of her unwritten legacy.

2

The Many Faces of the Soldadera and the Adelita Complex

Si Adelita se fuese ir con otro,
le seguiría la huella sin cesar,
en aeroplano, en un buque de guerra
y si se quiera hasta en tren melitar [sic].

[If Adelita were to leave with another,
I'd follow her footsteps endlessly,
On an airplane, on a warship,
Even on a military train].

—"La Adelita," Trío González, 1919

Va a la guerra, Marijuana
tras de su querido, Juan
va al compás de los clarines
del tambor el rataplán.

[Marijuana goes to war
Following her beloved Juan,
Keeping time with the bugle
And the drum's rat-tat-tat].[1]

—"Marijuana, la soldadera,"
Hermanos Bañuelos, 1929

Raucous whores high on weed and beguiling sweethearts: the most popular corridos of the Mexican Revolution of 1910 would have us believe it was quite a party. However, who the soldadera was in actuality and who she is now in the memory of Mexicans and Mexican-Americans are two very different things. The transgressive behavior of the soldadera, who was encased in either an abject domesticity or a slothful perversity, both resonated with and disturbed the people who relied on them because they seemed to incarnate the very struggles that propelled the Revolution. Their affront to Mexican patriarchy resulted in an historical negligence regarding their contributions to the war, as the prominence of their figures in the arts revealed the danger of their independence and promiscuity, provoking a real crisis for men of all classes. Despite the fear of their brash transgression, they were silently observed, derided but also admired. In a dialectic of blurry background images and strident individuals in the foreground, the aesthetic realm has made present—and consequently allowed us to critically read—what in history has remained negligible. Moreover, the soldadera is a trope that did not die with the Revolution or with the revolutionary political rhetoric. Because the notion of place can be "woven together through space by movement and the network ties that produce places as changing constellations of human commitments, capacities, and strategies," these women actually blurred the boundaries between public and private, between "place" as proper and "space" as abstract (Agnew 325). Indeed, through movement (*olin*) they created new places by transforming the old ones: the campgrounds, train tops, dusty roads, improvised barracks became "practiced places." By walking, cooking, trudging, and fighting they also forged a new spatial language that resulted in a new ontology for women in México.

To begin, I will briefly examine the way in which tropological criticism provides a fruitful framework for engaging the soldadera as a cultural figure and the predominant tropes that condition her appearance in the aesthetic realm. By placing female military participation within the social context of mainstream middle-class values, I interpret the representations of the soldadera as trope in diverse forms of cultural production, especially within the intersections of what is considered "high" art and popular culture. By reviewing the various avatars of the soldadera, starting with the eponymous "Adelita" and "Cucaracha" corridos and the texts they inspired, which in turn, closely follow the virgin/whore dialectic, I identify a cast of characters that are reproduced time and again across aesthetic genres. In addition to the Adelita and Cucaracha, the "noble mother/wife" trope developed in the texts by Rafael Muñoz and Josefina Niggli will receive special attention. The romanticized renditions of this character is arguably an attempt by writers and artists to soften the image of the soldadera, paying tribute to her sacrifices by using the language of a Westernized Christian patriarchy. This chapter ends by examining the provocative way in which Niggli's play *Soldadera* weaves together all the iconic—and acceptable—faces into one work designed for a U.S. audience, as well as the multiple possibilities this drama offers for reading into, and against, the prevailing soldadera archetypes.

Traveling Tropes

So ubiquitous they hardly need introduction, there are three main tropes that circumscribe the representation of the soldadera in the arts and historical imaginary: the "Adelita" as the young sweetheart, the "Cucaracha" as the harlot, and the abnegating wife or mother. From these master tropes or root metaphors emerge various sub-tropes that I will discuss in detail later on. In his book *Tropics of Discourse* (1978), Hayden White identified troping as "the soul of discourse," and hence the key to history, language, and ideas. Much like the perambulatory nature of the soldadera herself, the soldadera trope also travels, circulates, and contradicts itself. As expounded by White, a trope "helps us understand how speech mediates between our apprehension of those aspects of experience still 'strange' to us and those aspects of it which we 'understand' because we have found an order of words adequate to its domestication" (21). Furthermore, White's theory of tropological discourse is fundamental to my understanding of the soldadera and the mulata because a trope,

> is always not only a deviation *from* one possible, proper meaning, but also a deviation *towards* another meaning, conception, or ideal of what is right and proper *and true* "in reality." Thus considered troping is both a movement *from* one notion of the way things are related *to* another notion, and a connection between things so that they can be expressed in a language that takes account of the possibility of their being expressed otherwise. (2)

Movement is critical for discourse's "mediation" between supposed oppositions of error and truth, ignorance and understanding, imagination and thought, because it provides continuity between them. Tropological discourse is illuminating as a hermeneutic device because it examines what already operates in language and thought. Moreover, there can be multiple tropes circulating at the same time, in the same discursive gesture, and they can also stop operating at any given moment. "La Adelita" and "la Cucaracha," for example, function metonymically as discrete parts of a diverse whole. Tropes as understood by White account for nuance, but most importantly, for what is unknown or inexplicable "in reality." They account for the deviation "from" one meaning (Adelita/Cucaracha as sweetheart/whore) but also the deviation "toward" another (Elizabetta as complex rendition of camp follower). This contradiction manifests itself in the multitude of art forms that have produced this fraught figure. The soldadera as trope takes the different forms that White discusses: metaphor, metonymy, synecdoche, and irony. Rather than privilege one trope over another, I will reflect on how diverse figurative forms have emerged such that they result in conflicting representations of the soldadera.

Irony, which intentionally states one thing in order to say another, operates as one of the many privileged figures taken by the soldadera. For example, to avoid calling a woman a prostitute or a whore, she is euphemistically called a soldadera; to avoid saying soldadera, because of the very connotation it had with easy women, she is called a "wife." Similarly, to diminish the military nature of women's participation in the Revolution, you call a woman a soldadera instead of *soldada* or *coronela*. There is a tenuous space between one thing and the other because tropes, as White explains, account for these connections and contradictions. In the end, by officially redesignating soldaderas as "wives," the Mexican Army neglects their military participation by ironically relegating their unofficial status as soldaderas to an official anonymity and impotence as married women. As wives, they could claim pensions, but were prohibited from participating officially and also from remarrying. Very much as a father might offer his name to a bastard child, this official gesture does little to ameliorate the status of the illegitimate offspring. Irony implies that "other thing" the speaker wants to communicate; there is no need to state it. Elliptical language also functions ironically; through the discursive spaces occupied by the ellipsis one actually speaks euphemistically: "Esa mujer no es más que una. . . ." Literature is riddled with these pregnant ellipses. These gaps both connect and separate accounting for their constant movement "toward another meaning."

Although irony works powerfully in the cultural production about the soldadera, catachresis also appears as an important trope. In a catachresis the metaphor is mixed; one metaphor is employed in order to approximate another that in reality does not exist. The word soldadera, and the language surrounding these women, functions catachrestically; when you lack the language or consciousness to describe or understand a specific reality, you approximate it, or "domesticate" it into a language that is culturally and socially comprehensible, or that operates within the realm of your own understanding. Catachresis allows for women to take on multiple roles because it lumps them all under one erroneous title. In the case of the soldadera, that other reality, identity or ontology was unknown and perhaps unimaginable. They instantiate the catachresis; they are called "adelitas" by diverse members of society both during the Revolution and afterwards, when in fact they are many things. It is not just that the strictures of social norms prohibited these women from acquiring some kind of proper title and place: society has simply not created a "word" for them. They do not register within the vocabulary of cultural and discursive legibility. Language is working, in this case, *a posteriori*; war creates necessity, and necessity creates the conditions for social mores to change. Nonetheless, once the war ends, these social conditions return to normal. The soldadera was forgotten, relegated to paragraphs here and there in history books,[2] but given center stage as the prostitute or the sweetheart in cultural production. True to the form of catachresis, their participation in the Revolution was metaphorically domesticated by cultural producers into the sloppy diction of a cultural and discursive official grammar.

Finally, metonymy and synecdoche, as relationships that define the part for the whole, are what appear most often. In the case of metonymy, it can be identified through causality, origin, or contiguity; synecdoche uses an essential part, such as a hand, to represent the whole.[3] For example, the "Adelita" and "Cucaracha" become the parts that represent the whole in the case of the soldadera. The Adelita as the mythified doll-like or abnegating wife figure is predominant, and in fact the name soldadera is often replaced with "Adelita."[4] All of these figures of speech (metaphor, metonymy, synecdoche, catachresis, irony) seem to operate simultaneously in the cultural production that I examine.

The Adelita Complex[5]

Adelita se llama la ingrata
la que era dueña de todo mi placer
Nunca pienses que llegue a olvidarla
Ni a cambiarla por otra mujer

Y si acaso yo muero en campaña
Y mi cadáver en la tierra va a quedar,
Adelita, por Dios te lo ruego,
Que con tus ojos me vayas a llorar.

[Adelita is the name of the ungrateful one,
the one who owned my love.
Don't ever think that I would forget her
or exchange her for another woman.

If by chance I should die in battle
And my body be left on the land
Adelita, by God I beg you
To cry for me with those eyes of yours].[6]

—Trío González, 1919

"Adelita" is the name of the beautiful woman who stole the Sergeant's heart and that of every soldier who hummed the tune that became the unofficial anthem of the Revolution. Although "adelitas" became the polite name that was employed to describe the soldaderas (it was used to describe the soldier's sweetheart as opposed to the camp follower, servant, or prostitute), even as "adelitas" there is an underlying accusation of ingratitude that reflects a patriarchal fear of abandonment. The trope of the Adelita is still one of the most common and widely disseminated in the Mexican cultural imaginary; the image of the sweetheart awaiting her soldier has even inspired the contemporary Mexican punk bands to compose ballads.[7] In her book *Las soldaderas*, Poniatowska draws from her informant "Jesusa" and Elizabeth Salas to enumerate a few of the other names supposedly used to refer to soldaderas: vivanderas, comideras, galletas de capitán, soldaderas, chimiscoleras, soldadas, juanas, cucarachas, argüenderas, mitoteras, busconas, hurgmanderas, pelonas, guachas, mociuaquitzque [valiant woman] o auianime [woman of pleasure] (22). Despite Poniatowska's colorful list of nomenclatures, la Adelita became the metonymical sum of all the different parts, eclipsing the different faces, names, and histories that are often disguised by her sweet facade.

Leonor Villegas de Magnón, in her bilingual autobiographical narrative *The Rebel/La rebelde* (1994) chronicling her role in the Revolution, claims that the eponymous ballad originates with a fourteen-year-old girl who ran away from her home in El Paso, begging to form part of the White Cross Corps (founded by Villegas de Magnón herself) that was aiding the Constitutionalists during the Revolution (126–29). According to Villegas de Magnón, she "became the joy and pet of the brigade" by singing sweetly as she helped sew bandages, inspiring the composition of what would become one of México's most famous tunes by her young admirer, Antonio del Rioarmante, on their way to Torreón (130). It eventually surpassed the ribald Cucaracha in popularity (130). Adelita asks Villegas de Magnón for her permission, as head of the White Cross, to marry Antonio, and then secretly followed her sergeant to Torreón on the road to Chihuahua where they engaged in combat. But as fate would have it, he was felled by a bullet as he was about to cross the firing line to carry a canteen of water to his general. In Magnón's account, contrary to other versions where through her infidelity she actually causes his demise, Adelita witnesses her soldier's death:

> Adelita screamed for him to stop. A bullet ended his life. Brought back to town by the General's aide, Adelita fainted in the Rebel's arms. Later when she felt better, she decided to join the active fighting, to go to León, Guanajuato, where the fighting was thickest. Nothing else would console her. . . . (139)

In Villegas de Magnón's account, Adelita is strong-willed, faithful, and a fighter. Unlike the vision we perceive in the corrido, she chooses to continue fighting where it is "thickest." This rendition of the origins of "the Adelita" portrays a very different image; although she is still a faithful sweetheart, she is also resolute, impetuous, and courageous. She takes herself into battle and continues even after she has lost her suitor. Villegas de Magnón, like Poniatowska, recognizes the effect this simple music would have on the war, impressing itself into the imaginary cultivated by this culture of insurrection as the "song continued to follow Adelita, weaving its music into the fabric of the Revolution" (139).

Other historical texts (such as Salas) also support this version, although none have signaled Villegas de Magnón's text as an originary source. This is due, no doubt, to the inability of Villegas de Magnón to get her text published; she was rejected at least twenty-six times by American and Mexican publishing houses, not to speak of her daughter's multiple efforts to get her manuscript published posthumously. Sadly, Villegas de Magnón died without seeing her life's work published except as serialized newspaper articles, nor did she live to see it recognized as a contribution to the literature or history of the Revolution. She donated her whole fortune to the war, leaving her in dire economic straits after it was over. Up until her death, she was still fighting alongside other soldaderas to receive her pension as a Revolutionary veteran.

In truth, the origins of the Adelita corrido are unknown even when there are various hypotheses. Salas claims that the verses came from Villa's soldiers, but the melody might have been a traditional favorite. More important, by listing a few of the possible origins for one of the most famous corridos of the Revolutionary era, she highlights the very ambiguous and almost mythical nature of this figure. In one rendering, Adelita was a fourteen-year-old girl who nursed a soldier named Antonio del Río back to health. This version clearly coincides with Villegas de Magnón's account of Adelita as a nurse in her corps who worked alongside Carranza. In another, she was a twenty-one-year-old woman who was one of Villa's many paramours, and whose boyfriend, upon discovering her entanglement with Villa, committed suicide. In yet another related version la Adelita is a woman who disguises herself as an elite Dorado[8] and falls in the famous battle of Celaya. Upon discovering she is a woman, Villa honors her by claiming her as a Dorado. These last two versions were dramatized in the narrative by Baltasar Dromundo, *Francisco Villa y la "Adelita"* (1936). Finally, both Salas and Tabea Linhard in her book *Fearless Women in the Mexican Revolution and Spanish Civil War* draw from the account of a real soldadera named Tomasa García, who, in an interview with Marta Romo, claims that the true Adelita was a brave woman from Ciudad Juárez who, threatening to kill cowards, taunted fearful soldiers by telling them they should stay at camp to cook beans ["La mera Adelita esa decía—¡Órale, todos a entrar y el que tenga miedo que

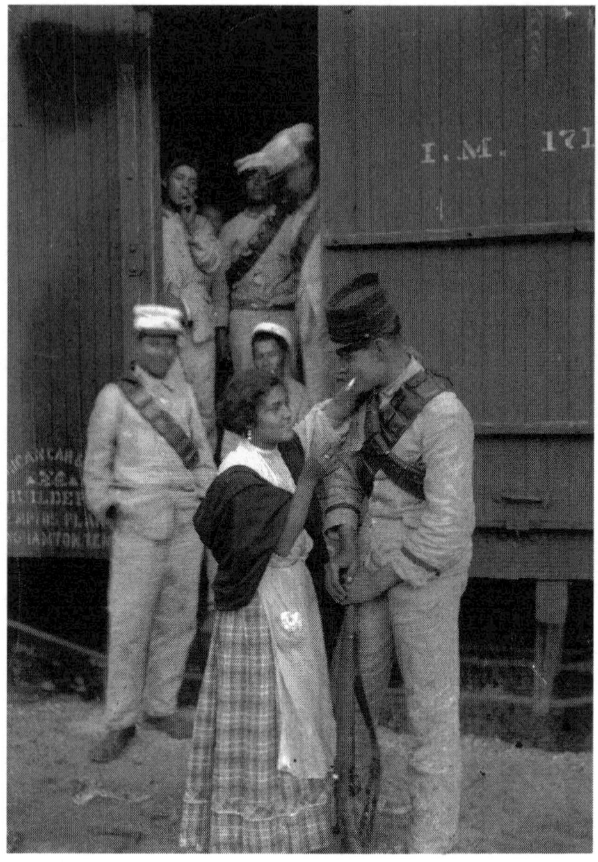

FIGURE 2.1. "A soldier says goodbye to his wife at the Buenavista train station," México City, D.F., 1913.

se quede a cocer los frijoles! Y balazos y balazos y el que no obedecía, ¡lo mataba ella misma!"] ("¿Y las soldaderas? Tomasa García toma la palabra" *Fem*, 12–14). What is fascinating about this interview is that despite García's intention to tell the "real" story about the Adelita, and by extension, the lives of the soldaderas, she reproduces these very stereotypes because "her own story cannot be told without reference to such mythical figures as Adelita" (Linhard 95).

The corrido, however, focuses not on Adelita's strength or role in the Revolution but almost exclusively on her status as a muse because "soldiers who sang about La Adelita did not focus on her valor, but rather on her beauty, desirability and loyalty" (Salas 92). The following verses from the corrido exemplify this (taken from María Herrera-Sobek, *The Mexican Corrido*):

"Conque quédate, Adela querida, / yo me voy a la guerra a pelear,/ la esperanza no llevo perdida / de volverte otra vez a abrazar" [So stay, my beloved Adela / I take my leave to fight the war./ I shall not lose hope / To once again embrace you] (105).[9] There are numerous variants of the Adelita corrido, but in general they follow two formulas. In one, Adelita is merely a love object, and the troubadour takes on the role of a medieval supplicant. Because life is ephemeral and short, he begs for her to love him, and to remember him after he has gone off to war. The other version, although considered more "literary" and less popular, recognizes Adelita as a soldadera, and actually hails her role as a valiant soldier: "una moza que valiente los seguía." In this version taken from Herrera-Sobek, la Adelita is described as following "her soldier" into battle, and because of her beauty and valor, is even respected by the Colonel: "Popular entre la tropa era Adelita / la mujer que el sargento idolatraba, / porque además de ser valiente, era bonita. / Y hasta el mismo coronel la respetaba" [Popular among the troops was Adelita / The woman the sergeant adored / Because she was not only valiant but beautiful / So that even the Colonel respected her] (107). Despite this reference to her valiance, the stanzas that follow have her depreciate into a stereotypical female hysteria as she quickly begins to sob and pray to God that her lover be spared, thus returning to her role as loyal lover and servile camp follower.

Herrera-Sobek theorizes that the *corridistas* incorporated women into popular balladry by adapting the poetry to this new political and cultural reality. Instead of completely ignoring their involvement, the bards neutralized their agency by either mythifying them or turning them into love objects (103–04). Catalina Giménez, among many scholars, contends that corridos are much more than popular musical traditions; she considers them collective histories as well as subaltern ideological expressions. They reflect the popular imaginary, but also create it. In an oral environment, popular song serves as an ideological vector of subaltern groups, a sign of mutual recognition and identification as well as an archive of collective memory (38). If we want to interpret the ballad tradition as not just a folk musical practice, but as an alternative history, it is incumbent upon us to understand the process by which female characters and folk heroes disrupt this tradition by insinuating themselves into epic folk ballads usually reserved for men. Despite the lyrical romanticism that the bards used to represent them, this change signals a small rupture; it constitutes an important departure from traditional balladry in a way that simultaneously includes and excludes them. In their ubiquity and real-life participation, the heroes and heroines indirectly forced change into a ballad tradition that responds, as argued by Giménez and others, to a regional collective memory. Moving freely out of their homes and invading the public sphere, these women made a radical impact on traditional gender conventions both in and outside of their communities. To appreciate the magnitude of this change we must consider the importance of the ballad tradition for not only recording historical events, but also interpreting them. Rancière puts it another way when he claims that "[p]olitics occurs wherever a community with the capacity to argue and to make metaphors is likely, at any time and through anyone's intervention, to crop up" (*The Politics of Aesthetics* 60).

Both "La Adelita" and "La Cucaracha" constitute two of the most well-known corridos of the time period, perhaps of all time, yet paradoxically some folklorists do not consider either of these ballads to be traditional corridos due to the fact that they do not follow the literary conventions established by corrido scholars. Furthermore, given that the narrative elements of the

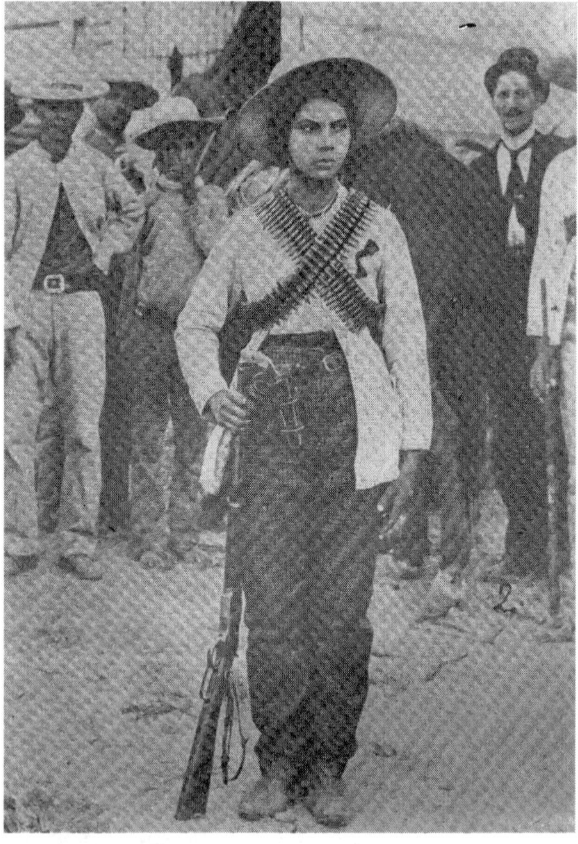

FIGURE 2.2. "Valentina Ramírez, soldadera," Sinaloa, México, 1911.

ballad tradition are subordinated to the sentimental or romantic components characteristic of *canciones*, they are considered more lyrical because they do not exalt the heroic qualities of their protagonists: "The transposing of the *soldadera* into a love object became problematic for the troubadour since he or she could not employ the classic form of the heroic corrido; a more flexible structure, a more lyrical framework, had to be employed to fit the romantic contents of the ballad" (Herrera-Sobek 104). According to Armando Duvalier, six of the primary formulaic structures of the corrido are: the initial call of the *corridista*; the formula that establishes the place, date, and name of the main character; the formula that introduces the speech act, which usually carries the ideological impact of the corrido or what Américo Paredes has designated the emotional core; the message; the farewell of the hero or main character; and finally, the farewell of the *corridista*.[10] Of the six formulaic motifs outlined by scholars and considered corrido dogma, "La Cucaracha" contains almost none; there is no "initial call" or "goodbye," no date or place is given nor are any heroic deeds recounted, and there is not much of a message or emotive core. Although many corridos do not contain all of these established criteria and frequently vary in composition, they usually contain at least three or more of these components and mostly adhere to traditional octosyllabic meter[11] and consonant rhyme scheme (although this is also variable). "La Adelita" contains a few more of these formulas, particularly the more "literary" variant which narrates the events of a battle and whose refrain could be interpreted as a speech act. It also contains more of the rhetorical flourishes that are typical of corridos. "La Valentina," on the other hand, contains none of the formulaic motifs; its stanzas are almost completely lyrical and narrate no particular events, "Valentina, Valentina, rendido estoy a tus pies / si me han de matar mañana / que me maten de una vez" [Valentina, Valentina, I beg at your feet / if they're going to kill me tomorrow / they may as well kill me now]. This verse merely communicates the plaintive laments of a forlorn lover, completely eliding the role "la Valentina" had as a combatant on the battlefield despite accounts that claim she was a real soldier. For example, Shirlene Soto maintains the corrido is based on the life of Valentina Gatica who was from Sinaloa and was a member of Obregón's troops (45). The photograph featured in figure 2.2 is identified by the Fototeca of the Mexican Institute of Anthropology and History as Valentina Ramírez, a soldadera from Sinaloa and we can appreciate that, although posed, she is dressed as a man and is wielding a rifle.

In sum, we see that balladeers did not completely ignore women's participation in the Revolution, although they certainly are marginal relative to the great heroic corridos composed for grandiose figures such as Benjamín Argumedo, Felipe Ángeles, Pancho Villa, and of course Emiliano Zapata.

Ironically, "la Adelita," "la Valentina," and "la Cucaracha" became the most popular songs crooned by the troops, invading the national imaginary while disrupting the traditional formulas for popular balladry. Because these figures are hailed as romantic objects or satirical figures, they become articulated in a more lyrical language rather than adhering to the conventions naturalized by balladeers. Even within a popular poetic genre, three of the most famous ballads within it (each of which was turned into a movie) are not considered authentic representatives of the genres from which they supposedly emerge. Not unlike soldaderas, the corridos that immortalize these figures are marginalized, considered "pop" versions if you will, but not true epic ballads. Notwithstanding their illegitimate status as true corridos, almost a hundred years later both Mexican and Chicano children still learn these corridos orally, while internationally these melodies are associated with Mexican culture.

Housed in the special collections for cultural heritage in the General Archives of the Nation in México City, exists a song titled "Las Adelitas" written by Prof. José G. Matus, with the music composed by Alberto P. Holguín. "Las Adelitas," labeled a "canción vals (corrido)" [song waltz (corrido)] by its composers, was published in 1951 in order to honor a female basketball team from Chihuahua: "Simbolizan a aquella heroína / que murió en nuestra Revolución. / Como Adelita, la inmortal Norteña, / son valientes y retadoras, / tienen porte de grandes atletas / y enloquecen a la multitud" [They symbolize that great heroine / Who died in our Revolution, / Like Adelita, that immortal Northerner / They are valiant and brave / and great athletes / Who inspire the masses]. Here the trope of the Adelita is employed in order to honor the women who became symbols of athletic excellence in a sport popular in the United States, but not common for Mexican women of the period. Ironically, "la Adelita" was a popular ballad precisely because she upheld the idealized vision of the sweetheart waiting for her soldier to come home. La Adelita as a sexualized muse, and not the *coronela*, is invoked as a symbol of these female athletes who transgress social norms by their show of physical strength. In effect, by invoking the trope of la Adelita, and not another figure who is bestowed with physical strength, the balladeer softens the perception of these athletes and effeminates them, so to speak, praising them as symbols of national and regional pride and prowess, both against Mexico's northern imperial neighbor as well as its "underdeveloped" southern one[12]: "bravas y bonitas como ningunas / han vencido a las gringas / a guatemaltecas y capitalinas" [brave and beautiful like no others / they conquered the gringas / Guatemalan women and ladies from the Capital].

The author of this *corrido/vals* simultaneously praises their strength and beauty, making the female presence and success in what historically has been a male public sphere (organized athletics) acceptable to a traditional Mexican public. By deploying the Adelita trope, the singer beckons a past that is both honorable and patriotic, allowing the revolutionary rhetoric to work its nostalgic magic for the images of women who won an international basketball championship. Adelitas are no longer revolutionary sweethearts; they are any women who display strength and courage, and metonymically become the moniker for those females who occupy the public spaces traditionally reserved for men. This domestication of athleticism allows for these women to represent México publicly through their show of strength, emphasizing their beauty and femininity by subordinating the trope of the Amazon to that of the doll, while simultaneously mythifying their force so that it can impress their rivals but still remain inoffensive at home.

Indeed, there has been some ambivalence with regard to the deployment of the Adelita trope by Chicana scholars. While some scholars have embraced the soldaderas as part of a cultural legacy, others have rejected it. According to Salas, the Brown Berets unofficially called female members "Adelitas" (116). The corrido "Mujeres valientes," written by Miguel Barragán, parallels the Adelitas with Chicana activists, and was a popular corrido for the United Farmworkers Movement (115). Others have found the soldadera imagery useful "to distinguish Mexican and Chicana feminism from Euro-American culture and the women's movement" (117). Others, such as Isabelle Navar connect the image of the Mexican woman to the soldadera, as they "had an enduring quality and strength in 'conserving and furthering human existence' " while academics such as Norma Cantú "lamented what she called the 'Adelita complex' in universities" (117).

In any case, it is impossible to disentangle the figure of the Adelita from that of the soldadera; even now, her legacy rings in the ears of contemporary Chicana artists. Poniatowska reiterates this: "Eso sí, los corridos suplieron la falta de reconocimiento y 'La Adelita' ejerció su encanto en los escuchas" [That's for sure, the corridos filled in the lack of recognition for women and 'La Adelita' enchanted her audiences] (22). Adelita certainly enchanted her revolutionary audiences, and continues to do so today. In 2005 at an Empowering Women of Color Conference at UC Berkeley, a young Chicana artist was selling a T-shirt she made with an image of a soldadera. Embossed on the T-shirt was the following statement: "Las Adelitas: A Tribute to Our Women Warriors." And in the summer of 2015, Chicana video/performance artist Nao Bustamante put on a multimedia exhibition dedicated to the soldadera that ran for over three months at the Vincent Price Museum of Art in East Los Angeles, and has continued to travel to other institutions. For better or worse, the figure of la Adelita is married to the participation of women in the Revolution, reproducing herself into a community of women as a symbol of strength and perseverance, and more importantly, Mexicana and Chicana pride.

"La Cucaracha" and the Other Animals of the Revolution

> La cucaracha, la cucaracha
> ya no puede caminar,
> porque no puede, porque le falta
> marijuana que fumar.
>
> [The cockroach, the cockroach
> Can no longer crawl,
> Because she ran out
> Of marijuana to smoke].

—Anonymous

Emerging from an old corrido, "La Cucaracha" is a stock character who embodies the trope of the drunken harlot that is brazen and fierce. Unlike "La Adelita," a ballad that is clearly linked to the Revolution of 1910, many scholars believe that the corrido "La Cucaracha" is quite old, going back to the nineteenth century. According to Salas, the first stanza was supposedly written by Fernán Caballero, the masculine *nom de plume* of a nineteenth century female Spanish novelist, but it became Mexican and gained popularity during the French Intervention when the federal soldiers sang about a soldadera who wanted money to go to the bullfights. During the Revolution, it reemerged with the Villistas in the North where it immortalized the figure of the stoned harlot who followed the troops (89). Since the war of Independence this trope has shaped the image of women involved in insurrection through multiple pejorative figurings: as a troublemaking whore, a racialized peasant scavenger or a defeminized soldier whose unnatural power and military prowess profoundly unsettles the gendered social order. In contrast to la Adelita, la Cucaracha became the model for the camp slut who entertained the troops even when she caused a little mischief.

As was the case with the corrido "La Adelita," within popular poetic expressions the emergence of women as salient participants and witnesses to war conditioned the transformation of the genre; in part, because women had not been acclaimed in such a fashion but also to remain acceptable to a more traditional audience. In effect, even the most ostensibly fluid of genres had to mutate in order to make way for these women. Of the thirty-seven corridos collected by María Herrera-Sobek that include the soldadera figures, there are only four that actually mention the women by name when depicting battle scenes, and only one, "El corrido de Petra Herrera," that includes both first name and patronymic, a veritable standard guideline for heroic corridos. In general, a traditional heroic corrido will use the person's full name and not just their nickname: this honors the character by establishing the veracity of the historical personage and relaying the details of a particular event.

The following Zapatista broadside "Vida y muerte de la cucaracha" printed by Antonio Vanegas Arroyo in 1916 quite comically sums up the sad fate of "la Cucaracha."[13] A riff of the original Villista corrido, it pretends to narrate the life and death of the Cucaracha by lampooning the *catrinas* (upper-class women) who had to turn into "cucarachas" in order to survive the food shortages of 1915. Many of the verses are even bawdier than the original, serving as a sad testament to the condition of our *pintadas* [painted-ladies]: "Nomás pongan atención / y aparen bien las de burro; / ya muero de insolación / y hasta los mocos escurro [. . .] / La cucaracha, la cucaracha / ya no puede patalear, / porque del viento una racha / de patas la hizo vol-tear [Hey pay attention / And get the donkeys in line / Because I'm dying of heatstroke / And I got snot running down my face [. . .] / The cockroach, the cockroach / Can no longer crawl / Because a strong gale / Has flipped her onto her backside] (357). As is revealed by these verses, the Cucaracha is in such a pitiable state that she is dying of sunstroke while riding a donkey with her nose running until an abrupt wind lands her on her back with her feet dangling in the air. Clearly the sexual double *entendre* brashly insinuates that the gales of war have landed her on her back as a prostitute, far from the comforts of home and the domain of respectable women. This corrido berates the *catrinas* for their decadent ways and mercilessly ridicules their sad condition. It also utters an undeniable threat: all women, regardless of class, are subject to the vagaries of war and can end up an unseemly cucaracha.

La Pintada Unmasked

> A testimony of the first kind: the character of The Painted One in *The Underdogs*. The Painted One is forward and blunt, she possesses mobility, affirms without reservation her love for her man, she is—in her own way and during battle—a woman in complete possession of herself, and the rest of the time she is manifested as a completely uninhibited individual.[14]
>
> —Carlos Monsiváis, *Amor perdido*

La Pintada [The Painted One]: mobile, passionate, self-confident, and talented in war but also uninhibited. Monsiváis pays homage to the character of la Pintada in this passage dedicated to the soldadera from *Amor perdido*. He honors her by qualifying her as strong and self-assured, a woman who is very different from her nemesis Camila in Azuela's *Los de abajo* (1915), a character who serves as a romantic rival for the attention of the novel's hero Demetrio

Macías. However, not unlike the other soldaderas, her figure is vulgar, inde-
cent, and inappropriate: "Una muchacha de carrillos teñidos de carmín, de
cuello y brazos muy trigueños y de burdísimo continente, da un salto y se
pone sobre el mostrador de la cantina, cerca de la mesa de Demetrio" (146)
[A very coarse-featured and very-dark complexioned woman, with rouge-
smeared cheeks, jumps up on the bar of the cantina, near Demetrio's table]
(74).[15] Monsiváis is certainly on to something: she is powerful, self-possessed,
and uninhibited. She knows whom and what she wants and even allows herself the liberty of changing her mind, a welcome contrast to the lachrymose
Adelitas or the "dark peasant scavengers." Her very name is a testament to
her bravery, and her sexual power does not undermine her military prowess.

As we might expect, she becomes a grave nuisance. She disrupts the
General's authority and is simply too much for him from the very beginning:
"Demetrio, sin comprender, levantó los ojos hacia ella; se miraron cara a cara
como dos perros desconocidos que se olfatean con desconfianza. Demetrio
no pudo sostener la mirada furiosamente provocativa de la muchacha y bajó
los ojos" (147) [Not understanding him, Demetrio raised his eyes toward the
young woman. They faced each other like two strange dogs sniffing around
with distrust. Unable to sustain War Paint's furiously provocative gaze, Demetrio lowered his eyes] (75).[16] Again, the animal imagery resurfaces, as they
"sniff each other like dogs," and similar to canines, stare each other down. Her
strength, however, cannot coexist with its male counterpart in the military
realm, let alone the romantic one. Her amorous intentions are spurned as it
becomes inevitable that he will be enticed by the sweet Camila. Similar to
the María Félix character in the film *La Cucaracha* we will examine shortly,
la Pintada is forced to leave the troop. Her character is vain, troublesome,
and unacceptable. The vulgarity of her name is illustrative of this inability to
incorporate female strength into the male realm, and her sexuality must be
relegated to its proper place as well. Despite Monsiváis's intention to recuperate this figure as an example of a strong revolutionary woman, she is not even
afforded a proper name; her power is entrenched in her "painted face." Her
authority is a mere pathetic simulacrum of male potency and honor. Only in
the chaos of a Revolution that has apparently lost its ideological purpose can
female figures emerge as travesties (and transvestites) of strength and honor,
social change and progress.

La Pintada, in sum, is an instantiation of the Cucaracha trope, and like
la Cucaracha, suffers a similar fate. La Cucaracha fills the pages of stories
and novels, is sung about in the corridos, and, alongside la Adelita, is the
star of feature films played by México's most treasured divas. She entertains
us with her lasciviousness, her insolence, and her audacious mouth. This is
amusing, of course, because she does not emerge from the middle or upper
classes and because she is always dealt with in the end. As maintained by

Castillo, the loose woman is insistently present in both popular and bourgeois cultural production, but is not assimilated into mainstream society. These characters traffic in a libidinous economy that allows for the public to watch in a sort of scopophillic fascination; while her subjectivity is always tenuous, she is the sacrificial lamb of her adoring public. Like the corridos that mostly omit the heroines' first names and patronymics, la Pintada's real name is never revealed. Furthermore, she is not constructed as a heroine, despite Monsiváis's (and my own) revisionist intentions that would rescue her from the abyss of ignominy. As a character, she is designed to impress the reader with her bawdy power, but only to reveal how degenerated the participants of this uprising had become. The perceived uncontrollable corruption and profligacy of the Revolution creates an environment where women may occupy unnatural positions of power, threatening characters such as Camila who would maintain the status quo and remain the flitting love interest in the background. This character, in sum, is the first in a long line of cucaracha types who will represent female strength and agency at the same time they incarnate the demise and corruption of traditional womanhood.

Indeed, we observe this trope repeatedly in the films and novels: Azuela's "la Pintada" is reproduced in Maria Félix's cinematic version of *La Cucaracha* (1958) directed by Ismael Rodríguez. The director of the film apparently created this movie with Félix in mind, as she was infamous for playing fiery divas with a penchant for vitriol. As underscored by Castillo, the figure of the loose woman became a way to interpret the thousands of women irrupting onto the public scene, and functioned, not unlike the Malinche, as a scapegoat and binary opposite of la Adelita. La Cucaracha as a figure is defamed, but is, nevertheless, entertaining. The negative elements of her portrayal are more illustrative of how women on the battlefield were considered a nuisance, creating trouble and vice among the ranks. Félix's film perfectly exemplifies this: she fills the screen in almost every shot with her expressive smirks and caustic repartee, challenging the virility of almost all the male characters. Although highly aestheticized and beautifully dressed, she is nonetheless powerful; she valiantly encourages the troops by getting their spirits up through a raucous party. She derides the soft-spoken and decent widow (played by another Mexican icon, Dolores Del Río) for her weakness and propriety; that level of domesticity does not belong on the battlefield, it is useless and even dangerous.

After a series of unsuccessful flirtations, la Cucaracha finally gets her way with el Coronel Zeta (played by alpha male Emilio Fernández) when he decides to come around and she, annoyed at his previous disinterest, plays hard to get. He bursts into her room, and after she rebuffs him, he orders her to undress, a command she willingly obliges. Then the scene cuts to the morning after, where shattered glass litters the room and the camera focuses in on a rose in a wine bottle while the extra-diegetic music is ebullient and happy. The aggressive male who sexually overpowers the shrewish female is portrayed as felicitous, bringing order to the disorder as she dons traditional "female" attire to signal this transformation when they tour the town as if newlyweds.

Not surprisingly, la Cucaracha will soon lose her lover to the meek and comely widow as he resents her for having been forced to kill an amorous rival in a duel for her hand. After this point she deteriorates dramatically; having been expelled from the troop she succumbs to her maternal instincts by completely abandoning the "masculine" clothing and giving birth to the Colonel's child. By the time she catches up with the troops in the hope that he might recognize the infant as his son, he has already died in battle. La Cucaracha, covered in a *rebozo* with her child in arms, goes off into the revolutionary landscape tamed by maternity, her fire squelched by her lover's rejection of her strength and her newfound identity as a mother.

For the Mexican public, it seems to be a sort of guilty pleasure to observe this sort of raw female power converting itself into an overwhelming sexual energy. Unlike the texts which allude to sexuality through elliptical language (such as Federico Gamboa's *Santa* written in 1903), this movie quite candidly exhibits Félix's ferocious sexuality, especially in the racy scene where the General tries to make up for his personal affront by wooing her, and ends up forcibly taking her after she rebuffs him. At no moment is the middle-class widow exhibited in this violent manner, although there is one particularly erotic scene where she is washing clothes by the river, and the General chances upon her half-dressed. Nevertheless, this scene is sensual and romanticized despite the sexual threat that lurks in the background. While the widow's body is "abstracted into a play of trope," the Cucaracha incarnates a formidable, albeit evanescent, sexual energy. The lesson here is obvious: la Cucaracha's force is expedient for its wartime purposes, but is ultimately expendable. At the end of the film even the middle-class widow is forced to take up arms; however, this is only once the Colonel has died and is a product of necessity, not military ambition. The only female figure with social longevity is the kind, decent widow who will remain after la Cucaracha has been expelled. This mimics the fate of Azuela's "la Pintada," who is also expelled from the troops in favor of the soft-mannered "Camila," and is a perfect example of the Cucaracha trope.

The play *El corrido de Juan Saavedra* by María Luisa Ocampo contains a similar libidinous dynamic where promiscuous soldaderas abuse their sexuality in order to recklessly provoke mischief and vice. This play was written in 1929 and debuted May 29th in the Regis Theater as a part of cultural initiative called Comedia Mexicana, partially funded by the government, and led by important intellectual and cultural figures such as Antonieta Rivas

Mercado (*Perfil y muestra del teatro de la Revolución Mexicana* 144). It was written at a time when the revolutionary regime was attempting to create a cultural mystique that would mythologize the Revolution and legitimize the government that followed in its wake. Despite the important patronage of Mercado and the artistic collaboration of Diego Rivera on the set, the play enjoyed a lukewarm reception and only five performances, as the audience for whom Ocampo intended it—the popular classes—were not the attendees, but rather, the middle-class bourgeoisie looking for more refined entertainment. It was written almost as a didactic revolutionary pastoral, with a set of six "scenes" that are episodic instead of Aristotelian. Marcela del Río Reyes claims that the similitude with the theater of Bertolt Brecht is uncanny given that Mexican artists were unfamiliar with his work at that time. Nonetheless, the play is similarly constructed in episodic segments that create an effect of distantiation while representing a social denunciation that is both didactic and folkloric.

The corrido as a metatextual device once again operates as a narrative voice, but is also inserted as way to create folkloric ambience. While Juan Saavedra has his own personal history in the form of the corrido, "La Valentina" makes her way into the play but only as a musical backdrop, not as a storytelling device. The play reproduces rural speech and diction in what appears to be a "cuadro de constumbre"[17] that is ideologically motivated in its condemnation of not only the exploitative nature of the hacienda system and the "tienda de raya,"[18] but the early revolutionary state and the abuses perpetrated by those in power—whether they be the wealthy landed classes, the federal soldiers, or the unruly revolutionary troops whose excesses hurt the very people for whom they were seeking redress.

In the fifth act, or what Ocampo calls "cuadro," there is a poignant camp scene where we are given a rather disparaging image of the revolutionaries, and in particular, their women, whom she does not call soldaderas but refers to as *mujeres* or *muchachas*. Unlike la Pintada or the Cucaracha, the characters representing soldaderas have no identifying name, nor are they engaged in the military activities, but are simply referred to in generic terms as girls or women. In this scene a young woman ["muchacha"] entertains herself by mischievously manipulating the soldiers in order to see which man she can get to fight for her, and ends up getting one revolutionary to kill another in order to win her hand (similar to the duel in the film *La Cucaracha*). When the General happens upon the scene and courts her, promising her pillaged riches from the rich folk of México City, she lets him hang the second soldier who killed the first in order to win her over in a ruthless *tour de force* of sexual power. In this scene we witness the raw violence that became stereotypical of the Revolution, where the peasants lose sight of their ideals and become engaged in rampant banditry, a free-for-all of crime, corruption, and disgraceful sexuality. As the young "Cucaracha" gets two men killed in order to win her hand, an aging soldier complains to one of the older women: "¡Epa! ¡Va a hacer una tarugada! (A la mujer primera) Todas las indinas viejas tienen la culpa de las desgracias que suceden" [Epa! He is going to do a stupid thing! (To First Woman) All these Indian broads are responsible for the misfortunes that happen] (327–28).

Although this play is written in order to exalt the righteous figure of Saavedra based on the events narrated by the metatextual corrido, which in turn is inspired by the figure of Emiliano Zapata, similar to Azuela's touchstone novel, this scene details the ideological morass the Revolution had become. The soldadera, although never explicitly called so, suffers a similar shameful fate: she becomes a heartless troublemaker, conniving her way to the top of the food chain and needlessly sending men to their death. Rather than advance the revolutionary cause she contributes to its chaos and corruption. The soldaderas appear only as secondary characters in this act that takes place in a revolutionary camp because the scene is designed to highlight Saavedra's (Zapata's) unflagging integrity amidst the degeneracy and criminality. Several times throughout the act ["cuadro"] a male character complains about the presence of women in war: they are disruptive, unruly, and the cause of vice. The complaint is issued initially when the girl flirts with the men and causes them to quarrel, but also when one woman lays dying from a bullet wound. This moribund woman is not considered a victim of war but a pathetic burden and constitutes another category of the Cucaracha trope.

Indigenous Scavengers Meet Armed Street Dogs

Unlike the singularly heroic yet vulgar figures of la Cucuracha and la Pintada, there are other soldaderas who appear in an abject, dehumanized state or as racialized indigenous scavengers, what I would call another avatar of the Cucaracha trope. They too are sexualized, but are seldom characterized as brave or take up arms. For example, José Clemente Orozco (rumored to find soldaderas particularly reprehensible) depicts these women in his murals, paintings, lithographs, and illustrations. He dedicated one etching to la Cucaracha (1915–1917), where, as can be expected, half-drunken soldaderas appear next to neatly dressed soldiers. In a similar illustration he made for Azuela's *Los de abajo*, "Bandit and Girl" (1929), a bandit cum revolutionary appears sitting down with a drink in one hand, and a girl in the other, lasciviously positioned on his knee with her legs on either side of him. All we see is the back of her head, with the two black braids coiled together, a hairstyle typical of indigenous women (and showcased in paintings by Diego Rivera). His right hand, which bears his *trago* [drink], is suspended on high, almost as if it were a military salute, and his left hand holds the girl tight and low around the waist. We observe only half of his face, as the other side is covered by back of the girl's head. His look is decidedly serious, with only half a moustache peering downwards. It almost resembles a revolutionary lap dance, reflecting the sort of rowdy, libidinous behavior we might imagine the *cucarachas* instigating. Interestingly, Orozco was chosen over Diego Rivera to illustrate Azuela's novel as the person in charge of selecting the painter (Enrique Munguía) accused Rivera of being too "simplified to the point of affectation [. . .] while Orozco is skittish [. . .] his artistic world is still in chaos [. . .] He comes close to drowning in a tropical cascade of virgin colors, when suddenly he decides to get lymphatic" (Renato Mello, *José Clemente Orozco in the United States* 84). Orozco's perceived style was raw and chaotic, and the publishers apparently wanted raw, exotic images to accompany Azuela's novel. This drawing reflects the racialized and sexualized image that circulated in the national imaginary: poor indigenous women with the typical markers of indigeneity—their braids and *rebozos*—not surprisingly positioned with their backs to the spectators and their faces devoured by the chests of the revolutionary males. Raw and exotic is exactly the kind of image that not only foreign audiences, but also domestic ones, wanted to see.

Monsiváis, in the same short section on the soldadera previously referenced in *Amor perdido*, provides another image: "La soldadera, suma de órdenes: busca agua, prepara la lumbre, fornica al aire libre, ve pariendo entre breñas" [The soldadera, replete with orders: find water, prepare the fire, fornicate outdoors, give birth in the brush] (22). He draws on the miserable camp follower stereotype and combines it with the sexualized image of Azuela's "la Pintada" in order to decry the sad legacy of these women. He portrays these miserable camp followers as loyal canines, following their men without complaint, providing them with everything at the expense of their humanity. In contrast to the sexually promiscuous cucaracha figure who abuses her power and holds little interest in politics, there is a sub-trope within this figuring that casts the cucaracha as servile, abject and pathetic.

Los de abajo once again stands as the literary precursor of this image of the pathetic camp follower, especially when we consider the way in which the soldaderas are animalized, such as we see in the following description after a battle: "La vertiente, de seiscientos metros, estaba cubierta de muertos, con los cabellos enmarañados, manchadas las ropas de tierra y de sangre, y en aquel hacinamiento de cadáveres, mujeres haraposas iban y venían como famélicos coyotes esculcando y despojando" (Azuela 143) [The steep slope to the side, six hundred meters in length, was littered with dead men, their hair in tangles, their clothes covered in dirt and blood. Among the heaps and piles of bodies, most of which were still warm, women in tatters went back and forth like starving coyotes, searching and stripping the corpses of their possessions] (68). The soldaderas are likened to starved coyotes, desperately stripping their dead victims of whatever valuables might remain on the decaying corpses. This description is morbid, dehumanizing these women as vile contributors to the violent realities of war. In addition to being animalized as entities that are hardly redeemable, they are racialized as dark, indigenous scavengers: "mujeres de tez aceitunada, ojos blanquecinos y dientes de marfil, con revólveres a la cintura, cananas apretadas de tiros cruzados sobre el pecho, grandes sombreros de palma a la cabeza, iban y venían como perros callejeros entre los grupos" (146) [women with olive-colored skin, bright eyes, and ivory teeth—with revolvers at their waists, cartridge belts across their chests, and large palm-leaf sombreros on their heads—roam from one group to the other like street dogs] (74). The dark skin and white teeth resemble the portrayal John Reed makes of Elizabetta in his book *Insurgent Mexico*, but in this description they are likened to armed street dogs, who beside the cockroach and the vulture, are the most reviled of scavengers. The image of the "cananas cruzadas" and "revólveres a la cintura" is hardly heroic or noble, but rather dark and depraved. These women are denaturalized, thrust into the animal kingdom and out of the world of man. The only redeemable woman in this novel is Camila, a hopeless girl in love with the white *curro* (dandy), who of course, manipulates her naïveté in order to please the hero Demetrio Macías who would like to make her his soldadera—in spite of the fact he has a proper wife at home waiting for him.

In the previously referenced play by María Luísa Ocampo, there are other female characters in the same "cuadro" that are illustrative of the stereotype of the camp follower as the "indigenous scavenger." Besides the troublemaking cucaracha girl I discussed earlier, the other soldadera figures in Ocampo's play parallel this pathetic, degenerate state: one serving as a sort of gossip and the other dying in an abject, undignified manner. As the soldadera called "Mujer Segunda" agonizes from a bullet in her belly, the others merely look on, actually anxious for her to die because they find all the noise she makes in her final death throes annoying:

Mujer Segunda: "Ay, Demetrio . . . ay, Demetrio . . ."

Muchacha: (Tapándose los oídos) "¿Por qué no la matan de una vez?"

Mujer Primera: (Encogiéndose de hombros) "Ya le falta poco. En un rato se muere."

[Second Woman: "Ay, Demetrio . . . ay, Demetrio . . ."

Girl: (Covering her ears) "Why don't they kill her already?"

First Woman: (Shrugging her shoulders) "It won't be long now. She will die soon."] (328)

They do not even waste a bullet to put her out of her misery. Again, these secondary characters do not have proper names, but curiously, are not identified as soldaderas. This could reflect a class bias on behalf of Ocampo, or her desire not to pigeonhole these characters into the pejorative term "soldadera," in part because it was written with the popular classes in mind. But as we will see with Josefina Niggli, the soldaderas are ambivalent to the dying woman's pain, signaling yet again a callous vulgarity that points to the corruption of womanhood; in particular, the nurturing sensibilities of women as wives and mothers. This play, as opposed to Niggli's drama I examine later on, takes up the adverse effects of the Revolution on women, but is not about women; rather, it is concerned with the general problems of the peasantry, abstracting from the Zapata myth to create a character whose integrity is born of the injustice of the hacienda system and whose story will be told only through popular balladry.

Orozco's illustration for *Los de abajo*, "Las soldaderas" (1924) which later served as a basis for his oil painting likewise reflects this sad image. The women follow behind their soldiers, hunched over from their bags. The soldadera who occupies the visual center of the painting is the most burdened because she appears to carry a child in her *rebozo* in addition to her bundles. The rifles of the men stick out oddly behind the women's heads. They are tired, over-burdened, and obedient, but unlike the cucarachas, they are noble: they constitute a piece of the topographical and revolutionary landscape. By employing somber earth tones, the painting allows the color of their skin to blend into the background; they almost function as synecdoches of a larger, natural, and revolutionary landscape. Unlike the fecund mother earth images that are sometimes associated with femininity, this landscape is drudging and bleak. Showcased in the center of the painting is a soldadera wearing a pink skirt, contrasting radically with the solemn background and reminding us, in a splendid intertextual gesture, of la Pintada's pilfered blue silk dress and sullied torn stockings. This out-of-place pink skirt also resonates with the bourgeois hats some soldaderas pillaged from the mansions of the *catrines*, whose poignant image makes its way into films like José Bolaño's *La soldadera* (1966). Perhaps this skirt belies the futility of the war and the absurdity of bright apparel in the midst of violence and despair, or simultaneously disavows, in the same gesture, this image of the soldadera as part and parcel of the natural landscape. Or, alternatively, perhaps it is intended to represent the colorful clothing typical of indigenous women. Although she occupies the center of the painting, filling it with her voluminous *rebozo* and pink skirt, she remains in a subordinate position, strategically behind the soldiers, with only one shadowy profile visible while in the drawing "Bandit and girl," the woman's face is completely devoured by the soldier's chest.

In sum, we have observed cucarachas as loutish harlots, as singular, impressive but tragic characters, as miserable camp followers, or as racialized peasant scavengers hardly differentiated from their animal counterparts.

Whether they are *la* Cucaracha, or *las* cucarachas, they embody a legacy that is, although not monochromatic, nonetheless undesirable.

Las Guadalupanas: In the Custom of Her Sex and Country

Despite the fact that thus far I have emphasized the negative aspects of the soldadera's striated cultural representations, there is another sub-trope that emerges in cultural production, which is that of the noble soldadera who sacrifices all for man and country. Although I have already hinted at this model of womanhood in the mural discussed above called "Las soldaderas," there are other representations which favorably depict the soldadera, casting her in a romantic light that underscores her heroism and fealty. In these texts the soldadera is figured as a mother/warrior who nobly subordinates her needs to those of her mate for the love of *pater* and *patria*. These women symbolize the future of the nascent nation-state, the poor stalwart women who will tend to the emergent national family. Much like the "Marianne" of the French Revolution, they are iconic of liberty and sacrifice.

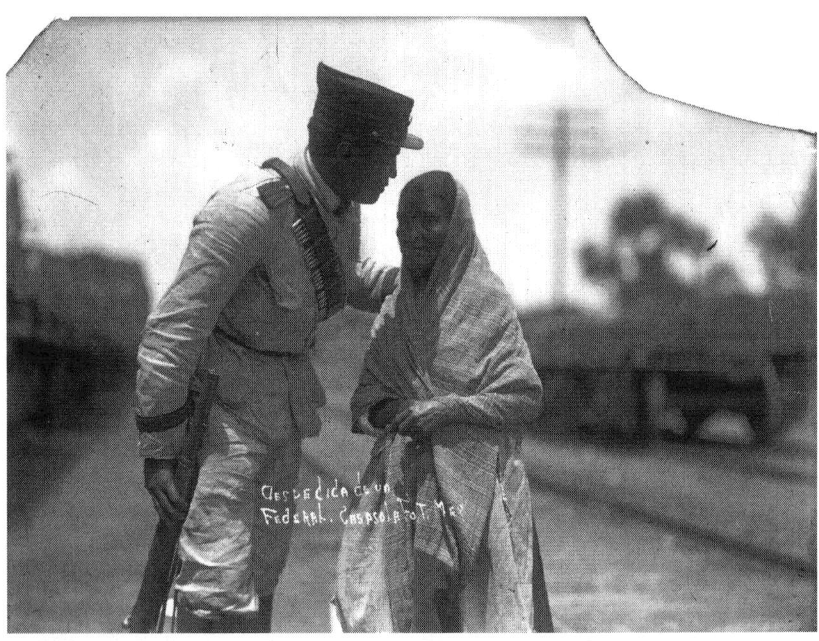

FIGURE 2.3. "Federal soldier says goodbye to a woman," México City, D.F., 1914.

Rafael Muñoz, one of the canonical writers of the Revolution, produced a few of these touching short stories that exalt the compassion and heroism of the soldaderas. "Agua," ["Water"] "Villa Ahumada" ["Smoked Village"] and "El Niño" ["The Child"] are all very beautiful, albeit profoundly romanticized representations that problematically bind these women to their traditional roles within the patriarchal state. "Agua" is a moving narrative that recounts the valiant sacrifice of a soldadera who crosses the firing line in order to retrieve water for her parched sergeant and the troops:

> Victoria corrió, avanzando el pecho firme, con los cabellos al viento; repentinamente se detuvo al oír un golpe seco y sentir la pierna húmeda; una bala le había quebrado el jarro y en su mano derecha quedaba solamente el asa, inútil . . . Y luego, ahí mismo donde estaba la arena húmeda, se recostó Victoria para siempre, con una flor roja en la blusa cubierta de polvo.

> [Victoria ran, pushed forward with strength and resolution, her hair flying in the wind; suddenly she stopped when she heard a dry thump and felt her leg get wet; a bullet had broken the water pitcher, and in her right hand only the handle had remained, useless . . . Later, in the same spot as the wet sand, Victoria lay down forever, with a red flower on her dusty blouse]. (25)

She runs heroically in the wind to find her companion when, all of a sudden, the enemy strikes down both Victoria and the pitcher of water she carries in her arms. Sadly, the specter of the Adelita haunts her sacrifice when the soldiers tease the Sergeant, accusing Victoria of having abandoned him for the enemy due to her hunger and thirst:

> Todavía hasta ahí le seguía la burla de sus compañeros:
> –¿Dónde está Victoria, mi sargento? . . .
> –¿Ya estará haciendo la cena?
> –se me hace que la Victoria fue de los rebeldes . . .
> –Claro, ya tendría ganas de agua . . .
> –. . . y debe haber quedado muy satisfecha, por cierto. . . .

> [He was still followed by the derision of his companions:
> –Where is Victoria, dear Sergeant?
> –Could she be making dinner?
> –I reckon she went off with the rebels . . .
> –Of course, she must be thirsty . . .
> –and of course quite satisfied, for sure . . .]. (25–26)

Her sacrifice is left in a state of derision and shame, called into question by the association of thirst with sexuality, as the mocking of her "thirst" insinuates that her Sergeant left her sexually dissatisfied. The story concludes with the soldiers gathering around the campfire to sing "Me abandonaste, mujer, / porque soy muy pobre" [You abandoned me, woman / because I am poor]. Rather than be recognized for her efforts, her absence raises suspicions and she is rendered a traitor.

As is typical in these narratives, the female figure operates as the Madonna who sacrifices all, including her life and her reputation, in order to provide the man she loves with water. Rather than recognize her sacrifice with honor, she becomes the sacrificial lamb whose intentions are called into question by the very soldiers she tries to help. By exceeding the limits of female valor she became too public a figure, too active a participant, and the water for which she gave her life is spilt vainly into the desert sand, along with her dignity as a human being. She dies with her chest decorated by a flower of red blood, while her sergeant, besides suffering the loss of his mate, is likewise ridiculed as a *cornudo* [cuckold]. These narratives commend female military engagement and contain a latent criticism of the social order that humiliates them even as they fight selflessly for others. However, it is this discourse of abnegation that once again is deployed in order to validate the sacrifices of women; while this story focuses on Victoria's valor, she is romanticized beyond all recognition. A symbol of an unrealized and unsung "victoria," she is born of a long tradition of tragic female characters that prevailed throughout the nineteenth century.

In contrast, Josefina Niggli wrote and produced the play *Soldadera*, a full-length one-act drama that purports to display the diverse range of personalities and experiences of the soldaderas of the Mexican Revolution. Born in 1910, Niggli was a native of Monterrey, Nuevo León, who witnessed the Revolution as a small child when her family, along with other wealthy border families, moved to San Antonio in 1913 as a result of the violence. Although she was an upper-class woman whose parents were not themselves Mexican, she identified strongly as a Mexican national. She received her undergraduate degree in San Antonio and worked in the local theater and wrote for the radio. In 1935 she began her graduate training with Professor Frederick Koch of the Carolina Playmakers in Chapel Hill, granting her access to a nationally recognized and prestigious theatre group. Koch's mission was to make American "folk plays" that portray the "folkways of our less sophisticated people living simple lives not seriously affected by the present-day, complex social order" (Quoted in Orchard/Padilla, *The Plays of Josefina Niggli* 7). Koch's influence left a heavy imprint on her work as he was insistent on portraying the rural "folk" in a way that was clearly reductionist and ethnographic, but nonetheless, at the forefront of theatre for the time.

The drama in *Soldadera* takes place in a mountain pass in the Sierra Madre range in Coahuila where a camp of soldaderas are guarding the ammunition of their rebel military chief, Hilario. They have captured a Federal soldier they call the "Rich One," and much of the plot revolves around the treatment of the prisoner and the discovery of a traitor in the camp. Niggli wrote all of her work in English, and this play was designed specifically for a foreign (U.S.) audience, which might partially explain the essentialized nature of the main characters. The Carolina Playmakers at Chapel Hill produced and performed *Soldadera* in February of 1936. Unlike many other female writers and artists such as Leonor Villegas de Magnón and Nellie Campobello, Niggli enjoyed tremendous success in her profession and was recognized as a great writer and dramaturge, even if her work would be largely forgotten later. She received major awards and the attention of the literary scene in New York and abroad, in addition to piquing the interest of Hollywood (16).[19]

Some critics have recognized the ambivalence of her position as an early Chicana/Latina writer because Niggli lacked "the ethnic and class markers that later Mexican Americans would regard as central to their cultural identity" (4). Academics such as Maria Herrera-Sobek have given her the "sympathetic status of 'border writer'" (4) while others such as Alicia Arrizón contend that her image and work is a product of a "bifurcated" identity ("'Soldaderas' and the Staging of the Mexican Revolution" 107).[20] Niggli was evidently beholden to a particular image of a nostalgic, rural México, both by her mentor but also her own aesthetic volition to validate and uplift México and its people in the eyes of prejudiced U.S. citizens. Moreover, she was the first writer to translate Adelita as a cultural figure into English, and the first literary voice on either side of the border that attempted to bring the reality of the Revolution for women—in all of its complexities—to the stage. This is remarkable for many reasons: first, it was written barely twenty years after the Constitution of 1917 was signed and the violent stage of the war ended, and second, because she was a woman. Rodolfo Usigli, a prominent Mexican dramaturge with whom she worked for a few years, was so impressed with her talent that he nettled her in his forward to *Mexican Folk Plays* (1938) to write in Spanish and adapt her writing for a Mexican audience. Her response to this was that the "United States needed the folk drama more than Mexico" (Quoted in Orchard/Padilla 10). Niggli's defense of this choice was born of her concern with the pernicious stereotypes of Mexican barbarism and the infamous "bandido" that permeated the North American cultural and political imaginary, and thus, she seemed intent on dispelling these harsh stereotypes, of course while relying on folkloric ones of her own (11).[21] Although the Mexicanness of her plays can sometimes feel canned, Niggli's accomplishments as a Mexican-American woman and her genuine concern for the struggles endured by women of the time period are extraordinary, and despite her professional successes, ironically resound her overall condition as a subordinate actor in a male-dominated Anglo-American field.

This play produces seven different female characters spanning the gamut of all the iconic faces of the soldadera. There is "Concha," the strong mother/warrior type who is their leader and the most complete of all the characters: she is fierce, brave, but battle-weary. She is not ingenuous about the destruction and death that war exacts. She supplies ammunitions for the rebels, and after having been discovered by the enemy, plans to execute a suicide mission where she, or one of the other soldaderas, will save the ammunition and the other women. Maria is the sentinel who shoots the "rich" prisoner and operates as Concha's second in command while the "Blond One" is also a feisty character who backs up Concha. There is a cucaracha figure, "Cricket," who is a flirtatious traitor who demands the same rights as men to be sexually promiscuous. She is the troublemaker, and naturally, the weakest link in the group. Upon revealing the facility with which Cricket is willing to betray the women, Concha plans to have her execute the suicide mission. The character Adelita, in turn, is a hardly dissimulated effort to incarnate the corrido. She is innocent, uncorrupted, and completely naïve. She spouts patriotic rhetoric, and it is she who, stealing the bomb from Concha after Cricket begs for her life, will save the rest of the group and sacrifice her body for the good of all: "What do you know about the Revolution? It's beautiful, it's glorious, it's heroic. It's giving all you've got to freedom. It's dying with the sun in your face . . ." (189). This play reveals the irony of this sacrifice, as the other figures are so embittered and bent on revenge that any change the Revolution might effect would be wasted on them. She represents the vanished youth and idealism of a Revolution that has lost its light; she is the martyr whose sacrifice was made in vain. Bickering over how to torture and kill the prisoner, these women hardly appear heroic but more like demented harpies, however Tabea Linhard suggests that "the disregard for life and death, together with the violence that permeates the words of the soldaderas, does not mean that Niggli's characters are essentially evil or bloodthirsty femmes fatales, as representations of women who participate in revolutions and wars often suggest" (108).

Despite being designed for a U.S. audience, the play accomplishes three major points: first, it constitutes the corrido as the legitimating source of information from which knowledge about these women is drawn. Second, it recognizes the symbolic nature of the Adelita figure as an abstract, glorious ideal that mitigated the bloody, vulgar aspects of war and the place of women within it. The soldaderas in this play idealize Adelita even as they poke fun at her; they see themselves as little more than callous shells searching for redress. Finally, it creates a range of female personalities that operate in relation to the tragic loss of a man (son, husband, brother): for example, the Old One saw her son crucified, while Tomasa witnessed her son torn apart by dogs only to be taunted by the soldiers afterward to make soup out of his bones. Although the loss of a male figure looms over the older characters, in the case of the two foils the loss changes: Adelita loses her mother and is brought up in the camps while Cricket loses her virginity, honor, and innocence when she is gang-raped. Impressing this profound sense of loss that creates the need for revenge, the play weaves in a discourse of redemption and hope that simultaneously condemns and dignifies the pain and victimization of these women.

To begin, throughout the play the corrido performs a powerful metatextual role, which not only accentuates the dramatic theatricality of the production by operating as a musical leitmotif, it acts as an evidentiary source and legitimating agent. Other literary texts, such as the play *The Corrido of Juan Saavedra* by Ocampo, weave the corrido throughout the narrative in an effort to lend it a popular authenticity, a technique that also is evident in *Soldadera*. Moreover, Niggli draws her main characters directly from the corridos ("Adelita" and "Cucaracha") and at first glance does little to complicate their personalities. As discussed, male heroes in the corridos usually have a first name and patronymic, and some evidence is generally provided with regard to the date of the event, place, and action that transpired. For example, the corrido dedicated to the figure of Benjamín Argumedo is still active in the oral repertoire a hundred years later despite the fact that he was notoriously ambivalent in his ideological proclivities, switching sides innumerable times. In a famous verse, his last few moments are immortalized by the corridista who narrates that when his petition for a public execution was denied, he smiled in the face of death ("antes mejor sonreía"). The "mañanitas" (last goodbye)[22] dedicated to Argumedo have remained popular in oral tradition because he was revered by the people for his valiance. Few corridos featuring female protagonists provide any specific information regarding the identity of these women, focusing instead on the role women play in service to men and the Revolution. Not unlike Azuela's Pintada and Camila, Niggli pairs both Adelita and Cricket as musical foils, and although the name "Cricket" is chosen over "Cockroach" (perhaps as a euphemism that would better appeal to U.S. audiences), Adelita as a symbol prevails.

War brings women—both in their degenerate and idealized forms—into a story that exceeds the boundaries of these archetypes. The play showcases the Adelita and Cucaracha while simultaneously unbinding them from the strictures of these flat models. Even Cricket, the abject Cucuracha, has a story behind her name:

> That Tomasa and the Old One! All they can do is talk about
> their sons. What's a poor woman who never had a son going to
> say? The only thing that ever happened to me was when the Rich
> Ones carried me off on my fourteenth saint's day. They brought
> me back quick enough, I can tell you. (*She sighs.*) One of them
> used soap that smelt like violets. Every time I smell a violet now
> I can remember the feel of my knife going into his stomach. Oh,
> well, the poor sinner's getting more rest than I am . . . be damned
> to him! (Orchard/Padilla 176)

Although traitorous and weak, the origins of her nickname are revealed: gang
rape, post-traumatic stress, and promiscuity. The Cucaracha corrido never
elicits such a complicated and painful history even when it is well known that
rape was an unforgiving reality; it only croons that she can no longer crawl
because she is out of marijuana. The concept of "Adelita" slides over these
violent elements of the soldadera's reality, and while the abnegating, suffering
mothers lament the murder of their precious children through the morose
and tortured memory of flashback, they intend to enact their revenge on
the Rich One not in the theatrics of a heroic battle, but in the way in which
female agency is often codified: as unnatural and perverse. They consider
letting him get eaten alive by red ants or tying him to a cactus so that the
needle can grow through his heart.

The corridos repeatedly interrupt the play and force us to reflect on
both the symbol and the reality because, as aptly expressed by Linhard, "the
myth of Adelita lies at the crossroads of history and fiction" (115). Whereas
the original corrido simply refers to Adelita's status as a muse, "la mujer que
el sargento idolatraba," Niggli's version does not disavow the sweetheart, but
rather, exalts her even as she emphasizes destruction—the "thunder" and
"bones." The revised ballad is testament to this ambivalence: "If Adelita should
go with another, / If Adelita should leave me alone . . . / I would follow in
a boat made of thunder, / I would follow in a train made of bone" (192).
The Adelita character recognizes herself in the romantic lyrics, and despite
the absence of wartime heroics in the corrido, she is inspired by "her" song
to valiantly exercise her strength as a military actor, if only for a few tragic
minutes. The symbol, the child, the angel, and the woman are all blown to
pieces with nothing remaining except the words of a song that does not even
belong to her. However, these voices, shards, bits and pieces—while impossible to reconstitute—provide the refractory evidence of what was, of what
had been, and what could be again. The absence of a complete body, as we
will see later on with the figure of the mulata, both provides the possibility
for change and action while erasing it.

La Adelita, then, dominates the play at the same time she is blown up; she is at once a beautiful political and social ideal and its impossibility. Her naïveté leads her to self-sacrifice after having poignantly inscribed her name into the air with her fingers, spelling out the letters of her name for the first and last time. Concha coerces the Rich One (the enemy) into singing the corrido "La Adelita" only to abruptly silence him, disgusted by his *voice* performing *their* song with a pointed irony; he was belittling the idealistic beauty and glory of the Revolution incarnated by Adelita. After her death, the "harpies," the soldier-women, the old cook, the traitorous slut, remain—all transmuted as they sing their homage to Adelita in "her" corrido.

As we have seen, Adelita even charmed the women, for her presence as an adopted orphan in a makeshift family, frozen into a childlike state, keeps them "human." It also reminds them of an ideal they can never become, because war and its concomitant atrocities for an ideal five hundred years in the making is so removed, so impossible, that one requires the symbol, the emblem, the "fire" to keep going. Thus, she is not just the symbol for lustful soldiers; she is the inspiration for women and their redemption from the ignominy of cucarachas, or even from the word soldadera, pejorative in itself. Why would one identify as a cockroach when one could be a valiant Barbie? The multiple layers to the Adelita figuring and legacy are indeed much too complicated to cast aside, and while Niggli (and others) appropriate this unidimensionality as a sign and signifier, she likewise blows it up. To be *otherwise* in revolutionary and post-revolutionary Mexico was certainly possible, even when there was no "name" for it.

Linhard, in turn, proposes a provocative reading of Adelita's voluntary death as a counterhegemonic graphemic act that is both self-effacing and singular. By drawing from Gayatri Spivak's interpretation of the suttee, she reads Adelita's inscription of her name into the air, the dramatic climax of the play and Niggli's rewriting of the corrido as reason alone not to disregard this play for its romantic foray into Mexican stereotypes:

> [A]ny attempt to reconstruct the stories and histories that the mythical Adelita conceals will result only in silences, fragmented narratives, thunder, and bones. Like the voices in Juan Rulfo's *Pedro Páramo*, Adelita's voice is a voice of death. She is constructing a counternarrative with her own body, since she does not have access to the written world. Still, can Adelita be heard? (114)

Linhard's reading theorizes female immolation as the ultimate act of writing; a speech act that goes unanswered. Like Munoz's "Victoria," Adelita's corporeal speech is left unrecognized and unremunerated, legible only in the language of a transgressive or romanticized sexuality. Linhard concludes that "[t]he point is that the play does not resolve the ambiguity between an act of counterwriting and a heroic sacrifice that is part of the dominant narrative of the Mexican Revolution" (116). Nonetheless, these acts are precisely the ways in which women throughout this period "spoke." Hundreds of thousands of women, unrecognized and unsung, made an impact on the places they occupied, and the spaces they created. These tactics, practices, and spaces left a lasting imprint on the cultural imaginary that created an unwritten historical legacy or as Debra Castillo describes, "historical catachresis"; even today Mexican and Chicana women still look to them as models of female agency.

Adelita is the lone martyr, who like Muñoz's "Victoria," did not live to see the fruits of her sacrifice. As I have been arguing, these images focus on the patriarchal idealization of women who give themselves to the cause not for their own personal or political self-aggrandizement as women, but in order to advance more lofty and generalized ideals that relate to the community. They are redeemed through their sacrifice to the state and to their men.[23] However, even with the Adelita and Cricket/Cucaracha as the leading ladies, this play showcases the multifaceted nature of the female participants in the rebellion at the same time it reveals a fundamental disenchantment with the Revolution. In the same camp we have a woman who dreams aloud about a night of passion (akin to a wet dream) while having flashbacks of rape and murderous self-defense; we have women who, orphaned and alone, forge new kinship ties built on the bonds of death and others who suffer daily flashbacks that witness the torture and murder of their sons and husbands. The dialogue written for the Old One is particularly moving in this respect:

> Sometimes in the night I wake up and hear him crying for
> me . . . small mother, small mother . . . until I have to cover
> my ears and scream to God. (*Rocks back and forth.*) When those
> Federals took him away I ran after them until I fell to the ground,
> and then I crawled on my knees for miles and miles until the dear
> Virgin sent sleep to cover me. (Orchard/Padilla 166)

Besides the role of the abject and abnegating mother, the Old One also possesses the important job of feeding the women and the troops. However, the strongest and most developed character in this play is the pragmatic and skilled military leader, Concha. She is invaluable to her rebel chief and is the leader of her group. Other fearless women such as María are loyal subordinates to Concha and operate as spies, sentinels, and intermediaries; and then there are those such as Adelita and even Tomasa that really have nowhere else to be. By repeatedly turning back to the abnegating mother, the heroic doll and the traitorous slut, male complicity in the machinery of exploitation, objectification, and degradation of woman is ignored, even absolved.

So while Niggli does not deviate from the stereotypes present in canonical texts like those of Azuela and Guzmán, but rather, doles out healthy doses of what Mexicans at the time were used to seeing and hearing (she claims to have read all the novels published up until then and even to have had a lover who was a revolutionary officer that served as her informant), she doubles those stereotypes with other, more powerful possibilities. Certainly, the very staging of the play reproduces the role of the soldadera in truth and in fantasy: in the background, guarding the ammunition, relaying messages, in a treacherous mountain pass wearing vibrant folkloric dresses with beautiful cacti as a backdrop. But by bringing them all together, Niggli provides a hologram of female participation where we simultaneously see the nurturing mother, the sweetheart who reminds the women of their humanity, the fierce warrior and strategist, the traitor who will do what is best for herself, and the passionate impulsive girl who sacrifices her life for the good of all. This play—one of the few literary pieces dedicated entirely to the female experience of the Revolution—allows the spectator and reader to appreciate both the complexity of the soldadera figure and the straightjackets that bind her tightly into a legible, cultural narrative. The fantastic possibilities that belie the dogged reproduction of Mexican womanhood become apparent in the cliché's that begin to fray, in the seams that tear, in the twisted translation from Mexican Spanish into American English.

Finally, in the character of Concha, the drama poses its most provocative question in the superb dialogue she has with the Rich One:

The Rich One: But you are women . . . not hardened soldiers.

Concha (*more to herself than to him*): Are we women? Sometimes I wonder. (180)

This line provides a rich point of departure for an unanswerable question: what constitutes womanhood in revolutionary México? Concha continues her reflections on the contradictory nature of female heroism, sacrifice, politics, and identity:

The Old One who cooks our food . . . she saw her son crucified by men of your kind . . . another one saw her son hunted down by dogs for the sport of it. That doesn't make women, my friend. That makes something worse than the devils in hell. [. . .] You called Adelita a symbol of the Revolution. Well, you're a symbol

to us. You're a symbol of all the hate and horror that the Rich
Ones have made for us. There are no men here to tell us what
to do. We stand alone. You are merely the victim. That is not
our fault. (181)

Unlike other texts that might emphasize the soldaderas apolitical stance, ignorance or lack of ideological fortitude, this conversation, as noted by Arrizón
and others, is the most suggestive: are we women? Indeed, these words become
the center of a polysemic code that interrogates the fundamental nature of
womanhood. While the answer seems to turn back around to loss and pain,
it is also deeply problematic. Why are womanhood and war constructed as
mutually exclusive? Time and again we see that women took up arms, moved
from soldier to soldier, and then returned to their duties as caretakers. Indeed,
the domestic space *par excellence* is transformed into a military train top: the
hearth, the home, and the kitchen are all ambulant. Others rejected motherhood and womanhood completely, such as the transgender Amelio Robles,
who fought in the Revolution with Zapata and was recognized as a male
veteran (and dandy womanizer) despite being born female (Gabriela Cano
49). Concha seems to ask of herself: did war destroy my "womanhood" by
making me fierce and callous? Or the other side of the question would be:
does the desire for redress and perseverance abound from my womanhood?
As witnessed by these lines, womanhood can no longer be defined in such
mutually exclusive terms. The boundaries slip and the categories are twisted
and turned. She states toward the end that when the men are absent, they
command themselves and "stand alone." The static signs—the Adelita, the
abnegating mother, the Cucaracha—all fold into each other even as they that
lay in contradistinction.

In a visual and historical parallax, these women appear to move slowly
in the background even as they keep pace with the rest; in a moving horizontal visual field amidst trains, horses, and troops, the shifting perspectives
create uneven close-ups and blurry background clips. The distortion of their
images is manipulated by the visual and historical optic privilege of he who
observes, while the oral record in popular music is equally distorted. Not
always as beautiful as the Adelita and Victoria, these women made the Revolution possible. They were an embarrassment to the Federal troops in the
presence of foreign observers (a sign of Mexico's backwardness with official
troops carrying women and children in tow), and they were rendered oppor-
tunistic traitors by the rebel bands, but they were nonetheless *there*. While
Benjamín Argumedo is provided the individuating singularity of a specific
time and place despite his ideological inconstancy, the adelitas are blown
up and blown off: yet, "her" song is still being sung and has been covered
innumerable times. From rockabilly bands, to *rancheras*, to punk rock and

even Brazilian samba, Adelita and Cucaracha have traveled the musical globe a hundredfold.

The invocation of the Adelita trope to pay homage to a female basketball team from provincial Chihuahua, to denounce the subordinated position of Chicana activists and intellectuals in the '60s and '70s, or as an inspiration for the indigenous Zapatista women who are advocating for the return of their ancestral lands and change in their own communities, belies the flat ways Adelita's legacy has been represented and interpreted. However, despite being lauded as sweet companions or despised as subservient vermin, soldaderas began to inseminate change into a patriarchal cultural grammar that did not know how to interpret the new language they were forging. From this history of disfigurings we, as perceptive spectators, readers, and listeners, can begin to discern the possibility of being *otherwise*. Tropological discourse, as White reminds us, allows us to "understand how speech mediates" that which is strange: women on the battlefield, women participating in war, not in singular numbers, but by the thousands, sometimes forced, sometimes of their own will, sometimes out of a sense of adventure. As long as the catachresis remains unwritten, as long as the legacy of these women remains in the crucible of historical neglect and aesthetic misrepresentation, there is a discourse in the making, creating new metaphors while resuscitating old ones. The following chapter will compare these mariological models with an examination of the more ambivalent soldadera figures found in the works of John Reed (*Insurgent Mexico*), Elena Poniatowska (*Hasta no verte Jesús, mío*) and Nellie Campobello (*Cartucho*), personages who provide a striking discursive counterpoint to the flat character models discussed here.

3

Beyond the "Custom of Her Sex and Country"

This photograph (see Fig. 3.1) is yet another of the many snapshots taken during the Revolution, and unlike other, more bleak images, is almost sweet.[1] We see a young couple resting, perhaps preparing to leave together or saying their last goodbyes. The girl hardly looks fifteen years old, while the federal soldier, what the revolutionaries called "changos" [apes], cannot be more than

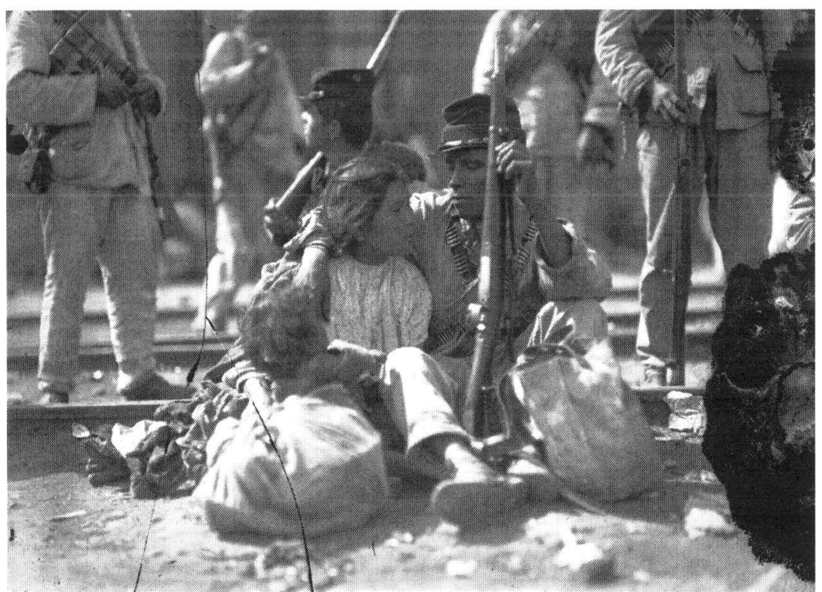

FIGURE 3.1. "Federal soldier and his family," México City, D.F., 1915.

twenty. Their young child, whose back is to the camera, sits among their scattered bags looking up at them. As with other popular revolutionary images
that have become stock icons in the revolutionary imaginary, we do not know
much about these people. It nonetheless provides a feeling, an idea or *saber*, a
flicker of knowledge that is fueled by affect that feeds into the Adelita myth:
young girls in love bravely following their soldiers into battle, or waiting
patiently—and loyally—behind. Regardless of the affective impact this image
may wield on the viewer, we can hardly know the *truth*. This young man could
have kidnapped the girl, she could have followed her lover/husband/rapist
into war or she could be a young soldadera who, like the figure of Elizabetta
we will see shortly in John Reed's historical vignette, might have only just
picked him up as a client when the camera shutter clicked. But as I have
been arguing, the Adelita and Cucaracha myths are far too restrictive, paying
little mind to the vast array of women and children who followed the men
but also fought alongside them. It glosses over rape and romanticizes what
in many cases was a transaction or a convenient arrangement. It beautifies
female heroism in a wash of dreamy colors and denigrates ferocity and promiscuity. In his book on the photography of the Revolution, John Mraz avers
that "[w]ithout identifications that 'anchor' photographs to their reality, their
aesthetic force generates myths, and they become decontextualized symbols
that disfigure our understanding of the past" (240). While the romanticizing
gesture prevails, this image along with many others like it provides a very
specific knowledge—*saber*—that cannot be simply defined, that *twists* the
predominant common sense and *turns* it into something unknown and undefinable by giving "the thing a name that belongs to something else." Moving
beyond the Adelita and Cucaracha tropes, I will examine a few examples of
revolutionary women who exceed the confines of common sense, who are
both concrete and an abstract ideal, who fulfill their womanly obligations
while blowing traditional womanhood apart. They occupy the *tlacticpac* (the
slippery earth) and provide slippery models of womanhood, of being female,
that move between divergent ontological modes. By examining the ambivalent
behavior of a soldadera named "Elizabetta" from a chapter in John Reed's
landmark chronicle *Insurgent Mexico* (1914), Elena Poniatowska's interpretation of Josefina Bórquez as "Jesusa" in her novel *Hasta no verte, Jesús mío*
(1969), Nellie Campobello's historical and literary figure in her novel *Cartucho*
(1931), and a portrait of an Afro-Mexican soldadera (1913), we will consider
the radical ruptures to the patriarchal tropology that has produced seemingly
immutable metaphors for women in the Revolution.

All the women in this chapter suffer the violence of the Revolution,
however, they are not lachrymose, hysterical, promiscuous, or motherly; they
have very different notions of how to accept violence, how to interpret death,

and how to accommodate it. Indeed, they are very sophisticated examples of revolutionary women whose literary and visual stories illustrate how to be—and how to *saber*—otherwise in traditional México.

Revolutionary Womanhood: Turning Away from Adelita

John Reed's *Insurgent Mexico* (1914) is considered a landmark journalistic text on the Mexican Revolution. A Harvard graduate, Reed was also a North American journalist, writer, and radical activist who reported on—and participated in—various labor strikes in the United States. He crossed into México for four months in the winter of 1913 and traveled with the troops of Francisco Villa. After his experience in the Mexican Revolution, he travelled to Russia and in 1919 published *The Ten Days That Shook The World*—his account of the October Revolution. *Insurgent Mexico* was inspired by his experience with the Villistas after joining the march south to Torreón, a battle city important to the insurgent cause. Nestled between the intimate descriptions of revolutionary life, a profile of the infamous Pancho Villa and sympathetic look at the peasantry, Reed's account offers a vivid and powerfully ambivalent depiction of the soldadera figure in a chapter titled "Elizabetta." This incident subsequently became the model for the soldadera episode that was supposed to be produced in Sergei Eisenstein's 1931 film, *¡Qué Viva México!* (which was actually never filmed because production halted), José Bolaños's *La soldadera* which premiered in 1966, and other literary pieces.

Reed's impression of Elizabetta is based on prevailing notions of what it means to be a woman, indigenous and a soldadera. In short, he sees Elizabetta straggle in behind the Captain of the troop he is accompanying and makes small talk with her as she prepares the Captain's food. She suddenly implores Reed to take her in for the night, and the sight of the two leaving together elicits an oddly joyful response by the townspeople who witness it. The next day she returns to the Captain and the normalcy of revolutionary living remains intact. That is what Reed reports "happened." However, the rich and multilayered nature of the following episode narrated by Reed proves to be both disturbing and illuminating for our understanding of these women and deserves a closer look:

> She was a very dark-skinned Indian girl, about twenty-five years old, with the squat figure of her drudging race, pleasant features, hair hanging forward over her shoulders in two long plaits, and big shining teeth when she smiled [. . .] Now she was trudging stolidly along in the dust behind Captain Felix Romero's horse

> [. . .] he had found her wandering aimlessly in the hacienda,
> apparently out of her mind; and that, needing a woman, he had
> ordered her to follow him. Which she did, unquestioningly, after
> the custom of her sex and country. (88)

Subsequently, Elizabetta asks Reed to take her in for the night, as she is
sickened by the thought of sleeping with her new man while her lover is
not yet cold in the ground. Reed cavalierly agrees despite inciting the ire of
Captain Romero, but awakens the next morning surprised to find her gone,
preparing the tortillas for the Captain—her new "Juan." Reed confronts her:
" 'Are you going?' I asked curiously. Elizabetta looked at me with wide-open
eyes. 'Of course I am going. Seguro! Is he not my man?' She looked after
him admiringly. She was no longer revolted [. . .] Elizabetta had forgotten
her lover" (91). The intricate layers in the warp and weft of revolutionary
living are brought into sharp relief in this anecdote. First, we must ask: did
Elizabetta actually say "lover," which in Spanish would be "amante" or did
she say "hombre," "juan," or "esposo"? Weaving in a discourse of love changes
the nature of the episode and certainly colors the way Reed, and the reader,
will consequently interpret her actions.

Elizabetta had forgotten her lover. Is Elizabetta the classic *ingrata*
[ungrateful woman]? Merely childlike? The submissive servant or just adven-
turous? How do you explain this particular episode, so poignant, yet so hackneyed in the rolodex of images that portray women in the Revolution? Recall
the language Reed employs: drudging, wandering aimlessly, out of her mind,
wide-open eyes, revolted. This image produces an almost childlike subject and
recalls the role played by Dolores del Río as the forlorn widow dragged into
war alongside María Félix in *La Cucaracha*. Moreover, this is exactly the image
we get of the soldadera in José Bolaños's film, *La soldadera*, starring Silvia
Pinal, which the director had designed as a realistic counterpoint to Félix's
Cucaracha and had partially based on Reed's account. Bolaños's rendition,
however realistic it purported to be, portrays a whiny blond who gets kicked
over the head and dragged along into the whirlwind of the Revolution. While
his neo-realist aesthetic is dreary and intentionally portrays the Revolution
in almost real-time, with slow, lingering shots that create the feeling of an
observational camera following the belabored, staggering movements of the
soldadera, Reed's vignette is much more provocative than the film made by
Bolaños would lead us to think. Indeed, Reed is unclear if she was just a peon
working on the hacienda displaced by the battle, or if she was a "vieja,"[2] the
term he uses to refer to the camp followers (111). Reed's account produces
several striking questions: was Elizabetta childlike in her decision to follow?
Would a child have disobeyed a Captain of the revolutionary army and spent
the night with another man? Or would only a whore have done that? Was

her change of heart a product of her indecision, or simply her desire to continue participating in the Revolution? How do we explain her loyalty to her dead "lover," and then subsequent decision to continue on with another man? Here we have the trope of la Adelita and la Cucaracha simultaneously present in the same woman, offered to us in the eyewitness account of a North American embedded journalist.

Elizabetta's body, however, is not sexualized; at least it does not comply with Reed's notion of a desirable, sexual body. Although she has "pleasant" features, her figure is described as the squat body of a "drudging" race. Furthermore, he makes an even more problematic remark regarding her expression: "Her teeth flashed as she smiled, and yet, there was a puzzling vacancy about her expression. Indians have mask-like faces. Under it I could see that she was desperately tired and even a little hysterical. But she spoke tranquilly enough" (111). At the same time she constitutes stalwart Mexican womanhood, her Indian "mask" is not exalted, but rather, seems to constitute the source of her subjugated and almost abject stoicism. In another part he describes her position in the social order as if it were below even that of a horse: "Captain Felix let his horse drink. Elizabetta halted, too, knelt and plunged her face into the water. 'Come on,' ordered the Captain. '*Andale!*' She rose without a word and waded through the stream" (111). In this passage she resembles the sub-trope of the miserable camp followers described in the last chapter, who are repeatedly likened with animals. Reed's very abstract appreciation of her indigeneity does not include information regarding what kind of Indian she might be, if she speaks another language besides Spanish, or if she herself even identifies as an indigenous person, or if in fact, she would refer to herself as something else: perhaps a mestiza, ladina, or *mexicana*? She is simply rendered a prototypical example of a childlike woman who belongs to a drudging race of people who are stoic, vacant, and unknowable. Despite this racialized description she is still reduced to a sexual animal; one who loses her lover, takes on another, begs for a foreign man's bed for comfort, and then willingly goes back to the man who callously tore her from her dead lover's arms. What kind of woman would do such a thing? Clearly not a *mujer decente*, the self-abnegating wives described by many novelists—clearly not an Adelita. How can history or art account for this kind of power, perhaps even sexual agency?

Whereas, in one interpretative frame, Elizabetta could embody the classic *ingrata* or mindless, subservient Indian, in another we could interpret the exchange as Elizabetta standing up to Captain Romero, humiliating him by leaving him for a foreigner. Rather than assume she had forgotten her lover, we could imagine she honors her dead "Juan" by mourning him for one night, recognizing that in the tumult of a vertiginous war, time acquires different dimensions. In one night, she recuperates her composure and her strength.

Perhaps her Juan would have liked for her to wait a little longer, like the supplicant in the Adelita corrido entreats, but war has its own imperatives. She had not "forgotten" her lover as Reed accusatorily claims because in her own way, she was still honoring his sacrifice in death by revering his cause and moving on with the survivors.

Michel De Certeau describes the infinitesimal changes indigenous peoples effected in the dominant cultural economy after the Conquest. This could be a useful parallel for understanding the *scenario* created by women like Elizabetta:

> Submissive, and even consenting to their subjection, the Indians nevertheless often *made of* the rituals, representations, and laws imposed on them something quite different from what their conquerors had in mind; they subverted them not by rejection or altering them, but by using them with respect to ends and refer- ences foreign to the system they had no choice but to accept. They were *other* within the very colonization that outwardly assimilated them; their use of the dominant social order deflects its power, which they lacked the means to challenge; they escaped it without leaving it. (*The Practice of Everyday Life* xiii)

Elizabetta humbly serves her "man," recognizing her otherness, both as a woman and as an indigenous person within the cultural economy created by colonialism, mestizo society, patriarchy, and the improvisational *modus vivendi* generated by the Revolution. On the other hand, she also perceives the possibilities where she might, if not rebel, fleetingly transgress traditional norms. She does not abandon her dead mate or her new man. Whereas in another place or time she might not have left her new "husband" for the night to run off in the arms of a white foreigner, she allows herself to do just that, and then return to her life as normal. This episode is even more provocative when we consider that, on the twenty-ninth of December 1914 (a few months after), revolutionary General Venustiano Carranza issued a decree that legalized divorce, alimony, and the right of women to own and manage property believing this would reduce the large number of free unions (like those of the soldaderas) and illegitimate children as well as emancipate woman " 'from the slavery in which she finds herself' " (Soto 58). Although Carranza's doctrine was hailed as progressive, the pressure for it largely came from male colleagues, and many of the provisions blatantly discriminated against women. For instance, a wife's *one-night absence* would constitute legal abandonment, while a husband could be absent thirty nights.

This unorthodox change in gender conventions was impressive and did not go unnoticed by the inhabitants of the village, with news of Elizabetta's departure with Reed spreading like a sonic boom. Within seconds of Captain Romero vociferating against Elizabetta and Reed, the home where Reed was being hosted began to bustle in preparation for their arrival as if they were "newlyweds": the floor was swept, candles were lit, and the house festooned with old Christmas decorations. As Elizabetta left the Captain's food uncooked and paraded through the town accompanied by the white foreigner whom the soldiers referred to as "Meester," many villagers and soldiers gazed curiously on the scene: "We passed the ledge where the soldiers and the wounded sat, grinning and making rough, genial remarks as at a marriage. It was not coarse or suggestive, their banter; it was frank and happy. They were honestly glad for us" (113). Someone contracted a group of musicians, who played outside their door. This then turned into an occasion for a dance: as the wounded, wretched soldiers straggled into town the "romantic" event gave way to a party. Bizarre, almost carnivalesque, the next day everything returned to normal. Reed, in turn, describes the intimate encounter with Elizabetta alone in the bedroom with the following words: "Without the least embarrassment, Elizabetta lay down beside me on the bed. Her hand reached for mine. She snuggled against my body for the comforting human warmth of it, murmured, 'Until morning,' and went to sleep. And calmly, sweetly, sleep came to me" (114). While he does not describe sexual intercourse, claiming that she only held his hand and snuggled against him, he leaves the impression that she sought out the *gringo* for comfort but returned to the Mexican alpha male for security.

This small change, this rupture to traditional gender norms, impresses the young American journalist enough for him to dedicate a whole chapter to her, and consequently accuse her of flightiness. I would not interpret this act as capriciousness or promiscuity. Elizabetta, "after the custom of her sex and country," follows her *juan(es)*, provides him (them) with food, but is (and is not) just a "bundle of misery" as Poniatowska describes them. In the same way De Certeau considers the subversive use of Catholic ritual by the Indians in the colonial regime, Elizabetta as a soldadera lacks the means to completely challenge the social order, but nonetheless escapes it without leaving it. Consequently, by inseminating an ambiguity into the cultural, social, and political order she produces an alternative "language" through her actions. She makes something "quite different" than what a traditional patriarchy might allow: she rebels against the Adelita, but is still not quite the Cucaracha. In the "custom of her sex and country" Elizabetta's behavior, like Adelita and la Cucaracha, becomes metonymically congealed into a national standard of conduct for its female compatriots. As a product of a "drudging race," she represents inwardly and outwardly, in this case to the North American observer, the expectations of Mexican—but also indigenous—womanhood. However, the interpretative ambivalence of her character as described by Reed is striking, permitting us to rethink the real position of women throughout the Revolution and in its aftermath. Reed's static interpretation but slippery words reveal powerful possibilities of being, and knowing, otherwise. We shall see this disruptive ambivalence and radical potential even more profoundly developed in the character of Jesusa Palancares, narrated by Elena Poniatowska. To be sure, both the episode narrated by Reed and the novel by Poniawtowska were based on the writers' interactions with real soldaderas. This makes it possible for us to appreciate how the conjunction of art, real-life, and history, in all of its forms and manifestations, can at once figure and disfigure its characters, operating as both a discursive disruption but also instrument of hegemony.

Jesusa: "Tan contenta volando
en las tripas de los zopilotes"[3]

Jesusa Palancares, the protagonist in Elena Poniatowska's proto testimonio-novel, *Hasta no verte Jesús, mío* (1969), proffers one of the most complete and profoundly compelling accounts of the soldadera, where unlike the other versions I have examined, the sexual component of the persona is remarkably absent. This novel, which is based on weekly interviews between Poniatowksa and Josefina Bórquez, truly unravels many of the polarizing stereotypes of women in the Revolution, and likewise, unwittingly highlights a latent indigenous cosmology that points to the fissures in the national narrative of a *mestizaje* that epistemologically elides indigenous culture. This protagonist is another compelling example of why women may have joined the Revolution, and the simultaneous revolutionary and tragic consequences of their participation. Her memories of the Revolution are nostalgic; it represented a moment of excitement, of hardship, but most important, of freedom. Jesusa narrates:

> Platicaban, y yo sentía que los ojos se me habían llenado de polvo, de todo el polvo del Defe, y que ya era hora de ganar pa'l campo. Como los balazos son mi alegría, pues hablábamos de balazos. La balacera es todo mi amor porque se oye muy bonita. Los primeros balazos sí se oyen, pero el fuego cerrado ya no se oye. Nomás se ve la humadera, los humitos que salen de los distintos lugares. Sólo de acordarme me daban ganas de irme a la revolufía. Por eso yo les dije que cuando salieran de México me avisaran, para irme con ellos a la primera balacera. Tenía ganas de andar fuera de México.

> [They would chat, and I'd feel like my eyes had filled up with dust, all the dust of México City, and that it was time to head out to

the countryside. As gunfire makes me so happy, well, we would talk about the shootouts. I love the gunfire because it sounds so pretty. You can hear the first gunshots, but later you can't hear anything in closed fire. You only see the smoke, the little billows of smoke that come from all different places. Just remembering it made me feel like going back to the Revolution. That's why I told them that when they left México City to let me know, so that I could go with them to catch the first shootout. I felt like getting out of México City]. (255)

As revealed by this passage, it is Jesusa who feels the desire, urge, and even need to escape the tedium of "el Defe," to wipe the dust from her eyes and rejoin the "revolufía." In her account, she never speaks about taking on men, in fact, the only man she had was her first husband, and never mentions being seriously involved with any particular man after that. Her description of the *balacera* is poetic and brimming with excitement; she describes the *balazos* like fireworks, as if the whole scene were a symphony of bright lights, smoke, and sound. The lyrical beauty of the *balacera* inspired her to return, to "andar fuera de México." This is not the wide-eyed, hysterical image of the *ingrata* who is lost in the war. Nor is this the foul-mouthed Cucaracha, Azuela's "la Pintada," or the *pueblo*'s sweet beguiling Adelita. Jesusa is a woman filled with a sense of wanderlust, a desire for adventure and above all, independence. Although her language is coarse and colloquial, she is not vulgar. She is strong but somewhat bitter about the human condition. Although she finds more beauty in the vultures than in her fellow compatriots, she does not seem to give up. Unlike Azuela, who likens the human condition to an animalized state, she finds transcendence in the animal kingdom, admiring their beauty and independence. In the following passage she describes the beauty of the *zopilotes*[4] even as they appear to be flying closer and closer, adumbrating her imminent death: "Me caen en gracia desde chiquilla [. . .] Ya parece que los estoy viendo volar en ruedas cada vez más bajito, cada vez más bajito [. . .] Los jóvenes brillan bonito, como chapopote caliente" [I've liked them since I was a little kid [. . .] I can just see them flying in circles lower and lower over me [. . .] The young ones shine beautifully, like hot tar] (394). She imagines the young vultures flying in circles above her head, announcing her death and threatening to devour her, as beautiful beings. She even nurtures what society has abandoned: orphans, a coyote, a street dog, and a pig.

   She is initiated into the Revolution by tagging along with her negligent father, and then follows her abusive husband who rises in the ranks only to fall on the battleground, dying uncovered underneath a tree. When he expires, the troop looks to her to lead them. She rejects this leadership position, preferring to follow her own path only to make her way back as a cook. Long after she has left it, the Revolution and its intrinsic movement, both ideological and physical, marked her life so profoundly that it continued to iterate itself in her multiple crossings, travels, and ultimately, self-instantiated philosophy on life. Similar to the ancient Nahua notion of *olin*, both as a cosmological concept and as a deity, travel and movement function almost as a *modus vivendi* for Jesusa; they are what constitute her purpose, what relieve her from her horribly oppressive situations, but what simultaneously reveal themselves as opportunities for transcendence. Let us recall how Diana Taylor explains this concept:

> *Olin*, meaning movement in Náhuatl [. . .] Olin is the motor behind everything that happens in life, the repeated movement of the sun, stars, earth and elements. And Olin also manifests herself/himself as a deity who intervenes in social matters. The term simultaneously captures the broad, all-encompassing nature of performance as reiterative process and carrying through as well as its potential for historical specificity, transition and individual cultural agency. (14–15)

Rather than constituting her cross and burden, like the peasant scavenger trope or the abnegating wife/mother model, movement and change is what fulfills and liberates her. Movement for Jesusa is what marks her life, yet it paradoxically constitutes a brand of domesticity. Through the historically specific moment of the Revolution, she appropriates its chaos as a form of personal agency, as a set of possibilities that defines her quest for individuation.

When she reflects on her imminent death toward the end of the novel, she describes how she would like to be consumed by a *zopilote* and fly in the belly of this magnificent yet repugnant beast, reaching immortality by traveling in its entrails:

> Tengo muchas ganas de irme a morir por allá donde anduve de errante. ¡Qué Dios se acuerde de mí porque yo quisiera quedarme debajo de un árbol por allá lejos! Luego me rodearan los zopilotes y ya; que viniera a preguntar por mí y yo allá tan contenta volando en las tripas de los zopilotes.

> [I would love to return to the places where I wandered in order to die. I hope God will remember me because I really want to wind up under a tree somewhere far! Then the vultures would surround me and that's it; they'd come looking for me and I would be so happy out there flying around in the guts of the vultures]. (395)

The violence of this morbidly graphic, yet sublime image is somehow beautiful and poetic. She wants to continue her life after death in the same way she lived her mortal life, traveling errantly in the belly of a beast, ultimately returning by being scattered across the land in its feces. Jill Furst, in *Natural History of the Soul in Ancient Mexico*, informs us that ancient Mesoamericans believed "the dead became hummingbirds, other birds with precious feathers, or a wide variety of butterflies" (25). Jesusa likewise wants to entrust the destiny of her soul to a winged scavenger with brilliant feathers the color of hot tar. Although *zopilotes* are not hummingbirds or butterflies, she considers them beautiful and believes that she will find peace flying about the world in their guts. Neglected by her father, abused by her mother-in-law, employers, and benefactors, beaten by her husband, and abandoned by her adopted son, she entrusts the afterlife of her soul to a parasitical beast of prey. The following passage further illuminates Jesusa's notion of cosmological balance:

> Ésos son los que limpian los pueblos de las epidemias; viene la mortandad de la indiada, de la caballada, de la juanada, del animalero de cristianos y de bestias y los zopilotes se lo embuchan todo . . . Ojalá los zopilotes pudieran tragarse la maldad cuando nos dejan limpios como calacas, pero ésa siempre se queda en la tierra.

> [They are the ones that clean the towns of the epidemics; death comes to the Indians, the horses, the peasants, the Christian animals and beasts and the vultures devour it all . . . I wish the vultures could eat all the evil as well when they leave us as clean as bones, but that always stays in the earth]. (394)

The *zopilotes* do not discriminate; they eat animals and people alike leaving only the bones and, in so doing, cleanse the earth as well. However, for all their work to purge the land of its excess and sickness, not even the *zopilotes* can rid the earth of human evil, which Jesusa contends remains in the earth.[5]

This resonates with the Mesoamerican—specifically Nahua—notion of death and understanding of the "soul," where one does not so much die as get absorbed by other elements of the natural world. Moreover, the soul is manifest in the body, not separated from it:

> A man or woman does not die so much as *dissolve into constituent parts whose nature is to live, with or without an intact body* [. . .] The soul, as part of the human organism, travels to other realms after death, but other *spirit fragments remain on earth as birds or as moving air or shadows.* (Emphasis added, Furst 182)

Much like the Mesoamerican notion of evil lodging itself in the earth, manifesting in certain places, in bad air, or as spirits, she believes the earth to be the recipient of the bad deeds of humankind. Although Jesusa practiced her own form of spirituality under the guidance of "la Obra Espiritual," claiming to have been already in her third incarnation, her notions of immortality resonate strongly with many indigenous religious practices and ideas. She accepts her mortality, even beckoning it rather than belaboring it, but she does not want her neighbors or anyone to watch her agonize, "porque la mayoría de la gente viene a reírse del que está agonizando. Así es la vida. Se muere uno para que otros se rían" [because most of the people come to make fun of the one who is dying. That's life. One dies so that others can laugh] (395). The cruelty of war might lead to a callous appreciation of life, where people laugh at the pain of the dying, such as we saw depicted in a scene from Ocampo's play studied in the previous chapter, where the soldaderas and soldiers find the death throes of a dying woman tedious, or in Niggli's drama, where one soldadera jests that it might be a good thing if the elder soldadera were to die because she was hardly useful in her decrepit condition. Jesusa, in turn, wishes to die outdoors not out of a feeling of wartime heroism, but because she knows there is no place for her in the holy ground. Like both her father and husband, she wants to return organically and symbiotically to the earth: "servirle de pasto a los animales del campo, a los coyotes, como Pedro el que fue mi marido" [serve as pasture to the farm animals, to the coyotes, like Pedro, he who was my husband] (396). Similar to the ancient Nahuas, who believed that "[s]ouls are not singular, indivisible, and of some other substance, but form a continuum from internal to external phenomena" she also believes a bit of her "soul" will permutate and remain on earth in the viscera of these beasts and in their excrement that fertilizes the land (Furst 182). Her notion of personal transcendence, which is moving from one spiritual plane to another, is mediated by the earth's most repugnant animals. There is no Manichean polarization between good and evil, the spiritual and material realm: they mutually constitute each other as immanent forces.

Jesusa clearly reflects the multiple contradictions inherent in dwelling and traveling as explained by James Clifford. Although travel was difficult and arduous, she poeticizes it by appropriating it. In other words, through her recollections of the beauty of the revolutionary *balacera* she creates "music," the rudeness of her "comportment" is conditioned by the rudeness of her surroundings, yet her tenderness within that chaos is her mitigation of that violence. "Knowledge" comes from experience and empirical data but also from what cannot be seen or proven, from the spiritual world and from the dead. She hopes to die in the open air so that vultures may devour her, and thus, travel in perpetuity in their entrails. She appropriates travel by becoming it, albeit in the viscera of a vulture. Through its travels, a detestable beast paradoxically turns into the angel of her salvation and that of humanity.

Jesusa is radically different from other prevailing visions of the soldadera: she created her own epistemological worldview out of poverty, abuse and revolutionary chaos, but also through her travels to the past, her communications with the dead, and her will to live. Her experiences reflect the traces of Mesoamerican cosmology that continue to be a part of Mexican culture. She is singularly heroic in her fight with life yet she never disavows the violence, she simply sees it for what it is: part of a complex macrocosm where she recognizes all things are predestined, where equilibrium will somehow restore itself. Yet her power and strife metonymically seem to reflect that of indigenous communities across the Americas. She creates her own self-referential cosmological system out of what she has culturally inherited from her indigenous and mestizo forbearers, but also from what she learns from her own experiences, where she etiologically explains the ill-fated destiny of what she calls her third life: "Mi deuda debe ser muy pesada ya que Dios me quitó a mis padres desde chica y dejó que viniera a abonar mis culpas sola como lazarina" [My debt must be quite large because God took my parents away when I was a young girl and left me by myself to repay my guilt alone like a leper] (8). Resonating with the Nahua notion of *olin*, her myriad travels and life movements constitute what is at once the source of her pain and her deliverance. She instantiates *olin* as a movement that weaves her in and out of family, political, and spiritual dramas; it places her as a historical agent within the specificity of the Mexican Revolution, but also in the timeless and universal struggle of humankind to understand its place in the cosmos. Her vision of death, her ambivalence toward dying, is also present in the writings of Nellie Campobello, who, unlike Jesusa, enjoyed a privileged life as a writer, dancer, and choreographer, and was the furthest thing from a soldadera. Nonetheless, Campobello's rendering of mortality and the brutality of war through the narration of its effects on the human body and collective memory bears a profound reminiscence to Jesusa's unflinching attitude toward the brutality of life, and what she considers to be the almost liberating possibilities available in death.

La niña Nellie y sus muertos[6]

Nellie Campobello, in her sublime novel *Cartucho, relatos de la lucha en el norte de México* (1931), creates a discursive ambivalence and distance by narrating her personal account of the Revolution from the point of view of herself as a young girl. These fifty-six short stories, some not even a page, build into one longer narrative where the author is simultaneously a character and narrator. In this way, both she and Leonor Villegas de Magnón (who narrates in the third person, calling herself "the Rebel") as authors created first-person narratives based on their lives that are paradoxically constituted by this critical distance. Rather than employing the imperative voice of a first-person narrator, this approach in fact mimics the fluid and confusing nature of the Revolution. This discursive and narrative technique creates a playfully oneiric prose that according to Campobello, allowed her to tell the most sincere, necessary truths despite the harm it might cause her: "Usar de su aparente inconsciencia para exponer lo que supe era la necesidad de un decir sincero y directo" [To use the apparent lack of consciousness to expose what I knew to be the necessity of a language that was sincere and direct] ("Prologo," *Mis Libros* 17). Although these stories are based on the experience of Campobello's family in Parral, Chihuahua, during the Revolution, it is difficult to disentangle myth from history; we do not even know if she was really a child or actually a teenager during this period as her exact date of birth is unknown due to the existence of contradicting birth documents. Tabea Linhard contends that "[c]ontrary to what the author herself would claim Campobello was born in 1901 (not 1909, 1910, or 1911), in Villa Ocampo in the northern state of Durango" (166). Campobello adamantly insists that the stories in *Cartucho* are based on historical facts witnessed by her: "Las narraciones de *Cartucho*, debo aclararlo de una vez para siempre, son verdad histórica, son hechos trágicos vistos por mis ojos de niña en una ciudad, como otros ojos pudieron ver hechos análogos en Berlín, o Londres, durante la Guerra Mundial; caso igual para mi pequeño corazón, que lloraba sin lágrimas" [The narrations in Cartucho, I should clarify once and for all, are historical truth, they are tragic events seen by my girlish eyes in a city, just like other eyes could have seen analogous events in Berlin or London during the world war; it was the same for my little heart, crying without tears] (22). Furthermore, she categorically states that she felt compelled to tell the truth in the face of the lies being told by the official government: "Por eso yo tenía que escribir, decir verdades en el mundo de mentiras que vivía" [That is why I had to write, tell the truth in the world of lies where I lived] (18). She and her mother were staunch supporters of Francisco Villa, whose figure at that time had still not been accommodated into the realm of revolutionary heroes as it is today. Much to the contrary, he was still considered a boorish bandit.

Jorge Aguilar Mora, in his prologue to *Cartucho*, reflects on these muddled facts and poetically concludes that the plurality of anecdotes, people, and events in these stories creates a dizzying *movement* of memory that no historical text can reproduce: the wavering rhythm of discourse makes it impossible to know what really happened, to pronounce a historical truth (38). This lack of hard empirical fact hardly seems to matter; her short narratives recount gruesome moments in war that do not cast judgment on the nature of violence. By utilizing the optic of childhood, with its concomitant innocence, she historicizes memories and popular lore and poeticizes history, weaving the two discursive realms so perfectly that it seems as if she never even hoped for them to serve as historical documents despite her declaration to the contrary. This tension between the perspective of childhood and her claim to historical authenticity creates a novel that excarnates her truth(s) in the bizarre and rattling language of simplicity, unlike what was considered the romantic language typical in female narratives:

> Los datos históricos que tenía que escribir debían ser narrados con toda atención y cuidado, sin caer en la bisutería tipo miscelánea, ni en la truculencia, ni en el sentimental plañir del que implora piedad. Tipos mexicanos de esta categoría no se pueden plantar en el melodrama, ni exponer en actitudes vulgares de folletín.

> [The historical facts that I needed to write had to be narrated with detail and care, without falling into a kind of miscellaneous fantasy, neither truculence nor in the sentimental lamentation that implores piety. Mexican men of that category cannot be inserted into a melodrama, nor exposed in the vulgar tone of a serialized novel]. (22)

For this reason, Poniatowska takes the trope of the soldadera and applies it to Campobello as an author, claiming that her historical and literary work was appropriated by the great writer of the Revolution, Martín Luis Guzmán (she gave him her notes and archive), but her own publication *Apuntes sobre la vida militar de Francisco Villa* (1940) was never appreciated as historically significant. Nellie, like the soldadera, was very much aware of her place in the intellectual social order. Like the soldadera, she was able to recount the atomistic parts of what to many was a massive, faceless peasant uprising, paradoxically narrating the stories of these individuals through their anonymity: "Los personajes de Campobello se distinguen por la asunción de su destino trágico, por el sentido colectivo de su personalidad, por su vocación irresistible hacia el anonimato" [Campobello's characters are distinctive for their acceptance of the tragic destiny, for the collective sense of their personality, for their irresistible movement towards anonymity] (Aguilar Mora 25). As signaled by Poniatowska, Campobello—like the soldadera—received little recognition for her work; although she was not completely ignored, her fellow intellectuals never recognized her as an equal. Until recently, she, like many of her characters, languished in a tragic anonymity. Only in the last couple decades did the criticism explode; Linhard claims much of it in response to her dreadful abduction and demise. Still, Linhard makes an important point when she reminds us that Nellie Campobello would probably not have approved of Poniatowska's metaphor that I have now appropriated in my reading: "The term soldadera bears certain connotations that associate Campobello with a social class to which she did not belong [. . .] Nevertheless, the similarity between Campobello's tragic disappearances in literary history and the ways in which women's participation was written out of the history of the revolution is more than a peculiarity" (164). The soldadera trope is a powerful way to consider the literary and intellectual place of Campobello: trailing behind the literary behemoths, guarding the ammunition but not rewarded for the battle.

"Nacha Ceniceros" is one of the many remarkable stories that comprise this novel, recounting a provocative vignette of a high-ranking female officer in Pancho Villa's renowned División del Norte. Ceniceros is a Colonel who, apparently distressed by news of her lover's infidelity, returns to her tent to clean her gun when it accidentally goes off and hits her lover, who is in a nearby tent talking to a woman, dead in the head. Villa orders Nacha's execution and she dies engulfed in sorrow, her arms covering her face while her two braids trail on either side of her body. Curiously, Campobello changes the ending of this story in the second edition of 1960 by adding a second part that, aside from doubling its length, divulges what she considers to be the real truth about the *Coronela*, and which she claims is the *only* historically erroneous part of her novel. In this addendum, Ceniceros did not die at the hands of Villa, but surely demoralized by the corruption of those who kept the triumphs of the Revolution to themselves, returned home to continue horse ranching: "Ahora digo, y lo digo con la voz del que ha podido destejer una mentira: ¡Viva Nacha Ceniceros, Coronela de la Revolución!" (67) [Now I say—and I say it with the voice of someone who has known how to unravel lies, *Viva Long Nacha Ceniceros, Coronela de la revolución*!] (22).[7] Casting herself as an author-character in her novel, Campobello shrouds this female protagonist in myth only to disavow it. She inserts another story *in medias res* purportedly to set the record straight.

As is true with the soldadera trope, this story is multivalent, ambiguous, and reflective of the myth that surrounds women in a world dominated by men. Did *la Coronela* "accidentally" kill her errant lover? Did Villa order her execution, or did she really go back home disheartened? Campobello, single-handedly cognizant of the fate of the Revolution's female warriors, refutes what she considers to be the lies that sully Nacha's name in addition to the propensity of patriarchal society to romanticize/eroticize strong female characters. Nonetheless, why Campobello did not include the second part in the first edition is unclear (she claims to have learned the "truth" about Ceniceros afterward), but by correcting the first edition in a self-referential manner, she intrigues the reader, forcing her to question all forms of discourse: official history, journalism, lore, and gossip. By rendering discourse duplicitous, she disavows her very medium only to make a strong final speech act, asserting her authorial voice and dispensing with the child's narrative voice. Linhard makes a strong argument that seeks to understand this as an effort to domesticate the role of women in the dialectic between agency and accommodation that is part and parcel of women's writing. She claims that this critical change, in addition to turning the old soldadera from whom Ceniceros seeks counsel in the first version into an old lady in the second, undermines the transgressive nature of Ceniceros and "literally rebuilds the boundaries between the domestic and the public domains" (171). However, Max Parra reminds us that the very act of re-membering is subversive, and that through the mother figure Nelly as a child and as a writer is linked—re-membered—to a bellicose tradition that is part of a familial, regional and geographical identity ("Memoria y Guerra en *Cartucho*" 177). Campobello then, in my reading, contributes to a chorographic memory where the mother and the child participate through the synecdochal re-*membering* of people to their body parts, of a regional rebellion to human dignity, of a specific place to a larger revolutionary consciousness.

Even when the mother might fill the role of the abnegating woman, we do not witness delicate, faint women typical of middle-class norms of decency. Campobello's mother has strong political affiliations and an ideological armature linked to the Villista cause. In the story "The General Rueda" she narrates how his soldiers threaten the children and insult her in an effort to find hidden supplies for Villa. In the face of an assault (Linhard claims rape) by the General Rueda in her home, she remains stoic—even icy—only to perish silently afterwards in the night "without being sick." Women, children, girls are a part of the daily life of war; they are witnesses to its atrocities and tragedies as well as its victims. Nellie the child dreams of becoming a man in order to fire a hundred shots into the body of the General that insulted (and perhaps assaulted) her mother; an attack that caused both her and her mother's eyes to "harden." Vengeance is present; but it is not depraved. She is innocent but not naïve. Linhard contends that by revising Nacha Ceniceros's story and alluding to, but never making the mother's rape explicit, the language of violence on female bodies, and by female protagonists, is deferred. However, the cumulative graphic and even grotesque violence reported by Campbello powerfully revises the traditional role of woman as agent, participant in, and in her case, eyewitness to the Revolution.

As in Azuela's novel, her characters live violent lives. Nellie the child witnesses this aggression, but although Azuela's novel only hints at redeeming its characters, Campobello's personages reveal a much more immediate and natural relationship to violence, death, and the ideology of the cause that brings them into such intimacy with each other. Her own character has a poetic, indeed intimate, relationship to death; she sees it as a form of redemption and transcendence, but more important, a quotidian reality. In "Desde una ventana" ["From the window"] she befriends a soldier's corpse that had been struck in battle outside her bedroom window and remains there for three days, appropriating it as her own special toy and lamenting when the cadaver is finally removed.

> Como estuvo tres noches tirado, ya me había acostumbrado a ver el garabato de su cuerpo, caído hacia su izquierda con las manos en la cara, durmiendo allí, junto de mí. Me pareció mío aquel muerto. Había momentos que temerosa de que se lo hubieran llevado, me levantaba corriendo y me trepaba en la ventana, era mi obsesión en las noches, me gustaba verlo porque me parecía que tenía mucho miedo [. . .] Me dormí aquel día soñando en que fusilarían otro y deseando que fuera junto a mi casa. (63–64)

> [Since he lay there for three nights, I became accustomed to seeing the scrawl of his body, fallen toward the left with his hands on his face, sleeping there, next to me. The dead man seemed mine. There were moments when, fearful he would be taken away, I would get up and run to the window. He was my obsession at night. I liked to look at him because I thought he was very afraid . . . That night I went to sleep dreaming they would shoot someone else and hoping it would be next to my house]. (37)

Rather than demonstrate disgust before the corpse that has been lying there for three nights, she befriends it, turns it into her doll. The cadaver acquires an identity in its abject anonymity. She laments when it is taken away, and then dreams that they kill another man so he can lay outside her window. Story after story in *Cartucho* describe in gruesome details the tortured body parts—flayed, shot, charred, hung, rotted—of the people she knew as a child. The anonymous cadavers live despite the reality of their rotting bodies. This infantile familiarity with death, although a product of war, also signals something more. It signals another worldview that does not fear death, but rather, appreciates its beauty. This discursive and narrative technique results in an oneiric prose which, in the case of Campobello, pays a gentle obeisance to those unsung heroes by beautifully narrating the ostensibly mundane details of their personalities, bringing many of them to life in the moment of their climactic apotheoses.

The complexity of her narrative voice lies in that it is neither patriarchal nor maternal, but rather, fragmented and anecdotal, and yet based on historical fact. It is one of the most exquisite novels of the Revolution because it is unsparing, brutish, and beautiful all at once. Like the bullets that blow out her characters hearts, or tear off their ears, it strikes at the Revolution's multiple truths and its concomitant paradoxes. Like the soldaderas, we appreciate the way in which her literary field moves in concentric circles from the intimate and domestic, as described by Max Parra, outward toward the public domain

(168). Suturing these men's body parts into a larger story, her writing simulates the traditional task of weaving; her words simultaneously rend in their brutalizing brevity and mend the parts into an indistinguishable whole. The sheer number of characters, vignettes, and deaths creates a narrative anonymity for her characters, as the reader sometimes gets overwhelmed by the myriad stories, forgetting that many in fact are related. Yet this anonymity dissolves into the singular individuating distinction of personages who each confront death on their own terms. They each acquire a subjectivity which makes them individually sublime, particular, irreducible, and irreproducible. Even her nameless cadaver becomes a character, acquiring subjectivity in his state of pitiable abjection. The following examples are just a few of the many bodies, enemy and friend, who are re-*membered*.

In the story "Los 30-30" [The 30-30] she describes how Gerardo Ruiz's ear was blown off, after which one of the soldiers threw what looked like a bruised piece of meat back to another soldier who then placed it next to his face, while in "El corazón del Coronel Bufanda" [General Bufanda's Heart], Campobello narrates how the Colonel's heart was blown out of his body, and in a graphic poetic twist, describes his left shirt pocket as having been shredded like a rose (82; 85). Afterward, a group of enraged men broke into the house where his lifeless body rest and dragged it out to the street to beat it to shreds, cracking his skull in pieces on the ground in return for his assault; yet, she notes that his mutilated skull still bore a smile of smug satisfaction. In another morose vignette, Nellie mourns the grime that appears to drown the once beautiful José Díaz, her feet saddened by the pestilent alleyway where his body lay face down. The handsome face of the man who was averse to the sun to keep from getting brown, ended up black and drowning in filth (91). While his aversion to the sun is clearly a product of the unquestioned racial hierarchy, Nellie too participates in his privilege, as her doll Pitaflorida denies having loved him after seeing him dark and grimy. Then, in "Por un beso" ["For a Kiss"], the narrator sadly exposes the endemic racism in Mexican culture that would condemn an innocent Yaqui soldier to death in a vacuous act of exemplary justice. She at once reveals the glory and depravity of a revolution that never finished, of the injustices committed against her family by also by them. This story re-members the nameless Yaqui Indian who died for a "kiss" he never stole: "de X regimiento sacaron a X soldado, el que nunca había visto a Luisa mi prima: ellos dijeron a la tropa: 'Este hombre muere por haber querido besar a una muchacha. El hombre era yaqui, no hablaba español, murió por un beso que el oficial galantemente le adjudicó'" (83–84) [they singled out soldier X from X regiment. He had never laid eyes on my cousin Luisa, but the troops were told, 'This man will die for having tried to kiss a young girl.' The man was a Yaqui Indian who spoke no Spanish. He died for a kiss the officer gallantly awarded him] (25). The "kiss" is a euphemism for the attempted kidnapping and rape of her cousin Luisa. She reports, with undaunted honesty, the injustice enacted by her aunt who would coldly allow the General to execute an innocent Indian in retribution for the attempted assault on her daughter, leaving the true culprit at large. She even describes her aunt coquettishly gazing upon the federal officer for the "respect" he paid her injury. Linhard makes an important point: "It also suggests that ultimately both the woman as well as the Yaqui soldier will be excluded from the kind of justice that will emerge out of this struggle" (185). The story ends with the townspeople blithely commenting that a "chango" was killed. She then explains that "changos," in the regional language of Chihuahua, is the epithet they use to refer to Yaquis. There is a searing critique embedded in her deployment of this epithet: the man was at once an "apish" Indian and an "apish" federal soldier, who was probably a conscript dragged into war. The fact that justice was not served is ultimately irrelevant; Yaquis are as dispensable as conscripted federal soldiers.

In comparison to Josefina Niggli's play, Campobello's childlike vision is nothing like la Adelita. She is young, but not innocent. While she almost morbidly scamps out of the house to peek at mutilated bodies, she claims she was not frightened, or even curious; yet, she nevertheless feels sorrow. In a touching passage from "Záfiro y Zequiel," she runs to find two dead brothers—Mayo Indians—whom she had befriended in childish pranks as they walked up and down her street, la calle Segundo del Rayo.

> Zequiel boca abajo y su hermano mirando al cielo. Tenía los ojos abiertos, muy azules, empañados, parecía como si hubieran llorado. No les pude preguntar nada, les conté los balazos, volteé la cabeza de Zequiel, le limpié la tierra del lado derecho de su cara, me conmoví un poquito y me dije dentro de mi corazón tres y muchas veces: "Pobrecitos, pobrecitos." (76)

> [Zequiel face down and his brother looking at the sky. Their eyes were wide open, very blue and clouded over, as if they had been crying. I couldn't ask them anything. I counted the bullet wounds, turned Zequiel's head around, cleaned the dirt from the right side of his face, which rather upset me, and in my heart said three or more times, "*Pobrecitos, pobrecitos*, poor things."] (19)

She closes their eyes and tenderly wipes the dirt off Zequiel's face. She then counts the bullet wounds, gathers the crystallized blood droplets as if they were little rubies restoring the bits of his blood to his body: "La sangre se le había helado, la junté y se la metí en la bolsa de su saco azul de borlón. Eran como cristalitos rojos que ya no se volvería hilitos calientes de sangre"

(76) [Their blood had frozen. I gathered it up and put it in the pocket of one of their blue-tasseled jackets. It was like red crystals that would never again turn into warm threads of blood] (19). Blood is a vital life force that lives through movement. Yet, in its crystalized dead form it becomes whole again. Similarly, the Huichols believe that their ancestors, even in life, live in deified stones. Indeed, the gory details are softened at the same time they are abrupt—almost too much. Synecdoche becomes the privileged tropological mode that connects these men, both figuratively and literally, to their bodies and to a larger chorographic memory. Nellie the child narrator is heroic before death, is valiant before the horror of hanging corpses, tortured bodies, charred carcasses. She is at once sad, tender, and virile, deploys a "macho" tearless silence, is frightened but distant.

Her character has a poetic relationship to death; she sees it as redemption but also a choice. In contrast to the late colonial attempts to sanitize death with decorative sugar skulls, mutilated corpses become beautiful, as illustrated in the story "El Centinela del Mesón Águila" ["The Sentinel of el Aguila Barracks"]: "Muy derecho, ya sin zapatos, la boca entreabierta, los ojos cerrados; tenía un gesto nuevo, era un muerto bonito [. . .] Tenía cinco cartuchos mohosos en sus manos y un gesto que regaló a nuestros ojos" (92–93) [Very straight, without shoes now, his mouth half open, his eyes closed. He was a pretty dead man in his new pose, his hands crossed [. . .] He had five rusty cartridges in his hands and a pose that was a treat to our eyes"] (31–32). His dead face "gifted" them a nice look as it lay inert. Indeed, there are *good* ways to die, and the majority of the fifty-six chapters end in death. This morbidity is not reflective of a disturbed child, a criticism the author once received, but of one who has an intimate relationship to violence, who finds beauty and honor in a courageous sacrifice. Aguilar Mora also underscores this notion of an honorable, dignified death by pointing to the soldiers' lack of agency within oppressive political and social regimes. The control the soldiers' exercised over their bodies by choosing to die (not senselessly, as critics would argue) for a cause, for a caudillo, was a way of prolonging their lives. This sacrifice was the only thing these men truly possessed, and they offered their bodies happily (25). Honor and courage were all these soldiers had for people to remember them by; oftentimes the *fusilamientos* [firing squad] were entertainment for the town, a kind of theatrical spectacle. The better the show they put on, the longer their name would be remembered in oral history, perhaps inspiring a *corridista* to sing their story. As Aguilar Mora affirms, this flirtation with death reflects a spiritual and even political agency that goes beyond a quest for manly recognition; it places them in something larger than themselves (25). Corridos from the Mexican Revolution further exemplify this: Benjamín Argumedo is one of the most famous of the revolutionary repertoire, still played in cantinas today all over México.

Soldaderas, on the other hand, were not even afforded the luxury or dignity of a *fusilamiento*; they died without pageantry and without acknowledgment. Nonetheless, this spiritual consciousness (within the gendered male sphere) also formed a part of why they too joined *la bola*.[8]

Reminiscent of Aguilar Mora's argument, in the *The Gift of Death* Jacques Derrida reminds us that one cannot give or receive death for someone else. Rather, it is a way of comprehending the irreducibility and uniqueness of the subject. However, in Campobello's novel, death constitutes an apotheosis of sorts, a single moment of recognition, but also, a return to a communal life, where bits of their body parts remain. The synechdocal re-membering of people to their mutilated body parts is like the re-membering of a local history to a national drama. It also re-members other ways of knowing, other *saberes* that have been submerged, invisible to the larger fabric of Mexican epistemes where the rhetoric of mestizaje incorporates all three roots but only recognizes one dominant episteme.

Snubbing melodrama and traditional female genres, Campobello nonetheless romanticizes and collaborates in the masculinist language of a "good death": *dime cómo mueres y te diré quien eres* [tell me how you die and I will tell you who you are]. An honorable death is the natural end result of an honorable life. Her character respects those who die with a smile on their face, even the detested General whose lifeless cadaver was beaten postmortem to shreds. Out of the many (people, political factions, ideologies, peasants, body parts) is born one; out of anonymity they become individuated subjects. Each death becomes a narrative and historical life. Sometimes a gruesome synecdoche emblematizes the whole of the character's personality: "La muleta de Pablo López" ["Pablo López's Crutch"], "Las tripas de General Sorbarzo" ["General Sobarzo's Guts"], "El corazón del coronel Bufanda" ["Colonel Bufanda's Heart"], and the beautiful blue eyes and crystallized blood of "Záfiro y Zequiel." Memory fuses itself with the material, and the material is imprinted onto legend through the particular pieces (intestines, hearts, crutches, eyes, blood) that link these men to their bodies. Her childlike perspective is not a woman's attempt to attenuate her narrative voice in the face of a patriarchal audience or female authorial vacuum, it is her technique for turning the quotidian death of her countrymen into more than a senseless carnage. She subordinates her own authority as a narrator so that other voices may emerge to narrate their own immortality. Sometimes, in the thick of the fray, those who are peripheral to it see it the best.

Indeed, travel is not just moving nobody or exploring new places, it is also about re-membering old ones, and telling stories about the places you have been as "[s]tories thus carry out a labor that constantly transforms places into spaces or spaces into places" (De Certeau 118). Through Campobello's narrative rendering of the events that took place in Parral, Chihuahua, on the Calle Segundo del Rayo, this provincial place transforms into a mythical space: "Travel (like walking) is a substitute for the legends that used to open up space to something different. What does travel ultimately produce if it is not, by some sort of reversal, 'an exploration of the deserted places of my memory'" (106–7). Campobello's travels into her childhood create a memory and a mythical revolutionary space out of a specific place, "la calle Segunda del Rayo," the main street where the drama unfolds. The men and women who walked for the last time down that street, the people who stopped by her home, the men who decomposed underneath her window. Nelly travels through memory, through her childhood, through her literary appropriations of death and through her translations of memory into language. In this way, she was a soldadera as well; unrecognized and unremunerated she watched the Revolution through her window, allowing her memory to convert this specific, confined place into a space, paradoxically giving the *juanes* who perished outside her window proper names that would become the stuff of legend and myth.

Whether she liked it or not, she wrote what the soldaderas could not; she witnessed the glory, depravity, humanity, and dignity of men who died for something important, something she believed in, and which she claims others distorted for their own interests as the unworthy "winners" of the Revolution. She honored that sacrifice in the terse, gentle language that, when rendered in a child's voice, made it at once dreamlike and graphically real. To conclude, in "El Cigarro de Samuel" ["Samuel's Cigarette"] she describes a painfully shy man whose last minutes were immortalized in a superb prose: "Yo creo que a él le dio mucho gusto morir, ya no volvería a tener vergüenza. No sufriría más frente a la gente. Abrazó las balas y las retuvo. Así lo hubiera hecho con una novia. El cigarro siguió encendido, entre sus dedos vacíos de vida" (133) [I think he was very pleased to die; now he wouldn't be ashamed again. He wouldn't suffer anymore in front of people. He embraced the bullets and held on to them. That's what he would have done with a sweetheart. The cigarette kept burning between his fingers drained of life] (66). A perfect metonym for the book, this terribly bashful man "hugged the bullets" that took his life even as the cigarette continued to burn in his lifeless hands. A man, like so many of the thousands who perished, who was too shy to speak, who perhaps knew his voice was powerless, but was earnest in his intentions and actions. These men continued to burn softly in the local memory of those who knew them, only to be blown away with time like the still glowing ashes of Samuel's cigarette. In a prolific literary tradition with myriad texts dedicated to the Revolution, only she was able to tell their stories in this unique way. While neither an historical document nor a memoire, she insists that her stories are all true, based on empirical fact: facts that she professes an obligation to tell in the midst of the lies propagated by the official story. Like her *muertos*, she perished in a violent death half a century later. Kidnapped and alone, her body languished in a common grave for almost a decade, like so many of the men whose stories she immortalized in bits and pieces, flickers and fragments, thunder and bones. Unlike Nacha Ceniceros, who enjoys a first and last name and whose "real" story Campobello attempts to rectify, there is one last soldadera I would like to re-member whose image is powerful but name was, until recently, lost, recalled only as a "soldadera from Michoacán" and whose undeniable racial attributes make her an exceptional figure in the Revolutionary iconography.

Revolutionary *Mulatez*[9]

This photograph of an Afro-Mexican soldadera, originally thought to be from Michoacán, is one of the many portraits attributed to Agustín Casasola

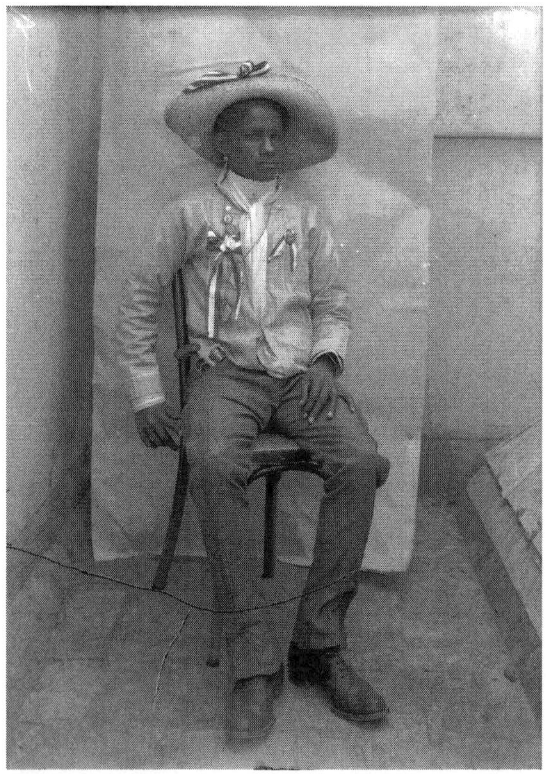

FIGURE 3.2. "Carmen Robles, soldadera," México 1913.

throughout the maelstrom of the Revolution.[10] Taken against an improvised, rustic white background, the first thing that arrests the viewer's eye, as with many portraits, is the subject's gaze. Her eyes, not quite "windows of the soul," are more like portals of danger. The sitter looks daringly at the photographer, her hand poised just a few inches from the gun she has holstered in her pants pocket, hovering below it in a menacing fashion. Not surprisingly, this portrait was showcased on the flyers for an exhibition titled, "The African Presence in México: From Yanga to the Present," which opened at the Mexican Fine Arts Museum in Chicago and travelled to San Antonio, Los Angeles, Oakland, and Washington, DC among other places between 2006 and 2011. Traveling throughout North America in this exhibition, and due in part to the burgeoning interest in Afro-Mexican history, she is almost a "cover girl" for Mexican blackness but has only recently been identified as Carmen Robles, Zapatista Colonel from Guerrero, by the Fototeca of Mexican Institute of Anthropology and History, after having languished for a century as a nameless soldadera. Far from certain, this identification is still under debate.

Not unlike the image of the soldaderas boarding the train in chapter 1, this photograph has traveled the visual globe and occupied divergent names, provoking an uncanny fascination in scholars such as myself and the general public. The congealing and reifying nature of the photographic image is challenged; her gaze speaks beyond the materiality of the paper on which her image is printed. This woman is strong and self-conscious and her eyes glow arrogantly, challenging any fool to cross her, but they do not burn with malice. Her chin is lifted with her head pointing slightly to the left, yet her gaze looks straight forward, piercing the materiality of the photograph, perhaps looking toward where the photographer, supposedly Casasola, may have been standing. Her gaze is imposing, and yet the language of her body is as impressive as her gaze. The sitter's body is positioned awkwardly, as she seems to almost be slouching slightly to the right in her chair, relaxed even. Nonetheless, the comfortable positioning of her body contradicts the threat hinted at by the lowered hand's proximity to the gun. Decorating her chest are what appear to be medals (both religious and military) while atop her head lays a floppy hat like those worn by the Zapatista peasantry. The hat is adorned with a bow, maybe from one of her medals, dramatically contradicting the drag of her masculine clothing. She even has donned long, dangling earrings for the event.[11] Not unlike the case of Antonia de Soto I will discuss in the following chapter, there is a dual transvestism. Donning male-gendered apparel permits her to showcase her strength, and in the case of Antonia de Soto, to travel unrestricted. Yet in the case of this portrait the performative nature of her drag does not undercut the equally performative nature of the vestiges of female attire. Similarly, Antonia de Soto performs the archetypical lachrymose female penitent in order to literally save her hide from the perils of the Inquisition.

In this portrait the subject looks defiantly at the photographer, communicating through her gaze what some people at the time might have considered to be perversion. Indeed, Cesare Lombroso and others after him believed that the body's features could be measured with scientific precision to reveal the nature of a person's instinct and intellect whether they are inherently civilized or criminal.[12] Physiognomy and other salient physical features allegedly determined a person's propensity for base conduct. Furthermore, Lombroso and Ferrero concluded in the first profile ever created of the female criminal that *arrogance*, *strength*, *eroticism*, and *masculinity* are the primary attributes of female delinquency: all qualities exhibited by many of the soldaderas we have examined. These "masculine" characteristics provide for the Italian criminologists a window into how criminal women behave. For our analysis of the representation of black women and mulatas in the following chapters, their theoretical framework, widely adopted in the social hygienic policies of early twentieth-century Latin America, adds another layer to how women of color were understood and represented in the arts.

Despite the original caption on the portrait informing she was a "soldadera from Michoacán," the strategic position of the gun in her pocket communicates that she was an active military participant, and not simply a "camp follower." Underscoring the multiple codes signified by the term soldadera, which in traditional parlance precludes military agency but often led directly to it, to call her a soldadera and not a soldier deflects the military nature of her position and thus, she is technically demoted. So often in the works we have observed, soldadera as a word choice is exchanged for another more dignified one, or in contrast, is used as an insult. But the medals displayed on her chest indicate that she was a recognized military officer within the revolutionary army and not simply a prostitute, wife, laundress, or cook. Certainly, what is intriguing about this portrait for the spectator is the fact that she is both a soldadera and a soldier, female and male, decorative but practical, and as a mulata, black and white, and yet, when compared to the gallery of photographic images that have been showcased of male soldiers during the Revolution, thoroughly "Mexican." She is quite comfortable in the traditionally male realm of war, yet is not quite ready to give up the *accoutrements* of a feminine aesthetic. The ribbon adorning her peasant hat and her earrings create a violent counterpoint to the gun she has not removed from her trouser pocket. Or maybe that is the point: perhaps the viewer is being instructed not to conflate the vestiges of female attire with weakness. This woman seems to embody the contradictions of war and the term soldadera—in addition to the post-revolutionary ideal of mestizaje.

It has been difficult to gain any information about this portrait beyond the few words written in the various captions and its current identification as Carmen Robles by the Fototeca and John Mraz, and at present it is unknown if its circulation could have reached novelist Francisco Rojas González, who wrote *La negra Angustias* [*The Black Woman Angustias*] (1944), a novel narrating the sensational exploits of a black *coronela* of the Zapatista army which is analyzed in chapter 5. Casasola and his team were the most renowned photographers who documented the Revolution, and at the time this novel was written it may very well have reached the hands of Rojas González in some form. Regardless of whether the novelist saw the portrait or not, this photograph certainly tells a striking narrative, in part because it could have almost served as the cover for the novel, and later, film adaptation by Matilde Landeta. Unlike soldiers such as transgender Amelio Robles, who actively performed a traditional masculinity in order to avoid the pitfalls of gender ambivalence and be granted his full rights as a man, this woman incarnates a fluid gendering that speaks to the ambivalent place of the soldaderas in Mexican history. This portrait then also serves as a powerful metonymy for the ambiguous place held by mulatas in the revolutionary and post-revolutionary social order: one that will shed light on other exceptional mulatas in México. This person, whoever she was, is still looking at us, and is still claiming her place in the making of one of the most important social revolutions of the twentieth century.

All three literary female figures—Elizabetta, Jesusa, and Nellie—are constituted by their movements: Elizabetta follows the soldiers, picks up after they die, makes tortillas for her new Captain, while nobody says anything about her "one-night absence" with the gringo journalist. "Jesusa" calls herself an itinerant leper, follows her father and then her husband into war, moves from town to town, leaves the Revolution only to return to its chaos. Nellie Campobello, both as a writer and a character, is constituted by her travels within her city, up and down her street la Calle Segunda del Rayo, the confines of her home, window, and memory. Like Jesusa, she moves in and out of personal, regional, and historical dramas. Even the portrait of the Afro-Mexican soldadera/coronela *moves* by defying a static iconicity that congeals and de-contextualizes, and instead points to another more powerful *saber*—one that has led to multiple identifications and a concomitant slippery truth: women were in the background, but also took fierce and strategic military roles. This portrait is testament to this woman's misunderstood and unwritten history, multiple names, and elided blackness.

Death, in turn, becomes another one of the unifying metaphors that bring these radically different figures together: all interpret it on their own terms. We witness Elizabetta's treatment of death when she mourns her dead "lover" for a night and then carries on the next day. We appreciate Jesusa's interpretations of the afterlife. We are overwhelmed by Nellie's self-proclaimed infantile "expertise" in all matters related to death and subsequent use of an almost morbid metonymy that creates a narrative subjectivity out of mutilated body parts. Then we view the casual—but strategic—positioning of the mulata's pistol holstered in her pants pocket. Moreover, all are interpreted by others: Elizabetta by a U.S. reporter traveling with the Villistas; "Jesusa" by an upper-class Mexican intellectual and writer who revised interviews with her informant to create a novel that narrates the life—both before and after—of a soldadera in the Revolutionary Army;[13] and Nellie, who interprets her own experiences and family history to tell the stories of the young men and women who die in front of her. A young child/teenager who witnesses the violence from her window, her work is recognized by literary giants such as Martín Luis Guzmán but ends tragically like many of the soldaderas: unknown, under-appreciated, and violated, put to rest in a common tomb only to be recovered—literally and intellectually—years later. Finally, the Afro-Mexican coronela/soldadera's photographer, supposedly Casasola, interprets the mulata warrior: the portrait is staged, but does not follow the tradition typical of military heraldry, such as the *contrapposto* or three-quarter positioning of the head. Yet, despite the improvisational staging of the sitter there is an undeniable power—indeed knowledge—communicated through the gaze. Considering how Mexican blackness is figured into the marginalized experience of the soldadera adds one more layer to the soldadera's already overblown and yet simplified legacy, as we will see in chapter 5 with the literary and filmic representation of the revolutionary leader la Negra Angustias; a story, like Adelita, Valentina, and so many others, based on a real woman. The portrait of this real woman, now (tenuously) identified as Colonel Carmen Robles from Guerrero, has traveled in the visual imaginary of Afro-Mexican scholars but has only recently recuperated a proper name. Alongside this excavated identity are only brief lines—fragmentary, inconclusive, and sometimes contradictory—to fill in the gaps of her story.

Conclusion: Adelita's Legacy

Formally unwritten, informally exchanged, commercially exploited, both private and public spheres blasphemed, idealized, romanticized, and effaced the histories of these women. Their contradictory legacies speak to the reality of the soldadera: she was all and no woman in revolutionary México. In the cultural texts, photographs, and eyewitness accounts we have examined women have been heroic, abnegating, promiscuous, saintly, miserable, mischievous, black, white, mulata, indigenous, and mestiza. The soldadera's movement, mutability, and dynamism created and simultaneously destroyed her as a stock character in literature and film. Caught between the Adelita and the Cucaracha, other possibilities like Elizabetta, Jesusa, the mulata Coronela or the Angustias character we will examine in part two of the book, get lost. Like White's definition of trope, her name moves away from one idea, that of the soldier woman, ("soldada") and toward something else. Woman becomes identified metonymically with that which she handles and is employed: the *soldada*. Woman equals object: she is exchanged, transferred but also paradoxically a free agent. As signaled by Castillo, she represents the catachresis, the unwritten, yet well-known story of almost half the women in México during the Revolution. How does this play itself out for the fate of Mexican women? The post-revolutionary era of the '20s was an effervescent moment in terms of the desire to forge a new, cohesive national identity. As Claudia Schaefer reminds us, the "despertar de una conciencia americanista" was the product of the liberal intellectuals whose confidence in democracy and progress was conditioned by the insistence on looking toward the future, thus neglecting the participation of women and further sedimenting their hitherto unchanged traditional roles (*Textured Lives* 6). Despite their contributions to the Revolution, women did not receive the right to vote until December 1, 1953, but it was not until 1958 that they voted in their first presidential election. This sounds very much like the cultural emergency to which Castillo was referring: neither faction of the Revolutionary party was prepared for the complete upheaval that the Revolution would mean, and actually produced, in the relationship between the sexes.

Women are still mobilizing themselves in order to effect change for the betterment of their communities. The Tzotzil indigenous group "Las Abejas" is a startling example of indigenous women organizing themselves by using global tactics of nonviolent resistance and placing their struggle within an international context of environmentalism and land reform. They started as a group in Acteal that fought for two sisters to have the right to own and administer their land that was being stolen by their brother. Las Abejas have been resourceful in their approach, using their native dress, the *huipil*, as a form of aesthetized resistance to neoliberalism. They employ the *huipil* as a unifying force among their members, and in striking gesture that recalls the soldadera's *rebozo*, as a symbolic (and real) weapon against mainstream mestizo society. Like the soldadera, they have impressed the world with the images of them in traditional dress forming human chains, with children in tow, fending off soldiers. They are testament to the continuing strife of women in México, both indigenous and other, and are the inheritors of not only centuries of Mayan resistance, but also the struggles initiated by the soldaderas of the Independence era and the Revolution of 1910.

Other young women today, such as "La Comandanta Bonita" from Apatzingán, Michoacán, are taking leadership positions in the community organized "auto-defensas" [self-defense groups] attempting to defend their neighborhoods and cities from the violence of narcotrafficking. She was one of the leaders who took back the city Nueva Italia from the drug cartel los Caballeros Templarios in 2014.[14] While not the majority, as a young mother of two her leadership is stunning. A year earlier, in 2013, over one hundred mothers and "housewives" in Xaltianguis (located thirty miles outside of Acapulco in the state of Guerrero) took up arms and joined these groups in order to defend their communities from drug and police violence.[15] And as has been witnessed in Cherán, Michoacán, an autonomous Purépecha village operating through an indigenous form of participatory democracy, the eruption of a few women one night in 2011 with literally nothing more than their *coraje*, sticks and stones, has led to four years of political autonomy and the expulsion of not only the narcotraffickers, but also the state. Tired and frustrated by the decimation of their forest through illegal logging by criminal organizations and the Mexican government's corruption and complicity, they stood up to the narcotraffickers and garnered the support of their community to take their streets back one by one with bonfires and their bodies. In 2015, these efforts led to the dissolution of all political parties. Alas, the soldadera represents a cultural heritage and female legacy that indigenous groups, Chicano/a artists, activists, and even contemporary Latin rock musicians have deployed as a symbol and icon of female agency, a good reason not to overlook the caricatured representations of her in the arts, but to reconsider her contemporary valence both for Chicanas and women in México today.

The portrait of the mixed-race soldadera/coronela has circulated in an odd visual odyssey, and through it we can appreciate both the complexity of the soldadera's divergent, even contradictory histories and representations as well as the ways in which race and gender overlap. Part two of this book will specifically examine the place occupied by the figure of the mulata in Mexican cultural production. Also lacking a proper name and patronymic, they, like the soldaderas, are identified through the obscurity of the monikers that have come to constitute their subjectivity, and substitute their proper place in history. Like the creation of the title "soldadera," which appropriates a word that belongs to something else, the word mulata means a person of mixed-race and literally comes from the word *mula*, which is a sterile crossbred farm animal designed for work. The anonymity or suppression of these women's titles reflects the erasure of their particular interventions from the official national narrative and popular imaginary. As women, we shall see how both soldaderas and mulatas have been figured in very specific and problematic ways at the same time that the slippery word will reveal other *saberes*, other possibilities and cracks in traditionally held notions of common sense. Blacks in México have fallen through these cracks but are nonetheless a powerful cultural force.

Part Two

The Blacks in the Closet

4

Black Magic and the Inquisition

The Legend of La Mulata de Córdoba and the Case of Antonia de Soto

Algunos aseguraban que la habían visto volar por los tejados, y que sus ojos negros despedían unas miradas satánicas mientras sonreía con sus labios rojos y sus dientes blanquísimos.

[There were those who were convinced they had seen her fly over the rooftops, her black eyes glaring satanically while her red lips and white teeth flashed a smile].

—Francisco Serrano, "La Mulata de Córdoba" from
Cuentos de espantos y aparecidos

This children's ghost story reinvents the spectacular legend of a Mexican mulata from the coastal region of Veracruz who, besides curing the poor, entrances the men folk with her spellbinding beauty and perturbing sensuality. As a result, she is denounced to the Inquisition, but rather than marry the Inquisitor who has also fallen victim to her charms, she draws a magical ship on the wall of her dungeon cell and sails away into a cloud of smoke. The spooky story quoted in the passage above projects a more sinister side to the mysterious Mulata, interpreting her as a witch more in line with Western conventions of horror stories intended to scare young audiences. These are the hallmarks of what is left of the African legacy in México since emancipation: legends, witchcraft, and myth.

In 1640, New Spain contained the second largest population of enslaved Africans and the greatest number of free blacks in the Americas.[1] By 1810, free blacks numbered approximately 634,000, or 10 percent of the total population. Contrary to popular notions of race and mestizaje in México, Africans and their descendants have had a long-standing and important role in forging the culture of contemporary México. Hardly an emerging area of academic interest, studies of Afro-Mexican history and culture materialized with the seminal work of Gonzalo Aguirre Beltrán, *La población negra en México* (1946), and have been constant throughout the last few decades, with a renewed interest emerging in the 1990s that helped to consolidate its place as a vibrant scholarly discipline. Nevertheless, many scholars still preface their work by acknowledging that in spite of the explosion of excellent and diversified contributions to the study of Africans in México, it is still a "new" discipline. Perhaps this somewhat ambivalent acknowledgment is, rather than a statement about the "newness" of the field, in fact more of a defensive gesture: a product of the overwhelming invisibility that marks the place of blacks in México. This bears testament to the fact that México as a nation, and Mexicans as a populace, do not accept the substantive contributions of Africans and their descendants, including the mulata,[2] to their culture.

The mulata is a person of mixed racial heritage whose body bridges the gap between whiteness and blackness in a colonial regime born of racism and xenophobia; it incorporates the forbidden desire that mediates the contact between master and slave. Within the context of the Caribbean, the mulata is intimately identified with her sexuality, and this sexuality operates as a means by which political, social, and racial binaries are negotiated. The figure of the mulata is present as a constant trope with regard to the constitution of both a national identity and cultural history in the Caribbean. Her physical presence mediates and incarnates two worlds that are still violently engaged. Similar to the "Malinche" figure (Cortés's translator and concubine) in México, the mulata's body has inherited the scars of this violent past, as literary representations of the Caribbean mulata have generally confined her to the sphere of mistress and mother of *mulatez*,[3] but not as a subject with agency. She incarnates that which the white woman does not: unbridled sexuality. As a person in-between two worlds, she enjoys a kind of tragic "mobility" that at once exalts and condemns her sexuality. Even in contemporary cultural production, the representation of the mulata cannot be divorced from a hyperbolic sexuality. In other words, her voluptuous body is synonymous with an exuberant sexuality that almost becomes defined as an ontological state; just her presence or mention in art invites and/or provokes the audience.[4]

Yet, almost no work has been done on this figure in México, in part, because her visibility is less striking than in the U.S. and Caribbean contexts. In México, the legacy of African culture and presence has been all but effaced in the national imaginary, especially as a result of the post-revolutionary rhetoric that proclaimed a brand of mestizo consciousness that would incorporate and ultimately assimilate all the diverse components of Mexican national identity.

The following chapters will examine how and why this exoticized other is celebrated and culturally consumed on a mass scale as quintessentially Mexican despite the invisibility of the African presence and the ambivalence of its legacy. To this end, I consider how slaves and free blacks began to erect a "creole" consciousness in the early colonial period, and then interpret the popularity of the legend of "La Mulata de Córdoba" in light of this emerging consciousness and the fictive kinships being forged by blacks themselves. In addition, I underscore the already proliferating tropes that constituted black female sexuality as perverse, linking blackness to the devil. I subsequently examine an unpublished seventeenth-century Inquisition case of a real mulata, Antonia de Soto, who was a runaway slave. The case of Antonia de Soto reveals that the less regulated regions of the viceroyalty, such as Nueva Viscaya, constituted a colonial crucible of emergent marginal identities and protean cultural practices as Spanish criollos, diverse indigenous groups, mestizos, and Africans as well as free and enslaved mulatos traveled and dwelled in this almost wild frontier, coming into intimate contact with each other. Both the legend of La Mulata de Córdoba and this Inquisition case shed light on the figuring of mulatas in the arts, but also unravel the continuous associations made between blacks, moral flaccidity, and witchcraft in the colonial period as well as the important impact this would come to bear on their representation in México until the present day. Moreover, this legend and Inquisition case underscore the contradictory uses of witchcraft as a discourse of knowledge, which was at once regulated and solicited by colonial elites, while also employed in counter-hegemonic ways that destabilized colonial authority. Indeed, recombinant and alternative *saberes*[5] by these very distinct and diverse groups of people become manifest in what appears to be the almost quotidian peddling of supernatural remedies and pacts with dark forces.

Blacks in México and the
Fashioning of a Creole Consciousness

Contrary to many misperceptions regarding slavery in México, Africans were instrumental to the consolidation of the colonial regime in the early years of colonization (1521–1640), even outnumbering whites and thus playing, as argued by Patrick Carroll, "a critical role in the economic take-off of the colony between 1550 and 1630" (*Blacks in Colonial Veracruz* xviii). Furthermore, they were not just restricted to coastal lowland regions as has been commonly assumed. They were spread throughout the whole viceroyalty. They worked in Guanajuato and Zacatecas primarily in the mines but also as farmhands in the haciendas and cattle ranches, and in the cities as textile workers, skilled laborers, artisans, and domestic workers.[6] In Michoacán they worked in the sugar, cacao, and añil plantations in addition to the cattle-ranching and textile industries.[7] In Campeche and Morelos they worked on the sugar plantations,[8] and in Colima they worked all along the coast in the sugar, cacao, and coconut plantations as well as in the salt mines.[9] In Tabasco they worked on the cacao plantations, in the cultivation of corn and *palo de tinte* as well as in the cattle ranches.[10] In Tamaulipas many Africans were reported to have arrived in order to work on plantations, but interestingly, runaway and shipwrecked slaves were also believed to have settled in this region. On the flipside, slaves were also introduced by the North American slaveholders who illegally settled in Tamaulipas, bringing their chattel with them. Furthermore, as was the case in Puebla and Veracruz, mulatos and *pardos* were even admitted into the colonial army in Tamaulipas in order to defend against the foreign intruders and "hostile" Chichimecas.[11] In Veracruz they helped to defend against pirate attacks: "La bamba"[12] (probably one of the most famous examples of *son jarocho*) is supposed to be a song about the pirate Lorencillo's attack on the Port.

In 1609, a runaway slave named Gaspar Yanga lived with his followers in the mountains for several decades and established one of the first *palenques* (fortified runaway slave colonies) in Veracruz. After negotiating a peace treaty with colonial authorities to be honored by the Spanish crown, Gaspar Yanga established the first free slave town, San Lorenzo de los Negros, which was renamed Yanga in 1930 to honor its founder. Furthermore, African-American slaves and Seminole Indians aligned themselves and migrated to México where they were granted liberty and land in northern México. They came to be known as "Indios Mascogos" and their descendants still live in "Nacimiento de los Negros." Africans have formed part of México's history from the very beginning of the Conquest, as the infamous story of the black conquistador Francisco Eguía reminds us. This man accompanied Cortés in his invasion of México, but rather than bask in the glory of the military victory, his shoulders carry the weight of the death of millions of natives as history blames him for having brought smallpox to New Spain.

What is noteworthy about the history of slavery in México is that there was a sizeable slave population in urban areas, including the capital of the viceroyalty as well as Puebla, Guadalajara, and Veracruz. In fact, they had the largest urban presence in México City, as it was common for artisans, craftsmen, and of course rich families to own one or two slaves. Even fruit sellers might acquire a slave, or rent one out from a widow to assist them in selling their wares. It was considered a sign of wealth or nobility for individual families to have slaves. The quality of the dress worn by the slaves also pointed to this class distinction: slavery became a social necessity for many members of the early colonial *noblesse obligée*.

Carroll reminds us that despite the restrictive legislation applied to blacks, whether free or enslaved, they were the most "socially outgoing of any of the racial groups in the emerging society" (xviii). Consequently, this immediate social interaction, acculturation, and miscegenation "contributed much more heavily to the racial and ethnic integration of the colonial community than their slave status would have implied" (xviii). Urban blacks began to create familial ties based on ethnic kinship (both real and imagined) quite early in the colonial era, familiarizing themselves not only with the dominant language and cultural norms, but also with the bureaucratic and legal maze created by the viceroyalty and the rule of canon law. They began to navigate the juridical labyrinth that regulated their bodies as private property, but also those of the fully recognized members of colonial society: peninsulares, criollos, castizos, and mestizos. However, the Church's paradoxical commitment to converting Africans into Christians created the possibility for these very same Africans to embrace Christianity and its social practices, such as baptism and marriage, which in turn, they used to circumvent their status as property in order to invoke their rights as Christians. Herman Bennett, in his account of Africans in México City during the sixteenth and seventeenth centuries, insists on the profound juridical knowledge of the colonial system possessed by enslaved and free Africans and their descendants, as well as the phenomenon of acculturation. In the following passage Bennett explains this skillful juridical navigation on the part of African-descended slaves:

> Obligations fostered rights that subjects employed in their defense and desire to modify their life circumstances. In the closing decades of the sixteenth century, mulattos in particular displayed this acquired acumen, a hallmark of their creole consciousness [. . .] the deft manner in which persons of African descent handled the tribunal's proceedings navigators underscores a legal acumen usually associated with the most skillful cultural navigators. But this consciousness also reflects a degree of cultural immersion among persons of African descent that has been overlooked. (181)

With this emerging "Christian-inflected cultural and legal consciousness," slaves who inhabited the cities began to advocate for varying degrees of autonomy and became supremely conscious of their rights and obligations. They requested rights ranging from having free time to spend with their families on Sundays, urging their masters to sell them to someone closer if they found themselves distant from spouses or children, or time to consummate their marriages consecrated by the Holy Catholic Church (2). Thus, they were able to initiate litigation in order to improve their positions and utilized this legal consciousness to establish "family and friendship networks predicated on an imagined identity" (2). By strategically performing a Christian identity they were resourcefully able to mobilize the Church not only to obtain rights, such as conjugality, but to undermine the masters' authority to treat them according to their own whim: "No Christian subject stood above the law [. . .] In the face of the canon law, even a powerful royal judge had to bow" (139). This insistence on their rights as Christians would eventually constitute the "hallmark of a creole consciousness" (139). However, this should not diminish the cultural and spiritual violence enacted on those who were forced to abandon their native identities, nor should it suggest that slavery was any less harrowing, but that the nature and scope slavery took in New Spain would be quite different from the Spanish Antilles and even Brazil. While México was among the first countries to abolish slavery, the latter were the last countries to legalize manumission.

This ability to assimilate on the part of the Africans and their descendants is what cemented their participation in the construction of colonial México's culture and history, consequently guaranteeing them a little more flexibility than in regions where slavery was primarily rural and based on the chattel plantation model. Due in part to the urban nature of slavery in New Spain, enslaved families lasted a generation or two at the most. But this astute maneuvering of the colonial state, in their fashioning of a creole identity, also paradoxically sealed the invisibility of the slaves' fate. Their absorption into the general populace left few traces as miscegenation began early on, especially among mulatos and mestizos, and slowly increased throughout the colonial period. This trend occurred not only in the capital, but as Carroll describes, in provinces such as Veracruz during the late colonial era, where he claims that marriage patterns suggest an erosion of the caste system due to an "[i]ncreased incidence of interracial marriages among all groups but Indians" (122). Whites, however, did not stray far from the color line. When they engaged in interracial unions it was usually with castizos[13] or mestizos, and those who did mix tended to be from the lower economic echelons of Spanish society, leading to a "dual reality in the late colonial meaning and application of race" where whites refrained from miscegenation but the racially mixed groups became combined into the "casta"[14] category (129). It would be whimsical to think that through the lumping of the mixed groups that race did not still rigidly constitute one's place in society. Nonetheless, the strict caste system for which New Spain is infamous, with much cited but in reality seldom used racial taxonomies as absurd as "torna atrás"[15] and "tente en el aire,"[16] began to disintegrate in order to create this dual system described by Carroll. After Independence, the Mexican state's second president, Vicente Guerrero, an Afro-Mexican himself, instituted the official abolition of slavery in 1821 as one of his first presidential acts (although the traffic of slaves had already been abrogated) and consequently insisted on the elimination of race as a category in the official census. This act, although intended to dismantle the strict caste system that had operated for two hundred years, also erased Afro-Mexicans from the ethno-historical map.

As might be expected, mulatas posed a threat to the racial hierarchy of the colonial order. As early as 1571 the colonial administration enacted sumptuary laws that were mostly directed toward free black women and mulatas prohibiting their use of fine stuffs such as silk, pearls, gold, or mantillas as well as dressing above their station. These laws were justified by authorities who were indignant about the "immodest" and "lascivious" dress of mulatas and black women. This reflected a fear on behalf of the administration that these lavishly attired mulata women would become "irresistible to 'decent' men" (Susan Socolow, *The Women of Colonial Latin America* 142). Moreover, mulata and black women who could afford this type of fine clothing were clearly engaged in (at least in the mind of colonial elites), and even worse, profiting from illicit and morally depraved behavior.[17]

The colonized subjectivities that were being fashioned in light of this racial amalgamation set the stage for the rhetoric of mestizaje that would be heralded by the Revolutionary state of 1910 and would lead to the subsequent historical amnesia regarding Afro-Mexicans. But long before the homogenizing discourse of mestizaje took hold, the colonial period proves that mulata women had a formidable presence that became articulated in the courts through the numerous inquisitorial cases involving them, and through the language of legend and witchcraft.

Mesmerism and *mulatez*:
The Legend of La Mulata de Córdoba

According to legend, "La Mulata de Córdoba" was a stunning mulata who entranced every man who laid eyes upon her ageless beauty. She lived alone on the outskirts of town (Córdoba, Veracruz) as an herbalist, working up potions to cure the country folk of their ills. But no man would win her hand, as she was beholden to a strange image that would not allow her to marry. When the town mayor fell victim to her charms, he ordered her to wed him. When she refused, he denounced her as a witch to the Inquisition. And once in the grasp of the Inquisition, her inquisitor, an aged fellow, also fell in love with her, promising to set her free should she marry him. She similarly refused the inquisitor and he, along with the other spurned men, condemned the wretched woman to death due to the insolence she displayed by rejecting such eligible white suitors. She was supposedly sent to the prison in the fortress of San Juan de Ulúa, founded in the port city of Veracruz in 1511.

This legend is such an indelible part of local lore that, while I was touring the former fortress of San Juan de Ulúa, the guide made sure to include a visit to the cell where the Mulata de Córdoba supposedly had been sequestered. According to legend, it was from this cell that she mysteriously escaped through witchcraft. By drawing a ship on the wall, she conjured a spell that would allow the vessel to whisk her away from the deadly punishment that the Inquisition had meted out for her. Our tour guide even ventured to point to the place on the cell wall where the Mulata might have drawn this mysterious ship, although by this point she was clearly enjoying her embellishment. These sinister hallmarks of the African legacy in México, while leaving much to be desired, reveal the profoundly complex nature of the roles played by Africans in forging the culture and history of the colonial enterprise in New Spain. The legend of the Mulata de Córdoba is well known in México, particularly in the Gulf Coast region of Veracruz and is even included in a compilation of children's ghost stories, not just from México, but across Latin America. The epigraph quoted at the beginning of the chapter is taken from this children's ghost story ("cuento de espanto y aparecido"), re-telling the legend of the infamous Mexican Mulata for the ghoulish enjoyment of young Spanish-speaking children across the Americas and Spain.

Not only retold as a ghost story for children, it has inspired art forms as diverse as ballet, film, and even opera. According to Luis Leal in his introduction to a version written by José Bernardo Couto in his anthology, *El cuento Veracruzano*, the legend was even said to have inspired a story by Guatemalan writer Miguel Ángel Asturias in his *Leyendas de Guatemala*.[18] It was the basis for a ballet written by Blas Galindo in 1939 and a Mexican opera written by Pablo Moncayo in 1948 (both were students of Carlos Chávez), in addition to one of the first Mexican films about an Afro-Mexican, *La Mulata de Córdoba* (1945) featuring the iconic Mexican singer Toña la Negra (a native of Veracruz) and directed by Adolfo Fernández Bustamante. The renowned Mexican poet Xavier Villaurrutia was compelled on several occasions to write about the legend, having authored the screenplay for the film, and together with Agustín Lazo, collaborated with José Pablo Moncayo to create the libretto for the opera.[19] This legend, aside from representing a quaint ghost story, is a fascinating account of the place held by mulatas throughout the colonial period, highlighting the specific role they played in forging the complicated concept of race in the national imaginary.

The Mulata de Córdoba, as the legend is told, was socially marginalized, living in isolation on the outskirts of the city, but was well known to all, perhaps because of the great mystery that surrounded her strange, almost miraculous, healing powers. Joan Bristol claims that Afro-Mexicans were ironically able to exercise a considerable amount of authority as medical practitioners despite their status as people without *calidad* (2).[20] In fact, there was a dearth of doctors and learned medical professionals, and the empirics (those who provided basic medical help as midwives, bonesetters, and tooth pullers) were not always successful in their treatments. Moreover, by drawing from Julio Caro Baroja and Solange Alberro, she explains that the authority they enjoyed as healers was due in part to their identification as racial "others" that were perceived to be "closer to nature." This provides a fascinating window into the ways in which, time and again, many Afro-Mexicans were intimately associated with witchcraft. Furthermore, it speaks to the relationships that blacks and mulatos (both enslaved and free) fostered with other non-white members of colonial society, such as Indians and mestizos. Indeed, it appears that Spaniards and criollos regularly consulted with mixed-race servants and slaves for help not only with their health, but also with their love lives. This subversive "knowledge" also generated a deep-seated anxiety in those who enjoyed a superior class and racial distinction because colonial elites often depended on these medical and spiritual curers, leading to a conditional and temporary authority that "often put Afro-Mexican curers and clients in difficult and dangerous situations" (12). Thus, this legend offers a unique insight into the social and cultural tensions that existed between those who possessed *calidad* and those who did not; it explores the imputed connection (in the minds of the Spanish and white criollos) between the irresistible sexual allure of Afro-Mexicans and black magic. In addition, it underscores the real problem of the dependence of colonial elites on racial inferiors to assist with their physical, mental, and spiritual health. By cultivating power through their talents as healers, Afro-Mexicans made themselves an intimate part of the lives of these racial superiors who at once beckoned and resented this intrusion. This shift in power undoubtedly made elites uncomfortable and vulnerable; in this way, the legend exposes the multifaceted nature of the problems facing Afro-Mexicans in the context of their contingent power as medical practitioners, but also, as exotic sexual objects.

In Vicente Riva Palacio's poem published in 1884 in collaboration with Juan de Dios Peza, the Mulata is portrayed as remarkably lovely, and her beauty is identified as "strangely" foreign. It is quite fitting that the legend unfolds in the state of Veracruz, which is likened to a tropical paradise, thus reflecting the place it has occupied in the national imaginary as a region marked by sensuality, decadence, and the movement of diverse peoples.[21] It was the point of entry for the nation's first invaders, and the last place from which its exiles departed. In Riva Palacio's poem, the mulata's body emerges *sui generis* in the tropicalized space of Veracruz, and she becomes the embodiment of this tropicality. The poem points to her eyes as emitting the rays of the African sun, and her brown skin bears witness to her mixed-race origin: "En Córdoba, jardín veracruzano, hermosa villa cuya sien adornan / del trópico los frutos sazonados, una linda doncella que en sus ojos / del africano sol lleva los rayos, / con su tez morena va diciendo / que es también de la raza de los blancos [In Córdoba, garden of Veracruz, lovely village whose temple is adorned / by sumptuous tropical fruit, / A beautiful maiden whose eyes / contain the rays of the African sun, and whose tawny skin reveals that / she is also of the white race] (vv. 2–8). As seen in these verses, the sensual signifiers point toward a tropicalized otherness where an African sun radiates its heat from the eyes of this voluptuous, mixed-race beauty.

In all the renderings of this legend, the Mulata is orphaned; no one can identify her parents, her family line, or anybody that might know of her past. She seems to appear out of nowhere: "Nadie a sus padres conoció; mas todos / al mirar sus cabellos encrespados / la morbidez de sus graciosas formas, / y su ondulante seno y rojos labios, / la Mulata la llaman, pues sospechaban, / que hija fue de morena y castellano" [Nobody knew her parents; however all / who gazed upon her curly hair / her delicate and charming curves, / her voluptuous breasts and red lips called her "the Mulata" / as they suspected that she was the daughter of a mulata woman and a Spaniard] (vv. 9–14). She immediately is identified through the sexualization and racialization of her body: her curly hair, sensual curves, voluptuous bosom, and red lips are descriptors rife with latent sexual desire, and in the case of the Mulata, this can only translate into sin. Her unknown origin is attributed to the union of a black or mulata woman with a Spaniard whose identities are also unknown. Villaurrutia and Lazo's libretto also focuses on this point: "Sin familia, sin esposo. Sin nombre que nos distinga, no se vive en nuestra tierra. Sin un querer" (32). The trope of orphanhood is widespread in new world narratives regarding blacks and mulatos, and in México, the disruption of traditional families and alternative kinships are also prevalent when narratives include African-descended characters. A single woman, especially a woman of color, living on her own poses a threat to the social, cultural, and religious order: she could only be a witch or a prostitute. Divested of a proper name, and with no man, and more importantly, no family to vouch for her, the place of the mulata in formal society was naturally rendered suspect. As expressed by the opera, one cannot live in this social order without a *name*.

Mulatos were often born of the sexual aggression that was inflicted on black women, and the mulata embodies the wounds of this original violence. The white fathers almost never gave them their family name, which in a patriarchal colonial order, is tantamount to social annihilation. Despite being "from Córdoba," there is an insistence on her foreignness, of coming from somewhere else, "del africano sol" (Riva Palacio), which places the source of her unearthly power elsewhere, thus making her alien and not autochthonous. This ironically naturalizes the Mulata's inherent otherness. Although her name indicates that she is a native from the city of Córdoba (she has no proper first or last name), she and her "dark" power must come from "somewhere else," in effect, ontologizing blackness as sexual, sinful, and foreign. That is, both the Mulata and the sin she unleashes have no traceable genealogy; the black mother is as nameless as the white father. Therefore, the mother and lascivious father become metonyms for sexually desirable black women and corrupted white men. The anonymity of this coupling creates and disseminates fear: black female sexuality will corrupt the delicate society's white patriarchs and their young sons. In a colonial society trying to rid itself of its barbarous others, miscegenation is likened to a plague, and worse, a moral sin against the law of god. The idea of having no past or discernable genealogy, in addition to her reported supernatural powers, leads to the association of the Mulata with diabolical forces. Accordingly, in their opera Villaurrutia and Lazo name her "Soledad" as a consequence of this real and metaphorical orphanhood.

Leonora Saavedra explains that Moncayo's musical interpretation of the opera written by Villaurrutia and Lazo renders the sound foreign through the use of hemiolas and pentatonic scales. This rhythmic and tonal choice suggests foreignness because the sesquialtera is common in sub-Saharan African and Afro-Latino music (including *son jarocho*) from all over the Caribbean and Latin America (although we should remember that it is also common in European music, especially baroque music for example). She also notes that Moncayo incorporated the *son jarocho* (Afro-Mexican music that originated in Veracruz) as a way to insert the "local color" of the Gulf Coast but also to bring in the sensuality of its women. However, alongside the insertion of autochthonous music from Veracruz (which is ironically not openly acknowledged as Afro-Mexican in origin), is the paradoxical orientalizing gesture implicit in the use of a pronounced hemiola, or sesquialtera (3/2 time) throughout the opera. The sesquialtera begins after an abrupt change in tempo interrupts the slow introduction that "heralds the new musical materials" (7). Moreover, the use of pentatonic scales—common in Native American, pan-Asian, West African and Eastern European music—are prominent in the music written for the Mulata leading-lady. In Moncayo's opera, the pentatonic scales and "modal melodies with lowered leading tones" produce a sonic blackness imputed to the Mulata that recalls the orientalist musical racialization in Puccini's *Turandot* and *Madame Butterfly* (8). In addition, Saavedra highlights the rhythmic constitution of the Mulata's sensuality:

> Most of the time Moncayo's almost random alternation of rhythmic groupings of two and three within a binary meter remains in the bass line, where the rhythmic juxtapositions drive the music forward in a dancelike movement. Indeed, these rhythms appear especially when Soledad engages in the sexually charged bodily movements that so enchant the men of the town. (7–8)

Hypersexuality is a significant key to the construction of mulata (and mulato) characters: it defines their very being, constituting the core of their subjectivity as it continuously appears at the center of their personal dramas.

Although mulatos and African descendants were often able to mobilize their status as Christians to their advantage, this also made them subject to

the Inquisition. Given the multiple stereotypes surrounding blacks and mulatos, especially with regard to their sexual availability and supposed depravity,
this made their status particularly vulnerable because "as a tangible manifestation of mestizaje, mulattos stood firmly in the jurisdictional vortex of the
Inquisition [. . .] In constituting Africans, particularly mulattos, as subjects
with defined Christian obligations, the tribunal bestowed rights that individuals manifested in the narratives they created for the inquisitors" (Bennett 181).
Mulatos appear frequently in the archives of the Inquisition and Bennett's
book is an excellent account of the contexts in which they were summoned
before the tribunals. In many of the cases, mulatas were charged with bigamy,
sexual misconduct, or witchcraft. Bristol avers that the denunciation of black
Mexicans for witchcraft was a way to maintain superiority over the very
people colonial elites procured for medicinal treatment and spiritual guidance
because "[b]y denouncing Afro-Mexicans to the Inquisition for witchcraft,
Spaniards tried to discursively push people who played an important role,
especially in times of affliction, back to the less significant positions where
they belonged according to the logic of Spanish rule" (14). Nonetheless, her
insight reminds us that these witchcraft denunciations were not just discursive
moves to be taken lightly, because they represented real threats that could
produce severely adverse situations for those accused (14). Throughout history, independent and powerful women have been demonized as witches, but
when this is combined with racial difference, it leads to a virulent persecu-
tion. The legend testifies to this fact as the Mulata de Córdoba was charged
with witchcraft not only because of her reported powers to cure—which had
actually endeared her to the community before her ageless beauty took its
malefic toll on society's menfolk—but also because of her rejection of the
men who accosted her, demanding her love.

The legend insists that her spectacular beauty had a maddening effect
on men, particularly white men who enjoyed positions of authority within
the colonial administration. Bristol cites several cases where Afro-Mexicans
were accused of invoking witchcraft to exercise telepathic power over the
minds of their superiors or owners. For example, there are instances where
they are accused of mentally coercing their masters to release them of their
duties or to delay a punishment. One case is the priest Tomás Cárdenas's
denunciation of the slave Juana, whom he believed was using witchcraft and
mesmerism in order to mentally coerce her owner Antonio Calderón. The
priest reported that the slave Juana confessed to having used magic to steal
from her owner, and the priest feared that the owner's delayed punishment of
Juana upon discovery of the theft was a consequence of his dulled senses. He
believed Calderón to be in danger of further mental manipulation provoked
by the sorcery of his bondswoman (Bristol 19). In other instances, blacks

and mulatos were charged with retaliating against their masters for punishing them by making them ill.

Villaurrutia and Lazo's libretto likewise emphasizes the unearthly mental powers of the Mulata, while also highlighting her sexual magnetism when Anselmo, the main protagonist, falls prey to her beauty: "Tengo celos hasta del viento que te ciñe el cuerpo ondulante, que se confunde con tu aliento y te abraza como un amante" [I am even jealous of the wind that envelops your voluptuous body, that becomes part of your breath and that embraces you like a lover] (Moncayo 16). Her sexuality is so powerful it exercises preternatural effects on nature and the elements: even the wind becomes her lover. Later, Anselmo valiantly tries to "save" Aurelio (another character who has fallen in love with the Mulata) from her charms by attempting to kill her so that Aurelio might be spared from falling under her spell. Suddenly, the Mulata "dissipates," or vanishes, and Aurelio is struck instead. This unleashes the operatic climax whereby Anselmo is compelled to rally the townspeople in order to apprehend the Mulata, as he believes it is her fault that Aurelio has been killed.

Another interesting case documented by Bristol involves a slave named Antonio, who is accused of casting a spell on a Spanish woman named Gertrudis (of low or questionable social status), inciting her to engage in sexual relations with him. Elements of this case indeed shed light on the popularity of the legend, underscoring that the ascribed hyper-sexuality of mulatos is not just a product of the cultural imagination: the sexuality and attractiveness of the colonies' black and mixed-race members became the motive for an irrational fear among Spaniards. Bristol maintains that the language of witchcraft was often strategically deployed to exculpate Spaniards from their own sexually illicit behavior (28). For example, in this case Gertrudis is a married woman who was already sent away due to marital problems, which is how she met the slave Antonio in the first place. Therefore, her behavior is rendered "suspect" from the beginning, although we cannot possibly know or judge the conditions of her original marriage that would compel her to find outside sexual partners. Notwithstanding, her mother Francisca instigated the proceedings against Antonio, and Gertrudis was later sent to a *recogimiento* (a house for poor, shamed, adulterous, and divorced women or prostitutes). In what might appear to be a last-ditch effort to rescue her "honra" and virtue, accusations were leveled against Antonio in order to explain how only through the compulsion of "a diabolical entity" could Gertrudis have possibly *consented* to such unthinkable and egregious sexual acts with a racial inferior (28).

In a further twist, the spell that Antonio allegedly cast was witnessed and reported by a fellow slave named Magdalena. It is not uncommon to see accounts of slaves or servants informing on each other; still, we should note that people in subordinate positions could also be pressured, put under duress, or bribed to testify in favor of their superiors. In any case, Magdalena reported that she had seen this man cook and pulverize birds and then pour the powder into Gertrudis's drinking water and sprinkle it on her body. After imbibing the potion, Gertrudis, who had held Antonio in disdain, became giddy and seduced him. Here we witness the indigenous practice of utilizing desiccated birds in potions and amulets for love being incorporated by blacks and mulatos in their own medicinal practices. Therefore, as we will see in the case of the runaway slave Antonia de Soto, there was a profound level of interpenetration and transculturation of cultural and medicinal practices among blacks and indigenous groups, leading to the cultivation of alternative knowledges that are manifested not only in the form of medicines and witchcraft, but in a transculturated and mutually constitutive African and indigenous *saber*.

The language we hear in the poem and opera of "La Mulata de Córdoba" likewise resonates with these accusations of sexual compulsion and witchcraft, as the mesmerism associated with her beauty is considered a product of the devil. Indeed, what this real Inquisition case initiated by a Spanish woman against a male slave signals is that black sexuality is intimately linked with witchcraft and pacts with the devil, permitting white or "almost" white colonial subjects to release themselves from any responsibility. As illustrated by scholars such as Laura Lewis and Bristol, Afro-Mexicans and other people *sin calidad* did in fact operate as health and spiritual practitioners in the absence of a strong medical community. Nonetheless, this legend bears testament to the sexual cupidity of the colony's Spanish and criollo members and illuminates how they were able to exploit the language of witchcraft in order to justify their own wayward erotic compulsions. In the eyes of the white aristocracy, mulatas exercise an almost diabolical sexual allure that can only harm those who fall prey to their enchantments. As evidenced by these multiple Inquisition cases and the various iterations of the legend, black female sexuality constituted a serious threat to non-blacks; it is not just a convenient drama for a ghost story or an opera.

Despite these cultural paradigms that hyper-sexualize mulatas (and mulatos), the legend ironically insists on the refusal of the Mulata to be with any man, as she states that she has made a promise to an image, or what she calls "her father." This ambiguous promise leads people to believe she has made a pact with the devil to whom she owes her ageless beauty and powers. In Riva's poem, the town *alcalde* loses his mind over her, and after she spurns him, he denounces her to the Inquisition due to the rumors circulating about her powers to cure. Afterward he leads the police on an all-night chase through the forest, where it seems some diabolical force embodied by a man dressed in black is protecting her. In all the versions under consideration, a powerful authority figure (in Riva Palacio's it is the *alcalde*, in Lazo and Villaurrutia's it is an aged inquisitor) agrees to free her from the clutches of the Inquisition if only she will consent to be his wife or lover. In each case she refuses and is therefore condemned to death for her arrogance: "Entonces el alcalde se imagina / que aquel desdén con desdén se paga" [And thus the mayor imagined / that her disdain should be paid in kind] (Riva Palacio vv. 70–71). To be spurned by what they consider a racial inferior is the height of emasculation; a mulata like she certainly cannot afford any supercilious sentiment and should be grateful that a white, distinguished man would take her as his "bride."

The legend ends with the mysterious disappearance of the Mulata from her jail cell when she sails away in the boat she sketched on her prison wall with a stick of coal. She beckons her jailor, or in other versions, inquisitor, to reveal what they think might be missing from the ship she has drawn. In all the versions, the person answers that the only thing the vessel needs is to "set sail." This spoken answer operates as the final ingredient of the spell she has cast to escape, as it is at this precise moment that the incantation becomes complete: the Mulata sails off into the night, escaping her sentence, never to be heard from again. This ending may forgive her from any dire punishment, but it also eliminates her presence from society. She disappears into a cloud of smoke, releasing the male population from her insidious threat.

The children's story quoted in the epigraph highlights the more macabre aspect of this legend with descriptions of her flying like a witch over roof-tops, resonating with Riva Palacio's poem through its allusions to the devil. However, the poem establishes a direct connection to blackness: the poet describes her strong gaze as radiating African sunrays, her body as morbidly sensual, and her lips as deep red. The description in the ghost story is analogous, except that her gaze emblazoned by the "African sun" is replaced by a "satanic glare" and her white teeth contrast with her red lips. These diabolical signifiers, like those of a vampire, qualify black beauty as pathological and clearly have the intention of scaring young children with a less than subtle racist lesson. Furthermore, this version of the legend, although intended for children, is reminiscent of European gothic fiction, with its penchant for melodrama, horror, and romance.

The legend of the supernatural Mulata inspired one of México's first original operas about an autochthonous subject matter. For this reason, it is imperative to comment briefly on the aesthetic context in which this opera emerged, coinciding ironically with a moment of nationalist effervescence that nurtured the fine arts as the privileged place this identitarian drama would unfold. Composer Carlos Chávez entered as a prodigy in the Mexican musical scene, becoming estranged from his former mentor and teacher Manuel Ponce and replacing Julián Carillo as conductor of the National Symphony Orchestra. At the end of 1936 and the beginning of 1937 he published a series of articles that Alejandro de la Madrid maintains performed a "kenosis" of México's musical past, because rather than acknowledge the continuity between the arts cultivated by the Porfirian regime and the post-revolutionary musical tradition, Chávez declared himself the "true representative of the 'authentic' Mexican identity" (*Sounds of the Modern Nation* 165–66). During the decade of the 1930s the Mexican government developed a policy that sought to symbolically recuperate the importance of indigenous cultures as part of its national identity, and Chávez's *Sinfonía India* (1935)[22] is the culminating moment of this *indigenista* impulse (149).

Chávez became the first director of the Instituto Nacional de Bellas Artes (INBA), a federal institution designed to protect and administer Mexican fine arts, and in 1948 published a series of articles in *El Universal* declaring his intention to create a national opera company under the auspices of the INBA.[23] In these articles Chávez announced the inaugural performance of three one-act operas commissioned by him to showcase Mexican musical genius, with themes inspired by autochthonous stories, to take place on October 3, 1948: *La Mulata de Córdoba* by José Pablo Moncayo (1912–58), *Elena* by Eduardo Hernández Moncada (1899–1995), and *Carlota* by Luis Sandi (1905–95). The prerogative of Chávez and his nationalist zeitgeist was to create an "authentically" Mexican music inspired by the ideology of the Mexican Revolution of 1910, one that would exorcise the fine arts from the evil spirits of the Porfirian Eurocentric past. Compelled by this desire, he commissioned the work of Moncayo and others. Clearly, this bears witness to the important political intervention played by the arts: boasting an independent cultural and aesthetic tradition becomes tantamount to acquiring entry into so-called modernity. As argued by Leonora Saavedra, opera in México has a long, conflicted history that involves simultaneously acknowledging the elite's foreign tastes when it comes to opera, while trying almost desperately to make it "Mexican." The impulse by Chávez to accomplish this was never consummated—apparently he did not consider writing opera himself—as these three operas were the beginning and end of these commissions. Although Mexicans have written opera before and after, these works would remain largely unpublished and underperformed.[24]

Internationally recognized, José Pablo Moncayo was a second-generation student of the famous workshops held by Chávez. Although less experimental and modernist in his musical aesthetic, one of his most famous pieces, "Huapango," is a popular favorite that incorporates *son jarocho* as its major musical theme. Moncayo's *La Mulata de Córdoba* opened with the two other operas mentioned, and indeed, they all had the intention of showcasing an authentic Mexican subject matter. However, the other two were romanticized visions of the ill-fated reign of the emperor Maximilian (the imposed Hapsburg monarch backed by Napoleon III of France), although *Elena* was based on a corrido and did incorporate elements of the oral ballad tradition into the music. As discussed, Moncayo's musical score makes use of pentatonic musical phrases that have the effect of racializing the sound with an "orientalist" and othering tonality and rhythm, particularly when the leading lady sings.[25] This is not unlike the way different composers invented indigenous music, such as Miguel Bernal Jiménez's fabrication of pre-Colombian Purépecha music in *Tata Vasco*, which created stereotyped renditions of what was imagined to be indigenous. Nonetheless, unlike the preeminence of an important historical figure like Vasco de Quiroga (the famous colonial Bishop of Michoacán who created craft guilds so that the indigenous communities could sustain themselves economically), or the Emperatriz Carlota (wife of the tragic and romanticized Emperor Maximilian), or even the exalted Guatemotzín (based on the Aztec figure of Cuauhtémoc who has been historically rescued as a symbol of indigenous pride and resistance), this Mulata was a nameless, anonymous woman who turned into a legend of black deviance. Almost seamlessly, a racialized discourse of mulata womanhood gets causally woven into this nationalistic attempt to reclaim art music and highbrow aesthetic forms. That a mulata woman could yet again wind her way into a highly contested musical form trying to break away from the grasp of imitative Italianness is a fascinating twist in the expression of Mexican arts.

Although not the first opera written by a Mexican about a local legend,[26] according to the reviewer Mauricio Magdaleno (an important writer himself), it premiered as one of the first original operatic pieces written by a Mexican that was not a poor imitation of the Italian genre. For the first time, according to Magdaleno, Mexican composers managed to pull off original, authentic pieces without devolving into simplistic clichés:

Al fin y al cabo, dentro del actual renacimiento artístico mexicano necesitamos contar con una *expresión operística nuestra, auténticamente nuestra*. En otras épocas, se escribió ópera en México. Desgraciadamente, la tal ópera tenía tanto de mexicana como ustedes y yo de astrólogos; eran simples, infortunadas imitaciones de los italianos [. . .] Esta vez, en pleno 1948, dueños ya de una pintura que pasea el genio del mexicano por el mundo, de una música que cuenta con creaciones de muy subido cuño, de expresiones literarias más y más crecientes, Carlos Chávez comprometió a un grupo de compositores, todos de primera y dueños de una indudable experiencia sinfónica, a escribir ópera mexicana [. . .] sobrias, nobles y elegantes, son las tres piezas estrenadas el sábado.

[In the end, within the recent artistic renaissance of Mexican art we needed to count on an authentic expression of opera that is *genuinely ours*. In other moments, opera was written in México. Regrettably, this opera was as "Mexican" as you or I are astrologers; they were simple, unfortunate imitations of the Italian operas [. . .] This time, in 1948, proud owners of painting that exhibits Mexican genius throughout the world, of music that boasts pieces of an exquisite quality, of literary expressions that are every day growing, Carlos Chávez involved a group of composers, all among the best and endowed with an indubitable symphonic experience, to write Mexican opera [. . .] somber, noble and elegant were the three pieces that premiered on Saturday]. (*El Universal*, October 26, 1948, Mauricio Magdaleno,[27] emphasis added)

Published a week after the premier of the opera, this review is a radiant appraisal of José Pablo Moncayo's opera and the trilogy as a whole. The reviewer gushes at how finally, in 1948, México had stopped being a poor imitator of a European genre and was now a creator and producer of this fine musical tradition. This fascinating cultural critique marvels at the creation of an authentically Mexican opera; yet how this "authentic" cultural expression registers race becomes the site of an identitarian quandary. How could blackness be so marginal, so insignificant to the nation's history if, within what many would consider to be one of Western culture's most prestigious musical forms (despite its deeply popular origins), one of the first top-quality, seemingly autochthonous cultural products of this genre is based on a colonial legend of a mulata, female deviant accused of contaminating the social fabric with libidinous desire and witchcraft? Despite embodying an historically irrelevant racial identity, the Mexican version of *Carmen* or *Aida* is a mulata from Veracruz; but unlike Carmen or Aida, she has no name or any discernible origin. Similar to the soldadera, who inspired corridos, novels, plays, and films, this figure is socially, historically, and politically marginalized and nameless. Yet why she is worthy material for an opera is a fascinating cultural conundrum born of a negrophobic coloniality.

While the Mulata de Córdoba started as a local legend that has influenced children's stories, an opera created in the height of musical nationalism in México, a major motion film and ballet, her mysterious figure and abstracted figuration has a very real and formidable presence in the Inquisition archives with a factual story that defies belief and contemporary credulity. The legend of the Mulata de Córdoba corresponds to a perceived sexual and magical threat posed by Afro-Méxicans for colonial Mexican society, and we will see the tangible repercussions of this threat in the Inquisition case of Antonia de Soto, whose physical prowess exceeded even the danger of her sexuality. Yes, Antonia de Soto's true-life case seems almost more unbelievable than the mythical powers of the legendary Mulata de Córdoba.

The Magical Adventures of Antonia de Soto

Preguntada quantas fueron las piedrecitas, y demas rosas, ierbas, que dice le dio [el susodicho] Indio matias, y que palabras le dijo que dijiesse o que havia de decir, para usar de ellas, y pa ser sacada de la casa de su amo, y como fue la salida, y con que circunstancias, y requisitos; dijo que las piedrecitas fueron tres, una negra, otra colorada, y otra medio blanca, y que quando las echaba en el agua, la piedra negra se bolbia verde, y con pelusa, y las sacaba el [susodicho] Indio, y se bolbia a su primer color, y que el agua la bebia el [susodicho] Indio, y con la espuma que hacian [estas] piedras, la hacia untar a esta declarante los brazos, y le decia, agora haz lo que quisieres, y esta declarante cojia entonces potros, y los ensillaba, y nunca la derribaron=Preguntada quantas fueron las flores, o ierbas, que le dio [el susodicho] Indio, dijo que tres, la una colorada, otra negra, y la otra blanca, preguntada, que palabras le dijo, que avia de decir para usar de ellas, y para ser sacada de la casa de su amo, dijo que: YUMARA. La otra palabra, y la otra; ACHULA.²⁸ Y que diciendo estas palabras, y teniendo las flores y piedrecitas en la mano, se salio de la casa de su amo por la puerta, estando su amo en [dicha] puerta, y que no le dijo nada, viendola salir. Y que fue a buscar al [susodicho] Matias a la parte, que tenian senalada, y desde alli se huyo con el [susodicho], y esto responde.

[Asked how many small stones, and other roses, herbs, that she says the Indian Matias gave her, and what words he told her to say or that she would need to say, in order to use them so that she could be removed from the house of her Master, and how the escape was, and under what circumstances and conditions; she said that there were three small stones, one black, one red and one off-white, and when these stones were put in water, the black stone became green, and acquired a downy film, and the Indian would take them out of the water, and they would return to their original color, and the Indian drank this water, and with the foam that these stones produced she was told to anoint her arms, and he would say, now do as you please, and this deponent would tame colts, and saddle them, and they never threw her= Asked how many flowers or herbs the Indian gave her, she said three, one red, another black, another white, asked what words he told her she needed to say so that she could use them to be removed from her Master's house, she said: YUMARA. The other

word, and the other; ACHULA. And by saying these words, and
having these flowers and small stones in her hand, she fled her
master's house through the front door, while her master himself
was in said door, and he said nothing to her, he just watched her
leave. And she went to find Matias in the spot they had planned,
and from there she ran away with him, and this hereby stands].
(Archivo General de la Nación, Vol. 525, exp. 48, 1693)[29]

Housed in the National Archives of México City exists a spectacular
account of a runaway slave who not only escaped her master, she outwit-
ted most of the men with whom she came into contact, perhaps even her
inquisitors. The story of Antonia de Soto is a seventeenth-century Inquisition
case related by the confessors of a cross-dressing, female runaway slave from
northern México. This document tells the unique story of how a mixed-race
slave woman escaped her master, Francisco de Noriega, with the help of a
Tepehuan Indian man named Matías de Rentería, and then proceeded to
find refuge in his village in northern México in a region known as Nueva
Viscaya. Beyond the fantastic and breathtaking adventures of a swashbuckling
mixed-race woman in the wild frontier of Northern México, this case, like the
legend of La Mulata de Córdoba, brings to light the important place of those
who have remained in the shadows of Mexican history: blacks and women.

In the statement above we witness the detailed description of the
incantation in conjunction with the application of the flowers, herbs, and
small stones used to liberate Antonia de Soto from her master, Francisco de
Noriega. The small stones are black, off-white, and red (curiously the "colors"
of the colonies three dominant races) and she reveals the magical words that
will incite the conjuration. Using this spell Antonia is able to simply walk out
of her master's house and meet up with Matías. When she is found in Parral,
she claims that the flowers ("cacomites") provided to her by Juana Golpazos
(a mestiza woman who aided her and Matías) cast a spell on the overseer
Pedro de Minjares who went to retrieve Antonia in Parral, so that he would
not identify her. According to her testimony, he inquired about Antonia de
Soto's whereabouts directly to her, and despite having lived on the estate
throughout her entire residence there, was unable to recognize Antonia and
thus departed without his charge.

In the indigenous and African world, language was powerful and could
be used to summon the supernatural, as is evidenced by Ruiz de Alarcón's
complaints regarding the continued usage of spells and magical language
by indigenous groups in the seventeenth century.[30] Viviana Díaz Balsera
contends that the *nahualtocaitl*, or magical language used by the *hechiceros*
[witches], executed part of its magical power by naming, or inciting a "confluence of things" that would change their immediate identity and reveal their

connection with, "las distintas fuerzas, espacios y tiempos del mundo" [the distinct forces, spaces and time of the world] (165). In Cuba, the Palo and Regla de Ochá traditions as well as those in West and West Central Africa likewise employ magical language that appeals to the "society of the dead" and communicates with supernatural forces ("Prendas-Nyganga-Enquisos" 390). The fact that the Inquisitors asked explicitly about the magical words she uttered, and then recorded them in capital letters, reveals the substantial fears that existed throughout the seventeenth century regarding witchcraft, and highlights the critical role of language as one of the important components in its execution.

According to Antonia de Soto it is this magical spell that permits her to slip out of her master's grasp and remain uncaught for six years. Whether we choose to believe in magic or not, it certainly is a convenient way to undermine, but also, impose a brand of power and authority over those colonial superiors who wielded brute political and social power, but lacked the supposed intimacy "with nature" that the colonies' marginalized, and "less civilized" members still possessed. This supposed intimacy with nature permitted them to cultivate supernatural faculties, while inciting a proximity to, and complicity with, the "devil."[31] The spiritual talents of mestiza Juana Golpazos, and the stones and peyote procured by Tepehuan Indian Matías de Rentería, for example, provided Antonia with the physical, mental, and even supernatural means to escape bondage, both that experienced as a slave and also as a woman. In a peculiar twist, the colors of the stones described above become profoundly symbolic as we see the unique way Nueva Viscaya, as a loosely controlled hinterland, allowed the "red," "black" and "off-white" members of this colonial society to operate in a fascinating complex of spiritual, cultural, political, and supernatural networks. José Rabasa's notion of plural-world dwelling provides a useful framework for appreciating the multiple epistemological and cosmological regimes that are bumping, but also, bleeding into each other.

Plural-World Dwelling in the
Backlands of the Northern Frontier

In his Morrison Library Inaugural Address, Rabasa explicates the idea of plural-world dwelling in his appraisal of the role of the *tlacuilo* in the early colonial moment and his "capacity to create a discursive space that does not react to, instead adopts elements from Western codes to communicate the specificity of a plurality of worlds" (33). The *Codex Telleriano-Remensis*, for example, reveals the *tlacuilo*'s ability not only to inhabit two worlds, but also to understand them by "codify[ing] in his own pictorial language a Western cultural modality by means of a symbolic use of perspective" (33). This lucidity, Rabasa claims, disarmed the colonial authorities. Many critics want to see this symbolic command on behalf of the *tlacuilo* as an in-between stage, as a "loss" of "authentic" indigenous practices through the contagion by Western modalities. Rabasa proposes a different perspective that does not succumb to a transitional epistemological nomadism or what he calls a "demand for recognition":

> However, the concept of *nepantla*, neither here nor there, neither in the ancient order nor in the Christian, can also be understood in terms of *a-not-being-really-convinced-of-the-necessity-of-dwelling-in-only-one-world*. The exteriority and incommensurability of the subaltern world engenders fear of insurrection (the war of the Mixton or the Zapatista uprising today), as well as anxiety in the face of epistemological lucidity that captures the relativity of Western forms of life—not by denying their truth but by inhabiting them and acting on them without abdicating one's own. (33–34)

This "not-being-really-convinced" of why we should dwell in one world also reflects the multiple worlds that the *tlacuilo* points to as coexisting on the same plane. The *tlacuilo* does not pretend to ignore alphabetical writing; he uses pictorial language and Western alphabetical writing to add perspective, not to pretend to exist in-between two worlds or to lament the state of *nepantla* in which he resides. When considering the diverse groups that were cohabitating in Nueva Viscaya—indeed cross-pollinating, mixing but not always combining—we can appreciate Rabasa's notion of occupying multiple worlds simultaneously without abdicating one's own.

This Inquisition case tells the story of slaves and women outside the center of Mexican society, which at that moment would have been México City. The northern frontier fell beyond the immediate purview of colonial authorities, and the existence of this amazing document bears testament to the fluidity of gender, racial, and cultural identities in a country that is marked by a strict code of cultural norms that subordinate women to men, blacks and indigenous groups to Spaniards and mestizos. Susan Deeds makes an important argument regarding the specificity of the space that Nueva Viscaya provided for the emergence of these new and often syncretic practices because the Spanish state exercised an "uneven jurisdiction"; in the countryside it was almost absent while it did wield some power in the mining centers, *reales*, and to a lesser extent the missions (96). The Tarahumaras in the Sierra Madre and Tepehuanes were indigenous communities that often sheltered non-white refugees of Spanish law, making evident that absolute control over non-white people in the region of the Sierra Madre Occidental was difficult to impossible (100). Not only that, both Tepehuan and Pueblo Indians (in addition to others) enacted fierce rebellions that almost decimated Spanish control at two different times in the seventeenth century: the Tepehuan uprising of 1616–1620 and the Pueblo revolt of 1680. Daniel T. Reff maintains that the Pueblo revolt apparently annihilated eighty years of Spanish investment on this frontier in one fell swoop, leaving both the Pueblo and the Athapaskan people free of Spanish dominion for a decade ("The 'Predicament of Culture'" 63–64). Indeed, the permeability of the borders between indigenous territory and regulated colonial areas, as well as the contact between diverse groups in the missions and mining centers resulted in almost unrestrained, protean social formations.

The colonial state ostensibly separated Indians from blacks, Spaniards, and mixed-race individuals ("República de Indios" vs. "República de Españoles"), and these discrete cultural and political spheres, according to many scholars and colonial records, resulted in antagonistic relationships among Indians and blacks. This case unravels the notion of a strict separation (at least among marginal members of the colony) revealing that in fact, these socially and culturally bound arenas bled into each other, reflecting a profoundly complicated coexistence and cohabitation that flourished in the far-reaching provinces outside of the seat of colonial power. In Nueva Viscaya, Deeds contends that "[w]hile authorities sought to impose social control on the lower echelons of society, Indians and mixed-race migrants commingled with immigrants from the south (e.g. muleteers, itinerant vendors and artisans) and attempted to forge new social networks" (105). An example of this is a Jesuit Mission called San Miguel de las Bocas where Antonia and her consort Matías spent some time. Campbell W. Pennington writes that this well-known mission, founded in 1630, is currently located near what today would be the city of Villa Ocampo, in the state of Durango and was established with the express purpose of caring for the Tarahumara and Tepehuan indigenous groups who were brought to this area as workers for the Spanish farms that produced food for the mining communities in Parral, which was fifteen leagues from the mission Las Bocas (*The Tepehuan of Chihuahua* 4). Despite being under the stewardship of the Jesuits, these missions created opportunities for significant racial and cultural contact due to the fact that "[a] good deal of cultural and ethnic interchange accompanied their farming and herding activities as they worked alongside mestizos, mulatos, Nahuatl-speaking peoples from Central México, and other Indians" (Deeds 97). Furthermore, early in the seventeenth century Alonso de la Mota y Escobar reported the presence of Tepehuan as far as Mapimí in 1602, and that later Almirante Matheo de Vesga referred to these Tepehuan communties as "Tepehuan negritos" in his account provided between 1620 and 1622 (Pennington 12). Given that they were known to shelter non-white refugees, it is possible that this particular group of Tepehuan that ended up as far as Mapimí had either mixed with, or fully incorporated, black and mixed-race members into their community. Pennington suggests that they had intermingled with the black slaves working in the mines of Mapimí.

Patrick Carroll contributes to the discussion surrounding the cohabitation of blacks and indigenous groups by distinguishing between black "ladinos" and black "naturales" and the degree of integration by blacks and mulatos into native communities. Hispanicized black "ladinos" were regarded suspiciously, while black "naturales" were those who married into indigenous villages and adopted their cultural practices. He contends that although evidence abounds regarding the antagonism between indigenous communities and blacks, in fact, there is also other "mundane documentary evidence" that points to relationships that were "commonly peaceful and consensual" (73). This belies the commonly held assertion that blacks and indigenous groups sustained antagonistic relations and existed in discrete political, cultural, and social spheres. He counters that indigenous social regimes were more concerned with culture and ethnicity than phenotype, and blacks who assimilated indigenous practices and culture were successfully integrated into some native communities. However, why this social phenomenon was underreported is unclear: he suggests that perhaps they remained unnoticed and that complaints and hostilities were more readily registered than peaceful incursions into native communities. In addition, Spaniards did not penetrate the more remote indigenous communities, particularly those that were removed from the colonial metropole. Besides obvious fears that collusion between these subordinated groups would lead to revolts as Spaniards were outnumbered ten to one by non-white others (for example, there were riots by mulatos, mestizos, blacks, and Indians in reaction to food shortages in México City in 1624 and 1692), Laura Lewis further elucidates a few of the many reasons why Spaniards would pit blacks and Indians against each other (97). For example, the colonial discourse that rendered blacks and mulatos in a masculinized, villainous language and Indians in feminized, passive terms operated to keep these groups separate by heralding Spanish authorities ironically as both exploiters and protectors of the wretched Indians, such as expressed in this Spanish decree of 1578 lamenting black aggression against, and contact with, the Indians: "their bad customs and viciousness and some errors and [ways of] life that can spoil or hinder the fruit desired for the Indians' salvation, as well as their cleanliness, because from similar company nothing can take hold that improves [the Indians], as mulatos, blacks and mestizos *are universally inclined to evil*" (qtd. in Lewis 98, AGN, RCO vol. 6, exp. 292, fol. 597). Thus, with the intention of "protecting the integrity of Indian communities by barring [. . .] black, mulatto and mestizo interlopers" the Spanish and colonial elites were really protecting themselves (98). Caste proximity would not only undermine Spanish efforts to "improve" Indians but also curtail their power to control racial "inferiors" (98). In addition, blacks and mulatos, Lewis argues, were positioned as intermediaries between Spanish and Indians, utilizing and peddling indigenous witchcraft, but also serving as henchmen for the Spanish *hacendados* and authorities. In sum, beginning early on in the colonial enterprise, the competing spheres between Indians and blacks as colonial subordinates overlapped and intersected in vital ways bringing the Spanish and Indian worlds together, since "[t]hrough reciprocal processes, then, these intermediaries 'contaminated' or 'cross-pollinated' the Spanish and Indian worlds, the sanctioned and unsanctioned lineages" (174).

Returning to Antonia de Soto's story, we can appreciate how it constitutes the stuff of legend and fantasy. She ingests psychotropic plants and has visions where she makes a pact with the devil in order to escape her master, dances with beautiful ladies and flies up a mountain to encounter an ominous man cloaked in dark, religious attire. As stated, she successfully eludes Noriega through the use of magical herbs and stones, dressing as a man in order to travel freely for six years. Among other activities, she becomes a mule driver, runs off again with Matías in order to become a bandit, and in their adventures, she kills a few men and finds treasure only to lose it along the way. She disavows her status not only as a slave, but also as a woman, rebuffing attempts by her partner Matías to make her his lover and almost beating him—the man who helped her escape bondage—to death.

When she was in Parral, Chihuahua, a Jesuit priest named Tomás de Guadalajara convinces Antonia to turn herself in to the authorities and to repent to the Holy Inquisition. She strategically confesses and offers profound and "sincere" repentance for her crimes, as it was known in that time period that those who repented of their own accord were often spared the severe punishment the Inquisition meted out for people who committed witchcraft or made pacts with the devil. By astutely deploying a Christian identity, she saves herself from an even more dire fate. After her confession is taken—she offers it twice, because the first friar does not "absolve" her—she is returned to her master, who, as it turns out, will no longer have her (he probably deems her to be far too much trouble). Her story comes to a close when she is sold off to a captain and the paper trail abruptly ends.

The salient motifs of the devil that appear in the poem of "La Mulata de Córdoba" and in this Inquisition account underscore that accusations made against others (and even oneself) for making pacts with the devil were, in fact, commonplace at the time, as were appeals made to the devil during beatings. Apparently slaves would often renounce God and invoke the devil during a beating because this act would technically oblige the owner to stop the punishment and turn the blasphemer over to the Inquisition. At this time the slave could then file her own complaint against the master (Deeds 104). This strategy to interrupt a painful punishment is ironically double-edged, as it signals an act of subversion on behalf of the aggrieved slave, but also compounds the association of blacks with malefic witchcraft in the minds of the colonial masters.

There did exist, nonetheless, a blurry line between what constituted black magic, complicity with the devil, and folk medicinal practices. The ambivalence surrounding the practices of traditional medicine, *curanderismo* and *hechichería* is brought into sharp relief with a case Bristol refers to that was documented in 1696 (but occurred five years earlier). In this case a Spanish woman named Doña Sebastiana Martínez de Castrejón claims her mulata slave, Dorotea, used black magic against her in retaliation for a beating. Doña Sebastiana testifies that after punishing Dorotea, the latter immediately retaliated by picking up an ant and rubbing it between her fingers, at which time, Doña Sebastiana felt a shooting pain throughout her body and welts began to appear on her flesh. What is supremely insightful in this case is that she solicited the help of two mulata curers who applied ointments to her body as they invoked the name of Santa Teresa (17). Here we see the irony of a complex social, cultural, political, and spiritual situation: Spaniards and white criollos have to defer to the medicinal and spiritual help of the colonies' non-whites in order to counteract the "black" magic of the very slaves who retaliate against the beatings their masters mete out as punishment for their insubordination as in this instance, or who try to improve their lives (as evidenced in the case by the priest Tomás Cárdenas's against the slave Juana for mentally coercing her owner). However, this case takes place in Guanajuato, quite a distance from the northern frontier where Antonia de Soto was roaming. As previously discussed, what was interpreted as "witchcraft" versus what was considered a "medical" practice operated on an ambivalent, and sometimes arbitrary continuum. In effect, there existed a tenuous difference between curing and witchcraft, and varying levels of both were not only permitted but also operated in conjunction with each other. This is evident in the invocation of Santa Teresa's name in the application of the ointments by the two mulata curers in the case waged by Doña Sebastiana against her rebellious slave. Bristol claims that medicinal powders and herbs often treated not only the physical ailment but also the supernatural cause; thus, physiological ailments could be treated "legitimately" despite the supernatural etiology of the illness. Moreover, we should bear in mind that all three groups—Iberians, Mesoamericans, and West and West Central Africans—believed in the nefarious and beneficial possibilities of human and supernatural intervention (7). Because folk medicine and spirituality, or what the colonial elites might deem witchcraft, were so intertwined, "witchcraft" could include activities that ran the gamut from demonic involvement and divination to folk medicines. This resulted in somewhat arbitrary assessments by individual inquisitors, "who interpreted cases and issued edicts" to determine what was considered acceptable "medical" practice or not (10).

Even contemporary ethnographers and anthropologists do not maintain clean divisions between what is considered traditional healing, a spiritual practice, witchcraft, or indigenous philosophy. James W. Dow avers that the term "shaman," for example, is hardly precise: for contemporary indigenous groups, there may exist magical and non-magical healers, and some who employ elements of both (66). A shaman might use herbal medicines in a magical treatment, where the practitioner leads the patient to consider the herbs as an instrument in the magical solution (66–67). Therefore Dow concludes that there exists a distinct epistemological bias on behalf of the individual ethnographer, and the fact that different ethnographers can represent the same ritual or belief system in radically different terms is "an artifact of ethnographic style" (68).

Furthermore, witchcraft or *curanderismo* was not uncommon in Europe either. In fact, Díaz Balsera reminds us that medieval Europeans commonly resorted to alternative healers, *curanderos* and the like. Besides obvious differences in time and place, what makes the context different in seventeenth-century México is that the *curanderos*, *hechiceros*, and *chamanes* operated within an established tradition of healing and witchcraft, to which they only inserted new figures from the Christian pantheon, the technology of writing and other modifications, such as African-derived knowledge, healing practices, and spells (160). The component of writing is important given that the notion of a *firma* or signing of a pact becomes part of the mythology surrounding witchcraft. It was common in this time period that Satan employ a " 'Devil's letter,' a written contract or statement of Satan's intention to dispatch eminent demons to counsel and assist evildoers" (Reff 77).

"Black" Magic and the White Devil

A repertoire of tropes exists regarding the apparition of the devil as well as his disguise in colonial México. Stemming from the late medieval and counter-reformation period, a recurrent iconographic image was "a black man, who, at times, had saucerlike eyes that glowed or shot fire" (76). In the northern region of the viceroyalty, these images were summoned by Tepehuan indigenous informants who reported to Spanish authorities, as in the case of the Tepehuan rebellion of 1616, where these exact images were employed by two indigenous men who were caught ferrying messages at the beginning of the rebellion (68). In order to explain the causes for rebellions, such as the Tepehuan revolts of 1616, rather than look inwardly at the infrastructure of colonial and spiritual violence "the missionaries consciously tried to shift the blame for the revolts from themselves to a third party by indicting Satan" (64). Indeed, we see that the Tepehuan groups with whom Antonia de Soto not only mingled, but actually lived, were well-versed in the late medieval Christian iconography that invoked the pervasive fear of the devil's meddling in human affairs, as "[t]he idea that no Christian was safe from Satan's machinations was part of the cultural baggage the Spaniards brought to the New World" (65).

These tropes of the black devil, however, do not appear in this Inquisition text or in the legend of the Mulata de Córdoba. In these cases, the devil appears as a dashing white man, who bears an uncanny resemblance to the masks featuring a Spaniard, or "catrín," with a dastardly countenance and striking blue eyes. In both the legend of the Mulata de Córdoba and this real Inquisition case, reference is made to a man in a black cloak. The Mulata de Córdoba, makes no mention of him being a black man, only that he is dressed in black. Furthermore, she reveres an "image" that she calls "her father" (recall that her father was supposed to have been a Spaniard, or could simply be a reverential term). In Antonia's case, the document makes an explicit point of stating that she is not given a *prenda* [fetish or object-charm], but rather, makes a promise to a *white* man, or *demonio* "dressed in black." This reminds us that blacks in México often sincerely, or strategically, appropriated a Christian identity and displayed a strong knowledge of Christian iconography and spiritual practices, and were consequently able to deploy them to their advantage. In the cases under consideration the men who represent the devil bear an important resemblance to their colonial oppressors.

Thus, Antonia is beholden to a dashing white man dressed in black who promises her freedom if she "will be his." This deal with the devil turns her into a skilled horse(wo)man, gambler, bullfighter, and bandit. Her physical prowess is so developed that she overpowers her indigenous consort, Matías, and practically kills him in the altercation, leaving him for dead. She tracks and kills a man who stole her booty from a raid, in addition to at least two other men. Despite dressing as a man in order to roam freely, she does, nonetheless, seem to identify as a woman in several key moments of the text. Moreover, it is in her capacity as a sexually alluring woman that she is courted by the devil. The following description from the document details the seduction of Antonia by the demon after an application of hallucinogenic drugs on her body:

> Dijo que un dia que se habia untado las coinunturas de su cuerpo
> con peiote, y lechugilla, se le aparecio el Demonio en figura de
> hombre blanco vestido de negro, y con golilla, y la empeso a alagar
> el rostro, y hacerle amores, y le dijo que si queria ser suya; a que
> le respondio esta declarante, que si=Preguntada si le dio palabras

de ello, dijo que si, pero que no le dio ningun papel, ni prenda. Preguntada si en alguna ocacion le habia vuelto a decir el Demonio, o el hombre en su figura, que le cumpliesse la palabra suya, dijo que si, que en una ocacion se le avia buelto a aparecer en figura como antes, y le habia dicho, que le cumpliesse la palabra a lo qual respondio esta declarante que ella se la cumpliria con condicion que no la dejasse bolber a casa de sus amos, a que el Demonio le dijo, sea en hora buena; y que esto le sucedio en el Parral.

[She said that one day after she had rubbed the joints of her body with peyote and herbs, a Demon appeared to her as a white man dressed in black, and with a smart hat, and began to compliment her pretty face, and seduce her, and he asked her if she wanted to be his; to which this deponent responded yes= Asked if she was given a verbal affirmation, she said yes, but that she was not given any paper or fetish. Asked if on any occasion the Demon, or the man in his figure, had returned to demand that she keep her word, she said yes, that on one occasion he had returned in the same figure as before, and he demanded she keep her word, to which this deponent declared that she would keep it on the condition that he not allow Antonia to be returned to her master's house, to which the Demon responded, let it be thus; and this took place in Parral]. (AGN, Vol. 525, exp. 48, 1693)

In addition to the pact we witness a seduction: a sexual provocation by the white man who compliments her beauty and asks if she would be "his." As in the example of the Mulata de Córdoba and so many other literary texts involving mulatas, we see the lasciviousness of a white man—corrupted in this case because he is the devil himself—inciting sinful behavior in the adolescent mulata. Despite denying sexual involvement with the men with whom she is associated (including Matías and his brother), she does indeed admit to falling prey to the devil's advances in exchange for her continued freedom.

This description of the invocation of the devil, his appearance, and the pact that was made between the two is multivalent and complex because some elements demonstrate a clearly Christian notion of sin, as is evidenced by the idea of a sexual seduction and pact with the devil (although it was not ratified through the exchange of a document, or what might be interpreted as a contract or letter), while other elements of the pact appear to reflect non-European cultural and spiritual references. For example, the use of peyote was an indigenous practice, and besides being a hallucinogenic ritual plant referring to a sacred deity, it was considered an aphrodisiac, although Aguirre Beltrán claims there is no pharmacological basis for this and that it is purely a mystical belief. Nonetheless, among indigenous groups such as Tepehuanes or other Chichimeca peoples, it was perceived to create an irresistible sexual allure. Another example of non-European influence is the apparition of the demon in multiple forms and guises. In this case he first appears as a well-dressed white man, but he also incorporates as a *sombra* [shadow or vital force] or a voice, and at others as a growling bear.[32] Antonia claims to have seen the devil at one point manifest as a *sombra*, and that the *sombra* then materialized into the body of a man. These manifestations as a *sombra* and bear are fascinating insofar as they refer to *nagualismo*, an important and widespread spiritual and cultural belief amongst Nahuas and many indigenous groups across Mesoamerica. According to this belief and practice, people have an animal essence or counterpart that can roam outside of the human body. In turn, the notion of a *sombra* as a vital force, or component of the soul, is primordial in African-descended thought systems as well as Mesoamerican ones. These multiple demonic entities incarnated in a white devil, a shadow, and bear highlight the point made by Deeds regarding the level of cultural and spiritual mixing among blacks, mulatos, indigenous groups, and mestizos. In fact, Deeds claims that the presence of a mulata runaway slave garnered little attention at the mission where she stayed after her initial escape. Moreover, help from a magical potion provided by mestiza Juana Golpazos allowed her to become invisible to the man who arrived in her pursuit. The document says that "he did not see her" although she spoke directly to him.

I find this point crucial in the case of Antonia de Soto, as her particular account reveals that there was a cultural and spiritual cohabitation as well as a rebellious cooperation between indigenous groups, blacks, and mixed-race people. Picking up on Aguirre Beltrán's cues, Bristol argues that many colonial medicinal practices remit directly to Afro-Mexican beliefs, "such as ancestor veneration, ideas about the vital force (the shade or *sombra*), divination practices involving ventriloquism, and mystical possession" (5). Bristol references a case in which a mulato practitioner put sticks in water in the form of a cross in order to identify a thief, and she points to the ubiquitous use of amulets as belonging to all three traditions: in the Congo, ritual specialists used "minkisi" or protective amulets, in West Central Africa pregnant women wore amulets with animal hair, feathers, and claws to influence qualities in unborn children, Christians wore scapulars, and Nahua priests carry bundles with the power of certain gods (5).

Despite Aguirre Beltrán's contention that the *sombra* and other beliefs were a product of Afro-Mexican thought, scholars such as Alfredo López Austin argue that they are of indigenous origin. He denies that the African notion of the *sombra* could have influenced indigenous metaphysics as the beliefs regarding vital energy are widespread and constitute the heart of Mesoamerican thought both before and after the conquest: "It is in perfect harmony with the rest of the elements of ancient indigenous conceptual systems; there are coincidences between the belief in question and others that are manifestly native" (228–29). The *sombra* and vital force (or *tonalli*) that López Austin describes is a predominant belief among Mesoamericans (Jill Furst calls it a "body-double"), as is ancestor veneration. Huicholes believe that the revered shaman actually becomes manifest in stones and mountains during life as well as after death. For the Africans taken to New Spain, similar animistic ideas regarding a vital force and ancestor veneration must have resonated strongly.

We should remember that the relative absence of indigenous groups in the inquisitorial records is attributable to Indians being exempt from prosecution due to their neophyte status. Even so, they often appear as witnesses or, as in this case, accomplices. Some scholars like Laura Lewis, however, claim that Indians actually provided most of the recipes for the sorcery used by Afro-Mexicans. Regardless of origin, these accounts bear testament to how these groups worked together, particularly in the backlands of the northern frontier. In her multiple travels and encounters, Antonia shares these spells, stones, and charms with various people she meets along the way. At one moment she exchanges them with an Apache man, and at another she shares her magic with an unnamed mulato slave. I believe there are striking correspondences between the two traditions that resonated both with Afro-Mexicans and indigenous groups. What seems most likely is that the beliefs and rituals that became prominent and widely practiced were precisely those that were easily assimilated by the diverse groups of blacks, Indians, and mixed-race people who came into contact with each other.

Another interesting point that merits further attention is that in Antonia's transcript it is reiterated that she was *not* given a *prenda*. *Prendas* are fetishes, charms, and ritual objects that can be traced back to African practices from the Congo basin and have different meanings and usages across the Caribbean and Latin America. In México, the importation of slaves in the early part of the seventeenth century almost doubled the entire number of slaves brought in the whole of the sixteenth century, when slavers began to procure more of their victims from the Congo. Alongside the emergence of *cofradías* [brotherhoods], a diverse social and cultural network of slaves began to appropriate the ethnic designations they were assigned by Europeans who classified them according to the port city that was their point of embarkation before arriving to the Americas (6). Bennett explains that names such as "Terra Nova" (Lucumi or Yoruba in other places) and "black from Congo" became important ethnic signifiers that proliferated as "ethnic tropes" by which masters identified *bozales*,[33] who in turn appropriated the designations to identify themselves to the ecclesiastical scribes who registered their marriages and other important cultural events (98). As a result, the large number of slaves imported from the Congo who accepted these designations facilitated the creation of filial networks.

Prendas, which are also known as *ngangas*, or *enquisos* (from *nkisi* or the plural which is *minkisi*) in Cuba, are items such as grave dirt, animal and human remains collected in a cauldron or pot and invested with a sacred power to summon the dead in both supernatural and corporeal form.[34] In exchange for the gifts and reverences, they operate in the benefit of their keeper. Each is unique to the individual person who has invested it with power, and as explained by Nathaniel Murray, initiates receive their *nganga* from a previously existing one (150). This is not a relationship of domination, and once entering into it, the spirit expects to be fed and admired, and "can adopt personal mannerisms: it can be flattered, petitioned, actuated, insulted and humiliated" (150). There is "a general understanding that the spirit will be helpful, or will 'work' for the palero in some unique ways" (150).[35] Murray claims that in the African Congo the *nkisi* were "object-charms [. . .] that practitioners held sacrosanct because they were charged with spiritual power for defense" (118). Indeed, these *prendas-ngangas-enquisos* exact obeisance and attention, but in return will intercede on behalf of their keepers. Lydia Cabrera conducted extensive fieldwork in Cuba, and in her seminal work, *El monte*, reveals that a common element in all of these objects is the presence of a stone, or "matari": "de preferencia una piedra de rayo o de centella, a la que se da sangre por separado" [a striped stone, that has to be fed blood separately] (118).

This case sheds light on the diverse, yet at times minute ways in which Afro-Mexicans might have contributed to the magical and epistemological milieu of the time, for example, through the use of amulets, *nkisi*, or *prendas*. Taking into account the manner in which the possession and practice of the *prenda* was deployed both in the Congo as well as in Cuba, there seem to be important resonances that I cannot help but underscore for their possible usages in México. Antonia is given three magical stones, and when dipped into water one turns from black to green, acquiring a downy film, and they all begin to foam. The Tepehuan Matías imbibes the water that the stones are bathed in, and the foam they exude is used to anoint Antonia's body. Similarly, Cabrera describes a scene told to her by an historian who procured the help of a "congo muy viejo" [very old black man] who gave him a medal as a protective amulet. In the interview he states that the older black palero begins to foam at the mouth after a spell, "Se sentó a mi lado, frente a la calavera y a los palos; se inclinó sobre ellos murmurando en su lengua, y a poco lo vi agitarse y echar espuma por la boca" [He sat next to me in front of the skull and sticks; he leaned over them and murmured in his language, then right after I saw him become agitated and began foaming at the mouth] (124). When the historian goes back to return the amulet, the elder "congo" inquires about the amulet's location. As the historian shuffles through his pockets he sees that the medal has moved of its own accord; it is no longer in his pocket but appears in the palero's hand.

I would like to point out that, although not identical, there are parallels between these particular indigenous and African religions insofar as they make use of similar elements: the use of stones, magical language, transmutation, foaming (of the stone and of the palero's mouth), and either the ingestion or expulsion of a liquid substance. For example, in Antonia's account, Matías drinks the water the stone was bathed in, the stone acquires a thin down and then foams, and in Cabrera's account the old palero foams at the mouth as he utters something unintelligible to his client, but that clearly constitutes some sort of magical language. In the scene narrated by Antonia, magical language is important, as the words "achula" and "yumara" are pronounced as part of the spell, and are of utmost interest to the inquisitors. In contemporary Palo practices, chanting and song are integral ingredients for summoning the dead.[36] The stones are transmuted into a liquid substance, their mineral materiality transformed, and the palero's medal actually acquires its own subjectivity, moving of its own volition.

In his research on the practices of Palo and the specific usage of the *prenda*, Todd Ramón Ochoa disavows their "objecthood" and describes them as a force that imbues the living with the dead; they are of a porous materiality that exists outside of the tense distinction between subject and object. Both now, as in the past, the force of the *prenda* is beckoned to intervene on behalf of those who require healing, or who need to free themselves from some kind of debt: "But the transfers of force over which prendas preside are ambivalent and hold no easy formula for healing. Rather, they promise only disruptions of what has become inevitable" (410). Ochoa identifies the practice of *coartación* (a gradual self-purchase according to Rebecca Scott) as the problem that the *prendas* addressed in nineteenth century Cuba (404). In the case against Antonia, she enters into a pact with the demon, man, *sombra*, or voice and agrees to do his will if, in return, he will keep her owners from finding her. Furthermore, it is through this "transfer of force" that she is able to tame horses, flee from her pursuers, and develop an extraordinary physical strength that will allow her to challenge men at a time when roles for women were strictly defined. The "pact" she makes with this devil-man requires her attention; he inquires if she will comply with her promise and Antonia replies "yes." She and her companion Matías manipulate the stones which then come to life and "echan espuma." She frequently picks new magical flowers ("cacomites") and wears the stones, flowers, and peyote-filled amulets on her person. In the same way the *prenda* can be transferred or reborn for the patronage of another. She shares her stones, flowers and charms with others that need them, such as an Apache man and other indigenous people (who are not Tepehuanes). However, the magic does not always work. She tries to share them with another Indian named Pascual who ends up getting wounded by a bull. Subsequently, she retracts her recommendation. The belief in these magical flowers, stones, and amulets provided a way for people like Antonia to escape the marginalization imposed by a patriarchal, colonial and slave-holding regime. Ochoa claims that *prendas* were born in the context of debt; as a way to relieve oneself of an oppressive situation one made recourse to a *prenda*.

While distinct, the practice and use of the *prenda* in Cuba bears a compelling resemblance to the usage of these stones, flowers, and amulets in seventeenth-century México, and indeed, the idea of reciprocity as a relief for some sort of debt or hardship provides a convincing parallel for understanding the way they were interpreted and deployed at the time. In the end, Antonia's inquisitorial record states that she was not offered a *prenda*, however, I suggest that its invocation signals that it was a possible item in the pact with the "devil" (although its presence is denied). This brings to mind the salience of other components of witchcraft that she did exercise and were employed on her behalf, such as the stones, amulets, and magical language used by the Tepehuan and others. As mentioned, the Tepehuan also coexisted with the African slaves and Hispanicized mulatos, both in the mines and in the missions. As a result, it is more than likely that they exchanged ideas about magical rituals, and probably mutually enhanced previous spells or practices that were similar. Although the influx of Africans from the Congo intensified in the first few decades of the seventeenth century, I do not know if Antonia's progenitors were a product of this surge in the slave trade or if the slaves in her immediate milieu identified as Congos. However, what I am suggesting is that rather than make a discrete link to one or another magical tradition, we should consider the ways in which these diverse groups worked and dwelt together in a world marked by epistemological and cosmological plurality, and interpret this case as an example of how women, mestizos, diverse indigenous people, blacks, and mulatos developed networks that helped each other not only escape slavery, but also improve their position.

Algo De Simple[37]

> [D]e mi parecer acerca de el estado en que se halla Antonia de Soto, digo que me ha parecido tener algo de simple, por lo qual el demonio puede aver introducido enella facilmente tales operaciones.

> [In my opinion regarding the current state of Antonia de Soto, I say that she seems to be somewhat of a simpleton, such that the devil could have easily inducted her into his operations].

> —Joseph de Arcocha, AGN 1693

Why did Antonia de Soto repent and turn herself in when she had been living freely for over six years? Both Deeds and Lewis suggest that the imposition of a quasi-religious state and Spanish discourses of morality may have clenched her Christian conscience, inspiring her penitence. In light of the egregious nature of some of sins she had committed—such as the murder of at least three men—Antonia may have harbored real worries about the state of her soul, having internalized Christian morality (Lewis 172).[38] However, it is also true that she may have been at risk of someone else denouncing her, and she stood a better chance of getting a weak sentence if she demonstrated real and profound repentance for her act. This is a likely scenario given that the records reveal that few people were actually punished for complicity with the devil. I believe that the latter is more probable when considering that she went from being a common slave to an adventurer of sorts by the age of twenty precisely by utilizing magic and subverting church dogma in order to acquire the necessary "male" prowess to be liberated and to not only survive, but even thrive (Deeds 104). Hence she had to defy her Christian identity in order to redress her status as a slave and a woman. Lewis suggests that rather than illustrate the subversive nature of witchcraft, Antonia's cross-dressing banditry and use of magic ultimately operates within, and even reinforces, colonial institutions and discourse. I suggest that the cultural and spiritual practices throughout the colonial period that were violently intersecting, but also cross-pollinating, rend asunder what has become, even today, the privileged and manipulated use of mestizaje as a racial discourse, as well as the uncontested role of Mexican motherhood as the staple guideline for female behavior. Indeed, Antonia's desire to cross-dress in order to acquire a "manly" strength would allow her to exercise untold liberty. Even when operating within defined discourses of gender and race as underscored by Lewis, Antonia's case nonetheless points to epistemological resistance and simultaneous conformity; she and others moved in and out of competing and diverse cultural, spiritual, and epistemological spheres in ways that were beneficial to themselves.

The quote above taken from Antonia's document is by the inquisitor Fray Joseph de Arcocha, who states that he found her to be somewhat simple, and for this reason alone the devil could have easily utilized her to do his bidding. This is a problematic assessment of her competence given that it is highly unlikely that a simpleton could have eluded her master, escaped with an Indian, lived in a mining town and a Jesuit mission undiscovered, and once again elude those who came to recapture her. All this in addition to becoming a muleteer and fearless bandit who convinced the men with whom she worked and marauded that she was indeed a man—not to mention the various "masculine" activities she performed such as taking psychotropic drugs, taming horses, riding bulls, and transporting goods over long distances. It is remarkable that those who interviewed her were completely convinced by not only her repentance, but her helplessness: "al parecer que da con Verdad arrepentimiento, porque quando hizo su declaracion, luego que sele empezo a preguntar por el Ynterrogatorio empezo allorar copiosas lagrimas, y con el mismo dolor y arrepentimiento volbio en la ratificacion allorar" [it seems that she gave her confession with true repentance, because when she gave her declaration, after she began to respond to the interrogation, she began to weep copious tears, and with the same pain and repentance began to cry in the ratification].[39] Either he simply mistook her "copiosas lagrimas" for the innate flaws of a weak woman, or he tempered his words so that she might be spared a harsh penance. In fact, it is recommended that she be sold to a virtuous woman who might reinstruct her in the virtues of Christian life in order to avert any possibility of recidivism. She must have appeared completely harmless or dimwitted, or simply have put on a superb show for such a suggestion to even be registered: a violent, cross-dressing bandit under the supervision of an elderly *beata* [pious church-goer] seems almost absurd.

Life for women in this region in general could be particularly dangerous as it stood at the crossroads of trading and marauding indigenous groups such as the rebellious Chichimecas (a term that was often applied indiscriminately to diverse nomadic or semi-sedentary indigenous groups), and the fearless "Toboso" (one of eleven different groups of hostile Indians that were given this name). The Toboso dominated the ranges and mountains east of the Camino Real that extended from Cuencamé, Durango, to Hidalgo del Parral in Chihuahua, which constituted a large north-south stretch of land that was almost lawless. They were known to raid parties of travelers going to and from Guadiana, Zacatecas, and Hidalgo de Parral by way of the most easterly route (Pennington 12). Consequently, women were frequently taken captive as forced labor, slaves, or as members of the tribe for the reproductive possibilities they provided in the preservation of kinships (Deeds 103). In any event, the relative freedom (or lawlessness, however you choose to interpret it) of the northern frontier changed in the eighteenth century when Spanish rule pushed harder as a result of the increase of the non-Indian population, and a harsh patriarchy supplanted the unruliness that had become a *modus vivendi* of the region (114). A lachrymose, repentant woman could hardly have survived, let alone flourished, in an environment as rough as this, thus casting doubt on both the motive behind Antonia's repentance and portrayal as a simpleton.

Despite the reduction of this brave woman's transgression to a tearful idiocy, this case bears testament to how this mulata slave walked in and out of radically divergent identities: a slave, *cimarrona*, free mulata woman, Indian, transgender person, man, sinner, bandit, practitioner of indigenous and African witchcraft, and repentant Christian woman. Although she began her life as a mulata female slave she learned to live among diverse indigenous and mestizo communities by participating in their cultural practices, ingesting their "magical" drugs and existing within the confines of their, and her own, conceptual systems. Indeed, the fact that a Tepehuan Indian and a mestiza collaborated in her escape from bondage proves that she formed part of a diverse, transculturated society even before she took flight. That is to say, her epistemological and spiritual universe had multiple and diverse influences: a medieval Spanish Catholic consciousness, an African cosmology in addition to indigenous medicinal practices and witchcraft. It is difficult to discretely identify which of the practices and beliefs she learned from her indigenous and mestizo peers, and which ones were derived from African spiritual systems, in part because she seems to blame the indigenous peers for the witchcraft she exercised, which may have been strategic since they were mostly immune to the persecutions of the Inquisition. The authorities were, however, using her testimony to mount a case against Juana Golpazos, the mestiza woman who first provided her access to the magic that would make her invisible to her pursuers. Furthermore, so many of the magical practices and cosmological beliefs resonate strongly with each other: the belief in the *sombra* in African thought and the *tonalli* or *sombra* for Mesoamericans in addition to the magical language in the performance of spells, for example, the *nahualtocaitl* for Nahuas or the chants and incantations in Afro-descended rituals still practiced in Cuban religions such as Palo.

In the end, the tropes linking blackness to witchcraft, mesmerism, and pacts with the devil proliferate in the colonial imaginary of the sixteenth and seventeenth centuries, and continue up until the twentieth century, when legends like la Mulata de Córdoba found in poetry, opera, and film continue to represent the contours and limits of the black female presence in México. As noted by Deeds, the marginal people that Antonia encountered both as a slave woman and as a free man all mutually participated in this "world of syncretic magic," and "the folk practices of diverse racial groups often intersected and brought Indians, mestizos, mulattos and Spaniards into close contact" (104, 105). While the Mulata de Córdoba disappears into a cloud of smoke and is eliminated as a provocative nuisance, Antonia, no longer a criminal, disappears from the record once she is recaptured. Despite her astute maneuvering within a region plagued by arbitrary laws and mutable frontiers, in addition to her fantastic feats as a runaway slave and fearless bandit, this Afro-Mexican woman ends up enslaved once again and is partially forgiven by the Church authorities because they see her as a lachrymose moron. Perhaps her "copious tears" were dissimulating an ironic wink, however, she is not, nor is she likely to ever become, a hero/ine or icon of Mexican womanhood. Black women exist as exotic exceptions, invisible in spite of their presence in the Inquisition records and their paradoxical recuperation by the arts.

5

"Dios pinta como quiere"

Blackness and Redress in Mexican Golden Age Film

This popular saying, translated as "God paints as he pleases," refers to a phrase common in México, but especially prevalent in a small town in central Veracruz named Coyolillo. In his article "Dios pinta como quiere," anthropologist Alfredo Martínez Maranto claims that in Coyolillo at least 50 percent of the inhabitants show phenotypical signs of African ancestry.[1] While Coyoleños identify themselves as racially different from other communities in the region, they do not consider their community as having descended from any African heritage. Rather, this expression seems to explain their blackness away as an almost arbitrary act of God. Nonetheless, a few of the people interviewed attribute their African features to the ambiguous and almost mythical migration of "Cubans" after the Mexican Revolution (Martínez Maranto 531). As a result, among the various racial appellatives that describe dark-skinned Coyoleños, "cubano" is one of the many racial taxonomies—such as *prieto, moreno, trigueño*—that define blackness.[2] It is paradoxical then that this town is considered one of the exemplary cases of Afro-Mexican culture, and has since been all but invaded by anthropologists and historians. Furthermore, it is emblematic of México's relationship to blackness: even in its most obvious cases, there is a tacit, albeit misinformed acknowledgment of Africanness that is overshadowed by a revolutionary rhetoric proclaiming the mestizo as the natural synthesis of centuries of colonization and oppression. The mestizo became the representative of the nation, both to itself and abroad.

The first important Mexican film to feature a strong mulata character was *La Mulata de Córdoba* directed by Adolfo Fernández Bustamante in 1945, with the screenplay authored by Xavier Villaurrutia.[3] Loosely inspired by the colonial legend analyzed in the previous chapter, it triangulates the racial panic evident in nineteenth-century drama with the exotic fetish of the *rumbera* film into a lesson on racial inequity and tragedy.[4] The film is set in a small village in Veracruz called Rincon del Brujo (the Witches' Corner), home to a seductive black woman who catches the plantation owner's eye. As the titles roll, the camera pans across the horizon with images of coconut and palm trees to establish the place as what can only be described as a tropical paradise. The scene then opens to an outdoor dance—a rumba in honor of the seductive black woman named María Belén. Toña la Negra, whom I will discuss at length in the following chapter, sings the opening song, but does not play the part of the enticing mulata but rather that of the soulful *nana.* The film cuts to an extreme close-up of black hands beating the bongos, a common visual trope in many *rumbera* films throughout this period. However, when the sequence ends, the music transitions from an Afro-Caribbean inspired dance to a number featuring *son jarocho,* a genre traditional to the region of Veracruz (and only recently reclaimed as an Afro-Mexican musical form). The abrupt musical change serves as a sonic counterpoint that firmly juxtaposes blackness and Mexicaness, unlike the other films we will examine in this chapter.

The mulata, who is the orphaned progeny of the plantation owner and the seductive black Belén, is presented early on in the film reclined in a hammock while stroking her favorite cat. Even while laying sensually in a hammock, the "corpo-mulata," as discussed by Melissa Blanco Borelli, is not indolent, but rather "actively labors by problematizing how definitions of beauty and purity affect [her] interpellation and how the machinations of history amplify said interpellation" (218). We witness then, the juxtaposition between a languid white mulata body and the industry of the black mulata mother, servant, and *nana,* and we see that, even when "God paints as he pleases," the beauty of the former is constituted by this very otherness, and by the tension it generates in the spaces she fills and the lines she crosses. As evidenced in the legend of the Mulata de Córdoba, and repeated *ad infinitum* with mulata characters, her irresistible allure attracts all the white eligible men and wreaks havoc for upper-class elite families.

Indeed, the mulata body labors as the battleground for colonial fetish, new transculturated identities, contested whiteness, and a mythical blackness. Her body constantly provokes violence: between families, among lovers, and onto children desiring redress. Thus we see that the listless tropicalized body, despite the fantasy it invokes, cannot untangle itself from the very real anxiety invoked by its unwanted introduction into private and public places. The mulata figure's body labors for revenge, but also seeks to accommodate the privilege her whiteness affords her subjectivity and social rank. In different ways, these films will each address the tragedy of mulata bodies, both white and "cinnamon"—painted according to God's will—but do not seek to fill any historical vacuum. Rather, they appropriate this racial tension as a mechanism for subverting real discussion about racial privilege in México.

This chapter continues the analysis begun in the previous one by critically engaging the figure of the mulata as an embodied trope within the context of Mexican cultural production and history of the first half of the twentieth century, by comparison to the figuration within abolitionist fiction from the early nineteenth century Caribbean and United States, where the figure of "tragic mulatta" furthered the aim of highlighting the evil nature of slavery and the politics that legitimized it in the polarized United States South. As such, in this latter context, the mulatta became a stock character through which both abolitionists and anti-abolitionists dramatized the politics of race and its untenable oppositions. As Eve Allegra Raimon wrote in her book *The Tragic Mulatta Revisited*, in the United States the mulatta "functions as a device to investigate what place mixed-race persons are going to occupy in the new republic and indeed whether the Union itself can survive such profound divisions in race" (5). The embodiment of a tragic liminal state, she is usually portrayed as an educated, almost white, martyr because as Raimon noted further, "[t]he sexual vulnerability of a female light-skinned slave is essential to propel the plot forward and to generate the reader's sympathy and outrage" (5). Her tragic nature clearly reveals the ultimate fate of this figure, and thus expresses a prevailing view regarding the limits of racial reconciliation. Moreover, mulatto figures are often depicted as depraved; even when a kind benefactor incorporates them into mainstream white society, their black blood comes back to haunt them and their vile behavior sabotages both themselves and their race.

In the years since the early nineteenth century, African-American writers have attempted to resurrect this fraught figure of United States and Caribbean abolitionist literature by pointing to her racial hybridity as a quintessentially American attribute that casts doubt on racial purity, and more importantly, on the construct of a hegemonic whiteness. Bearing in mind the prevailing construct of the "tragic mulatta" as a narrative and filmic device, I explore the portrayal of blackness in Mexican arts by unraveling the contradictions inherent to the literary and cinematic projects that inform a selection of key works produced during the effervescence of México's Golden Era of cinema, and discuss how each signaled the aporetic status of México's black history through the figuration of the tragic mulatta. Beginning with a close reading of the 1944 novel, *La negra Angustias*, and its adaptation to film, released five years later, I proceed to a consideration of common themes linking them to the aforementioned *La Mulata de Córdoba* (1945), and to two additional films of the immediate period: *Angelitos negros* (1948) and *Negro es mi color* (1951). In a span of six years, four films were made that signaled the painful aporetic status of México's black history.

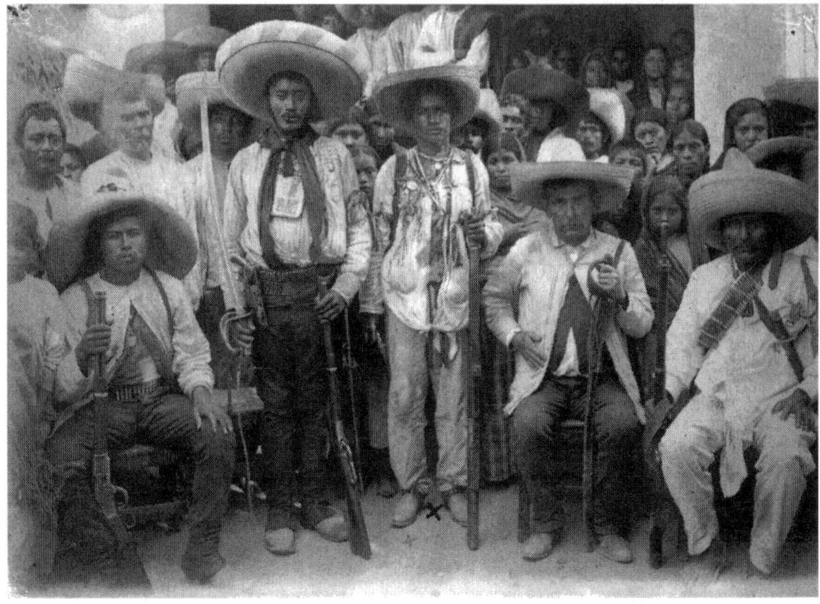

FIGURE 5.1. "Revolutionaries and soldadera in front of a home," México, 1914.

Exceptional Blackness: *La negra Angustias*

The Mexican Revolution of 1910 was arguably one of the most important peasant uprisings of the twentieth century, and as we examined in the first part of this book, it was fundamentally impacted by the participation of women in breathtaking numbers. The above image, although titled "Portrait of revolutionary soldiers and soldadera in front of a home" by the Mexican National Archive of Photography, or Fototeca, is differently identified by John Mraz as a portrait of Carmen Robles, an Afro-Mexican Zapatista Coronela from Guerrero, pictured in the center with fellow soldiers after the battle of Iguala in May 1911 (*Photographing the Mexican Revolution* 118). Basing his conclusion on an inscription written on the photograph that was featured on the cover of the Mexican news magazine *Proceso* in 2009, Mraz provides two different dates—1911 and 1913—while the Fototeca put 1914 in the caption I observed, leading to a total of three different dates attempting to situate this photograph in a specific historical moment. Agustín and Gustavo Casasola likewise identify the image as, "The Valiant Revolutionary Carmen Robles and Her Chief Officers after the Take of Iguala, Guerrero" in *Historia Gráfica de la Revolución* (750). Furthermore, if the current caption by the Fototeca is indeed correct, and if also she is in fact Carmen Robles, then the woman in the center of this image is the same woman who is on the cover of this book. Yet again, we see that the identities of women—both soldaderas and mulatas—have been obscured through misnaming, resulting in an historical odyssey of discovery, neglect, and recovery. As was the case with the image of the soldaderas boarding the train I analyzed in chapter 1, locating the specific name and date of this photograph does little to change the overall indexicality of the image; with or without a name it registers the fact that women played active roles in the Revolution, and despite the mythologizing or disappearing of their figures, were nonetheless *there*. That the captions accompanying their images would result in a long history of conjecture and palimpsest further illustrates the violence committed against their memory, but it does not invalidate their evidentiary quality.

The shadow of the Revolution altered the trajectory of Mexican cultural production, even generating its own literary genre: the novels of the Revolution. *La negra Angustias*, written by Francisco Rojas González in 1944 and awarded the National Literature Prize the same year, is not, despite the prestigious award, one of the hallmark novels of the Revolution. It does not rouse the same critical attention as Mariano Azuela's touchstone novel *Los de abajo* [The Underdogs] (1915), or *El águila y la serpiente* [The Eagle and the Serpent] (1928) by Martín Luís Guzmán and is generally not included in the bibliographies of Mexican literature courses. According to many accounts, this remarkable story of a black *coronela* of the Zapatista army, who fights for justice for the poor and rural peasantry and also deplores the violence enacted upon women, is based on the story of a real revolutionary colonel of the same name—Remedios Farrera—of whose actual life little is certain except that she hailed from the southern state of Guerrero. Anna Macías, in her landmark book on women in the Revolution, *Against All Odds*, claims that Rojas González based his character on the real Remedios Farrera, who, in turn, bore striking resemblances to María de la Luz Espinosa Barrera (La Coronela de Yautepec), given how both rose to the rank of colonel, were orphaned, and raised goats (42).

Aside from being a novelist and short-story writer, Rojas González was trained in ethnography and collaborated on several books about indigenous culture. Furthermore, he wrote another novel, *Lola Casanova* (1947), which similarly showcases a strong female protagonist whose story is based on the legend of a white woman taken captive by the Seris (an indigenous group from Northern México), how she acculturated into Seri society and subsequently rose to power. *La negra Angustias* is exceptional due to its powerful mulata heroine, and yet, paradoxically typical in its representation of blackness, ultimately relying on hackneyed tropes of victimization and mulato perversion. In order to illustrate how blackness is figured in the novel by Francisco Rojas

González and the eponymous film directed by Matilde Landeta five years later, I examine a few salient moments in which the representations of race are crucial to advancing the plot. Blackness is figured in the novel and film (both negatively and positively) through the deployment of classic tropes like that of the Amazon woman. Furthermore, the female protagonist and the community in which she is raised display a keen awareness of racial difference. Elizabeth Salas reports that the historical Angustias (or Remedios) was reputed to be a valiant colonel who was foul-mouthed and crass.[5] The choice to present the protagonist simultaneously as a pitiable victim and depraved seductress highlights the impulse on behalf of the novelist to favor the portrayal of the sexually provocative yet victimized mulata, rather than focus on her as a "butch" military hero like the real Angustias was rumored to be. In turn, the feminist gesture of Landeta's film chooses to focus on her military prowess by truncating the storyline presented in the novel, strategically cutting out the end where Angustias succumbs to the white teacher and the fire of maternity (not unlike many of the soldadera narratives). Despite this critical consciousness, Landeta paradoxically has the actress wear skirts for most of film instead of the trousers worn in the novel and witnessed in many of the photographs of female military engagement. We will see, then, that both the novel and film adaptation traffic in blatant stereotypes that tangle gender and race at the same time they almost unwittingly celebrate the role of blacks and women in the making of the most important historical movement of the last century in México.

Cedric Robinson and Luz María Cabral, in their 2003 article, "The Mulatta in Film: From Hollywood to the Mexican Revolution," compare North American filmic representations of mulattas with those of Mexican cinema, and claim that in both the novel and the film versions of *La negra Angustias*, blackness gets lost in the rhetoric of Mexican nationalism and class struggle (16). Indeed, the protagonist's mixed-race identity is submerged in the post-revolutionary quest to craft a cohesive Mexican national identity and the five-hundred-year struggle over agrarian reform. However, the powerful rhetoric of mestizaje espoused by Mexican officials did not only affect Afro-Mexicans by flattening regional and racial identities; it also impacted indigenous communities through the creation of the National Indigenous Institute (INI) in 1948, which initiated a number of social programs of cultural and linguistic assimilation for indigenous peoples that were only dismantled in 2003.[6] Nonetheless, an attentive reading of the novel and the movie reveals striking evidence to the contrary: blackness *is* figured prominently in the novel and the film, but it becomes quickly disfigured by its inevitable framing according to racist stereotypes as well as its subordination to class struggle. In both versions of *La negra Angustias*, blackness becomes mired in revolutionary disenchantment and the filmmaker's privilege of a more feminist perspective. It is clear that neither novelist nor director considered blacks an important component of the social fabric. In an interview with Luz Cabral, director Matilde Landeta claimed that the contributions made by blacks to Mexican history and culture were insignificant, even despite her having chosen to make a feature film about a black Mexican. This "insignificance" is borne out by Landeta's casting of a non-black actress who wore blackface for the part. In fact, Eli Bartra references another interview where Landeta recalls her meeting with the real Angustias, and comments that she "is dark, dark, but not that she was black" ("How Black is La Negra Angustias?" 282). Other female artists and writers in Latin America have been charged with subordinating race to gender equality: feminists Rosario Castellanos (México) and Clorinda Matto de Turner (Perú) have been criticized for their treatment of indigenous subjects, and Gertrudis Gómez de Avellaneda for her treatment of blacks (Cuba). Regardless of the author's or director's intentions, what makes the display of blackness different in this novel and film is that, unlike the classic "tragic mulatta" genre, neither one dramatizes a mixed-race figure who "serves as a chiaroscuro through which the tragedy of slavery is sentimentally experienced by white readers" (2). Neither does the novel or film make reference to a community but to an extraordinary mulata individual.

Not unlike the now almost famous portrait of the Afro-Mexican soldadera/coronela, *La negra Angustias* operates like an interesting metonymy that parallels the state of black consciousness in México: although Africans have been in México since the conquest, they are often regarded as anomalous coastal communities that are either leftover from the colonial era or descendants of shipwrecked Africans.[7] With regard to the constitution of racial difference in México, Robinson and Cabral write that "[p]aradoxically, this lacuna in awareness has enabled the creation of a female Black character who is allowed a full agency and range of emotion and activity that, hitherto, most Black filmic representations had been denied" (17). They argue that it is ultimately Angustias Farrera's muted relationship to blackness that allows for her to become so powerful, contrary to U.S. depictions of mulattas. Subsequently, this tenuous relationship to race, in Landeta's rendition, allows for her to relinquish her quest for self-fulfillment as a black woman slighted by her community and accosted by predatory men in order to continue her fight for justice within the imaginary of Zapatista revolutionary ideals. I contend, however, that it is the protagonist's personal awareness of her blackness in critical moments of both texts that creates the conditions for the fulfillment of her subjectivity, and the possibility of her participating as a military actor in the Revolution. For example, the appropriation of her black father's legacy through the history provided by the corrido legitimates her place as an agent of revolutionary justice. The individuality and subjectivity that facilitate this participation are predicated upon the acceptance of her black body and her pride in the legacy of her father.

Alongside the nascent power of Angustias as a revolutionary woman, we witness the insidious characterizations of the mulata that subvert the agency of the Angustias character at the same time, such as the trope of hyper-sexualization and that of the Amazon, in each case a process analogous to the representations of mulattas in the Caribbean and the United States South. As in the legend of the Mulata de Córdoba and the case of Antonia de Soto, this hyper-sexualization of mulata figures is not new to México, although the cinematic rendition one encounters in *La negra Angustias* seems to bear the influence of the North American movie industry. As a filmmaker, Landeta must have been familiar with popular movies that portrayed mulattos (such as D. W. Griffith's *Birth of a Nation*) because the critical moments in which she engages race parallel the representation of race relations in the United States. This similarity may be pertinent since Landeta herself seemed to have no knowledge of the presence and impact of Africans and their descendants in México. Contrary to Robinson and Cabral's assertion that the legacy of the opprobrious mulatta was swept aside, allowing for the Angustias character to emerge with full force, I contend that the influence of North American representations of race insinuates itself into certain moments in the film (and novel) because of the perceived historical absence of blacks in México. However, if blacks were as inconsequential to Mexican history as some critics, and even the filmmaker maintain, why would they emerge as prominent protagonists in cultural production? This reminds us that blackness in México has a very complex history and the arts merely reflect the paradoxical nature of this simultaneous invisibility and extraordinary presence.

It is my hypothesis that these artists looked to the North (and in the case of Rojas, perhaps to the Caribbean) in order to determine how to weave the issue of blackness into their texts, and then, due to its supposed irrelevance for México, submerged these issues within the rhetoric of Mexican nationalism. Race relations in the United States have historically been defined by this striated perspective, especially with regard to bloodlines (the one-drop policy, for example).[8] Although race and racism are fundamental components of Mexican culture, they do not identically parallel the United States case, particularly because Africans integrated quite early into the colonial regime and slavery in México did not take on the same mythic dimensions that it did in the Caribbean and the United States. As such, the cultural products examined in this chapter reflect the tensions of the dominant discourses of race that emerged from the hegemonic North and from the Caribbean as well as those discourses that emerged from the Mexican nationalist rhetoric that proclaims a "cosmic race" as the model for its citizenry.[9] The distinctive way in which race is obliquely acknowledged and simultaneously dismissed through the trope of the Amazon and through the refiguring of the "tragic mulatta" permits us to appreciate the fraught nature of racial discourse in Mexican film.

Angustias the Amazon: The Mulata as Excess

Francisco Rojas González, author of *La negra Angustias*, deploys quite an arsenal of problematic tropes with regards to black women. As in the colonial legend of the Mulata de Córdoba, the trope of the Amazon in this novel is immersed in stereotypes of African, but more specifically, mulata women as lusty, power-hungry, and dangerous. Although the tragic mulatta genre in the hands of the abolitionists in the United States focused on her virtue and purity, and encased her within the Christian paradigm of martyr, there is a stronger current of racist literature that contends that black women are immoral and that the mulatta's blackness contaminates the whiteness with overt sexuality and moral depravity. According to Robinson and Cabral, "[b]y the end of the seventeenth century [. . .] the mulatto had come to signify an abominable spiritual contamination as well as the spurious violation of the boundaries between property and human identity" (2). In effect, it appears that the Negra Angustias character is indelibly marked by many of these same categories.

Furthermore, Robinson and Cabral notice how in order to make Angustias powerful, her blackness must be "swept aside":

> Culturally, in North American eyes, the mulatto was a figure of opprobrium, who subverted 'Old South' mythical history and whose physical appearance significantly problematized the dominant racial hierarchy. She was an unnatural being, too erotic, too sexualized, too much an advertisement for a sexual congress that was never supposed to happen. In Landeta's hands, all that is swept aside—but so, too, is the awareness of a specifically Black contribution to Mexican history. (9)

I would argue, however, that in this novel the exuberant sexuality of the mulata figure, which according to Robinson is part of what problematizes the dominant racial hierarchy, is not at all swept aside. Rather, it is her attractiveness to non-black men that creates her social predicament and actually leads to her first crime, forcing Angustias to leave her community.

While the exuberance of the mulata in the Caribbean is pervasive and almost unavoidable in the arts, in México the appearance of the mulata is more selective. Nevertheless, Rojas González's *La negra Angustias* aggressively deploys the stereotype of hyper-sexuality when constituting its heroine, as is evidenced by one of the first descriptions of the young woman: "La mujer grande y cuadrona alzóse de su incómoda postura para levantar en alto los brazos llenos de carne juvenil. Su cintura, perfectamente contorneada, tuvo movimientos felinos, por elásticos y graciosos, cuando echó hacia atrás su admirable torso" [The large and hippy woman stood up from her uncomfortable position in order to lift up her young, fleshy arms. Her waist, perfectly rounded, took on feline movements, at times elastic and graceful, when she pulled back her admirable torso] (43). Oftentimes in Caribbean cultural production the robust body and physiognomic hint of blackness is almost a provocation in itself, suggestive of a latent prurience of character and thus reifying black female sexuality as derelict. In the case of the United States, Robyn Wiegman insists that the role of the public gaze is part and parcel of constituting black female subjectivity. She refers us back to the previous century with the figure of the female Hottentot, whose body circulated throughout Europe and "became the primary signifier for black sexuality in the nineteenth century, and it was through both popular and scientific dismemberments of her body that a normative sexuality—heterosexual and quite specifically racialized—was pursued" (57–58). The same sort of energy goes into the early characterizations of Angustias, the way the townspeople observe, interpret, and malign her body, which ultimately lands her in the clutches of lascivious men. However, unlike the "tragic mulatta," these characterizations also determine her heroic destiny. Rather, the defense of her virtue is what inspires her rise in society and indeed it compels her to become a military leader.

Angustias's problems in her village commence with her incredible rejection of a marriage proposal offered by one of the town's most eligible bachelors. The would-be suitor and the villagers are so affronted by the fact that such an insolent rejection would come from a poor mulata that they mercilessly defame her by accusing Angustias and her father of incest. Subsequently the crowd charges her with committing various sorts of sexual depravities such as chasing and molesting young girls and urinating upright against a tree. This masculinized, hyper-sexuality is indubitably perceived as a product of her mixed-race status: mulatos and blacks were commonly accused of and associated with sexual perversity throughout the early colonial period, and there are countless cases against them in the Inquisition records. We have only to recall the cases examined in the previous chapter that accuse mulatos of sexual turpitude and witchcraft. In the case of Angustias, the protagonist and her father are ostracized from the community and she falls victim to a brutal attack instigated by the village girls until Doña Crescencia, the *curandera*[10] who raised her, comes to the rescue by performing a "limpia" (cleansing ritual) that purges Angustias of her supposed deviance.

Later in the novel, when Angustias is taken hostage by the rural police, the men fight over who will get to rape her first, before ultimately they have to relinquish her to their superior, Don Efrén. The men then conspire to distract or remove Don Efrén's wife so that he can have his way alone with Angustias. When Doña Chole (Don Efrén's wife) figures out the ruse, she naturally mistreats Angustias, accusing the poor girl of trying to steal her husband. When Angustias rejects Don Efrén as loathsome, Doña Chole becomes even more incensed:

¿Qué?—dijo desolada doña Chole—, ¿desprecia una negra un hombre blanco y cabal como don Efrén?
Sí—repitió agresivamente la Angustias—, me chocan su facha y su modo. ¡Le tengo miedo!

["'What?' said Doña Chole desolately, 'a black woman would dare spurn a consummate white man like Don Efrén?' 'Yes' repeated Angustias aggressively, 'I don't like his face or mannerisms. I am afraid of him!'"] (67)

Doña Chole is offended by this black girl's rejection of her white husband. The absurdity of this situation is telling: a racially "inferior" woman—indeed, girl—is expected to feel honored to be the object of sexual assault by a man such as Don Efrén. Her negritude, indelibly marked by this exuberant, if unwarranted sexuality has provoked his desire. As was the case with Rito Reyes (the young bachelor who wanted to take Angustias as his wife), she is repudiated for not appreciating that a "white" man could deign to desire, even if through violence, a black woman.

Furthermore, her blackness in the eyes of the white and mestizo populace makes her naturally inclined toward inciting sexual perversity. The following passage from the novel clearly illustrates this accusation of connivance:

La mulata, provocativa y aparentemente despreocupada, pasó casi rozando con sus caderas las piernas de Laureano, que obstruían la estrecha senda. El hombre no tuvo más que estirar la mano para cogerla por el brazo [. . .] ¡Ahora no te escapas! La mulata detuvo bruscamente el paso, bajó los ojos y sonrió equívoca. Laureano, dueño de bestial orgullo, hincó sus dedos en el macizo brazo de la mujer. Ella, impávida, dejó hacer.

[The mulata, provocative and apparently not preoccupied, almost brushed Laureano's legs with her hips as she tried to get past him because he was obstructing the narrow road. The man had to do nothing more than extend his hand in order to grab her by the arm. [. . .] "This time you won't escape!" The mulata stopped abruptly, lowered her gaze and smiled equivocally. Laureano, fiercely proud, sunk his fingers into the strong arm of the woman. She, undaunted, let him]. (46)

This passage strikingly reveals what is regarded as Angustias's complicity in arousing the lust of Laureano (the man who had been threatening to rape her); her large hips almost touched his legs as she passed by him. He had to do "nothing more" than extend his hand in order to clutch her by the arm. This scene is narrated as if she were teasing him, and later, after he savagely digs his fingers into her strong arm, she relents.

The beginning of what is about to be a rape scene is sensually recounted and has the clear intention of titillating the reader's imagination; it is an erotic provocation that implicitly places partial culpability on the girl. Laureano, her sexual aggressor, "had to do nothing more than extend his hand to grab her" (46). The choice of "coger" over "agarrar" also points to the underlying threat of sexual violence, as "coger" means to grab, but in México and other parts of Latin America, it also means "to fuck." He then tries to drag her into the brush so that they may fornicate like animals: "—Allá—dijo el hombre mientras empujaba a la mulata—. Allá, entre las breñas, como los chivos y como las pastoras" [" 'Over there,' said the man while he pushed the mulata. 'Over there, in the bushes, like the goats and the shepherdesses' "] (46–47). Angustias *did* set him up: she had the intention of killing him with her father's knife if he tried to rape her, which is ultimately what transpired. The aging black father symbolically killed Laureano by placing the knife in her hands for self-defense (although in the film she steals the knife from her father while he sleeps, foreshadowing her rise to power in his stead). By invoking the sexual promiscuity that is often attributed to mulata figures, the sexualized violence of this scene is also racialized, appearing to be almost inevitable. Due to this perceived sexual allure, Angustias could not expect to be left alone for too long.

Furthermore, the sexual perversity she inspires is considered "hereditary." Again, unlike the traditional mulatta narrative from the early nineteenth-century United States or Caribbean, where the mixed-race figures are generally a product of a white male's "dalliance" with a slave woman or amorous fling with an irresistible mulatta, Rojas presents the attractive allure of the mulato male as instigating a fetishistic desire in white women. The stereotype of overwhelming black sexuality and prowess is played out here to explain why Angustias's white mother fell in the arms of a mulato bandit: "¡y mi mujer—Dios la perdone—sola, triste y con la debilidad que sentía por los mulatos!" ["and my poor wife, may God forgive her—alone, sad and with that weakness she had for mulatos"] (13). Antón himself recognizes this fetish by lamenting the tragic fate that befell his late wife as a result of a "weakness" for mulatos. In this respect Angustias, like the tragic mulatta, is the result of a perverse sexual desire that is marked on her body despite her virtuous pretensions. She fights off the "coyote," a metaphor for the potential rapist (Laureano), and kills him in the process. As a result of her self-defense, she is forced to flee only to encounter another round of antagonists who are soldiers in the Revolution.

In her book *Scenes of Subjection*, Saidiya Hartman theorizes the relationship between black slave subjectivity and criminality. Although her example comes from the United States South with an account of the rebellion waged by a slave woman against an attempted rape by her master, the link Hartman establishes between the pathology of the black subject's will and criminal behavior is telling for the Angustias narrative, particularly when we consider it against the chaotic backdrop of the Mexican Revolution. Hartman explains:

> Thus the fashioning of the subject must necessarily take place in violation of the law, and consequently will, criminality, and punishment are inextricably linked. Furthermore, Sukie's [the slave woman] performance exploits the charged linkage of property and sexuality, challenges the will-lessness of the object of property, and induces a category crisis for the spectators whose enjoyment is defined by wanton acts and the promiscuous uses of property. (41)

Hartman's argument underscores that criminality is the only form of slave agency recognized by the law, while it also highlights the relationship between female sexuality and the notion of property. Not surprisingly, a fellow slave recounts the attempted rape of Sukie as a seduction, much like Rojas Gonzalez's staging of the attempted rape of Angustias through the language of seduction. The slave recalls that the master tried to "make Sukie his gal," exemplifying how rape is often conflated with concubinage in the sexual economy of slavery (40). Sukie defies her status as property by fighting her master, almost boiling his "hind parts." Then, lifting up her skirt to the slave traders as they poke and prod her on the block, asks them to see if they found any teeth "down there," in an ominous reference to the trope of the vagina *dentata* and, for the white master, to the threat of castration. This act subverts her status as property, as well as the enjoyment provided by the spectacle of domination.

Hartman's reading of Sukie's case bears a striking resemblance to the racial drama that unfolds in *La negra Angustias* despite the fact that it was written over a century after abolition in México. Her rejection of marriage to a racial and economic superior—arguably another form of proprietorship—is unheard of, especially considering that her father did not force her to marry Rito Reyes (the young bachelor) as might be customary. As with Sukie, who almost boiled her master's "hind parts," the struggle of Angustias against her potential rapist results in her initiation into crime, as she is forced to stab him to death in order to defend herself. Finally, the association between her self-fashioned subjectivity and delinquency is powerful, as it does not lead to just any kind of criminal behavior, but to a metaphorical rape and murder with her father's knife, and later, a literal castration of her pursuer.

Rojas fashions the trope of depravity by invoking the "unnatural" mixing of the races embodied by Angustias, who aside from exhibiting an exuberant sexual power, maintains what might be considered an unnatural military power over her male subordinates. This recalls Cesare Lombroso's discussion of the female born criminal who wields inordinate power over men, whether through force or insinuation. Rojas graphically illustrates this criminal power when Angustias castrates her former captor Don Efrén, teaching a lesson to all the soldiers.[11] In Landeta's filmic rendition of this powerful episode, Angustias laughs almost maniacally as the castrated man cries out while a bolero plays in the background as a sonic counterpoint, and sharp cactus leaves fill the visual field. Rather than revealing the irony of the act—which is a vindication for all women who have suffered sexual violence by men who abuse their authority—the morbid filmic pairing of a castration with a traditionally romantic musical genre illustrates the perceived pathological power of the mulata heroine.

Later in the novel a symbolic castration occurs during a sensational and melodramatic scene in which Angustias kidnaps the effeminate *catrín* [dandy] whom she loves unrequitedly. Clearly Rojas astonishes his readers with such brazen, "unnatural" female behavior that exposes the pernicious excesses of womanly power if left unchecked. This is similar to the characterization of the powerful soldadera characters such as "La Pintada" or María Felix's version of "La Cucaracha." Not content with her destiny in the hands of the *machos*, Angustias ultimately creates her own when she castrates her captor, making him an example of what happens to men who rape women, and later, when she takes as a captive the man who rejects her because she is black. In effect, her *mulatez* sensationalizes her audacity in the eyes of the Mexican reader/spectator. In contrast to the tragic mulatta, as figured in abolitionist fiction from the United States and the Caribbean, whose body is the untenable incorporation of two antagonistic races that leads to her inevitable tragic demise, Angustias is catapulted to success as a result of her blackness. She confronts her antagonists, kills or castrates them, and is empowered by her rebellion. It is her father's legacy that inspires her to lead an army of men whom she instructs to treat women respectfully.

Nevertheless, behind this commanding figure inspired by the pursuit of justice for her community and women lurks the peril of perversity associated with black female power. As Hartman illustrates with the example of Sukie, black female agency is also often intimately linked to excess and criminality. Although Angustias is a heroine, her subjectivity is compromised by her crime, simultaneously inspiring pleasure through the potential ravishing of her body—as we saw with the rape threats issued by Laureano and Don Efrén—but also inspiring fear of her carrying out her will, as evidenced by the castration scene.

Seeing is Believing: Appropriating Blackness

Upon Antón Farrera's return from prison at the beginning of the novel, he is informed that he has a daughter. Although reluctant to claim her because now that he is old he would prefer to find another wife to take care of him, Farrera nonetheless asks Doña Crescencia, the *curandera* who raised young Angustias, whether the girl is truly his child:

> –Pero, ¿es cierto que es mi hija? . . .
> –Válgame Dios, Antón Farrera!—respondió impaciente la vieja.
> –Es cierto, ciertísimo. Eso se sabe no sólo en Mesa del Aire, sino en toda la sierra . . . *No más véale la color.* Mulata como usted. La madre—que en paz del Señor descanse—era blanca y fina; de ella sacó Angustias las facciones y de usted los ademanes, la resolución y lo prietillo.

> ["But, it is true she is my daughter?"
> "For heaven's sake, Antón Farrera!" the old lady responded impatiently. "It is true, absolutely true. It is well known not only in Mesa del Aire, but throughout the whole sierra . . . Just *look at her color.* Mulata like you. The mother—may she rest in God's peace—was white and delicate; that is where Angustias got her features and from you she inherited her attitude, her resolution and her dark skin."] (emphasis added, 13)

The old lady responds with absolute authority that not only does *she* know the child is his, but the *whole community* does as well: her dark skin is proof. It is Angustias's skin color that determines patrilineage for Antón Farrera and, through Doña Crescencia's verbal confirmation, his doubts are assuaged. This is also notable because the narrative takes place in southern Morelos and Guerrero where there are many Afro-Mexican communities, although in the novel it is claimed that *morenos*[12] live mostly on the coast. In the small village where the plot unfolds, it is clear that Antón Farrera is the only known mulato. Again we see that the black presence is made singular and exceptional although there is tacit acknowledgment of a larger community of *morenos* living "elsewhere."[13] The heroic feats recounted and circulated in the corrido are what contribute to Antón's infamy as a "black" social bandit, a reputation that consequently, Angustias will claim as her birthright through the very legitimation provided by the ballad tradition.

Indeed, a critical moment in the novel occurs after Angustias arrives at a small town somewhere in Guerrero to take refuge after Güitlacoche (the man who will become her second-in-command) helps Angustias escape from her captor Don Efrén. Her father had told her stories about his exploits as a bandit, but it is in this community that she comprehends the importance of his remarkable legacy. The film narrates this event in a beautiful scene where the townsmen sing the "Corrido of Antón Farrera" around a campfire, and, afterward, Angustias listens to the balladeers discuss the ideals of land, liberty, and justice that prompted them to join the Revolution. Through camera close-ups on her face and ambient lighting, we witness the "birth" of her political consciousness. The corrido details the heroic nature of black Antón's exploits, and it is at this moment that she recognizes both his place as a local hero in a longer history of peasant insurrection, as well as her part in continuing this legacy as an agent of the Revolution. Indeed, the corrido acts as a protagonist in the preservation of community memory, a reference that is important because the corrido today still exercises an important role as arbiter of social conflict in Afro-Mexican communities and throughout the Costa Chica.

The following passage from the novel is striking in terms of character development and the appropriation of her blackness. In this scene, Angustias, inspired by her father's corrido, utters one of the first affirmative speech acts in the novel, commanding the *huespere* (innkeeper) to look at her face:

> –Mírame!—ordenó fríamente la mulata, mientras acercaba a su cara el mechero de petróleo—¡Veme mucho!—repitió imperante . . .
> –¡El negro Farrera, Antón Farrera! Sí, son sus mismos ojos, su mismo gesto . . . ¡Sangre de Cristo! Antón Farrera, el más atravesado pandillero . . . Parece que lo veo . . .
> –Silencio—cortó con energía la muchacha—, ya has dicho mucho, viejo del dianche. Cuela, dilo a toda la gente de Real de Ánimas; platícales que aquí está la hija de Antón el negro, al que cantaban los corridos de esta tierra; al que le alzan pelo todavía los mineros y los comerciantes ricos, pero al que quieren los *probes*. Anda, viejo, corre la voz por el pueblo, di a todos que aquí está la mulata Angustias, hija del negro Farrera.

> ["Look at me!" the mulata coldly ordered, while she hastened the oil-lamp close to her face, "Look at me good and well!" she commanded. "The black Farrera, Antón Farrera! Yes, they are his same eyes, his same face . . . Blood of Christ! Antón Farrera, the most ruthless bandit . . . it is as if I see him . . ." "Silence!" the girl commanded energetically. "You have said enough, old man. Spill it, tell everyone around Real de Ánimas; tell them that the daughter of black Antón is here, the one they sing about in the ballads of this land; the one whose name still makes the miners' and

rich business owners' hair stand on end, but whom the poor folk love. Go, old man, spill it around town, tell them that the mulata Angustias, daughter of the black Farrera, has arrived."] (79–80)

The ensuing scene is glorious; Angustias is treated regally, smiling benevolently to the women while the children greet her shyly. They welcome her as they might a queen, and it is through this moment of self-recognition that her agency and subjectivity are actualized.

Blackness facilitates and conditions this moment of self-recognition and empowerment, for it is the single-most important factor in her self-identification and her self-initiated introduction into society. The *huespere* looks at her face; however, it is her eyes ("ojos") and gestures ("gestos") that identify her as Antón Farrera's daughter. Yet, it is in the eyes of the mestizo innkeeper that her blackness is reflected back to her.[14] She forces him to recognize her blackness, and then proudly assumes it for herself. From this moment on, Angustias radically changes, having found her personality: "Angustias dejábase admirar por todos, echada en el taburete del mesonero, muda y altiva, dueña de su prestancia y de aquella presea que acababa de encontrarse muy adentro: la personalidad" [Angustias let herself be admired by them all, sitting casually on the barstool, mute and haughty, the new owner of a distinction, a precious jewel that she had just discovered inside herself: a personality] (81). Moreover, this image resonates strongly with the portrait of the coronela we examined in chapter 3, with the subject sitting confidently on top of the chair while gazing directly at the photographer. The novel's eponymous "negra Angustias" is literally born in the eyes of the innkeeper, as his public recognition of her legitimizes her claim to black Antón's legacy. The admiration *el negro* Farrera once inspired is now hers, as she appropriates his reputation and replaces his figure in name and person. From this moment on she becomes a formidable Zapatista colonel and the men rally to her side to join the social insurrection.

Although she creates a successful career as a revolutionary leader, Angustias's blackness eventually becomes an obstacle for her own personal fulfillment in love, ultimately leading to her demise in the novel. The filmic version, however, points more directly to racism as the culprit for Manuel Reguera's rejection of her marriage proposal. This is poignantly illustrated in the scene where la Coronela declares her love to Manuel de la Reguera, offering to marry him to lessen his financial difficulties. He cruelly rebuffs her amorous advances, after which, in Landeta's screen version, she screams for Güitlacoche and begs him to tell her the truth about her looks: "¿Soy fea?" ["Am I ugly?"] "¡Dime la verdad!" ["Tell me the truth!"]. She commands Güitlacoche to fetch a mirror and seizing it from his hands she holds it up to her face. Angustias lifts up the broken mirror, and in a moment of dramatic tension, stares into its depths, allowing it to reveal the truth about who she is. She then braces the broken mirror to her chest and wails, in what appears to be a declaration of self-loathing, "¡Soy negra!" [I'm black!], and the scene fades out. This statement resounds like a condemnation that constitutes the reason for her sentimental tragedy, for why she cannot find love in the delicate, white figure of Manuel de la Reguera. In the novel there is no scene with the mirror, Angustias is simply rejected by Manuel and then explodes in a torrent of pent-up emotion and tears. Beyond Angustias's uncouth manners and imperfect grammar, no dress could undo the fact of her blackness, making it impossible for her to be beautiful in the eyes of the man who she loves, and also in her own.

In this scene of the film version of Angustias's story, the mulata protagonist's climactic outcry reveals the undeniable truth that paradoxically allowed her to reclaim her father's place as a famous social bandit at the same time as it irrevocably barred the possibility of reciprocal love. Indeed, like a reversal of that initial Lacanian mirror stage, in which the child develops an ego upon regarding the wholeness of the body and mistakes it for a developed individual, in Landeta's film this double-edged truth is revealed to Angustias in the broken mirror, and the mirage of complete subjectivity discovered in the innkeeper's eyes dissipates in the mirror's jagged edges. Angustias's blackness granted her the power to claim the legacy of her father so that she could become an influential revolutionary hero, yet this same blackness demarcated rigid social limits that prohibited her from participating in the affective relationship of her choice, and denied her full incorporation into society.

After this powerful cinematic scene, Angustias catches up with Manuel in the funeral cortege for his dead mother, and as he laments his loss she naïvely repeats her marriage proposal. Once again he rejects her, uttering the same cruel words that appear in the novel: "En otras palabras, que mi unión con usted sería considerada por la gente más que un matrimonio como una cruza absurda . . . ¿Me entiende usted?" ["In other words, my union with you would not be considered by the people like a marriage but more like an absurd mixing . . . Do you understand?"] (176). Angustias completely understands the motives behind this brutal rejection; it would reduce their union to the unnatural miscegenation of two distinct farm animals. Despite the cultural animosity between the lettered, bourgeois Mexican society and the "hordes" of illiterate peasant revolutionaries that is a recurrent trope of the revolutionary literary genre, it is her blackness that becomes the determining factor that marks her, literally and figuratively.

Subsequently, Angustias breaks away from the cortege wandering aimlessly, and finally slumps pathetically under a doorjamb, as the camera zooms in from the street for an extreme close-up of her face, once again to underscore the reason for her rejection. The camera lingers as she slowly devolves into hysteria. Yet importantly, unlike some classic tragic mulatta narratives in which the mulatta figure is *almost* white, educated, and virtuous, Angustias is undeniably black (a fact rendered problematic, of course, by the minstrelsy of the actress). Her blackness, combined with her virility, overrides her willingness to be "tamed" through attempts at domesticity and literacy; she is simply not good enough for the white dandy despite his physical, economic, and political dependence on her. Ironically these insistent camera close-ups on the protagonist's blackened face creates what Eli Bartra calls a "racial transvestism" that results in a "strange ambivalence," because even though "the actress acts like a black woman [. . .] the audience do not respond in the same way as if she really were black" (281). This is replicated in the blackface employed in other films, where, for example, the abnegating *nana* (typically an Afro-Cuban) wears blackface, further distantiating the idea of blackness from the reality of Mexican audiences.

This rejection of the strong woman is echoed in the narratives of other soldaderas, such as "La Pintada" in Azuela's *Los de abajo* (1915) and María Félix's filmic performance in *La Cucaracha* (1959). Both are rejected by their lovers in favor of a more traditionally "feminine" and docile character, and likewise each ends up expelled from the troop by the very men they love or, as in the case of Angustias, tamed by maternity. But Angustias is not rejected in favor of anyone, but rather she is just flat out rejected. Clearly, her strength and vigor, like other soldaderas, is "unnatural" for a woman. But more importantly, her blackness—together with her social position as an uneducated, female peasant—prevents her from social recognition and self-fulfillment. In the film, as in the novel, the mulata protagonist lapses into hysteria until she is awakened from her hazy stupor by an attempt on her life as the Federal Army approaches in its take of the city. When her lieutenant Güitlacoche heroically defends her, he is shot and dies in her arms.

Unlike the version presented by the novel, in Landeta's film adaptation, the mulata figure recovers after her rejection. Although the film took much of the screenplay directly from the novel, hardly altering many of the lines, here it changes course radically. In "Faldas y pantalones: el género en el cine de la revolución mexicana," Bartra lauds this remarkable filmic recuperation: "In *La negra Angustias*, the Colonel Angustias could have ended up as submissive as Flor Silvestre or Beatriz, if the film had been made by a man" (14).[15] But in Landeta's cinematic rendition, Angustias does not end up submissive like the protagonist in *Flor Silvestre* (1942), or her counterpart in María Felix's *Enamorada* (1946). Landeta, facing her own struggles as one of México's first female filmmakers, had to pawn her car in order to make the film. She was subsequently blackballed by the sexist industry and did not make another film until 1991, forty years after her last film, *Trotacalles* (1951). Instead, Landeta's Angustias gives herself up entirely to the cause after Güitlacoche's death, as the film ends

abruptly with a low angle close-up of her riding astride a horse, valiantly rally-
ing the troops by shouting "¡Viva la Revolución! ¡Viva México!" She becomes
completely subsumed by the revolutionary cause and its concomitant nationalistic rhetoric. The rejection she faces due to her blackness becomes addressed
by the egalitarian and agrarian ideals of Zapatismo: liberty and land. However,
we should recall that Zapatismo was not a national movement, but rather it
was—and still is—a movement propelled by very specific regional demands that
include the redistribution of land, much of which was, or is currently, populated
by indigenous groups as well as Afro-Mexicans, and political autonomy based
on communal indigenous notions of participatory democracy. The "nationalism"
of this film made in 1949 reflects an already calcified "revolutionary" party that
had institutionalized the Revolution as a one-party dictatorship.[16]

In Rojas González's novel, Angustias deserts the tumult of the Revolution in order to become a "woman" once again. After she kidnaps Manuel
Reguera, she gives up the dignity she acquired as a revolutionary leader
in order to follow the white *catrín* and his commands. She bears him a
brown-skinned, blue-eyed child, and allows him to betray her as well as
her revolutionary ideals by hiding them away in a poor, dirty room in the
slums of México City while he collects her military checks. In an intentional
twist of gender roles, once Angustias surrenders her military prowess and
physical power, Manuel, who until that point had been an effeminate weak-
ling, acquires the "manly" vigor that he had been sadly lacking. For Rojas
González this ending was a clear allegory of the Revolution; the spirit of the
Revolution was reduced to superficial salutes and the erection of statues in
the hands of the same upper-class white bureaucracy who had always held
the power. The glory of one of the century's most important social upheavals
is carried on the backs of the rural poor who suffered, died, and ended up
not much better off than they started, while those who wore the regalia of
victory had been empowered to begin with, thus displaying Rojas González's
disillusionment with the Revolution. In fact, this conclusion becomes even
more metaphorical, as behind the cunning white man in power is a black
woman hiding in the recesses of poverty, invoking the inevitable tragic end-
ings of mulatta figures in the tradition of abolitionist fiction of the early
nineteenth-century United States and Caribbean. The product of this union,
the mulato child, similarly disappears into the shadows of oblivion. Following in line with the trenchant rhetoric of mestizaje, Rojas González's other
novel, *Lola Casanova*, ends in a similar fashion, with the white protagonist
teaching her adopted Seri tribe how to cooperate with the "Yoris" (their
white or non-indigenous countrymen) in order to avoid further conflict and
stave off annihilation.

Indeed, as underscored by Robinson and Cabral, it is the invisibility of
blackness within the national imaginary that paradoxically creates the conditions for the emergence of a superlative mulata figure; despite the elision of

blacks in México's historical consciousness, black characters emerge in its cultural production time and again. Similarly, this elision does not prevent the deployment of racist stereotypes regarding black female sexuality. The irony presented by Rojas González's *La negra Angustias* is that it is the protagonist's very blackness that defines her, creating the conditions for her respectful military success and rise in power while it simultaneously constitutes her sexual allure, criminality, and the motives that drive her ultimate decline. The influence of filmic negotiations of race produced in the United States could have resonated for Mexican directors, in part, because of México's already long history of black culture: an historical presence that had been dormant for almost two hundred years when slavery was abolished and the category of race was eliminated by México's second president Vicente Guerrero (ironically, himself an Afro-Mexican). But Francisco Rojas González's novel, *La negra Angustias*, almost unintentionally initiates an important discussion that Mexican cinema, among other cultural texts, will take up rather clumsily later on: the historically marooned presence of blacks in México.

¿Y los angelitos negros?

> Pintor que pintas tu tierra,
> si quieres pintar tu cielo,
> cuando pintas angelitos
> acuérdate de tu pueblo
> y al lado del ángel rubio
> y junto al ángel trigueño,
> aunque la Virgen sea blanca,
> píntame angelitos negros.
>
> [Painter who paints your land,
> if you want to paint your heaven,
> when you paint the little angels
> remember your people
> and next to the blond angel,
> and along with the brown angel,
> even if the Virgin remains white,
> paint me some little black angels].

—Andrés Eloy Blanco

The movie *Angelitos negros*, filmed and released in 1948 and then again in 1969, was directed both times by Joselito Rodríguez and based on the play written by Cuban writer Félix B. Caignet. It performs one of the first critical reflections on race in México and the title itself is inspired by the poem "Píntame angelitos negros" ["Paint Me Little Black Angels"] by the Venezuelan poet and politician Andrés Eloy Blanco.[17] Written in the 1940s, the poem is a critique of exclusionary racial politics in Venezuela, issued through a poignant dialogue between a black woman who has lost her child and her *comadre*,[18] who then, in an accusation directed toward a nameless painter, laments that there are no black angels. While the poem does not, however, contest the whiteness of the Virgin—it merely entreats for a few black angels—it is a direct criticism of those cultural agents who are authorized to represent Christian iconography for not including blacks and their transculturated experience as Christians in their representations of the afterlife. This is interesting, of course, because México's cult of the Virgin of Guadalupe is predicated upon her being a dark-skinned Virgin, "la Virgen Morena." According to Theresa Delgadillo in her article "Singing Angelitos Negros," this poem is supposed to contradict a proverb in Venezuela that states that "Blacks do not go to heaven" by calling into question traditional Christian principles of tending to the wretched and the marginalized. Moreover, it refers us back to the discussion of a "creole consciousness" in chapter 4 that highlighted how blacks in the colonial period deftly utilized canon law in order to invoke their rights as Christians. The poet Andrés Eloy Blanco not only asks that the painter draw black angels, but also include *trigueños* and *indios* eating mangos as opposed to an iconic continental fruit, like a fig, for example. In truth, he is asking for the spiritual realm to visually reflect the Venezuelan geographic, racial, and social landscape, not unlike José Martí's famous exhortation in "Nuestra América" (1891) that America create its own products rather than imitate European ones, and if it has to make sour-tasting wine made from plantains, then so be it.

Both of Rodriguez's filmic renditions are melodramas that despite the use of blackface and overacting performed much-needed preliminary work on the nature of racial politics for blacks in México. The 1948 movie features Pedro Infante as the main protagonist, a world-famous singer and performer named José Carlos Ruíz; Rita Montaner as Mamá Mercé, the mulata's suffering black *nana* who hides her true identity as mother to Ana María; and Emilia Guiú as Ana María, a mulata who has no idea of her black identity, and who, despite having been raised lovingly by her *nana* (who is actually her mother), harbors a virulent disgust for blacks.

Emilio García Riera, one of México's foremost film critics, believed the blackface and overacting on the part of Infante killed any impact the film might have, and furthermore, that it was more appropriate for the United States South than for México. He may be right about the structural problems of the film and the deployment of tragic mulatta and mammy stock figures, but Rodriguez's *Angelitos negros* still represents one of Mexican cinema's first attempts to deal with racism against blacks seriously. Likewise, although Mexican critics have been known to dismiss films such as this one and the *La negra Angustias*, in part, because they believe Afro-Mexicans to be irrelevant to contemporary Mexican society, this film is still widely viewed in both its original black-and-white form, as well as in the form of the color remake, released twenty years later. Regardless of its structural imperfections, it stands as an important initial attempt to grapple with critical issues regarding race that to this day remain ignored.

Several of the film's main flaws have to do primarily with the nature of the genre. Melodrama, especially in México, is known for its simplified narrative structure that proceeds carelessly and quickly to the climax with very little nuance, and for its abuse of *deus ex machina* and Manichean character development as well as its propensity for overacting and sentimentalist excess. Long a genre of choice for Mexican audiences, to this day Mexican cinema continues to churn out melodramas, and of course, today histrionic *telenovelas* are more popular than ever. It stands to argument that melodrama has performed a specific role in catalyzing social consciousness in México, as its cathartic effects have been fundamental toward the narration and identification of the predominant social ills.

Peter Brooks theorizes the important work performed by melodrama in his book *The Melodramatic Imagination* (1976), arguing that the popularity of melodrama corresponds to an "urge toward resacralization and the impossibility of conceiving the sacralization other than in personal terms," and is in part due to the way the Manichean impulse toward good and evil that is proper to the melodramatic mode takes place between characters who lack psychological complexity (16). As society becomes increasingly secular, he suggests, the conflict between good and evil plays itself out in these exceedingly flat characters that work out the daily dramas that we, as individuals vacated of a sense of spiritual urgency, actually need.

Brooks further distinguishes between tragedy and melodrama in order to elucidate the role the latter plays in contemporary society:

> Tragedy generates meaning ultimately in terms of orders higher than one man's experience, orders invested by the community with holy and synthesizing power. Its pity and terror derive from the sense of communal sacrifice and transformation. *Melodrama offers us heroic confrontation, purgation, purification, recognition.* But its recognition is essentially of the integers in combat and the need to choose sides. *It produces panic terror and sympathetic pity, but not in regard to the same object, and without the higher illumination of their interpenetration.* (emphasis added, 205)

Brooks makes an excellent point: tragedy requires that there be a higher spiritual significance that orders the meaning of sacrifice. Society needs to agree on what is to be gained by the sacrifice; the hero's illumination thus constitutes the community's illumination. But what happens in the face of a pluralistic, hierarchical, transcultural, transnational, and secularized society? How can one recognize his or her place in the cosmos if one's place in society is not always recognizable and stable? México is a place populated by holders of a multiplicity of worldviews and epistemologies, where one can dwell within plural worlds and inhabit diverse realities.

As Brooks observed, the melodramatic mode creates order where there is none; it sacralizes what is secular, and creates the possibility for heroism without a clear idea of what the stakes are either way. It presents antagonists with a nebulous idea of the ways in which they relate to each other, but nonetheless provides clarity through the finality of the conflict: "Melodrama cannot figure the birth of a new society [. . .] A form for secularized times, it offers the nearest approach to sacred and cosmic values in a world where they no longer have any certain ontology or epistemology" (205). In sum, melodrama does not destroy or create new worlds, or even possibilities, like classic tragedies might. It merely approximates these cosmic values, bringing us closer to them. Indeed, in the pluralistic word of Latin *América*, there has never been nor ever will be "any certain ontology or epistemology." In the melodramatic mode the hyperbole of the integers in opposition alerts us to the impossibility of their reconciliation. The "birth" of a new society would only enact new forms of violence to protean identities and spiritualities. When tackling issues of race, Joanne Hershfield argues, "film melodrama is able to accommodate cultural uncertainties surrounding issues of race in ways that fit within the limits of proscribed social attitudes and beliefs" (96). Mexican society is riddled with the phantasms of racial tension that creep back through the specters of coloniality, spiritual and epistemic violence, and the imposition of a univocal, yet uneven, "modernity." Melodrama plays out this "society reformed" that has not reconciled itself with its past, but rather, is disfiguring and disappearing it.

Angelitos negros purports to address—and redress—the insidious nature of racism in México by specifically identifying the invisible nature of it. But in order to perform this work, the director Joselito Rodríguez chooses to engage his actors in their own form of minstrelsy, lest the audience not be clear that one of the main mulata characters (José Carlos's dance partner Isabel and the suffering *nana*) are supposed to be black. Although blackface was still quite common in American filmmaking, even when the first version of *Angelitos negros* was produced in 1948, the reluctance on behalf of American filmmakers to employ black actors does not seem to be the only reason why the director opted to use it. Considering México's tenuous relationship to blackness, it is not startling that the director might choose to recur to this cinematic device. But in this film, it is the main protagonist—José Carlos— who dons blackface for his performance of the Caribbean-inspired acts in an effort to create a veneer of tropical authenticity. It is a meta-performance that mediates blackness through multiple spectators: the diegetic audience in his act, the film's spectators, and Mexican society in general. As a mestizo, José Carlos is a mediator who performs blackness in order to approximate it, but also, to incorporate and even instrumentalize it as a tool of exotic fetishism and consumptive desire—one that provokes taboo fantasies while simultaneously sublimating them.

Furthermore, the mulata actress who plays his partner, Isabel, also wears blackface. Although she is a Puerto Rican mulata, the director's choice to artificially darken her complexion clearly makes the racial dynamics of the film ironic. As Delgadillo argued, "the role of blackface in the film is the inverse of its function," and in in "*Angelitos negros*, blackface represents the desire to absorb blackness into the Latin American ideal of *mestizaje* rather than [. . .] to overcome marginality" (415). I, too, contend that the overall effect of employing blackface leads to a conflict of interest, undoing the critique it was hoping to effect and perpetuating the fraught mestizo ideal. Rather than simply absorb blackness, it seeks to make it disappear.

Saidiya Hartman's theorization of the role of melodrama and minstrelsy for white audiences in the United States is profoundly insightful in this case, even for a Mexican movie that is not dealing with the problem of slavery directly. She claims that "[t]he fungibility of the commodity, specifically its abstractness and immateriality, enabled the black body or blackface mask to serve as the vehicle of white self-exploration, renunciation, and enjoyment" (26). By donning blackface, one abstracts the very material nature of blackness, separates the body from the person, and the person from the reality of the social conditions that surround them; thus blackness is reduced to a performance for the enjoyment of white viewers. By reifying the body, or the face, blackface becomes a "vehicle" for white self-exploration; it stops being about black people at all, and is more about creating a safe place for white self-reflection. This is the trap into which Rodriguez's film falls victim. In his minstrelsy, José Carlos performs the very commodification of blackness that the film is trying to critique, but in this case, instead of providing a safe haven for white reflection, it transforms it into an ironic place for mestizo reflection.

It is the protagonist's performance of blackness that makes him an international star. This performance is capitalizing on the popularity of Caribbean music in México at a time when cabarets were exploding and Mexican music was appropriating Cuban *son*, *danzón*, *bolero*, and *cumbia*, exploiting México's privileged position as the key producer of cinema in Latin America. The cultural appetite of Mexicans at the time had them voraciously consuming these tropicalized figures. Many of the black characters in *Angelitos negros* are from the Caribbean, thus perpetuating the Mexican myth that blacks do not form a part of Mexican history, while the Caribbean, as a tropical space marked by a confluence of peoples and racial difference, is fetishized, and the influx of Caribbean entertainers and mixed-race dancers and musicians in the popular cabaret scene reflects not only the Mexican fascination with "tropical" music but also triangulates the construction of race in México. In this way, the Caribbean influence takes the blame for México's Africanness.

Finally, it is this blackness that simultaneously attracts and repels the racist mulata character Ana María, who begins the film as a mawkish prude afraid of both men and the outside world, and radically transforms into a bombshell after an encounter with José Carlos. As Hartman explains, the performance of blackness through minstrelsy and melodrama serves as sensual titillation because "[t]he punitive pleasures yielded through the figurative possession of blackness cannot be disentangled from the bodily politics of chattel slavery. Blackness facilitated prohibited explorations, tabooed associations, immodest acts, and bawdy pleasures," (32) and this is central to understanding the transformation of the mulata protagonist one sees in *Angelitos negros*. The immodesty of José Carlos and his act turns her on; the taboo associations and bawdy pleasures identified in the performance of blackness simultaneously thrill and repulse her by harkening back to the possession and domination of the black body through slavery. Although she is unhappy about both his minstrelsy and intimacy with a group of mulato coworkers who constitute a sort of surrogate family for him, it is this minstrelsy that mediates Ana María's pleasure and which ironically brings her out of her prudish shell, inspiring her incipient cupidity. The very same night she sees José Carlos's act for the first time, he asks for her hand in marriage, and she accepts. Although the sequence of events is forced and structurally awkward, its narrative expedience does not give José Carlos—who aside from being repulsed by discrimination, feels like a member of the black/mulato community due in part to his own orphanhood—time to ascertain the real nature of his lover's demeanor. Thus he discovers that she is a violent racist way too late; his daughter's suffering due to the rejection she faces by her own mother bears the cross of his fatal mistake.

Through this problematic characterization of the mulata the film accomplishes the destabilization of whiteness, and by extension, the rhetoric of an all-encompassing mestizaje. Regarding the former, Hartman writes that in the nineteenth-century United States, "the illusory integrity of whiteness facilitated by attraction and/or antipathy to blackness was ultimately predicated upon the indiscriminate use and possession of the black body" (32). The simultaneity of her attraction/antipathy toward blacks reveals Ana María's own deep-seated insecurities and self-hatred. Her proximity to a black mother figure, who in actuality is her biological mother, unravels her sense of racial purity despite the fact that throughout the film she insists on her whiteness by pointing to her white skin and balking at the possibility that her lineage may have produced a dark-skinned mulata child. In addition to José Carlos's intimate association with blacks and mulatos, which, through some sort of perverted reasoning, she seems to think has contaminated him, Ana María also expresses a belief that her mestizo husband's orphaned status makes him responsible for the skin color of their child, again invoking the trope of black orphanhood. In response, José Carlos agrees to maintain Mamá Mercé's dark secret by obliging in his wife's ill-founded beliefs, and fabricates a lie that his mother was of mixed-race.

Ana María never ostensibly questions her racial integrity, cruelly rejecting her own child, even refusing to touch her. This rejection slowly leads to the debilitation of Mama Mercé, who suffers quietly at the hatred her own daughter exhibits toward black people, and the cruelty she inflicts on her granddaughter. It becomes too much for her to bear. Similarly, Hartman states that her "reading attempts to elucidate the means by which the wanton use of/and the violence directed toward the black body come to be identified as its pleasure and danger" (26). The economy of enjoyment that creates excess, pain, and pleasure is a product of melodrama and minstrelsy's appropriation of black bodies. This dynamic is made manifest with the figure of the suffering black mother who is constantly humiliated and rejected, as well as the black grandchild who performs her own brand of violent minstrelsy, disfiguring her face with white powder so that, in an attempt to efface her blackness, her mother might love her. The spectators participate in the economy of enjoyment that constitutes, and is constituted by, black suffering as Hartman reminds us that "both minstrelsy and melodrama (re)produced blackness as an essentially pained expression of the body's possibilities" (32).

Ultimately, *Angelitos negros* falls within the scope of traditional tragic mulatta narratives, ending with Ana María slapping Mamá Mercé, the impact of which pushes her down a flight of stairs to her death. Only once Mamá Mercé lies dying on her bed does Ana María come to know the truth; that she is her real mother. And only in this moment does Ana María recognize her error, beg for forgiveness for her atrocious behavior, and call Mamá Mercé by the name she has longed to hear all these years, "Mamá." Although Mamá Mercé is unconscious while Ana María repents, a close-up on a single teardrop flowing down Mamá Mercé's face indicates that she has heard Ana María's petition, and that she forgives her daughter for her rejection. This moment is replete with sentimentalist tragedy; only through this sacrifice can black subjectivity become acceptable.

Through Mamá Mercé and Juan Carlos's complicity in silencing the truth, they facilitate the racism that manifests itself in Ana María, but also the unspoken racism that abounds in Mexican society. By not speaking the truth, they collaborate with the racism that excludes blacks from the national narrative. Mamá Mercé's death speaks to this point: she participates in her own suffering and thus cannot form part of the present, only part of the tragic past. Although having accepted her black heritage by the end of the film, Ana María can no longer be a heroine or be redeemed. She has already been tainted by her hatred, her vitriol, and her matricide. True to the melodramatic form, there is no social illumination; rather, the film registers the problem of the silencing of racism and identifies the social actors who perform this drama. The answers, and thus resolution, are to be found elsewhere.

The role of Belén, the mulata child, becomes part of this ambiguous resolution in the drama. She remains after the violence of the mother has consumed itself. What place will the child occupy in Mexican society? The film insinuates that Ana María will accept her child, but the violence of matricide makes her an unfit mother even after she has reconciled herself to the truth. This ending for the child is similar to that of *La negra Angustias*, as the white dandy relegates both the visibly black Angustias and their mixed-race son to obscurity. The equivocal place of the mulato progeny in these narratives mirror the empty placeholder held by blacks in Mexican society and cultural production. As a child, the fact that Belén remains after Mamá Mercé has died might indicate a positive future for her in society despite representing a kind of atavistic throwback. Nevertheless, I contend that this character signals an unresolved tension where she remains an innocent victim of societal racism and violence: a product of the colonial desire to produce, and to witness, black sentience. As with other "tragic mulattas," the tragedy of the family drama does not bode well for the future nor suggest any meaningful reconciliation; the film begins a discussion that it cannot resolve.

De colores: Performing Redress

Negro es mi color (1951) was filmed three years after the first release of Rodriguez's *Angelitos negros* and it constitutes a cinematic attempt to redress racial injustice head-on. In contrast to the other films examined here, *Negro es mi color* opens with a voice-over that operates as a preface that purposefully locates the story's setting in a nonspecific place within an ahistorical timeframe:

> La historía que aquí se relata es absolutamente verdadera. El país en que tales acontecimientos pudieron suceder existe, quizá.

Pero mencionarlo sería tanto como tirar la primera piedra sobre una sola de las muchas naciones en las que todavía, a pesar del progreso y de la civilización, el pensamiento de los hombres y el espíritu de las leyes naufragan en las tinieblas del prejuicio racial.

[The story told here is absolutely true. The country in which these events could have taken place exists, perhaps. But to mention the name would be to throw the first stone on one of the many nations where, despite progress and civilization, the thought of man and the spirit of the law drowns in the darkness of racial prejudice].

This meta-textual device initiates the film like a parable moralizing on the dangers of racial prejudice. In this way the film abstracts blackness from the very beginning, to speak about how black persons in general, in "any place in the world," have suffered the iniquity of intolerance and hatred. A few moments later in the film the camera zooms in on a signpost that reads: "Se prohibe el paso de perros y negros" [Dogs and Blacks Are Not Allowed]. Indeed, the film alerts the spectator to its missionizing project from the beginning (lest the spectator miss the lesson to follow) and through this self-referential gesture announces that this cinematic representation stages racial violence in an attempt to redress it. Markers of *mexicanidad* are presented only subtly in the accents of certain actors, but no specificity with regard to place and time are revealed. Unlike the films *La Mulata de Córdoba*, *Angelitos negros*, and *La negra Angustias*, which each specifically address issues of blackness in México, this film overtly rejects locating this racial quandary within a national context and instead universalizes the problem of race relations. This abstraction of race to an unknown time and place is a move that again seems to painfully mirror the actual state of blackness in México: even those, like these filmmakers, who recognize that blacks are part of the Mexican social fabric, distantiate blackness from daily life in México in order to moralize from afar. As is the case with other racial melodramas, imperfect verisimilitude, sentimentalist excess, and deployment of stock character types detract from the virtues of *Negro es mi color* as a work of artistic filmmaking, but unlike *Angelitos negros*, it attempts a more full development of the mulata figure although it does not stray far from popular paradigms regarding mulata turpitude, sexuality, and inevitable tragedy. In fact, it too relies heavily on tried and true renditions of the tragic mulattas and mammy types that proliferate in the traditions of work typical of the United States and Caribbean.

Unlike the main character in *Angelitos negros,* the mulata protagonist of *Negro es mi color*, Luna/Blanca, is fully conscious of her black heritage and utilizes her sexuality as a tool to manipulate men so that she may enact her revenge, complying with commonplace characterizations of mulatas as coquettish teases that use their bodies for their own personal ambitions, their flesh mapped by the inevitable crossroads of desire, shame, and loss. However, the only physical marker of her African lineage is manifest in her sultry, powerful voice, constituting a sonic blackness that bewitches her audiences and that is responsible for her immediate success as a cabaret singer. But although Luna performs and exploits this aural blackness in order to secure success as an entertainer, she rejects her family and black heritage, thus replicating the exploitation of chattel slavery.

The plot begins when Luna's mother Rita, also seduced and abandoned by a white man, has misgivings about the white sailor Luna has brought home to meet her and refuses to accept this man as her daughter's fiancé. Consequently, Luna decides to run away with her suitor and, as to be expected, is duped by the sailor and abandoned on ship. As a result, she refuses to return home but instead decides that this humiliation will allow her to be "born again." In her new identity as "Blanca" she has but one mission: to avenge her humiliation by the white man who abandoned her and to hide the truth about her origins. She becomes a performer and ironically makes her debut by singing a languid song she learned from her mother about the suffering of black folk. This melody subsequently operates as a musical motif throughout the film. Akin to the racial dynamics I will discuss in the next chapter with the figure of Toña la Negra, the acoustics of race become "evident" in her voice. One of her secondary love interests, an air force pilot who has lived in a black community, exclaims that he has only heard such a unique sonic texture in the voices of black women. Thus, the sonic equivalence of race becomes uniquely identified in the timbre of her voice, constituting the only corporeal marker of her blackness. It is precisely the racialized timbre and texture of her voice that catapults her to stardom and makes her the object of male attention, including her own father. So true to the melodramatic form and the tragic mulatta genre, *mulatez* becomes signified not only by wickedly manipulative behavior, but by the lust she provokes in her father, who has only just become aware of her existence through a missive sent by her suffering mother alerting him to her arrival. Despite the warning, he does not recognize Blanca as his daughter, and his interest in her as a star for his show is coupled with his fascination with her beauty—a clever narcissistic twist because she inherited his white body. When he asks her to go on a trip with him, the adumbrating threat of incest looms, although it never materializes because her mother Rita intervenes in the nick of time when she recognizes her former lover as he arrives to pick up their daughter. This reunion between Rita and the white lover who abandoned her years before leads to his unexpected repentance, as both parents lament the callous behavior of their daughter, which they believe to be a result of their illicit union and the father's rejection and abandonment. Thereafter Luna discovers that she is pregnant and attempts to commit suicide, unable to fathom the possibility that her child will be black. However, the doctor who attends to her in the maternity ward convinces her to accept the child as a blessing, regardless of the color it may turn out to be. Luna returns home to her mother but, alas, arrives too late. Her mother has died of a broken heart.

The melodramatic mode in concert with the trope of sexual perversion, incest, and unknown origins harkens back to Caribbean representations of *mulatez* in works such as *Cecilia Valdés* (1882), by Cuban writer Cirilio Villaverde, as similar tropes regarding blackness and whiteness, revenge and incest weave themselves in and out of this film. Rita Montaner (a light mulata herself and a *cuarterona*) is once more portrayed in blackface; yet again it seems that in order to authenticate the plight of the abnegated mother she must be "blackened up" like the identical role she plays in *Angelitos negros*. The deployment of the mammy figure invokes a pained black subject whose loyalty to her white masters and domesticity makes her an acceptable display of blackness both for white North American and almost-white Latin American audiences. Moreover, the image of the suffering mother is not unfamiliar to Mexican audiences. As already noted, Mexicans adulate the figure of the Virgin of Guadalupe, the brown-skinned patron saint of the Americas, and the portrait of an afflicted dark mother whose daughter rejects her would resonate loudly for a Mexican audience. However, the mother figure is loyal not to her patrons, as in the case of the mammy trope, but to her phenotypically "white" daughter. Rita begs Blanca to take her in as a servant and likens her loyalty to her daughter to that of a "faithful dog." Unlike the mulata figure in *Angelitos negros*, whose rejection leads to a physical altercation that accidentally results in matricide, Blanca's emotional rejection of her mother in *Negro es mi color* leads to the physical demise of the dejected woman. Neither mulata repents in time to reconcile with the heart-broken mother, but in *Negro es mi color*, Luna ends up accepting her pregnancy despite not knowing if the child will bear the "mark" of her race. Furthermore, her racist paramour also repents and accepts Luna despite her black heritage and embraces their future progeny notwithstanding the unknown phenotype of the child. Acceptance (or resignation) serves as a sort of resolution to the conflict constituted by racism and the problem posed by unknown or undisclosed origins. The piteous, abnegating mother is yet again sacrificed; her presence only constitutes itself as a physiological atavism that will give way to the cloudy future of a mixed-race grandchild. Once more, the mulata's villainous past ultimately places her outside of the models of acceptable motherhood and taints the child's uncertain future.

In her 2008 analysis of blackface in mid-twentieth-century Mexican cinema, Marilyn Miller writes that the use of blackface in these films serves to distantiate Latin American identity from blackness: "Through parody, substitution or caricature, Blackness is rendered superficial and thus empty; through blackface the Mexican or Latin-American collective subject is thus paradoxically whitened" ("The Soul Has No Color" 253). In contrast to U.S. film audiences, Latin American spectators do not identify with whiteness in such a clean-cut manner: audiences could be urban mestizos, indigenous people, mulatos, white, and not-so-white elite criollos, blacks, and Asians. Because whiteness in México is a construct that cannot be divorced from its colonial context—in México race was variably and subjectively determined by parish priests or scribes, and if wealthy enough one could almost purchase whiteness, rendering racial identifications much more fluid than has been imagined—it is not surprising that blackface is employed in all of these films. In this way, blackness is elided and "rendered superficial" through excess, but also whiteness as a paradigm becomes destabilized; in fact, there exists a profound insecurity regarding the stability of whiteness in Latin America that goes back to medieval Europe with the Spanish Reconquista.[19] In the last two films the mestizo/almost-white José Carlos in *Angelitos negros*, and the phenotypically white but mixed-race Luna in *Negro es mi color* are presented in blackface and blackbody for their most visually stunning performances, simultaneously seducing the audience and appealing to the spectator's desire to consume blackness. Racially mixed or almost-white characters perform blackness, which not only destabilizes whiteness; it unravels the ideology of mestizaje.

In particular, one striking scene from *Negro es mi color* calls attention to this complex racial dynamic. Blanca performs a cabaret scene in blackface and body while interpreting the music with gesticulations evidently supposed to invoke a powerful African woman, but at the end of the scene, she removes a brilliant white stole to reveal a strip of skin over her shoulder that has not been darkened in order to disclose to the internal, diegetic audience that indeed, she is a white woman. The doubled irony is startling, because the actual spectator knows that she is a mulata although her phenotype would indicate otherwise, thus signaling the racist gesture implicit in perform-ing blackness for the pleasure of a non-black audience. The deployment of blackface as an attempt to distantiate whiteness from blackness by, in fact, successfully performing blackness to the fictional audience—as opposed to traditional blackface where all spectators are fully aware that the performer is not black—is undone, as the protagonist herself is dissimulating her whiteness in order to complete the guise. However, this twinned racial performance reveals a deeply problematic depiction of blackness as it is at once consumed and instrumentalized as entertainment while ironically intending to reveal racial injustice. The film attempts to denounce blackface by underscoring the violence of the performance by the phenotypically white protagonist who invokes a powerful, beautiful, and elegant black woman, only to reveal to the cabaret audience that she is white, and that no such black woman exists. However, the external audience knows that the actress, Marga López, is not mulata but a white Mexican national.[20] Thus, although intended to shock the spectator, the white face of the actress portraying a mulata character performing in blackface results in a doubly painful performance of blackness, annulling any possible social denunciation the film might have achieved (not to mention the fact that Rita Montaner is once again presented in blackface). How then, does one define blackness? This film would indicate that it is sonically expressed; that her voice is testament to her racial origins. Although not a *cabaretera*, the movie highlights the protagonist in her role as a cabaret star through the astounding and racialized timbre of her voice, supposedly only found in those of black women. It also hints at blackness as an atavistic reality that cannot easily be buried in the past, or disguised by a dissimulated whiteness.

However, Jill Lane makes a different argument with regard to the strategic use of blackface in nineteenth-century Cuba, which is interesting for my consideration of these films. In *Blackface Cuba, 1840–1885* (2005), Lane contends that the use of blackface in Cuba's *teatro bufo*[21] was popular among Cuban whites and relied on racialized stereotypes, such as the *negrito* and the *mulata*, to coagulate an anti-colonial sentiment against the Spanish and strengthen the racial ideology of mestizaje which celebrated the new cultural reality that resulted from physical and cultural miscegenation while maintaining the racial hierarchy.[22] The use of blackface and Afro-Cuban musical rhythms in the *teatros bufos* created safe havens for white reflection and, in this case, spaces for crafting a cultural difference between white Cubans and the Spanish colonizers. But real social integration is rendered impossible by the use of blackface and the comedic elements of the *bufos* because racial hierarchies remain unchallenged. Furthermore, by claiming a mestizo identity rather than a mulato identity, blackness becomes subordinated to a romanticized indigenous substrate.[23]

And different from the libidinal economy of disgust/desire that the performance of blackface provoked in white North American audiences of the early twentieth century, these Mexican films move beyond fulfilling the designs of the white audience who will be ethically moved and outraged by this display of racist hatred at the same time they are empowered by the figurative and physical possession of a black body. Rather, blackface allows the insecurities regarding racial purity to be set aside, as the performance does not necessarily validate whiteness in the Mexican "mestizo" spectator as much as it confirms that they are *not* black. Blackface operates to invisibilize blackness and "paradoxically whiten" because blacks do not constitute a formative component of the Mexican ideal of mestizaje. Like the oversaturation of a sponge where the water overflows and slips away, an aesthetic of excess and hyperbole serves to distantiate mestizos from blacks and the racial politics of chattel slavery. Despite its design to reproduce U.S. cinematic renditions of racial conflict, the filmic trend of blackface and figures that simulate tragic mulattas and mammies—although similar in their execution—produce a very different effect in the Mexican and Latin American audiences for whom they were intended.

Let us return to the film that began this chapter, *La Mulata de Córdoba*, which was the first produced in this series and the only one to reference the historical role of blacks in México—albeit obliquely—relying loosely on the legend from the Gulf Coast of Veracruz that inspired the poem and opera examined in chapter 4. Unlike the others, it was not well circulated and even now is difficult to find. Still, it is the closest we will get in Mexican Golden Age cinema to a discussion about the contributions of Afro-descendants to the economic development and culture of the colony, in this case, through the sugar plantations in the Gulf Coast and the miscegenation in the countryside that led to the specific Afro-Caribbean heritage that many identity with the city and state of Veracruz. While the figure of Angustias is portrayed as a revolutionary colonel in the most significant political uprising in Mexican history of the last century, her blackness is exceptionalized, and not part of the longer history of slavery. It is, simply, an accident that provides the dramatic tension that will lead to her rape(s) and criminality.

As discussed in the previous chapter, blackness in México has had a decidedly urban expression, forming large communities in the vice-regal capital and other colonial centers, making the historical contributions of blacks in *La Mulata de Córdoba* largely reliant on generalized assumptions of chattel slavery, which was certainly present in México, but not as predominant as it was in the Caribbean, Brazil, and the United States. In this way the legend compounds all the prevailing tropes as they relate to black women not only in México, but throughout the Americas: opprobrious sensuality, diabolical allure, psychological perversity, and inevitable tragedy. These attributes are all woven into this film—indeed, all of these films—with little variation in form and content. Even in México, the visual traffic of black bodies serves much the same function it does in other areas of the world where chattel slavery was more prominent: it acts as a mechanism by which to spectate black sentience and to participate in the economy of subjection that simultaneously eroticizes wounded black bodies and exoticizes them as other.

The cinematic version of *La Mulata de Córdoba*, starring Toña la Negra and Victor Junco, is based on the original screenplay by Xavier Villaurrutia, although significantly adapted by filmmaker Adolfo Fernández Bustamante. The drama in this film involves two important rival families, and the mulata is the offspring of an illicit liaison between one of the town's most important patriarchs and his sensual mulata servant, Belén. Unlike *Negro es mi color* and *Angelitos negros*, here the white father officially recognizes his racially mixed daughter, and she inherits his fortune and the family patronymic, much to the disgust of the other members of his prominent family who disown her despite their own economic decline. When the town's most eligible bachelor from a rival family returns after a long absence, he falls in love with the Mulata and spurns her white cousin Emilia to whom he is betrothed. This unleashes a tragic amorous triangle because, as fate would have it, his own father has also fallen in love with the Mulata. In the original screenplay, the legend of the Mulata de Córdoba does not come in until the end, when it is revealed that it is her spirit, or *sombra*, that has inspired the mulata protagonist's plot of revenge against the family who has socially alienated and insulted her, despite her great wealth and kinship with them. Both the original screenplay and film confront the racial panic that is wrought precisely by the recognition and incorporation of the white mulata daughter into a family consumed with genealogy, prestige, and the concomitant expectation of whiteness. The acceptance of the mulata by her father as a legitimate—and loved—child is mitigated by his fetish for black female bodies. Both the screenplay and film note that his one "vice" was his attraction to mulata women, positioning blackness once again as a sexual indulgence and white womanhood as respectable and beautiful, but untouchable.

Due in part to the disappearing of blacks from the historical memory, if not the official colonial record, Bustamante's film centers on the allure of an imaginary blackness (the mulata is phenotypically white in the film while in the legend she is clearly mixed-race), in contrast to the reality of sexual violence and aggression that are the source of the hyperbolic sexuality imputed to the racially mixed body. Mulata mesmerism, such as that discussed in the previous chapter, comes in full force to explain her power, revealing nothing of the actual role of blacks and mulatos as folk healers and curers throughout the colonial period, preferring to exploit more familiar themes related to perversity and tragic *mulatez* in cultural production in the United States and Caribbean. For example, the verses from the *son jarocho* in the opening dance sequence speak to this notion of mesmerism, black magic and danger: "la negrita María Belén tu mirada me fascina / la quiero de medicina aunque me muera después / te daremos lo que anheles si nos miras con amor / tus ojos de engaño pueden matar" [oh black María Belén / your gaze fascinates me / I would take you as medicine even if I die afterwards / we will give you what you most desire if you were to only grant us an amorous gaze / your deceitful eyes are deadly]. These lines recall the "Son de la Negra," the *son jaliciense* (musical genre popular in the mariachi repertoire) cited in the epigraph to the introduction of the book, in which the supplicant cries: "Little black woman of my sorrow / with flickering paper eyes / Say yes to them all / but don't say when / Just like you said to me / which is why I live in grief!" Similar to the song in the film, this black woman's flirty eyes and sultry countenance provoke an unsated and treacherous desire; they insinuate a sexual buildup that will likely lead to frustration and violence by the male suitor.

The trope of mulata mesmerism is amplified not only through the effect she has on the white aristocracy but also through the power she wields over her subordinates: in this case, the love-stricken mulato manservant Juan Miguel. The mulato occupies the role of the loyal eunuch, or as the film says, "faithful dog," childlike even as an adult, harkening back to Gertrudis Gómez de Avellaneda's tragic mulatto *Sab* (1841) who, like the character of Juan Miguel, is emasculated by his unrequited love. Juan Miguel knows that Belén is too good for him; her white skin color puts him at a disadvantage, and renders her position untenable and irreconcilable in the society to which they both belong. He laments that "she is too good for the black people, but not good enough for the whites. What will become of her?" To be surrounded by only mixed-race and black peasants is tantamount to social isolation, and she is alone because blacks are not socially viable subjects. As in *Negro es mi color*, her father's perversion results in her malice, and in the end, the bullet issued by Juan Miguel in her defense accidentally strikes her. Over and over again, the mulata is the cause of her own disastrous fate, and only through her elimination can the temptation be removed and the social order normalize.

La Mulata de Córdoba (like so many other films) insists on the mulata's ire and quest for redress as a result of the inability of society to accept her despite her white skin. This anger is deployed as a weapon to destroy the purity and sanctity of the elite family lineage, and more importantly, the respectability of its members. The mulata character, unlike anything we see in the legend, refuses to step away from the legitimacy of her name. After being rebuked by her *nana* for flirting with the father of the bachelor who will soon be her lover, she seethes: "Sólo quiero sentir el placer de verlo rendido a mis pies. Quiero vengar en él todo lo que los blancos me han hecho sufrir. Lo que me dices le hicieron sufrir a mi madre, con su desprecio, me han inculcado tal odio que a veces siento deseos de . . ." [I only want to feel the pleasure of seeing him at my feet. I want to avenge in him all that the whites have made me suffer. The pain you say they inflicted on my mother with their disdain, has conditioned a hate so strong that sometimes I feel the urge to . . .]. She refuses to stop being part of a wealthy family despite their rejection of her as an illegitimate mulata. This pride necessarily results in the depraved love triangle she causes and the destruction of two important families.

True to the "tragic mulatta" trope, only misfortune can resolve the conflict her body represents. The mulata's legitimate desire for redress is, as is to be expected, rendered perverse and can only be redeemed by her subordination, or worse, self-sacrifice. Accordingly, the film ends with her heroically stepping in front of her nemesis, the racist white uncle who has rejected her since she was born, in order to take the bullet for him and save his life. Only through this self-effacing and singular act of heroism can she be redeemed. She knows this, as the last lines directed to the sobbing Juan Miguel confirm: "Estoy contenta por que me has dado la oportunidad de mostrar que tenemos el alma como ellos" [I'm happy that you gave me the opportunity to show them that we have souls just like them]. And with these words, the repentant uncle utters that, in light of Belén's selfless heroism, she indeed has the "sangre de los San Juan" [blood of the San Juan].

In all of the films, the black mothers die of heartbreak (or childbirth), making way for the phenotypically white or whitish family to continue. The mulata characters' subjectivity—despite their heroics, skill or smarts—is compromised by either their perceived crimes, their heartless behavior, or their insolence. Such as we see in *Negro es mi color*, the *Mulata de Córdoba* character seeks redress for the racism that has violently excluded her from her rightful place in the social hierarchy—without every really questioning the hierarchy. In turn, Angustias seeks redress for the violent nature of gender relations in a patriarchal society, and although she does not die in the end, nor induce the death of the abnegating mother, in the novel she is rendered completely subservient to the foppish white male who has recovered his masculinity upon her dejection. However, through her incursion in female sentimental weakness triggered by unrequited love, she indirectly causes the death of her faithful subcommander and servant, Güitlacoche. This feminine weakness in concert with the commission of unspeakable crimes, such as the murder and castration of her aggressors, makes her also impossible to redeem. In the film she is validated by her revolutionary fervor and valor through Landeta's revisionist ending.

Different from the film that was finally produced, the original screenplay of *La Mulata de Córdoba* penned by Villaurrutia concludes the drama by making reference to the legend from which the title is drawn. When the former lovers barge into her house to seize the black servant who shot her uncle, they are greeted with a maniacal laugh that resounds from every corner of the house, carrying an echo from a distant pass that speaks of centuries of violence and of the need for redress. Echoing the gothic tenor of a ghost story, the rooms reverberate the "wicked" and "diabolical" laughter that asserts its revenge. The famous legend appears only to incite tragedy and violence; the inevitable turpitude occasioned by a mixed-race woman who speaks from the grave, an aggrieved revenant that incites fear in order to achieve redress.

Insolence, tragedy, unearthly sexuality, and perversity: these are the proliferating, indeed, unavoidable, tropes that define mulata subjectivity. *La Mulata de Córdoba* does accomplish what *La negra Angustias* begins when it locates blackness in the Mexican national historical imagination and seeks to tell a story of racial inequity but, also, a story of truncated female agency. Powerful women, whether lowly soldaderas or wealthy mulata plantation owners, are impossible to reconcile with Mexican manhood and emergent civic and national culture. Tropicality, such as that witnessed in the feverish *rumbera* films, will be the outlet for this latent admiration and fear of blackness. While undoubtedly flawed, the film partially succeeds in proposing a tense counterpoint between Mexican culture and blackness through the *jarocho* culture and identity, and in particular, through the musical practices in the opening sequences of the film that serve as almost a sonic evidentiary material: back-handed proof of Mexican blackness. The Afro-Mexican characters that fill in the background provide an unmistakable Mexican context for this race drama, but only through their dress and the music. Moreover, the iconicity and diva status of Toña la Negra as the *nana* figures Mexican tropicality into the center of this drama even when, unlike *Negro es mi color*, she is not an abnegating mother, but more of a knowing and tough, cigar-smoking mammy who stands up for her protégé.

In these films, as well the famous *cabaretera* films of México's Golden Age, black actors form part of the background as supernumerary musicians and performers. In fact, some Mexican musicians in the *cabareteras* were replaced with more "authentic" looking Afro-Cuban musicians. Why mulato or black musicians were preferred to mestizo-looking Mexican ones elicits some interesting questions regarding the strategic appropriation of black bodies for the tropical background scenes and why, for leading roles, directors preferred blackface as a means to authenticate the performances by white or light-skinned mulata actors. The logic that undergirds why black musicians are coveted but black leading ladies are not speaks loudly to the phenomenon I discussed earlier: visible blackness in México is often deflected onto the Caribbean. But what remains crystal clear is that, in Mexican cinema, black actors were not afforded the luxury of representing themselves despite the filmmakers' exhortations to overcome racism. Toña la Negra is the only Afro-Mexican who is featured prominently in Mexican cinema. As aptly expressed by Miller, blackness is more easily "simulated" than "assimilated" in Mexican filmic culture of the twentieth century (245), and the prevalence of Afro-Cuban musical acts in these films and others, in addition to the use of blackface, point to "signs of recognition of the racial other and as the absorption of otherness into dominant forms of national and regional identity" (253). In spite of this absorption, these films are fundamentally ambivalent: on the one hand, their continued popularity indicates that they do successfully introduce Mexican and Latin American audiences to the problems facing black Latin Americans, although at a safe distance. On the other, the flawed attempts to address the marginalized black presence by utilizing U.S. models does little to redress the insidious nature of Mexican racism against blacks. The awkward fit of these filmic models and haphazard execution provokes the annoyance of critics like García Riera, but also functions against creating a real discourse regarding black contributions to Mexican history, culture, and thought. Afro-Mexican communities continue to linger in a narrative fragmentation while their presence is marooned, because, despite the filmmakers' "good" intentions, nothing substantive is revealed about them or their history in these films.

Unknown Origins

In his ethnographic work of the Costa Chica (on the Pacific coast of México), Bobby Vaughn finds that, in general, no consciousness of slavery or link to Africa exists among Afro-descendant communities living there in the early twenty-first century. Rather, locals "will invariably talk about any number of shipwrecks from which their ancestors escaped" and will even claim to have relatives that came from the remains of ships that can still be seen (4). Likewise, after conducting fieldwork in Veracruz (on the other side of the country) Vaughn claims that "most Afro-Mexican people that I have spoken to trace their origins to Cuba" (3). Similar to the inhabitants of Coyolillo, the small town in Veracruz, who, despite acknowledging their racial difference possess a very attenuated notion of blackness, preferring to deflect it onto the Cubans or explain it as the fate of "god's design," these extraordinary films, photographs, legends, poems, and Inquisition cases illustrate that blackness in México, despite the paradox of the nation's historical amnesia, has been a fundamental agent in its self-fashioning.

The persistence of the trope of unknown origins regarding black individuals or communities is one that abounds in the cultural production and imaginary in México and across the Américas: the orphaned mulata witch from Córdoba who vanished suddenly into obscurity (and literally into the air), Antonia de Soto's multiple names and identities, the African descendants from Costa Chica who would rather talk about shipwrecks than runaway slave colonies, and the orphaned leading ladies in Mexican films produced during the glorious *época dorada*, including those discussed above, such as Angustias, orphaned as a child and raised by a *curandera*, José Carlos from *Angelitos negros*, whose orphaned ancestry takes the "blame" for his child Belén's blackness, José Carlos's wife Ana María, who has no idea that the black nanny who has raised her is actually her mother, or Luna from *Negro es mi color*, who actively chooses to sever her familial ties in order to achieve a symbolic orphanhood. Indeed, orphaned and existing almost *sui generis*, Mexican mulatos take the blame for sexual depravity and social upheaval in the emergent colonial society, and continue to reflect these same anxieties in the representations they are afforded in the film and literature of the subsequent centuries.

Each cultural product examined in these chapters touch on the black legacy in México obliquely, and some deflect México's black history and culture onto a racialized Caribbean. The next chapter will continue to discuss the legacy of blacks in México, but will specifically explore the impact they have had on Mexican music and expand on this notion of black exceptionalism through its real—and imagined—ties to the Caribbean. We see then, that Mexican blackness is dressed in a tropical headdress.

6

The Music of the Afro-Mexican Universe
and the Dialectics of *Son*

Decía las canciones de una forma muy especial, siempre diferente. Ella era muy especial como persona y como artista, era figura, nació para ser figura.

[She performed her songs in a very special way, always different. She was a very special person and artist; she was a figure, she was born to be a figure].

—Pepe Arévalo[1]

Toña la Negra was an extremely influential singer from the state of Veracruz on the Gulf Coast of México who, beginning in the '30s up until the '60s, was famous for singing *boleros* and Cuban *son*. The figure of Toña la Negra, contrary to other Mexican mulata figures that I considered earlier (both fictive and real), is not marginalized in the popular imaginary, nor is she a victim or martyr. On the contrary, she is as both prominent and as *mexicana* as they come. Not only a practitioner of Antillean music, she is an embodiment of the tension that inhabits the assimilation and naturalization of tropical music in México. Indeed, she is an example of what Licia Fiol-Matta calls a "thinking voice."[2] Dressed in tropical fanfare for one of her publicity shots on a tour to Cuba, complete with flowers atop her head and ruffled *rumbera* sleeves, she embodies Caribbeanity (see Fig. 6.1). This publicity shot incarnates the kind of image projected both abroad to international audiences, and internally, to domestic ones. Born to be a *figure*, as expressed by Pepe Arévalo (a popular Mexican actor and musician), we can appreciate how she was also born to embody the paradox of Mexican blackness. In one of her first films, *Konga*

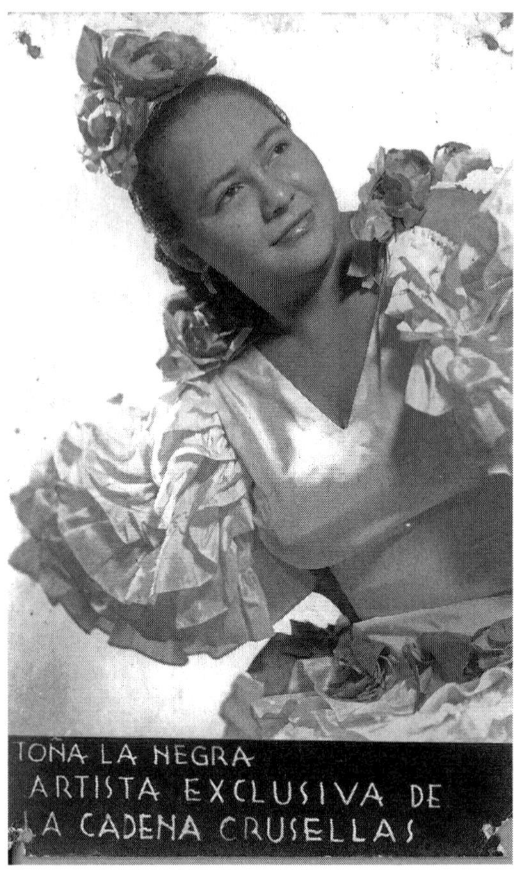

FIGURE 6.1. "Toña la Negra in publicity poster for her first tour of Cuba at the beginning of the 1940s."

Roja (1943), she played a nightclub *rumbera*, and two years later she starred in the *La Mulata de Córdoba* (1945) as the soulful black *nana*. Sometimes blackened up to perform her *mulatez*, and at others whitened to play the *jarocha*, her body performs this Caribbeanity through an incursion in all its signs, and yet simultaneously remains Mexican. We see, then, that the *jarocho* identity born in the city of Veracruz is at once celebratory of miscegenation and fraught by a racial memory that is lopsided. Furthermore, in the same way some soldaderas and other powerful woman such as Antonia de Soto transvested in order to gain access to privileged male domains, the performance of tropicality is a gesture tantamount to recognizing—and displacing—blackness.

In May of 2004, Charles Rowell and Marcus Jones conducted an interview of a man named Edgar Cano, from Santiago de Tuxtla in the state of Veracruz (south of the Port where Toña was born)[3] and asked the following questions:

Rowell: What does that mean to you, to be Afromestizo? What does that mean here in México?

Cano: For me, Afromestizo in México refers to the synthesis of *Africans, Cubans and Indigenous Mexicans*. I believe that a synthesis took place at some point way back. It did not just happen through the Spaniards' colonization, but I believe it took place long before the Spanish arrived. It wasn't so much colonization as it was possibly a commercial relationship among the towns, whether they were African or even Asian.

Rowell: Do the local people here in Santiago de Tuxtla or elsewhere in the State of Veracruz wonder why the Olmecs don't look like anybody else of the pre-Colombian period?

Cano: We could say that the whole coastal area of the State of Veracruz was more affected by the Afromestizo influence. I want to distinguish between the physical and the cultural. *The Afromestizo influence is not entirely a physical one; it is much more than skin color or the phenotype.* I don't know why I wasn't born with darker skin color. [. . .] I think the State of Veracruz is very rich in the physical and cultural diversity of its people. (emphasis added, 515)

The morsels of information gleaned from this interview turn out to be profoundly revealing, as it tells us that Cano identifies himself as an Afromestizo, recognizes Cubanos (as opposed to Spaniards) as an integral part of the culture of the state of Veracruz, believes the African influence in Veracruz predates the Conquest, and finally, that culture is not reducible to phenotype. The nonchalance and candor of this statement result poignant—even shocking—given the amnesia that has absorbed the contributions of blacks to Mexican culture. The responses evinced by the interview above underscore that the concept of Afromestizo,[4] so central to the *jarocho* culture, is a matter of great civic and regional pride. *Jarocho* refers to the inhabitants of Veracruz and means "mixed blood"; the mixture to which it refers is precisely the African and Amerindian. But it is after the Revolution of 1910 that the cultural life of the city actively sought to create cultural links with the Caribbean, particularly Cuba. It is through this exchange that Veracruz's "Afromestizo" culture marks its lasting contributions to Mexican culture and the national imaginary in its appropriation of *son, danzón, boleros,* and of course the creation of the *son jarocho,* whose very name and unique sound point toward a pan-Caribbean imaginary in a distinctly Mexican fashion. Through an analysis of "música tropical" as a vital contribution to Mexican music—specifically *danzón, son cubano,* and *son jarocho*—this chapter explores how Mexican musical culture reflects this African-inspired Caribbean influence while deflecting the autochthonous black presence. Building on many of the themes presented in previous chapters, such as a marginalized Africanness and the exoticizing of the mulata, these ideas are engaged through a discussion of music (both Mexican and Cuban) as the aesthetic form in which this tension takes place. I examine the various cultural movements originating from the state of Veracruz and interpret their regional identification as part of the *Gran Caribe,*[5] in addition to their insistence on honoring what they call their "third root," as a gesture that disrupts the discourses of national belonging. Indeed, the various artistic and cultural movements emerging from Veracruz act as a point of resistance to the Revolution's rhetoric of assimilation. Furthermore, the centrality of Toña la Negra as a figure, despite the insistence on her blackness as a *jarocha,* points to the fractures of mestizaje as a Mexican nationalist discourse. Winning innumerable awards and making countless records, she is a positive and foundational figure in the creation and dissemination of a national culture, making the paradox of the invisibility of blackness in México that much more acute.

According to the eminent anthropologist Gonzalo Aguirre Beltrán in his now classic study *La población negra de México* (1946), *jarocho* was the term that was used to describe the racial mixture between blacks and Amerindians. He claims that the etymological origin of the word stems from the epithet "jaro," which in Muslim Spain meant wild pig, to which they added the pejorative ending "cho." This was the term the Spanish apparently used to describe those Veracruzanos who were "mulatos" and "pardos," intending to call them wild pigs due to their multiple racial combinations. According to the Real Academia Española, *jarocho* refers to "una persona de modales bruscos, descompuestos y algo insolentes," thus signifying racially mixed people with "boorish and insolent mannerisms."[6] The etymology of the word in multiple definitions consistently evokes objects with a reddish hue, as "jara" denotes both plants and pigs that are a "pardo rojizo" [reddish brown].[7] *Pardo* was a euphemism strategically employed to describe mulatos that was less ominous, because mulatos were not allowed to enter the military but *pardos* were[8] (Aguirre Beltrán 173). Finally, the etymological origin of the term "jara" also refers to a sharp stick or lance used as a weapon, which some historians claim spawned "jarochos" in order to describe the crudely armed colonial militiamen who, due to their mixed-race status, were only allowed to be armed with sticks.[9]

Whether the word refers to the mixture between African and Spanish, or African and indigenous, it was a derogatory term used to describe people who physically reflected racial miscegenation. This was especially true in the countryside where many blacks were employed as cowhands in the ranching industry and may have been "burnt" by the sun, thus the added connotation to the insistence on reddish hues. Whatever the original intention (they might all be correct), as wild pigs, reddish-brown "half-breeds," or barbaric, stick-wielding militiamen, it was used to disparage the emerging community of racially mixed people that would create the particular culture of this region. Although it began in the countryside in the eighteenth century this moniker stopped being derogatory and actually became a term used to describe the residents of the Port of Veracruz, and then metonymically the whole population of the state of Veracruz. People today refer to themselves proudly as *jarochos*, and *son jarocho* is one of the unique musical forms that is a product of this contact between diverse peoples and the way in which an epithet became a source of pride, mutual identification and a dynamic regional cultural production.

The Permutations of *Son* in México

Jarochita, jarochita, baila este son.
Calientito y movidito, picosito y sabrosón.
Jarochita, jarochita, tú en verdad, sabes bailar
y en los ritmos tropicales nadie te puede igualar.

—Luís Alfonso Castillo

Son, in the Mexican musical vocabulary, can mean a number of things: it can refer to music in general, or music from any number of traditions and time periods, or music from a particular region or country. Thus, we have *son* Veracruzano, Jaliciense, Huasteco, Jarocho, Cubano, de Oriente, Montuno, among others.[10] According to the *Real Academia*, the word *son*, from the Latin *sonus* means: "a sound that agreeable affects the ears, especially that which is done with artistry."[11] The second definition claims it means "news, fame, divulgation of something" while the third defines it as a "pretexto" followed by "tenor, mode or manner." Finally, the dictionary also states that it in Cuba it means "popular dance music." The penultimate definition, "tenor, modo o manera" is provocative considering the vicissitudes the word as a musical concept would undergo in the context of Mexican music. *Son* as a word is all of these things: a tenor, a mode, or manner. It is also a divulgation of something, whether that be a rumor, sound, or song, and it is also a pretext to dance. In the musical landscape of Veracruz, Daniel Sheehy informs us that *son* refers to music that is accompanied by a *zapateado*,[12] while other danceable music is called *danzas* because they are non-*zapateado* dances that are performed by the middle classes. Eugene Rodríguez, in his introduction to an album by the internationally acclaimed *son jarocho* group Mono Blanco, explains that in Veracruz, *son* is not a song, but is "based on a repeating rhythmic and harmonic pattern with an infinite number of melodies and verses—depending on the creativity of the interpreter" (4). Therefore, one who improvises and creates within this genre is a *sonero*.

Indeed, the origin of *son* in México is disputed, but based on the work of Gabriel Saldívar, Sheehy suggests that the *letrillas, coplas,* and *coplillas*[13] are direct predecessors to the *son*. Even today, the term *coplas* is used interchangeably to refer to the *son* performance in Veracruz. Sheehy concludes that before 1766, the *son* had been associated with secular singing, dancing and instrumental performance, especially the latter, and that its shift toward a particular musical genre most likely occurred in the Caribbean-Gulf Coast. Furthermore, he claims that the performance of the *son* involved chordophones, particularly the diatonic harp and the guitar (23). Sheehy explains that the *tonadilla*, which was a theatrical piece that began to develop around the second half of the eighteenth century and fell into disuse by the 1830s, depicted scenes from popular life in a folkloric fashion and thus constituted a major form for the creation and diffusion of original Mexican *sones*. Adding to this theory, Vicente Mendoza claims that the "sonecitos regionales" appeared in the late eighteenth century as imitations of the *tonadilla*. He claims that "La bamba" is an example of this, as well as other *tonadilla* prototypes that are still played today as *sones jarochos* (31). *Son jarocho* became popularized nationally when the Mexican President Miguel Alemán—who is symbolic of a moment of hope in post-war Mexican politics—took "La bamba" as the theme song of his campaign, thus catapulting *son jarocho* to the national and, subsequently, international stage, when Chicano singer Richie Valens made it famous for U.S. audiences.

Truly, *son* becomes its own metaphor; it stands for tradition while paradoxically it requires improvisation. It constitutes musical forms as "traditional" as the sound that would come out of Jalisco, to be played internationally by Mariachis or other orchestras, or *son jarocho*, the recombinant musical form that is the product of Veracruz, or the Cuban *son* that would influence music both in the Spanish Antilles and across the Americas. Although *son* as a Cuban form did not make its way into México until the early 1920s, Antillean music was already quite familiar along the Gulf Coast. In fact, one of the earliest *sones* from which some claim the *son jarocho* is derived was the source of scandal in the seventeenth and eighteenth centuries, as Inquisition archives document the trouble a certain *son* named the "Chuchumbé" brought to whomever was caught humming its sexually provocative lyrics. As discussed by Rafael Figueroa, certain musical pieces such as this one and the "Jarabe gatuno" were popular among the lower classes, mulatos, and people of *color quebrado* ["broken color"] and quite possibly could have originated the diverse *son* tradition not just in Veracruz, but all over New Spain (10). Álvaro Alcántara López informs that of the twelve denunciations that were filed beginning in 1766, only one occurs in the Port of Veracruz while many others were made in México City, Toluca, and Acapulco. The intimate port relationship between La Habana and Veracruz in addition to the slave trade may be what led Alejo Carpentier, among others, to assume the Chuchumbé was brought from La Habana (189). It is unclear whether "El Chuchumbé" truly came from Cuba or not, but Sheehy cites documents from the Archivo General de la Nación (AGN) that discuss a European fleet in 1766 that stopped in La Habana to pick up some black and mulato sailors, and arrived at the Port of Veracruz with the blacks, mulatos, and the "Chuchumbé" in tow. Soon after, the religious authorities became outraged at the lyrics and the dance inspired by it, issuing an edict to prohibit it (Sheehy 23; Tomo 1297, foja 19).

Alas, it is easy to appreciate why the Church would bristle at this musical affront: everyone from the priests to virtuous church ladies was an object of ridicule. Sheehy informs us that in the AGN at least forty of the obscene couplets are still preserved (Sheehy 24; fojas 294 and 195 of Tomo 1052 of the Ramo de Inquisición). The following are a few of the more humorous and subversive stanzas:

> En la esquina está parado
> un fraile de la Merced
> con los abitos alzados
> enceñando el chuchumbé.

> [Standing on the street corner
> you'll find a friar of the Order of Mercy
> With his habit hiked up
> Showing off his "chuchumbé."]

> Que te pongas vien
> Que te pongas mal
> el chuchumbé
> te e de soplar.

[If you get better
and even if you don't
I will still blow
the Chuchumbé on you]

Esta vieja santularia
que va ibiene a San Franco [Francisco]
toma el padre, daca el Padre
y es el Padre de sus hijos.

[This old saintly woman
who comes and goes to St. Francis
The Father takes, and the Father gives
and he's the Father of her kids].

Estava la muerte encueros
sentada en el taburete
enun lado estaba el pulque
ien el otro el aguardadiente.

[Lady death was buck naked
sitting on a barstool
in one hand was the pulque
in the other the firewater].

Sabe Vmd que
Save Vmd que
meneadora de culo
le anpuesto a Vmd.

[Did Your Grace know
that Your new Title
is ass-shaker?]

Mi marido se murió
Dios en el Cielo lo tiene
y lo tenga tan tenido
que aca, jamas, nuncabuelba.

[My husband passed away
he's with God in heaven
and may he never return home!] (qtd. in Sheehy, 24–25)

As evidenced by these verses, there is no sanctity in the treatment of the Church or its priests. The first stanza begins with a friar of the Order of Mercy standing on a street corner lifting up his habit to show his "chuchumbé." This humorously invokes the image of a street prostitute in scanty clothing looking to "hook" a customer by showing off her wares. Drawing a scandalous parallel between a church official, proselytization, and a streetwalker, "El Chuchumbé" is a brilliant critique of the Church in the early colonial period and may still resonate for contemporary dissenters.

In any case, this friar is shaking "his thing," and, enjoying it. A subsequent stanza describes the speaker in the *son* addressing the person to whom the verses are directed as "Vuestra Merced" (a reverential title). In this case, "Vuestra Merced" could refer to the friar again, or any other person endowed with colonial authority; however, the verse that follows, "meneadora de culo" implies it is noble or holy woman. The stanza almost accusatorily informs "Vuestra Merced" (whomever this person might be) that she has been given the nickname "ass-shaker," satirizing the usage of the formal "Vuestra Merced" by contradicting the authority invested in such a title by immediately qualifying it with a nickname that is sexually explicit and playfully suggestive. Symbolically winking at those listening, singing, or dancing to the music, this verse validates the *son* and popular music by claiming that even the most respected authorities or members of the colonial elites—be they church leaders, governmental officials, or their wives—cannot help but boogie to this catchy rhythm.

In another stanza, the *son* teases about on old religious female parishioner who went back and forth to the Church of Saint Francis by drawing on the pun of the priest "giving and taking" ["toma y daca"] as the father of the church, but also the father of all her children. The song scorns the abuse of the chastity vows by the "fathers" of the church with their single, female devotees. In another impudent and humorous stanza, death is feminized, which is not uncommon, but rather than be treated with fear or respect, she is treated irreverently, described as naked on a barstool while getting inebriated with a bottle of *pulque* in one hand and *aguardiente* in the other. These lyrics mock death herself, one of the most important tropes in Mexican culture, spirituality, and psychology. Representations of death in the lithographs and cartoons of Guadalupe Posada appropriated the importance of the afterlife in order to criticize the Porfirian dictatorship and nineteenth-century bourgeois ideals, while the "Chuchumbé" was already using the image of death as a way to critique colonial political life. Finally, there is a stanza with a widow actually pleading with God to keep her late husband in heaven and not let him return, because she has been enjoying her freedom since his earthly departure. All of these saucy verses rebel against the social, religious, and political norms of the time, with priests enjoying secular music and dancing lasciviously, laughing at death although Catholic doctrine holds eternal life as the recompense for good behavior on earth, and even subverting gender norms, with the representation of a widow who is ecstatic—rather than mourning—that her husband is good and gone. Ángel Quintero Rivera, in his book *Salsa, sabor y control* (1998), looks at the sociology behind popular music such as *salsa* and other forms of "música tropical," illuminating the importance of emerging popular music like "El Chuchumbé":

> Históricamente, su apropiación y control (la mayor parte de las veces, indirecto) ha sido un elemento central en las luchas sociales, y la multiplicación de su ejercicio—componer, tocar, cantar y bailar—parte de las aspiraciones democráticas y la conservación ritual de la memoria.

> [Historically, its appropriation and control (which the majority of the time is indirect) have been a central element in social struggles, and the multiplication of its performance—to compose, play, sing and dance—comes from democratic aspirations and the ritual conservation of memory]. (34)

Taking into account Quintero's claim to the solidarity, resistance, democratic aspirations, and ritualized memory inherent in music, we can see these lyrics as an enlightening window into popular sentiment regarding the early colonial Church and government, as well as the imposition of Christian moral standards, as this *son* was not just played in Veracruz or La Habana, but was prohibited all throughout New Spain.

As suggested earlier with the legend of the Mulata de Córdoba and the case of Antonia de Soto, the performance of a Christian subjectivity by blacks and mulatos, although granting them a certain level of autonomy, also led to a fierce regulation of the cultural practices that these "músicas mulatas" were producing. The popularity of the *son* and the fear that this song incited is evidenced by the fact that the edict declaring its prohibition had to be reissued a dozen times after its initial ordinance in 1766.[14] Indeed, the intimate link established between people of "color quebrado" and these explicit lyrics leaves no doubt about the racialization of what the authorities perceived to be sexually delinquent social practices, firmly placing mulatos, *pardos*, and *jarochos* in the vortex of the Inquisition. If nothing else, the presence of these early *sones* proves that México early on was attuned to a popular, danceable music that, whether from Cuba originally or not, made its impact clear by punishing those who might defy the Inquisitorial mandate. Furthermore, the presence of these *sones* marks a space where, through music, and specifically *son*, the politically dissident attitudes of these early Afromestizos were manifested, carving out an aural space from where their voices would be heard. The relationship between race, the masses "de color quebrado," and the sexual explicitness of this music should be underscored as part of the way in which Afromestizos were signified in the early colonial regime by the authorities but also, by themselves. The insistence on the ties to Cuba will later give Mexican nationalists a place to blame the "exceptional" black presence.

As we have seen, *son* has myriad articulations, geographical spaces, and resonances. *Son jarocho* may have originated with the *tonadillas*, which were popular theatrical pieces, or with the *sones* that were danced in popular settings and were supposedly brought on the ships from Cuba, such as "El Chuchumbé" and "El Jarabe gatuno." This music helped to craft what may have been an early form of a *jarocho* identity founded on resistance to the colonial regime. We cannot disassociate these early musical genres from the Afromestizo communities that were promulgating them, and we will see how these forms will set the stage for the naturalization of "música tropical" in the Gulf Coast.

"El son tiene nombre y apellido: Veracruz, México"[15]

Son jarocho as we know it today really consolidated its form in the twentieth century in Veracruz. However, as discussed, its diverse origins go as far back as the colonial period. Notwithstanding regional discrepancies, the primary instruments in the *son jarocho* are: a *jarana* (which can be the first, second, or third and range from sharp to lower), *requinto* (or mosquito, a small *jarana* which plays high-pitched notes), *arpa jarocha* (jarocho harp), and *zapateado* (which is the percussive footwork against the wooden platform), and in the city of Tlacotalpan a *pandero* (tambourine). Although most musicologists claim the harp was added later, it has become one of the primary instruments in the execution of the *son*. In the southern region of the Sotavento, percussive instruments such as the *quijada* [donkey jawbone] and *marimbol* were added to the *son*. The melodies are usually in the form of *décimas*, which are ten-line octosyllabic verses, but can also go as low as three or four verse stanzas. The musical time is usually 6/8, but also varies. The vocals usually take the form of call-and-response, with one singer coming in as a second finishes with the same verse, and the topics can range from love to witchcraft to political satire. Although most groups play from a repertoire that is over a hundred years old with standard songs such as "La iguana" or "El colás," the lyrics are almost always modified extemporaneously by each singer to reflect the place, a recent event, or the interests of the musicians. The instrumentation in the *son jarocho* changes from region to region because many cities and communities within the state of Veracruz debate the authenticity and inclusion of certain instruments. For example, in the town of Alvarado (infamous for its colorful residents with a penchant for expletives), they insist that the *son* is composed of only *jarana, requinto,* and *arpa*; the only percussive instrument should be the *zapateado.*

Notwithstanding regional variances, scholar Figueroa defines this form for which Veracruz is famous—and which was internationalized by Chicano singer Richie Valens—as a product of the Afro-Andalucian peoples that populated the countryside of Veracruz, principally the region south of the Port in what is called the Sotavento. Figueroa emphasizes that renaissance and baroque peninsular music, in addition to the musical components traditional to West African music, were integral to the "Afromestizo universe" that was fashioning itself.

> In places like Santiago de Murcia, "sones de la tierra"[16] encompassed a dizzying array of transculturated sounds as Spanish *sevillanas, fandanguillos, bulerías, garrotines, peteneras* already reflected the fascinating mix of Arabic, Gypsy, Jewish, and Byzantine music. If you weave in the *coplas,* the strumming of the lute and guitar and the *zapateo* to the rhythmic fabric of antiphony, improvisation, jitanjáforas,[17] onomatopoeia that came from Africa, then Veracruz becomes a veritable crucible of diverse musical rhythms and traditions that gave birth to the *son jarocho.* (*Son Jarocho: Guía Histórico-Musical* 10)[18]

One critical component of this Afromestizo universe is defined by a particular space where these diverse musical traditions come together, both in the region of the Sotavento as well as all over the Huasteca: the "fandango."[19] This festive space is where these sounds meet to create a unique musical aesthetic proper to their transculturated reality. According to sociologist Alfredo Delgado Calderón, the *fandango* is the catalyst for music, dance, and poetry that creates community:

> The communal expression of the *son jarocho* is the fandango, where musicians, dancers and poets converge; music and dance is improvised around a wooden platform. There is no specific time to do a fandango: it could be during the day, after a wedding or baptism, or at night during a local holiday or at a veiling ceremony [or funeral], to bid farewell to the daylight.[20] (53)

There is some dispute among ethnohistorians as to whether the entry of *son jarocho* into the record industry did away with the *fandangos,* or if claims that the *fandango* traditions are still alive in the countryside are true. In either case, the space created around the wooden platform is the place where young and old come to dance the *zapateado* and the country folk who work the land by day can exhibit their musicianship by night. An older musician interviewed in the documentary *Son Jarocho* made by Francisco Viveros Domínguez in 2006, distinguishes between rural *fandangos* and those that take place on a stage, occur in a more urban setting, with professional musicians, performers, or dancers. He complains that although the tradition is making a comeback, "no son de los meros buenos" [they're not the really good ones] in effect recognizing, as do others, that although the tradition has changed, it has never ceased.[21]

The "Encuentro de Jaraneros" ("The Encounter of the Jaraneros") was initiated at the end of the 1970s by the band Siquisirí with the intention of revitalizing the *son jarocho* as well as continuing the tradition of the *fandango* during the *Festival de la Candelaria*.[22] It originally started out as a contest, but so many people from all over the country began to participate (in 2006 over seventy different bands signed up) that they decided to make it a musical and folkloric "encounter." Today, musicians, *trovadores*, *jaraneros*, *decimeros*, and *repentistas*[23] from all over the countryside gather in Tlacotalpan to play, some bringing their own rustically fashioned instruments. Others are professional musicians who have toured both around the country and abroad, but every year since its inception it has been steadily growing in numbers and popularity.

In the same documentary, Julio César Corro Lara from the group La Estanzuela laments the popularity of the festival, claiming that there is still much to be learned from the older musicians who are not professionals and play instruments made "a machete," or instruments they have crafted themselves with a machete. He regrets that the more popular groups, who are now internationally known, steal the thunder from these elderly, rural musicians who come from far away to participate, thus defeating what for him constitutes the purpose of the *fandango*. Nonetheless, this important festival has incited what since 1981 is being called a "movimiento jaranero" mobilizing regional musicians to not only preserve their tradition, but to revive it with the creation of new *sones*. The groups Mono Blanco, Siquisirí, and Los Negritos are all examples of local bands that are concerned with the composition of new *sones* as imperative to the survival of the genre. The leaders of many of these bands complain that they are playing *sones* that are over one hundred years old, and that for it to be a living musical form, composition needs to be ongoing. They claim that musicians (and the public) should not be so invested in only playing traditional *sones*, for if it does not evolve, *son* will die as a form that is preserved in an almost museological fashion. Mono Blanco, according to the Mexican journal *México Desconocido*, has been one "of the most musically daring groups, introducing some instruments that are different from traditional son instruments and working in the United States with musicians from Cuba and Senegal to produce a distinctive sound"

(Farquharson 41). Many older *son* practitioners, such as Cirilo Promoter, do not agree with these changes, not even the introduction of *quijadas* and *cajones* [box drum], as he believes they betray the traditional nature of the *son*. The existence of these very debates prove that the *son jarocho* tradition is very much alive and kicking. Indeed, the movement has moved beyond Veracruz, México, to Los Ángeles, California, where the Chicano and Mexican community has continued the tradition of the *fandangos* since 2000, hosting its own "Encuentro Jaranero" featuring local Californian musicians in the symbolic heart of the Mexican-American community, La Placita Olvera.[24] The East Los Angeles-based group Las Cafeteras, for example, is fusing *son* with ska, punk, hip-hop, marimbol, and bilingual spoken-word, revolutionizing the traditional sound into a politicizing, transnational musical force that has left some *son* purists bristling. They have even remade and modernized one of the most iconic songs of the genre, "La bamba" into "La bamba rebelde."

African Origins of *Son Jarocho*

Bobbie Vaughn found evidence of "La bamba" being played as early as 1816 by blacks in Veracruz, "where the observer describes a large contest of men and women" (5). During the Alemán years, "La bamba"[25] was the national hymn and signaled a political loosening due to his status as the first civilian elected to the presidency. It is now synonymous with the *son jarocho* and is intimately linked to the Afro-Mexican presence in México. Internationally, it is one of the hallmark songs of the Mexican culture. Its origins are contested, but as mentioned, it is thought to derive from a *tonadilla*, or to have been brought by the Afro-Cuban slaves. The more colorful version is that it was composed as a result of the pirate Lorencillo's attack on the Port of Veracruz in 1683, when the guard tower watchman fell asleep and failed to toll the town bells to warn the populace of the pirate's imminent attack. It is reputed that a military unit of *pardos* arrived to help defend the Port against the infamous pirate. In any case, it is the quintessential *son jarocho* that has symbolized through its presence, and despite its contested origins and myriad expressions, the contributions of Afro-Mexicans to a globalized *mexicanidad*.

Ethnomusicologists and historians alike have pointed to the *son jarocho* as a distinctly Afromestizo art form. I choose to say art form, because it includes multiple artistic media—some of which exist independently of each other—such as music, poetry, and dance. In my consideration of *son jarocho* as an Afromestizo form, I would like to reflect on what Quintero Rivera has theorized regarding the inherent hybridity of Caribbean music. He claims that "música tropical" manifests both traditionally occidental elements that are derived from Europe (specifically Spain with its insistence on melody) as well as Amerindian and African components that have other aesthetic preoccupations, such as an emphasis on multiple and often conflicting rhythms, leading to what he characterizes as "mulato margins of modernity" (62). The semiotics of *mulatez*, as understood by people like Lourdes Martínez-Echazábal, is signified as a hybrid state that underscores liminality and racial ambivalence. But the "mulato margins" also constitute a space where there is creativity, fluidity, and movement. Unlike the trope of tragedy that defines the figure of the "tragic mulatta," making future reconciliation or subjectivity impossible, this understanding holds the mulato margins as a generative space with endless possibilities. Indeed, José Buscaglia's notion of "mulataje" also renders mulato subjectivity as additive, ever-shifting and the "antidote to conquest and reduction [. . .] a movement of reverse colonization that is, although not utopian, keenly aware of the possibilities in the metaphorical 'double-crossing [of] coloniality' " (xvii–xviii). However, scholars such as Julio Ramos have eschewed this vision of *mulatez* as a kind of heroic intervention that neglects the tragic experience of Africans in the Americas; one that fetishizes polyrhythms and orality as a signifier of blackness that moves past racial inequity.[26] While this criticism is not only valid, but urgent in the face of the still prevalent myth of racial democracy in the Caribbean and Brazil that often finds its expression by touting hybridized musical forms as testimony, blackness in México is still so foreign that caricature and tragedy seem to constitute the only discursive modes in which Africanness can be expressed, when expressed at all. By invoking *mulatez*, which is not a proliferating signifier in México the way mestizaje is (recall, mestizaje in México includes the black third root but subordinates it to the mythical union of Amerindian and European people), we witness the loud possibilities for a generative otherness in Mexican music. Invoking Quintero Rivera's notion of a "mulata music" at the border of a "mulato modernity" in concert with Buscaglia's vision of *mulataje* problematizes the privileged racial ingredients heralded in the discourse of a Mexican mestizo nation. Unlike the Caribbean, where music has been the privileged place of the African diasporic voice, Mexican music—played and enjoyed worldwide—has unintentionally enjoyed the African voice but has not even felicitously considered *mulataje* a relevant source. Although music has been singularly celebrated as one of the premier products of black and mulato culture to the exclusion of other cultural, epistemological, and historical contributions, we ought to remember the power it wields as a transhistorical cultural force. Despite Ramos's lucid—and timely—critique of the reifying gesture implicit in the idea of "música mulata," I draw from Quintero Rivera's paradigm as a fruitful way to interpret the mulato universe in which Mexican music and culture has been forged by prominently placing blacks back into the cultural scenario.

Some of the most obvious African or Afro-Caribbean elements of the *son jarocho* are intimately linked to the specific rhythms of the *son*. The use of "contratiempo," that is, syncopation and simultaneous juxtaposition of double and triple rhythmic groupings is one of the most important. A common type of alternation between double and triple rhythm in a triple meter framework has been termed "sesquialtera"[27] (Sheehy 97). The sesquialtera, literally "altering sixes," has been described by E. Thomas Stanford as the "alternation of two groups of three pulses with three groups of two pulses with the basic pulse remaining constant" (qtd. in Sheehy 98). In his article on the black musical influence in *son jarocho*, Rolando Antonio Pérez Fernández engages in an extensive discussion of the importance of African rhythms and points to the presence of numerous rhythmic and metric patterns, that are both divisive and additive, as well the "contraritmo" [cross-rhythm] as seminal to the *son* (41). The way in which rhythmic patterns displace each other in a particular time span produce a polyrhythm which he relates to the multi-lineal rhythmic organization of African music (41). He concludes that these particular usages of poly- or cross-rhythms is exclusive to the *son jarocho* and therefore reflect an indubitable African imprint on Mexican music. Additionally, the way in which the instruments are played reflects this African musical presence. For example, there are two ways of playing the chordophones: one is "rasgueado" (strummed) and the other is "punteado" (plucked, as with a pick). Although most academics describe the "rasgueado" as a form that originates in the Iberian Peninsula, constituting a traditional way folk musicians strummed the lute, the particular *percussive* way in which the chordophones are played leads to a diversity of timbres, pointing to an African-inspired musical practice (42). The way in which specific rhythms enter a musical composition off beat is integral to the *son jarocho*, but also to the regional traditions in Western México, such as the *son* in southern Jalisco and the Tierra Caliente (hotlands) of Michocacán, where there were also sizeable African populations (41).

Aside from the complex rhythms, syncopation, and off beat musical entries, there is an important improvisational component of the *son*. Although there is wide discussion as to the nature of its musical form, the *son jarocho* as a genre not only permits, but almost requires a certain level of instrumental and vocal improvisation. Pérez Fernández contends that instrumental improvisation is key for specific instruments such as the "tamborita" from the Tierra Caliente of Guerrero as well as the jarana and requinto jarocho (which is called "tangueo") in Veracruz (41). Moreover, there is a similar structure to the *canto responsorial,* or call-and-response, which allows for interjections from musicians as well as the audience members. It is constituted by brief interventions by the chorus, and operates such that one singer repeats the phrase that another singer has just finished singing. The lyrics are also written so that they enter on what he calls the "segunda negra" or off beat, which confers upon it an acephalous nature (43). Furthermore, Pérez Fernández underscores the presence of certain African words and categories, most of which he claims originate in "Bantú" languages (42).

Improvisation in African-inspired music is, for Quintero Rivera, what defines "música mulata." Because Africanness becomes camouflaged, the "runaway" rhythms are what create music but are also what restrict it: under a colonial oppressor, one must resist this African impulse through "cimarronaje" [marronage]. Musically, this was accomplished through camouflage; that is to say, by limiting spontaneity and improvisation by "dulling its potential luminosity" (242). Once *son jarocho* became commercialized, the necessary improvisation of the *son* became truncated and sometimes eliminated. Many of the *sones* became congealed into a set form. For many musicians this is problematic, but as we shall see with the figure of La Negra Graciana as well as younger musicians both in Veracruz and Los Ángeles, this is not the case.

Finally, Pérez Fernández signals the presence of the *marimbol*, an instrument of unquestionable African origin that is still played today as a sign of the African influence. The *marimbol* is a wooden box with round sound hole cut in middle. Across the hole a number of metal strips are attached, and these metal strips are tuned to different pitches and plucked to produce a deep bass-like sound (Vaughn 5). Pérez Fernández claims that the percussive way in which the *marimbol* is played points to this African influence in Mexican music (42). According to musician Octavio Rebolledo Kloques, the usage of the *marimbol* (sanza) is unique to the Americas because in Africa it was played to carry higher, sharper pitches and the melody (the part in *son jarocho* a harp might perform), while the "American sanza" plays the medium and low tones and serves as a kind of musical support (94). However, Rebolledo somewhat controversially claims that the *marimbol* is not an old instrument indigenous to the area, but rather that it was introduced, or reintroduced into the *son jarocho* in 1928 with the orchestra Son Marianao. He contends that the *jaraneros* immediately recognized its sound (he recalls one case when he played it at a *fandango* upon the invitation of the musicians) and that musicians intuitively incorporated it into the *son jarocho* due to the natural affinity of the sound produced by the instrument with the nature of the sound produced by the rural *son*. There has been a renewed interest in the *marimbol* and there are now classes and workshops in México and Los Ángeles that teach students how to construct and play it as a "traditional" instrument. For Rebolledo, this is a telling phenomenon because it underscores the irony of the hospitable reception of an African instrument by rural communities into an autochthonous musical form. If Africans were so foreign and exotic as historical memory has made them out to be, why is an instrument like the *marimbol* so easily assimilated?

Others declare that the Cuban immigration in the mid- to late-nineteenth century left an unmistakable Afro-Caribbean accent in the *son*, especially in the southern countryside. Indeed, scholars such as García Díaz claim that beginning in the 1870s, Cubans skilled in harvesting tobacco and sugar began to migrate to the Sotavento, and that the Afro-Cuban *son de oriente* from the early colonial period was instrumental in the creation of the *son jarocho*, imbuing the son from the Sotavento region with an incontrovertible "guajiro" (Cuban country) flavor (300). In either case, the Afro-Caribbean presence had its hand in the formation of this unique genre, whether through the *son de oriente*, "The Chuchumbé, or the *marimbol.*

What Quintero Rivera considers to be revolutionary about these trans-culturated musical forms is the simultaneous fluidity and tension between the diachronic, synchronic, and successive. Indeed, the playful ways in which African-inspired rhythms, harmonies, sounds, tonality, and musical progressions found their way into Caribbean music is relevant for my consideration of *son jarocho* because this genre similarly participates in this musical game (63). Musicians such as Graciana Silva and groups like Siquisirí or Las Cafeteras interpret old *sones* in diverse respects: the former emphasizes tradition, while the latter privilege innovation. In both cases this music manifests an active rhythmic regeneration proper to a vital community, an Afro-Mexican legacy that is not only part of the colonial Inquisition archive of "moral" dereliction, but a vital, affirmative *present* in both Mexican and Chicano communities.

Playing the *Son* "a la antigüita": La Negra Graciana Silva

One of the most famous *soneros* from Veracruz was a mulata named Graciana Silva.[28] She was a superb harpist and singer of *son jarocho* who for most of her life never left the Port, and according to Mary Farquharson, interpreted the *son* following the old forms with a style even older than that of Andrés Huesca (*México Desconocido* 38).[29] La Negra Graciana trained as a harpist with the great master don Rodrigo, and was renowned in the Port for playing a more traditional style of *son jarocho*. Unlike modern *soneros*, who play the bigger harp that is able to stand on its own and is easier to transport, she played a smaller more traditional harp that is harder to carry because it requires that the musician be seated while playing. Her insistence on the original instrument, besides reflecting her desire to remain within an older tradition, allows her to play, as she states, "a la antigüita," or in a more traditional style: "her execution is slower and simultaneously profoundly sentimental, with structures that are more complex and addictive than modern versions" (38).[30] She played long, emotionally inflected sets with complex structures that invoke reflection rather than a quick thrill. This musical choice made her style different from modern repertoires that prefer shorter songs that are more adaptable to roving from bar to bar, and are hence more lucrative but less open to musical and vocal improvisation.

The recording industry in the early part of the last century truncated the traditional *sones* so that they could fit on the LP (vinyl record). In some cases the record company actually accelerated the original recording so that it might be more attractive to wider audiences. Silva refused to do this, thus endearing her to her local audience: the *pueblo* of Veracruz. She exclaimed that, "Lo rápido no es a fuerzas lo bonito. No se aprecia bien la música a esa velocidad. Lo mejor es la normalidad. Tocar el arpa es la gloria del cielo" [To play rapidly isn't necessarily what makes it beautiful. One cannot appreciate the music properly at that velocity. To play the harp is heaven's glory].[31] Perhaps because of her predilection to play "a la antigüita," she also preferred to perform on her own, becoming a local figure and icon associated with traditional *son jarocho* and appearing in the documentary *La raíz olvidada* (2001). Eduardo Llerenas, a musicologist and producer, heard her music and recorded her. This record landed her a tour in Europe where she played to an enthusiastic crowd in Paris. It is remarkable that so much international recognition would be given to a black woman who, up until that point, had never left Veracruz.

Her musicianship exalts her loyalty to the "tradition" of her art form, and as a black Mexican, her insistence on the orthodoxy of the form she practices places her at the heart of "traditional" México. Indeed, la Negra Graciana incarnates tradition; to impugn her authenticity because of her blackness would be to impugn the *son*, and everything "a la antigüita" symbolizes. As we will see with Toña la Negra and other mulatas, she seems to fall into the status of beloved "exception": another cultural icon who just "happens" to be black. Her performance of *tradition* constitutes a flicker of blackness in a genre that, besides the mariachi, constitutes the soul of Mexican musical heritage for the world. Before her death la Negra Graciana became an international success, signaling the important interjections of blacks in Mexican cultural history. We can appreciate the irony of her visibility as a musician of *son jarocho* when we consider the importance of the introduction of "foreign" sounds, such as *son cubano* and *danzón*, to the musical landscape of Mexican culture and their specific relationship to blackness in the Caribbean.

The Explosion of Cuban Music in the Port and the "mulatización de la gente pudiente": *Danzón, Son,* and *Carnaval*

The movie *Danzón* (1991), starring the popular actress María Rojo, is a beautiful homage to the *danzón*—both the musical genre and the dance—and a fascinating glimpse into the flickers of the Afro-Mexican presence. The film narrates the personal voyage of a middle-aged woman from México City named Julia, who, amidst the humdrum of her tedious middle-class life as a phone operator, finds respite in the poetry of the *danzón*. After winning many competitions and dancing together for years, her dance partner Carmelo (a mulato from Veracruz) all of a sudden disappears, and the rest of the film is constituted by her frantic search for him. This pursuit takes Julia on an odyssey back to his native Veracruz, where on the way we get glimpses and glimmers of the Afro-Mexican legacy. This search for origins is mediated by the phantasm of the mulato dancer whom she only rediscovers upon her return to México City, in the same place that she left him. This journey of self-discovery is also a telling voyage of the place held by México's African descendants: they stand phantasmatically behind the making of Mexican tradition and culture. Always a few steps behind her partner, he disappears behind the corners of every place she looks for him, only to emerge at the end in the heart of Mexican nation, far from Veracruz (his mythified place of origin), and quietly smack in the middle of its political center.

Danzón was introduced to México in the nineteenth century, sometime around 1879,[32] however, it originated in Cuba as a derivation of the "danza habanera" and it is traditionally played using the instrumentation of the "charanga francesa," basing its sound on a section of cords that accompany a solo flute. In 1879, a popular mulato composer named Miguel Faílde debuted a composition he called a "danzón" at a ball in Matanzas. He thus received the credit as the father of the *danzón* although it had already been around for at least ten years. It would subsequently become Cuba's national music for the following fifty years, until its popularity waned with the emergence of other danceable music such as the *chachachá* and *mambo*. According to Peter Manuel in *Creolizing Contradance in the Caribbean* (2009), the *danzón* overcame the monotony of the previous *danza* by introducing new material in the B sections of the musical score (93). Faílde's imprint on the *danzón* conventionalized these new sections, thus requiring new melodic material which consequently led to "predatory" musical practices where everything from operas and zarzuelas to "boleros, ragtime tunes, street vendor calls, *sones*, rumbas, Spanish *cuplés* and pentatonic Chinese-Cuban melodies" could be poached to make those open sections more interesting and familiar for audiences (94).

Around 1910, the Cuban musician José Urfé introduced additional variations to the *danzón* in the form of an ostinato-driven coda that permitted more compositional flexibility (96). Moreover, the prominent incorporation of the *cinquillo* both in the melody and accompaniment was vital, as its "two-bar *clave*-style format," which in addition to the "obstreperous percussion," and most important, the close, sensual couple dancing that replaced the line-dancing was part of the "afro-Caribbean tinge" that made it so ingeniously creole while provoking the indignation of conservatives (93). These profoundly recombinant musical practices that riff off radically diverse melodic themes, while maintaining unity and elegance as a musical genre, is part of the magnificence of the *danzón*. Indeed, this is probably why it was so seamlessly incorporated into the Mexican musical tradition not long after it was born in Cuba. Carpentier, in his famous treatise on Cuban music, describes the circuitry of the origins of the *danzón*:

> la *country-dance* inglesa, pasada por Francia, llevada a Santo Domingo, introducida en Santiago, rebautizada y ampliada en Matanzas, enriquecida en la Habana con aportaciones mulatas, negras y chinas, había alcanzado un grado de mestizaje que daba vértigo. Y sin embargo, el danzón mantenía su carácter y su unidad

> [the English *country-dance* which passed through France on its way to Santo Domingo, was introduced in Santiago, with new changes it was re-baptized in Matanzas, enriched in Havanna with mulata, black and Chinese additions, had reached a level of mestizaje that was dizzying. And yet, the *danzón* maintained its character and unity]. (161)

This rich description reflects the vertiginous movement of *danzón* even before it arrived to México, which was not long after it was created as a musical genre in Cuba, underscoring its musical itinerancy from the beginning.[33]

The story of *danzón* in México begins with the introduction of the Bufo Habaneros who started circulating throughout México by means of the colonial, commercial, and migratory routes between la Habana, Veracruz, México City, and Yucatán. Furthermore, the already established popularity of the *danza habanera* tuned the ears of Mexican audiences for the beauty of the *danzón*. The *danzón* first arrived to the Port of Progreso in the Yucatán peninsula, where it was fashionable for a while before dying out. Due in part to the Caste Wars that restricted access to the *danzón* from the popular classes, in Yucatán it acquired a more conservative musical interpretation (Flores Escalante 2). It simultaneously arrived to Veracruz but did not become popular until years later. *Danzón* was regularly played by Cuban orchestras in Veracruz only to be taken over soon after by Mexican bands (as the *son cubano* would later on), such as the Danzonera Veracruz and Los Chinos Ramírez (Figueroa, "Rumberos y jarochos," 385).[34] In México City it arrived as sheet music that was primarily written for piano, but became popular during the Porfiriato as the president was an enthusiastic patron of the arts, especially those he felt cultivated a European aesthetic. It is noteworthy that the Cuban population in Veracruz of the late nineteenth century coincided with the Independence movements, and both Mexican and Cuban musicians were employed to celebrate the fight for Cuban independence from Spain. In the Teatro Principal de Veracruz, Cuban artists such as Severiano Pacheco and his orchestra came to celebrate milestones in the fight for Cuban independence, such as "the deaths of the students from Habana" or the deaths of Antonio

Maceo and José Martí,[35] despite the protests of the powerful Spanish colony that was a prominent part of the Port's population[36] (García Díaz 313–14). In a talk given during the "Festival de Música Popular Barbarito Diez" that took place in Manatí (Eastern Cuba) in 2005, the Cuban musician Eduardo Rosillo Heredia discusses the importance of race in the constitution of *danzón*, as well as its place as a "mulato" music; a genre that coalesces not only the various musical influences and movements, but also, the emergent political sentiment of an island desiring autonomy:

> Existen publicaciones de prensa de ese tiempo, donde los órganos que obedecen al poder colonial, al poder gobernante entonces, arremeten contra el danzón, calificándolo como música de negros, por el nombre, y como música inmoral por el abrazo. ¿Por qué arremete contra el danzón, calificándolo como música de negro y música inmoral? Porque ve que es la expresión de la cultura de un pueblo que acaba de pasarse diez años peleando por su independencia

> [Publications from that time exist where organs obeying colonial power, the governing power of the time, attack the *danzón*, qualifying it as music for blacks because of the name, and immoral because of the embrace. Why attack the *danzón*, charging it with being music for black people, and even immoral? Because they see it as the cultural expression of a people who have just spent ten years fighting for their Independence]. (43)

Thus, the creation of *danzón* in Cuba seems to represent one of the first truly "Cuban" sounds, although the *contradanza* had already been sufficiently creolized in the preceding century (Manuel 26). Moreover, a majority of the musicians were black and mulato in addition to the fact that the "father" of the *danzón* was a mulato. Indeed, we witness the close, almost simultaneous, development of the *danzón* in Cuba and México; while for many in Cuba it represented a sonic unity that came to symbolize a nascent political independence and fictive national brotherhood, for Mexicans it represented a familiar sound that was negotiated through the triangulated sonic renderings of a displaced African heritage.

Roberto González Echevarría in his article "Literatura, baile y béisbol" also underscores the relationship between *danzón* and its black roots:

> Frente a la pacatería peninsulur de la última década de XIX, sin embargo, el danzón era algo peligroso, exótico, decadente y demasiado cubano. Se trataba, nada menos, que de la incorporación

abierta de lo africano a la vida social de las clases acomodadas; una incipiente mulatización de la gente pudiente.

[Faced with the peninsular scrupulousness of the late nineteenth century, *danzón* was something dangerous, exotic, decadent and entirely too Cuban. It was about the open incorporation of the African to the social lives of the upper classes; an incipient mulatization of the powerful people]. (*Jornada Dominical*, México, March 26, 1995)

The connection González Echevarría makes between African identity and its incorporation into upper-class musical forms provides a critical lens through which we can appreciate its ardent acceptance by the populace of Veracruz and México City. While it represented an emergent "cubanidad" that under-scored its *mulatez* (or what some Cuban ideologues would herald as *mestizaje*) on the island, for Mexicans it signaled a deflection of *mulatez* onto the Caribbean. However, the "mulatización" of the powerful Cuban elite seems to have struck a chord amongst those who performed and consumed *danzón* in México; it may have begun as "demasiado cubano" but it ended up as also entirely Mexican.

In Cuba, the popularity of *danzón* faded earlier (after the first couple of decades in the century), and although a sonic marker of Cuban independence and wildly popular early in the century—at one point cages had to be built to house the bands that accompanied the silent films because audiences could become aggressive with the musicians should they refuse to continue playing a popular tune—it did not sustain the same longevity as in Veracruz and México City (Rodríguez 150). Cubans however, are seeking to reclaim their patrimony over the *danzón*, as its entrenched popularity in México has inspired a renaissance of *danzón* in Cuba. This is evidenced by reports of the fifth annual 2008 *Festival Danzón Habana* dedicated to the state of Yucatán as well as the municipality of Madruga in Cuba: "The recuperation of the genre that lives in the very roots of traditional Cuban music just rose in status when it was celebrated and dedicated to the Mexican state of Yucatán and the municipality, Madruga, that belongs to la Habana" (Sonia Sánchez, *Cubarte*, March 15, 2008).[37] The 2007 *Festival de Danzón Habana* was similarly dedicated to the city of Guadalajara, México, for its role in the preservation and dissemination of the genre. José Loyola Fernández, president of the organizing committee, claims that "México and Cuba are culturally very close and the *danzón* is one of the best examples of this, the Mexicans are very organized in their development and practice of the *danzón*" (*El universal*, March 9, 2007).[38] In their attempts to reclaim *danzón* as part of their musical roots, the Cubans acknowledge the seminal role played by Mexican music and culture where it is still a lived cultural tradition and whose popularity, since its initial introduction, may have faded but has never died out.

The popularity of *danzón* is an important antecedent to the acceptance of *son cubano* in Veracruz, moreover, its continued and increasing popularity has cemented *danzón* today as part of the regional culture. The local schools will often teach children *danzón* as a traditional dance, and the municipal government as well as the Veracruz Institute of Culture ("IVEC") hold workshops and cultural events in order to maintain what they consider to be a crucial part of their cultural patrimony. A few times a week *danzón* is played in the *zócalo,* the "Plazuela de la Campana" and occasionally in the "Parque Zamora" for free to be enjoyed by the Port's residents. These efforts by the local government have the intention of maintaining and reviving for the younger generations a fundamental component of their cultural legacy and patrimony. During carnival, "chilangos" arrive from the capital in order to see how "jarocho" *danzón* is performed and danced.³⁹ Carnival, which began in 1925 and has been on-going ever since, is proof of the permanence of *son cubano* and *danzón* in this city and state, as almost every form of *música tropical* reigns supreme during this popular festival.

In sum, the history and movement of *danzón* as a musical tradition tells a fascinating story of twin ports, creative musicians, avid audiences and dancers, as well as an at once celebrated and manipulated *mulatez.* Arriving in México with the Bufo Habaneros, which relied on tried and true tropes of staged blackness, it became the preferred music of the *arrabales* [marginal neighborhoods], cabarets, and brothels. It rose to ascendancy in the country's capital with the opening of the club "Salón México" on the twentieth of April 1920 (Flores Escalante 101). The League of Decency in México had already lamented the invasion of dancing halls and salons as an "acute cabaretitis" and *danzón* became the musical signifier, despite its elegant beginnings, of the tawdry impulse of the city's rapid urbanization and imminent modernity (101). Moreover, the eponymous film *Salón México* produced in 1949 by director Emilio Fernández indexes this part of México's cultural history by metonymically immortalizing, in the first few minutes of the film, the dancing feet and rhythmic sway of the *danzón* as a corporeal practice indebted to its mulato past. The "sin" of the growing city is unmistakably racialized with this "tropical" music.

While in Cuba it reflected a history of blackness that was useful in the wars of Independence and as a strategy to coalesce a "mestizo" identity in the face of a Spanish colonizer; for Mexicans, it seemed to represent a recognition of a latent blackness that was then deflected back on to the Cuban émigrés. *Danzón* is not just a dance for the elderly, and it is ironic that, despite its Caribbean origins, films like the one directed by Maria Novaro insist on the transmission of the dance to younger generations lest the tradition be lost.

Although often considered a music of nostalgia, *danzón*, like the *son jarocho*, is still alive and making a vibrant comeback as an indelible part of México's musical heritage.

Danzón wove its way into México in the late nineteenth century; however, the official entry of Cuban *son* in México wasn't until 1928, with the arrival of Son Cuba de Marianao. The first organized orchestras played in México City, but really took off in the Port of Veracruz, where, according to Figueroa it unleashed a veritable craze absolutely remapping the terrain of Mexican music in Veracruz (386). Musicians immediately began to incorporate Cuban *son* into their repertoires and, as soon as they could, began forming their own orchestras, working with and independently of the Cubans, even starting children's groups, such as the one begun by José Macías, the "Tapatio" who would later direct Son Clave de Oro (386). Figueroa not only underscores the immediate incorporation of Cuban *son* into the musical landscape of Veracruz as well as México City, but he emphasizes the Veracruzanos' insistence that they were not merely copying a Cuban musical form. As he reiterates, the musicians claim that the Cubans may have brought the music, and the Mexicans may have learned from their musicianship (often indirectly), but the Cubans never *taught* them: "nosotros aprendimos de los músicos cubanos a tocar esta música, *pero ellos no nos enseñaron*" ["we learned from the Cuban musicians to play this kind of music, *but they never taught us*"] (Emphasis added, 387). Thus *son*, now *son veracruzano*, is born in a way that does not deny its obvious Caribbean origin, but naturalizes it.

One of the first bands to be created was Son Clave de Oro formed by Agustín Lara. It featured Antonia Peregrino or as she was later known, "Toña la Negra," as well as other of members of her family, but there were many other bands that followed. Figueroa has written extensively on what he calls the "veracruzanísimos" ("the most authentically Veracruzano") Pregoneros del Recuerdo directed by Carlos Pitalúa, who started out by playing timbales in the *danzón* orchestra of his father. This band continues to play to this day, maintaining and reviving the Veracruz brand of *son cubano*, and the original leader's son is now the leader of the band. They revived the *son* by singing "a dos voces" (with two singers) and, through instrumentation including duets of trumpets and clarinets in the melodic part, as well as guitar not only in the harmony but also in the melody, created what would become the original mark of the Pregoneros' particular brand of *son cubano* (392).[40]

Furthermore, Veracruz hosts multiple festivals that honor its regional music, and specifically Antillean music, such as the *Festival Cómo suena la clave* in Xalapa, and the *Festival de Son Montuno*, also in Veracruz. According to Figueroa, "this festival has proven its capacity as a catalyst for a good part of the *jarocho* identity that finds its expression in this genre, which despite having come from the Antilles, we can now consider without reticence as

Veracruzano" (396).[41] To this day *son cubano* and *montuno* is played a few nights a week and is central to the weeklong festivities of carnival. Figueroa's statement accurately highlights what has come to be cultural patrimony for many *veracruzanos*, and part and parcel of *jarocho* identity. Thus, hosting a festival for *son cubano* and *montuno* is not just celebrating an international musical form, but celebrating a form proper to their own culture. Carnival would come to play an important role in making this music a permanent fixture of the musical landscape of Veracruz, as only tropical music is heard in the streets of the Port during this festivity. No mariachi, or even *son jarocho* band is to be found while the city celebrates carnival.

Carnival in Veracruz is one of the main cultural events that consolidated the primacy of *son cubano* and *música tropical* in Veracruz from 1925 to this day. From its first institutional beginning in 1925, all the *comparsas* or dance groups typically play *son cubano, guarachas, salsa*, and a unique *jarocho* form of the *conga*[42] that would accompany the *comparsas*. The *comparsas* are the heart and soul of the festival, as they emerge from popular and traditional neighborhoods and fundraise in order to participate and compete for their

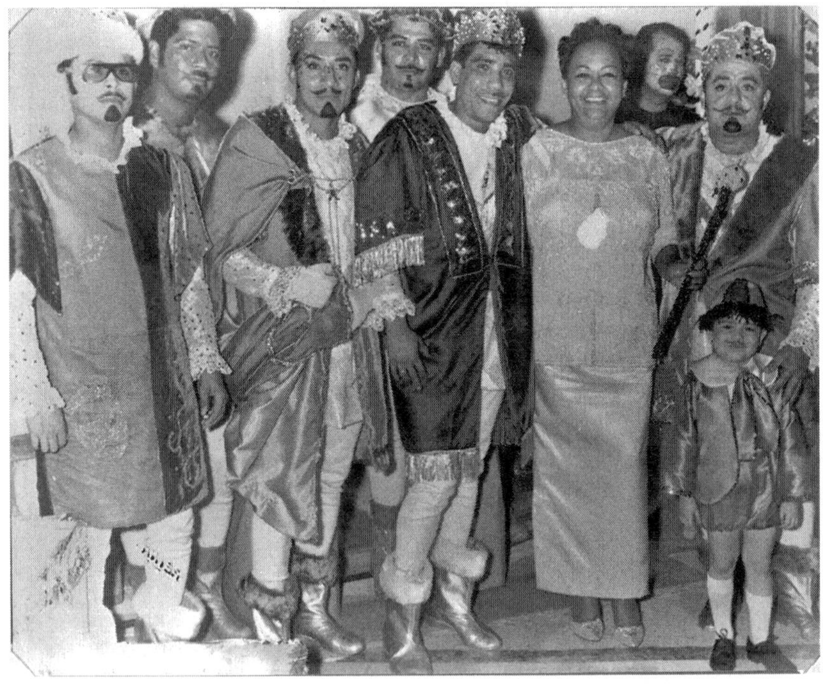

FIGURE 6.2. "Toña la Negra next to the carnival court of the 'ugly' King."

choreography and costumes, which can range from typical tropical fare to pachuco-style costumes.[43] Indeed, carnival in Veracruz is intimately linked to the explosion and subsequent naturalization and institutionalization of tropical music in the Port.

"Veracruz, por fortuna, es y seguirá siendo Caribe": Celebrating México's Third Root[44]

The last decade has seen an explosion in efforts by Mexican universities to retrace the contributions of what is now officially called México's "tercera raíz" or "third root": its African presence. This idea comes from José Vasconcelos, who, in his famous treatise *La raza cósmica*, proclaims the mestizo as the enlightened individual who is the product of all the races, including the African, coming together in the Americas. However, despite the homage paid to the African component, it did not constitute the most important element of this racial theory. There have been efforts in the last few decades to ameliorate this through programs like "Nuestra tercera raiz," although there are complaints that it is poorly funded and supported. Nonetheless, these efforts in Veracruz have been critical for the cultivation of a regional identity. The IVEC is one of the most important organizations of the region, sponsoring myriad cultural activities and events ranging from dance classes in *danzón*, *son*, and *zapateado*, in addition to workshops in *son jarocho* and the crafting of traditional instruments. Every summer there is an "International Afro-Caribbean Festival" sponsored by the IVEC that showcases all forms of cultural production, including dance, music, arts and crafts, exhibits, films, and academic roundtables and conferences.[45] It has been influential in shaping the cultural awareness of the region, and as the following quote from the 1997 anthology of the Afro-Caribbean festival illustrates, has made reclaiming México's "tercera raíz" a priority in its operations and programming, as well as cultivating a regional pan-Caribbean identity:

> Since its inception, the Veracruz Institute of Culture has encouraged innumerable activities that promote the different manifestations related to our black heritage, which is why since 1994, with the support of the government, it has organized the annual International Afro-Caribbean Festival as a way to *revindicate the African contribution to our culture*. One of the primary objectives is research, the appreciation and diffusion of the Afromestizo identity, which at the same time *affirms and recreates the common root of the different communities who belong to the greater Caribbean*.[46] (Rafael Arias Hernández 13, emphasis added)

As is evidenced by this statement made by the director of the IVEC in 1997, one of the foremost activities of this institution for the last few decades has been to revindicate the blackness that all Mexicans hold internalized as part of this "third root." Therefore, the IVEC considers its work as a "singular act of justice for a culture that until today has been marginalized" due to the prejudice and denial on behalf of Mexicans, who consider the black presence a result of idiosyncratic coastal communities that are remote and isolated (13). He concludes his presentation of the anthology by stating categorically that, "Veracruz fortunately, is and will always be the Caribbean" (12). In her ethnography of the Port of Veracruz conducted in 2013, Christina Sue claims that rather than celebrate blackness, Vercruzanos both "import racialized images of others, mainly African Americans and Afro-Cubans, to represent authentic blackness," and have also "co-opted recent efforts to draw attention to Veracruz's African root to achieve their goals of distancing themselves and their state from blackness" (*Land of the Cosmic Race* 116). Her research demonstrates that race is only obliquely acknowledged, that Veracruzanos are racist in practice but not in discourse, and that these local efforts have done little to raise the consciousness of blackness in the Port, but rather, have operated only to further displace it onto Cuba or other foreigners. Thus, according to Sue's research, even one of the "blackest" cities in Mexico refuses to identify as black. While this evidence is riveting, it is not a surprise. The art we have examined in these chapters all points to blackness as exceptional, foreign, tropical, and other. The fact that the IVEC and other institutions have tried to reclaim blackness, even if mediated by its connection to the Caribbean, is still remarkable. Moreover, it also ignores the fact that the intimate connection between Veracruz and Cuba as well as other port cities has existed for centuries; that Veracruzanos have allowed the Caribbean to take its share of the "blame" for their blackness is only part and parcel of a discourse that has been ongoing since the Chuchumbé.

In the Plazuela de la Campana, a colonial plaza that has been restored in order to host public dances and events funded by the local government in the Port, there is a plaque commemorating Celia Cruz, the famous interpreter of Cuban *son*. Given the previous statement by Rafael Arias Hernández and Figueroa's insistence that *son* is a part of *música veracruzana*, this recognition by the city makes perfect sense. This colonial plaza is the center of nightlife and music in the Port, with performances several nights a week that alternate between *son* and *danzón*. To place a plaque commemorating Cruz's participation in the festival is tantamount to erecting a statue to one of the nation's great heroes: Veracruzanos consider themselves part of the *Gran Caribe*.

To utter Veracruz and the Caribbean in the same breath is to also include an important contribution by blacks to the culture of Veracruz, despite the implicit and explicit attitudes of those who refuse to accept their blackness. As

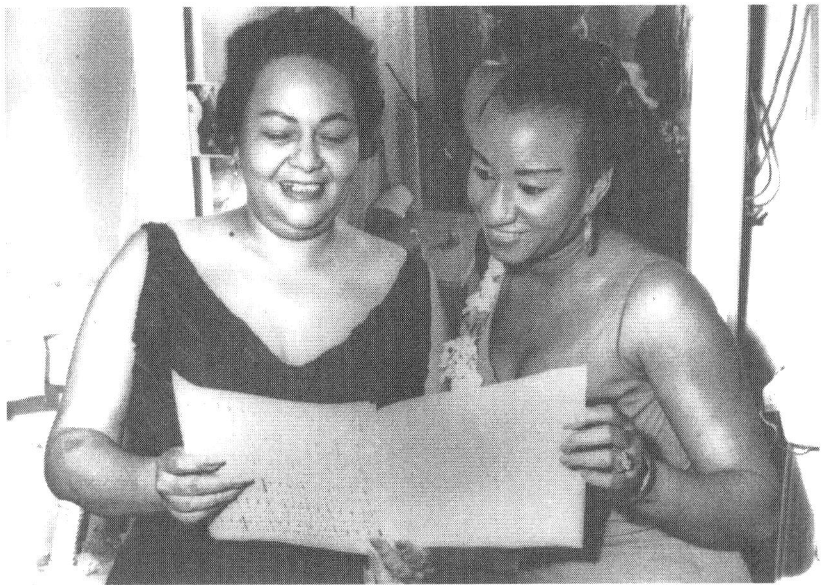

FIGURE 6.3. "Toña la Negra and Celia Cruz."

this image of Celia Cruz and Toña la Negra poignantly indexes, there is a profound cultural liaison between Veracruz and the Antilles that is more than mere affinity or desire to displace blackness; it is part of a long political and historical relationship that precedes the colonial transaction and continues today. Art, in the form of music, dance, and poetry, pulses and sings what has been part of the circuitry of bodies and sound for the last several hundred years: a mulato rhythm that has been moving back and forth between the Caribbean and Veracruz. However, it is easy to see how racial panic could attribute blackness to this Caribbean connection, and not as a presence proper to Mexican culture.

Performing Blackness: The Grand Figure of Toña la Negra

It is in this cultural and musical milieu that one of the most important Mexican performers of the first part of the twentieth century, María Antonia del Carmen Peregrino Álvarez, was born on the second of November, 1912, in the barrio of La Huaca. This neighbornood was well-known as a traditional mulato working-class neighborhood in the Port of Veracruz.[47] When she was ten years old she won her first prize, and later she is rumored to have abandoned medicine to become one of the most famous singers in México.

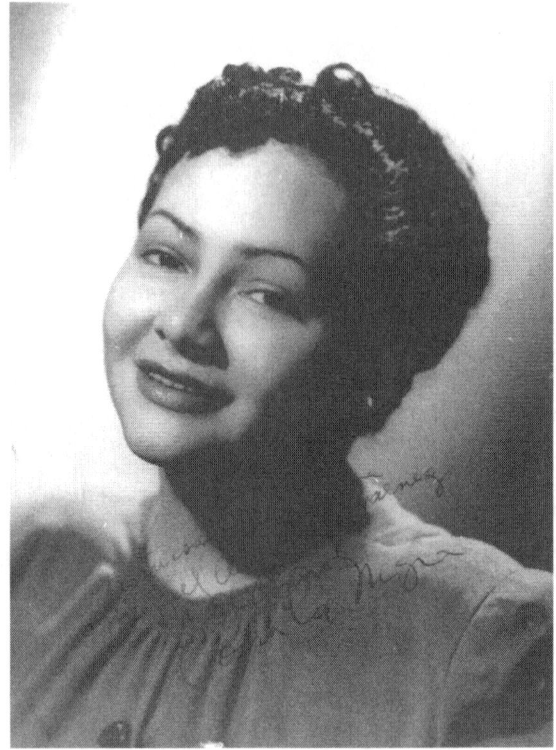

FIGURE 6.4. "Toña la Negra in publicity photo from her early period."

She started out singing *tangos*, but later sang *guarachas*, *sones*, *bambucos*, and of course, *boleros*. She formed part of the trío Uzcanga-Peregrino and Son Clave de Oro, and performed music written by México's most illustrious musicians including Agustín Lara, Rafael Hernández, Pedro Flores, Sindo Garay, Gonzalo Curiel, Ignacio Piñeiro, Son Clave de Oro, and even poet Andrés Eloy Blanco, who wrote "Píntame angelitos negros."[48]

Innumerable rumors circulate regarding the way in which she and her counterpart songwriter Agustín Lara met: some say her brother introduced them, others that they met in the center of town while hanging out in a bar or café, while still others claim that they met in a cabaret in México City called El Retiro.[49] One of the most folkloric versions of the story is that she arrived at the doorstep of Agustín Lara as a young mother, with her child in her arms, hoping he would give her an audition. Another myth is that she was singing while washing clothes in Boca del Río, and Lara passed by and

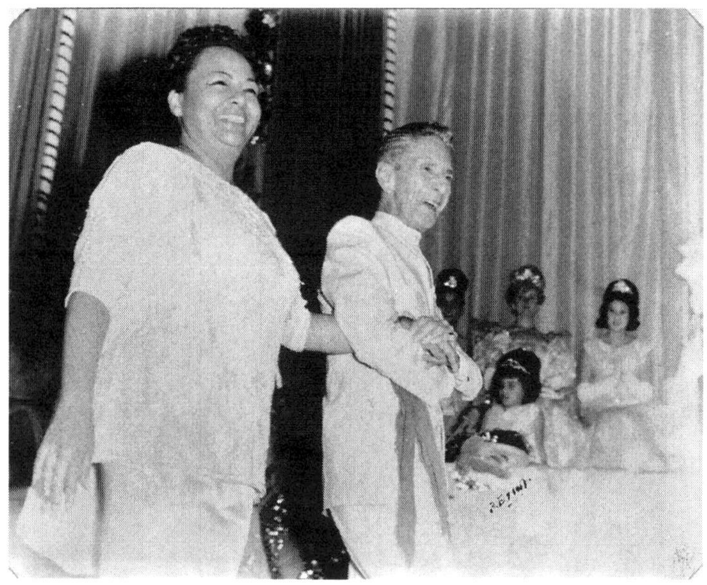

FIGURE 6.5. "Toña la Negra and Agustín Lara enjoying the applause after a performance in Veracruz."

exclaimed at what a shame it was a poor laundress should waste her talent. This last myth seems to be the most unlikely of all, considering she was from La Huaca, a barrio in the center of the Port and somewhat distant from Boca del Río. Moreover, while certainly not well off, she came from a musical family of *soneros*, *treseros*, percussionists, and singers. This problematic rumor supports a white, patriarchal mythology where the bohemian dandy "discovers" the poor black laundress.

The intersections of colonial history, music, race, and gender are important to understanding the grandiose figure of Toña la Negra because, as often happens with artists of color, their nicknames become the racial markers that define them. Critic Francés Aparicio comments on the importance held by the strategic inscription of blackness into her name: "[h]er stage name—La Negra [The Black Woman]—reveals her strategic racial self-objectification or essentialization, a racializing gesture that exhorted Mexican audiences to accept the African heritage of the Caribbean coast as a central element of their culture" (175).[50] Although she began her career as "la Peregrino," it is rumored that Agustín Lara convinced her to take "La Negra" as her stage name.[51] Indeed, the performance of blackness through the creation of her very name, although not uncommon with black musicians (her nephew David also took on "el Negro" as his stage name) does perform the work Aparicio claims it does: it requires that Mexicans rethink their own conception of race, and, through the link to the Caribbean, allow blackness to enter in as central to the makings of their own cultural traditions and people.[52]

Agustín Lara, her counterpart who was rumored to have had countless lovers and bore a long scar on his face carved by a prostitute in a fit of jealousy, is, despite this tawdry past, one of México's most beloved songwriters. Agustín is the king of the *bolero* who also wrote Cuban *sones*. Although he is not of mixed-race, he fashioned his identity based on having been born in the heart of the musical hub of Veracruz: Tlacotalpan, home of the finest *jaraneros*, *decimeros*, and, of course, *rumberos*. As such, it was the musical center of the "Afromestizo universe" that musicologist Figueroa claims has been forging itself since at least the seventeenth century. Agustín Lara is the maker of his own myth, practically fancying himself a child of that *herencia negra* although his actual birthplace is disputed with some records indicating that he was in reality born in México City.[53] Regardless, he claims Veracruz as his home and inspiration, having been lulled to sleep by the sound of the river Papoloapan—"the river of the butterflies"—with Toña la Negra as his muse. He thus appropriated the Afromestizo culture of Veracruz as part of his own musical heritage and birthright.

"La sensación jarocha"

The term *jarocho*, as discussed at the beginning, is a signifier with disputed origins that began as an epithet, referring to the racially mixed people born in the state of Veracruz, in particular, the Sotavento and the Port. On the jacket for Toña la Negra's album, *Lamento Cubano*, Bernardo Rivera claims it was Pedro de Lille who named her "The Jarocha Sensation" after a series of concerts because "Toña was the voice of the creoles, mestizos, blacks and mulatos from the barrio of la Huaca in Veracruz" (2004). Rivera's claim allows us to appreciate the irony of her almost immediate success and how, despite Toña's singularity as an exceptional black figure, she was metonymically identified with a larger community. Toña's first hit with Lara was "Enamorada," and on New Year's Eve of 1932, she appeared at the Esperanza Iris Theater singing "Lamento jarocho," a song Lara wrote especially for her. Jesse Varela, as it has been mythologized ever since, writes that "[h]er exciting and passionate voice tore the place apart with seven triumphant encores. The club management quickly hired her for 24 additional evenings" (*Latin Beat Magazine* 2011). Toña's repertoire also includes a few Afro-centric songs such as version of the poem "Píntame angelitos negros" by Andrés Eloy Blanco, which rebukes the church for not representing blacks in its religious iconography. There is also "La Negra Concepción," which is a paradigmatic song about a *mulata rumbera* (party girl) who gets all the menfolk ecstatic, as well as "Yo soy mulata," a song that manifests a veritable pride in her black body.

Despite the lack of recognition of black cultural contributions in México, Toña is the quintessential Mexican diva and icon; no one would ever deny Toña her *mexicanidad*, and yet her blackness is inscribed into her very name and sound. Aparicio underscores the maternal tenor of her voice as well as the stunning impact of her persona as an important element in Mexican culture because "the modulations of her voice and her almost matriarchal presence contributed to the inclusion of the Caribbean cultural heritage among Mexican listeners" (175). Aparicio astutely notes that she was "almost" like a maternal figure, not the sultry tragic mulatta of the North American tradition, but recalling a sort of "mother Africa" symbolism in a maternalizing gesture that is not unfamiliar to Mexican culture.

Yet this "almost matriarchal" presence is muted by the sensuality that is invoked by her throaty voice with its low timbre; the eroticism implicit in the music she sings challenges the maternal presence highlighted by Aparicio and others. Her music clearly reflects and invites the tropicality of the Caribbean, and it is her relationship to the Caribbean that both sanctifies and legitimizes her music while simultaneously legitimizing her blackness. In a way, it is as if the Cuban *son* and the tropical genres she became famous for were strangely responsible for her *mulatez*, hence explaining why blackness still does not figure prominently into the national narrative of mestizo subjectivity. Despite the claim by the IVEC that Veracruz forms part of the greater Caribbean, many nationalists looked critically at the "invasion" of Cuban art forms because they introduced music and dance that was inclined to what they considered relaxed moral standards while also introducing Afro-Cuban artists. In this way, Toña created and embodied the domesticity of Caribbean music at the same time critics signified it as a pernicious foreign element.

Caribbean as Foreign

The impact of the Mexican film industry on Cuban music is impressive, as the Golden Age of Mexican cinema is marked by a whole genre of melodramas that were almost excuses for musical numbers featuring Cuban music and acts. In his article on the relationship between the Mexican film industry and Afro-Cuban music, Francisco J. Crespo states that "[b]esides providing a simple musical framework that marked the different sequences of the film, Cuban music was used by filmmakers to represent cosmopolitanism, prosperity, and decadence brought on by the urbanization and modernization, reinforcing the new sets of urban sexual mores" (226). This modernization was viewed skeptically by conservatives, leaving little doubt as to the role that would be occupied by women should they leave the home.

Carl J. Mora also remarks on the integral role that music played in the creation of the film genre called the *cabareteras* (cabaret girls) showcasing films such as *Aventurera* (1949) that usually featured poor women fallen from grace or prostitutes with hearts of gold. These films, in their own way, were commenting on the destruction of traditional rural values that were epitomized by the *comedias rancheras* (country comedies) through the introduction of a foreign music that operated within a specifically decadent libidinal economy as "the cabareteras dramatized the breakdown of those [traditional] values" (85). Mora remarks on what was perceived to be the foreign influence of Afro-Cuban music on Mexican cinema by stating that most of the music "was Afro-Cuban—danzones, rhumbas, congas, mambos, cha-chas—musical forms with a high level of erotic suggestiveness, which in turn highlighted the freer sexual standards of postwar urban life" (85). Lest we forget that *danzón* had been around since end of the nineteenth century in addition to the

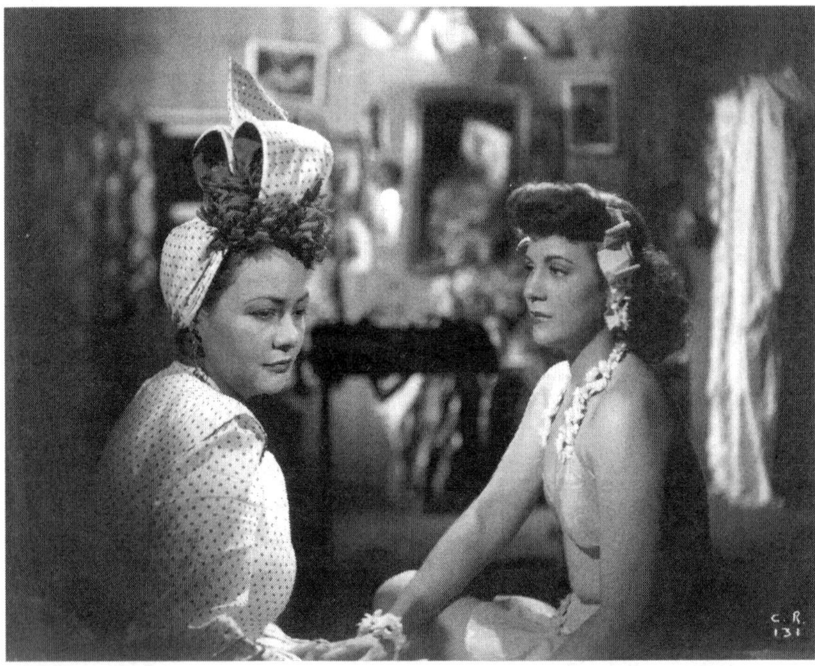

FIGURE 6.6. "Toña la Negra playing Marta la mulata alongside Antonieta Pons, one of the famous Cuban rumberas in the film *Konga Roja*," 1943.

fact that *son*, *rumba*, and *conga* were all practically formalized as traditional musical forms with the institutionalization of carnival in Veracruz in 1925, we might reconsider how truly "foreign" this music was. Furthermore, Toña's renditions catapulted many of the title songs from these films to the top of the charts: *Aventurera* is among the most famous films of the *cabaretera* genre and it is also the name of one of Toña's (and Lara's) most popular songs.

Not only a singer, Toña performed in over twenty movies, and held secondary roles in many of the most famous *cabaretera* films, including *Konga Roja* (1943) alongside Maria Antonieta Pons and the immortal *Humo en los ojos* (1946) with the Mexican *rumbera* Meche Barba. Filmed in Tuxpan, Veracruz, *Konga Roja* is one of the foundational *cabaretera* films that initiated this cinematic genre in an industry that was booming. It showcases several of the most iconic Mexican actors, such as Tito Junco and Pedro Armendáriz. In this movie, Toña la Negra plays the mulata cabaret singer who is caught in a love triangle with one of the film's alpha males, who in turn ignores her because he is in love with the white-skinned *rumbera* played by María Antonieta Pons. As is to be expected, the mulata cares selflessly for this man and, when he is killed in an imbroglio occasioned by union opponents and local rogues, she abandons her career as a singer, heart-broken despite the fact that he never loved her. The film is located in a place called "Puerto Largo," which operates as subsidiary of a large American company that follows commercial shipping routes between México and the Caribbean. Although it never explicitly claims to be Mexican and the only markers that situate the location are the vague name of the Port (which could be anywhere) and its proximity to Puerto Rico, the actors, accent, and attire are attributable to a coastal Mexican locale. The immediate allure and avid consumption of these tropicalized films reflect the anxieties of industrialization and urban decay, and, in this film in particular, U.S. economic hegemony and labor disputes.

However, this is not so different from the kind of warning Mexican women received at the turn of the century with novels like *Santa* (1903) by Federico Gamboa (Agustín Lara wrote the title song for the film version of this novel and Toña la Negra performed it) and films like *La mujer del puerto* (1934) which, yet again, takes place in Veracruz. In fact, narratives about prostitutes in literature and film are a cliché. But what makes this particular genre so remarkable is the way in which this fall from grace is racialized; or rather, the particular link that is made between mulato bodies, tropical music (what Quintero Rivera has called "música mulata"), and a seeming excessive eroticism that allows the filmgoer to enjoy the cinematic experience with the scantily clad *rumberas*, most of whom are white, while the musicians are often black or mulato. Indeed, all of the *reinas del trópico* are white, and Toña often played the mulata sidekick, rival, *nana*, or simply herself. By placing almost white, half-dressed female bodies in close, intimate proximity to black or mulato musicians, these films send a social message to the Mexican women who might be seduced by this tropicalized, glamorous representation of nightlife in the big city or international port, rife with infectious music, but also danger. Despite the "warnings," Mexicans continued to consume these "foreign" cultural products voraciously. Moreover, while melodramatic and formulaic, they brought Cuban music to the international stage and further contributed to the naturalization of tropical music in México.

Crespo emphasizes the importance of the Mexican film industry for Afro-Cuban dance and music as he claims that it strategically incorporated Cuban music into the quotidian listening practices of people around the globe, and attributes part of the continued success of Afro-Cuban music to these Mexican films (229). The point here should not be missed: not only was México appropriating Caribbean music (as well as actors and actresses), but Cuban music was becoming internationalized through its cultural and economic triangulation with México. This relationship created a cultural partnership and artistic mutualism that continues even today. But we must not neglect that the cultural, artistic, and economic flows of people and things have been going on for centuries between Veracruz and Cuba. While the Mexican cultural industries were booming, and urbanization and decay became a favored motif, tropical music became the conduit for the simultaneous titillation, outrage, and rural nostalgia felt not just in México, but across the Spanish-speaking world. The flourishing film industry, with cabaretera films more popular than ever, would make it seem as if tropicality only just arrived to México via their gyrating hips.

Caribbean as Proper

The history of tropical music in México begins right from the start, when Spanish boats began crisscrossing the Caribbean, creating a circuit of ports that became important gateway cities, but also transculturated cultural practices and rhythms, with the first important musical contact tracing back to the notorious Chuchumbé. In this ethnohistorical musical context, we can understand how Toña's voice operates almost as a sonic intermediary between the Caribbean and México, and the instant popularity of her landmark song, "Lamento Jarocho," speaks to the resonance this relationship has for her diverse Mexican public. The lyrics in this song as well as others written for her by Lara reflect this tension. "Lamento Jarocho" is a lamentation directed to those "bronzed jarochos" who "suffer" and "cry" their misfortune: "Canto a la raza / raza de bronce, raza jarocha / que el sol quemó / Alma de jarocha que nació morena / talle que se mueve con vaivén de hamaca / Boca donde llora la queja doliente / de una raza entera llena de amarguras / alma de jarocha que nació valiente / para sufrir todas sus desventuras" [I sing to my race / the race of bronze, the jarocho race / who the sun has burnt / The soul of a jarocha who was born dark / The torso that moves like the sway of a hammock / The mouth that moans a pained protest / Of an entire race full of bitterness / soul of the jarocha who was born valiant / in order to suffer her misfortune]. This song is written as a homage to the black soul of the jarocha singer who was born "valiant" in order to suffer her "misfortune," which in this case is the misfortune of being born black. The female figure metonymically represents the "bitterness of a people," while her body is simultaneously signified as a sensual and tropical object: her torso moves

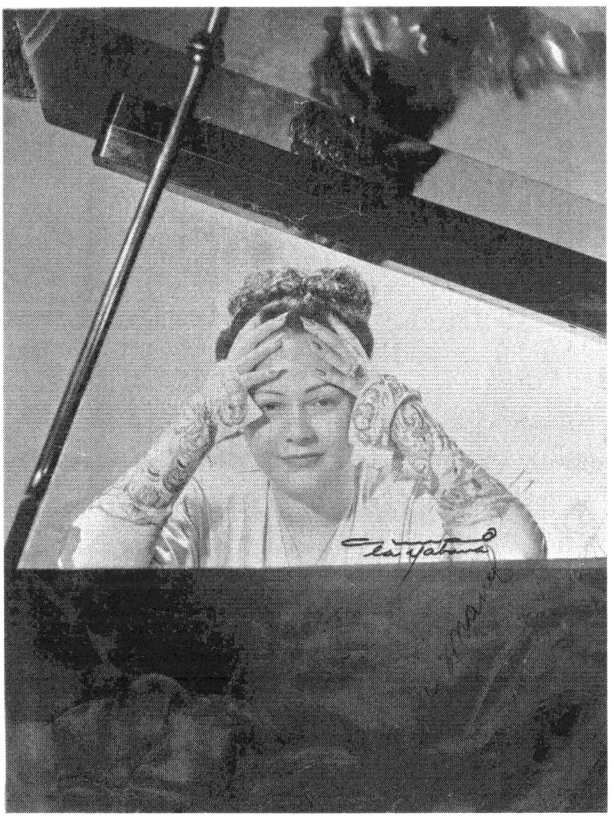

FIGURE 6.7. "Toña la Negra at the piano."

like the sway of a hammock, a delightful metaphor that points to the sway of her voluptuous body, an image typical of the sexualized descriptors that are used to describe mulatas.

Despite the "matriachal modulation of her voice," Toña's blackness inevitably operates within the libidinal economy of *mulatez*; her racial hybridity and the lower timbre of her voice beckon the listener to imagine her body. In addition to the swaying torso, it also describes burnt skin that has been perfumed by the kisses of the sand. All of these metaphors recall images of tropical beauties waiting listlessly in a sensual anticipation on the shore while suffering the burden of their poverty. As discussed in previous chapters, many of the mulatas in Mexican and Caribbean art forms are sexualized with references to their tawny skin and voluptuous bodies, titillating readers and spectators, or in this case, listeners. Vicente Riva Palacio's poetic rendition of the Mexican legend "La Mulata de Córdoba" similarly constitutes its protagonist through her phenotype and signifies Veracruz (where the drama unfolds) as a heady, tropical space that begets the same sort of listless sensuality described in the lyrics by Lara.[54] However, the poem also emphasizes the "African rays" that emanate from her eyes in addition to the voluptuous sway of her body, thus constituting her sensual tropicality as other at the same time it is autochthonous. In this way we see how the link to the Caribbean figuratively passes through Africa, and in this triangulation of desire exists a continual fetishizing of tropical spaces, making the role performed by Veracruz as its intermediary, and the gateway to the Caribbean, a place of racial and cultural contestation.

"Oración Caribe" is another one of Lara and Toña's greatest hits; it is written as a "prayer" offered to the Caribbean Sea, which, in the Santería and Candomblé spiritual traditions is embodied by the deity Yemanjá. Afro-Cuban drums operate as a percussive prelude to the ballad, providing a striking sonic counterpoint between the frenetic percussion and the plaintive oration. The "prayer" voices the suffering of blacks who plead for mercy and light in their lives: "Oración Caribe / que sabe implorar / salmo de los negros / oración del mar" ["Caribbean prayer / that knows how to plead / psalm of the blacks / prayer of the sea]. Both "Lamento jarocho" and "Oración Caribe" are like parallel homages to the latent Africanity, mestizaje, mulatez, or mulataje within the Caribbean and Veracruz. These twin "prayers," if you will, herald and even exhort their audiences to recognize and honor this "raza de bronce" (bronzed race), as the lyrics in "Oración Caribe" plead for a little "heat" (as in love) and a little "light" (as in recognition and illumination) for the black race. Toña's voice sounds a mournful lament to the sea, honoring those blacks who beg for mercy. These songs, in addition to others like "Veracruz," "Vereda tropical" and "Noche criolla" extol the beautiful tropicality of Veracruz through its ties to a black past. The tropical inflection in all of these songs does not invoke the image of a "Madre Africa" as much as it summons the fetishized tropicality of a Caribbean *mulatez*. This leads to a contradictory yet fluid musical combination where a matriarchal performer interprets music that is part of a repertory of musical genres considered romantic and sensual. While many of the songs (such as "Lamento Jarocho" and "Oración Caribe") operate within an immaterial, abstracted blackness that is signified by a pained mulato sentience; in general, most of the genres for which she is most famous are musically and lyrically provocative, constituting the stock favorites of the dancing clubs and brothels. Not to mention that she sang dozens of title songs for the famous *cabaretera* films that incited the ire of México's League of Decency. Toña's place as an intermediary exceeds even that between México and the Caribbean, blackness and whiteness; it is one that speaks to the stressed place of Mexican womanhood that is caught between illicit desire and unalloyed maternal instinct.

Racialization of Sound and Voice

Blackness is inscribed in Toña la Negra's voice as well as into the musical product she creates and that is created for her. While her voice proclaims the beauty of her native Veracruz, she equally offers "prayers to the Caribbean." As I have discussed, it is as if only through this call to the Caribbean that black culture could be summoned, and more importantly recognized, gesturing toward the performance maintained by the inscription of blackness in Toña's stage name. She somehow needed to be "la Negra" in order to sell her product by fetishizing and tropicalizing the black woman, but paradoxically requiring this identification of blackness so that, like blackface, it simultaneously might be elided in the same gesture. As Saidiya Hartman reminds us in *Scenes of Subjection*, the abstractness and immateriality of blackface serves to disassociate the reality of the black body from the performance of blackness, in this way providing a safe place for white reflection of, and on, racial purity (26). Toña's strategic naming operates in much the same manner; she is "la Negra" only because she is an exception and because blacks do not register within the nation's official history, leaving the sanctity of the mestizo identity (and its own problematic privilege of the European component) intact.

Toña's role as the primary interpreter (besides Pedro Vargas) of one of México's most beloved songwriters adds another layer to the problematic union of her voice, blackness, exotic tropicality, and motherhood because there is an intimate connection made between her and the sensual music written by Lara. She apparently complained that her audiences would not let her sing anything else. Quintero Rivera explains the role performed by music for people attempting to understand themselves and the world: "Music

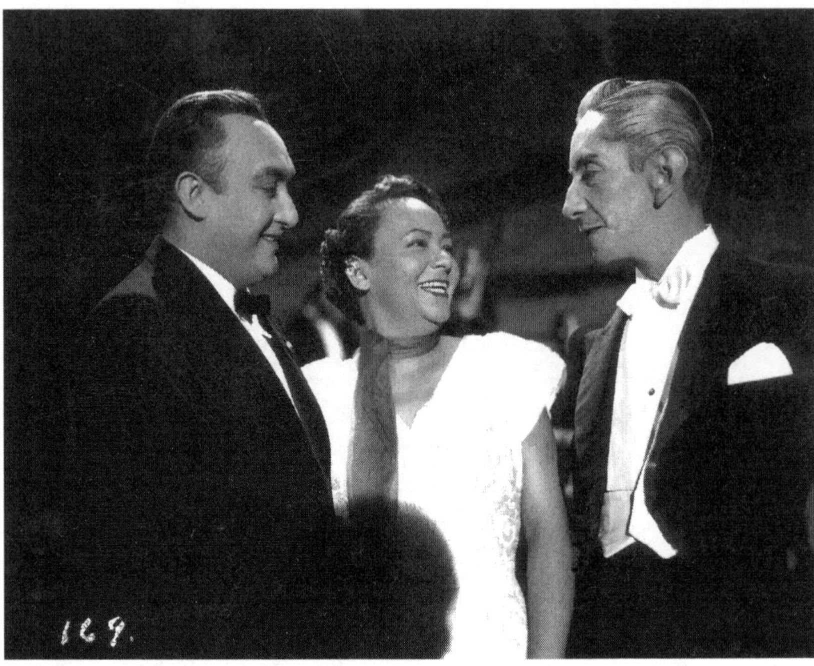

FIGURE 6.8. "Toña la Negra between Pedro Vargas (left) and Agustín Lara (right), in the film dedicated to Lara's love life, *Mujeres en mi vida*," 1949.

represents, then, a way in which people interact with their world and attempt to exercise control over their materiality, over their biology, collectively resignifying one of the essential elements of their existence. It has therefore, in all societies an enormous importance: the decisive function of the symbolic configuration of social reality" (34).[55] This theoretical intervention frames the way in which we might think about the role of Toña la Negra in the history of Mexican culture and music. If, by giving Veracruz its material tropicality in the form of her body, she also symbolically signified this tropicality with an inherent blackness both through her name and her voice. Consumed at this level, it remains aurally felt: at once symbolic, ephemeral, and intangible. Figueroa poignantly describes the power of the duet formed by Toña la Negra and Lara: "La fuerza y belleza de su voz y su personalidad—aunadas a la genialidad de Agustín Lara—nos brindaron la calidez y los aromas propios de una ciudad portuaria abierta siempre a los efluvios musicales y culturales provenientes del Caribe" [The strength and beauty of her voice and personality—linked to the ingenuity of Agustín Lara—provided us with the warmth and aromas proper to a port city that is always open to the musical and cultural flows that emanate from the Caribbean] (389). Figueroa conjures up a warm, aromatic voice that, coupled with the genius of Lara, invokes both the heat and smells of a port city open to the musical and cultural flows to and from the Caribbean. This description of her voice is marked by a gendered and sexualized image of the way in which Toña's voice and person, both as an intermediary and instrument, allowed for the Caribbean and Veracruz to intermingle, each leaving behind an aromatic taste, or *sabor*, in the mouth of the other. Moreover, her low timbre reflects and even creates an expectation for a particular kind of body. Nina Edsheim convincingly theorizes the performativity of racialized voices, claiming that "[v]ocal timbre is not the unmediated sound of an essential body. Instead, both body and timbre are shaped by unconscious and conscious training practices that function as repositories for cultural attitudes toward gender, class, race, and sexuality" (47). Thus blackness becomes produced through the content of the music that is written for her specifically (by Lara and others), through the association with a racialized Caribbean identity, but also, as suggested by Edsheim, through the performance of timbre. Edsheim posits that while timbre is not a quality exclusive to any race, it is nonetheless bound up with certain physical and cultural expectations of racialized bodies. This notion proves to be a provocative but not tidy theoretical intervention in the case of Toña la Negra because blacks simply do not register in the Mexican national imaginary in the same way their presence undergirds U.S. and Caribbean identity and racial politics. However, the identification of timbre with a specific racialized body could be part of a dormant repository of cultural attitudes reactivated by the ubiquity of North American and Caribbean musical forms which have always had a specific history of racial politics defined predominantly in terms of blackness and whiteness. In this way, Toña's la Negra's naturally throaty timbre, whether "produced" or not, becomes a performative element of her blackness, and it is therefore interpreted as such by the composers, songwriters, and consumers of her music.

Furthermore, Quintero highlights the salience of reception in music, especially *música mulata* where the role of the cultural consumers or "receptors" who interact and communicate with the composer and musicians is of paramount importance. Music is not just the result of a composer or musician's arbitrary artistic volition; it is the public who, through its "usage, consumption and communication" in the form of improvisational interventions such as *gritos* [yells] or a collective social will also contribute to the music that will be produced (338). In other words, Lara's tropical fetish and Toña's sultry voice are not the only reasons why they were so admired by their Mexican public; they reflected a deeper and more profound collective will, a sort of immanent popular aesthetic that created a mutual identification between the artists and the consumers.

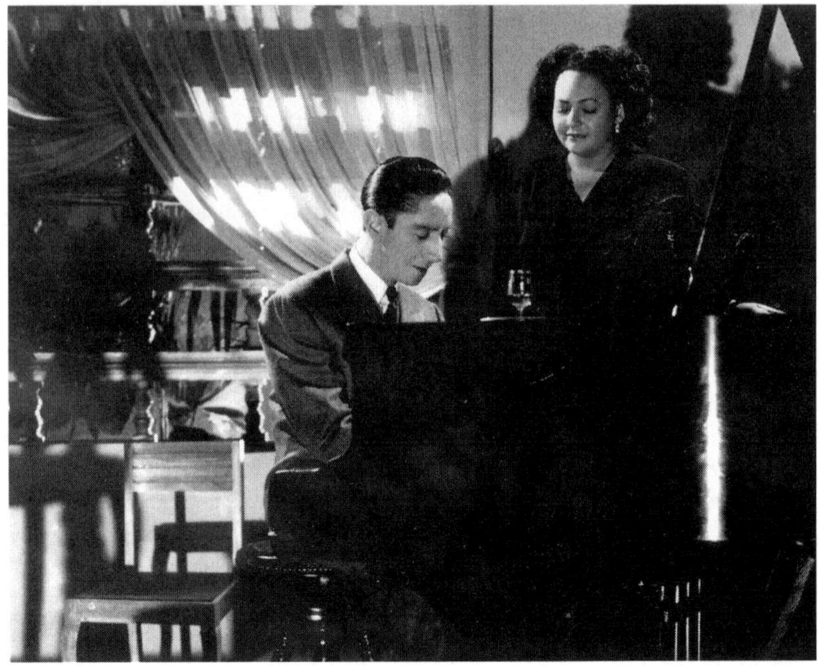

FIGURE 6.9. "Toña la Negra singing with Agustín Lara in the film, *La mujer que yo amé*," 1950.

Quintero also discusses the camouflaging of Africa within these *músicas mulatas* (16). I believe this point to be critical because, although it is a visual metaphor, it is specifically speaking to the disguised sonic renderings of an African past. In much of the music performed by Toña la Negra there exists a cultural acoustics full of tropicalized ambient sounds; yet there are moments, usually at the beginning and the end, when it is as if she were singing for you. This sonic significance excites the listener but also constitutes what Edsheim calls a "sonic color-line" that racializes and eroticizes her voice, as with the sensual description by Figueroa. Similar to the lyrics of Agustín Lara, the black voice is constituted as melodic and melancholic; part and parcel of what makes Veracruz a "tropical" space through the invocation of a pained black past that made its way to México through the Caribbean.

Sound and "sones" are powerful media for expressing the qualities of a specific time and place. Quintero explains the power of music and sound to capture time and organize human existence as an element that is both physical and invisible. He maintains that, unlike the other senses, the impact of sound is determined by the intensity of its physical vibrations in a specific temporal space (35). It can register a particular historical moment as well as prominent metaphors. Sound creates the possibility to feel and to organize; it can trap its producer (as is the case with the racialization of Toña's voice), but it can also release itself from its corporeal cast because the vibrations exist outside of the body and subsequently dissipate.

Much contemporary theory (and of course psychoanalytic theory) is heavily influenced by a scopic desire that is predicated on the visibility of the phallus. But what happens when you cannot see? The voice takes its place and appropriates space. Although voice can still be racialized and inflected, it maintains more open spaces that, according to Britta Sjogren in *Into the Vortex* (2005), deflect the "sadistic gaze." These open spaces are like uninscribed vacuums: silences that simultaneously fill and do not fill. In México, you cannot always "see" blackness, but does that mean it is not there? Does that mean there is no place for blackness in the making of modern México? When interviewed about his identity as an Afromestizo, the veracruzano Edgar Cano made an important distinction between phenotype and culture. There are other forms of "seeing" and "knowing." What prevails in México, at least in my reading, is the aural—the voice.

In her book Sjogren explains the power of sound in the context of film, and despite referring to a different artistic medium, she clarifies the role that aural recognition plays in the creation of an alternative paradigm or subjectivity that is not defined by an optic logic: "the voice is both of the unconscious and the conscious, of the body and of the Other's body (anterior to the placing of a sexualized value on that body). The recognition of these differences 'in' the voice, I argue, may remind of a state in which consciousness of self and Other does not imply dissolution for the subject" (14). Sjogren suggests aurality defies the specular or optic logic that orders our sensorial universe. The voice, as part of the conscious and unconscious, of the body but eerily outside of it, creates this possibility for recognition that within a specular libidinal economy is rendered impossible. Images do accompany sounds, like the ones that have been created through Lara's sexualizing lyrics, or the ambient tropical sounds that racialize the sound of the music, thus creating a visual context for the eruption of the voice. But sound, nonetheless, can elude its materiality, as its vibrations are felt but then dissipate.

In the case of Toña la Negra, the medium of sound becomes the mechanism for entertaining and for creating a specifically Mexican product; although her figure has been interpreted as maternal, her voice is simultaneously sexualized and forms part of an aural libidinal economy, a contradiction not incompatible with Mexican culture. Indeed, critic Roger Bartra theorized the paradox of the mother/whore dialectic in Mexican society when he coined the term "Chingadalupe."[56] Nonetheless, can sound possibly grant agency, or, as is suggested by Sjogren, be a liberatory medium by sustaining difference while deflecting optic sadism? I am not sure if Toña la Negra as a cultural practitioner is really effecting that, but she *is* pointing toward another México:

one that is present and absent, a México that is nominally—and sonically—black. Indeed, Toña's name does not allow her to escape this, yet it is through this performance of blackness that she helps to catapult Mexican music to its apex. Aparicio reaffirms this idea in her claim that tropical music has Toña "sing to the geo-cultural spaces of an Afro-Caribbean México that has remained marginal to an historical social reality invested in its indigenous, pre-Columbian past and in its very rigid European mestizaje" (175).

Toña la Negra deployed for Mexican audiences what Licia Fiol-Matta calls a "thinking voice." In her analysis of the importance of the role played by performer Lucecita Benítez for Puerto Rican culture, she claims that Benítez "danced around celebrity's strictures and kept the focus on vocal performance, impelling her public toward thought through the sense of hearing and the act of listening. This is, in Heideggerian terms, the 'gift' of the thinking voice" (1100). This notion of a "thinking voice" is profoundly revelatory for comprehending the impact of Toña la Negra as a cultural figure. Indeed, some Mexican critics of the time complained that Toña la Negra's performances were purely vocal; unlike her contemporaries such as Cuban Rita Montaner (rumored to be her rival), there was little "performing," affect or even exuberance to her gesticulations. She was almost entirely pure voice.[57] In a gesture parallel to that described by Fiol-Matta, Toña la Negra likewise impels her audience to think, to focus on her voice despite the visual and ontological impositions of a tropicalizing music and racializing stage name. Moreover, there is an important role played by the listener due to the participatory nature of sound which "can orient our sense of hearing to what is allegorical in the voice, to its pastness, tuning into the artist's call to restitution by listening to 'the contemporaneity of the audible'" (1100). Finally, Fiol-Matta contends that "Lucecita embodied and stood by voice's desire to articulate truth and speech in unjust late colonial modernity and its celebrity culture" (1100). Toña la Negra likewise embodied México's exceptional blackness, sounding a claim, if not to "truth," as Fiol-Matta suggests, certainly to a *presence* that sought to question and redress the violence of purposeful invisibility.

Although mestizaje and a museological indigenous legacy have provided the discursive markers for discussions of racial identity in México, this supposed investment is profoundly ambivalent. Like other mulata figures, Toña is paradoxically central as a cultural figure who both reflects the relationship between México and blackness as a part of the circum-Caribbean, yet deflects it through her status as an exception. The inscription of blackness into her name and voice, although intended to pay homage to her mixed-race ancestry, paradoxically erases it through this status as an exception. In other words, despite her racialized subjectivity, Toña, as a black woman, is not the rule. I would argue that although her blackness may be eclipsed by this idea of exceptionalism, her voice and aural presence prevail. Music problematically gestures and moves toward a slippery blackness that resides in the *sombras* of knowledge and sound; a blackness that is manifest as a diffused, but real, aesthetic presence.

Son como son

The dialectic between *son jarocho* as homegrown and *son cubano* as foreign reproduces itself in Toña's voice, a voice that sings both to the Caribbean and Veracruz as paradoxically and simultaneously the same and other, as a part

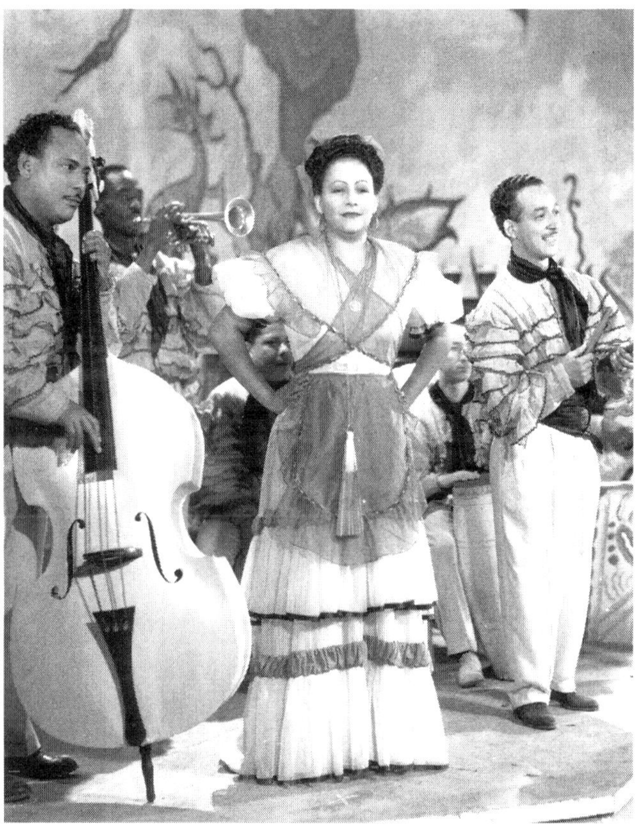

FIGURE 6.10. "Toña la Negra accompanied by Son Clave de Oro in another landmark *rumbera* film, *Humo en los ojos*," 1946. Her face is visibly whitened for this performance despite wearing traditional *jarocha* dress.

of her and her nation. Yet the African presence in the Americas, both in the Caribbean and in México, is what curiously links them together, although mediated through their distinct musical trajectories. Tropical music is racialized and sexualized, but Mexican music is considered autochthonous, even though ethnomusicologists have long studied the African components of the *son jarocho*. Nevertheless, Quintero Rivera reminds us in the case of *salsa* as well as other *músicas mulatas* in the Americas that it is not as important to trace the link to Africa as it is to critically recognize the eruption, creation, and circulation of music that is uniquely American, Caribbean, Mexican and, finally, "mulata." He argues that these genres are not musical traditions created in Africa and replicated in the new world, but rather they are instruments, sounds, and rhythms that in their transcultural form generate their own mulato style.

Music, then, is an important medium for expressing diverse—even contradictory—identities. On an extremely popular album, *Lamento cubano*, Toña sings an old *son jarocho* titled, "El cascabel" in a Cuban arrangement by her nephew Pablo Peregrino.[58] The entire album is composed of Cuban music, yet she includes a *son jarocho* and not only showcases her *jarocha* identity through an appropriation of its quintessential musical form, she refashions it. This particular arrangement, although Cuban in its rhythm while using the *jarocho* melody and lyrics, ends in a completely Mexican way. Her prolonged last note jumps up an octave; a distinctive style called *huapango* (a kind of falsetto where the vocalist stretches the final vowel sound). While originating in *son huasteco* and *jarocho*, it is also common in *sones jalicienses* and mariachi. This song symbolizes what I call the dialectics of *son*, as well as its relationship to Toña as its practitioner. It incorporates and appropriates a traditional *son jarocho* proper to the countryside of Veracruz and combines it beautifully with the rhythm of a Cuban *son*. The backup vocals in this song are also Cuban in style; perhaps the facility with which this classic *son jarocho* was appropriated is testament to the transcendent possibilities of music through the fluidity of aural movement. The antagonistic musical forces of *son jarocho* as thesis and *son cubano* as antithesis result in this song as its synthesis, as the product of historical movement and change, of a people's musical reaction to different social forces, and of the power of music to not only reflect what socially already exists, but to configure it as well.

The history of music in Veracruz and its relationship to the Caribbean, the contexts and vicissitudes of *son*, whether that be *son cubano, jarocho, montuno, huasteco,* or *jaliciense* is fundamental to understanding the importance of music in negotiating the black presence in México: *todos son como son.* It is critical for understanding the prominence of Toña la Negra and her status as the "Jarocha Sensation," diva of the *bolero* and the lone black female figure in the twentieth century who represents the contours of México's relationship to blackness. Blackness reaches far back, beyond the multiple waves of immigration of Cubans to México in the eighteenth and nineteenth centuries; yet even today it exists only as a residue, as phantasm, or in triangulation with the Caribbean. Her relationship to music—both Cuban and Mexican— reverberates this odd combination of proper and other, the ebb and flow, the comings and goings, the reciprocity and transculturation of Caribbean and Mexican music: "Veracruz, fortunately, is and will always be, the Caribbean" (12). Music becomes one of the privileged forms that allows *veracruzanos* to appropriate *mulatez*, to assume blackness, if only through this back-handed gesture. The association of *danzón* and Cuban *son* with blackness as well as Toña's identity as the "La sensación jarocha" helped to create Veracruz's identity as a port city with an African past. Furthermore the *son jarocho* as an autochthonous musical expression with distinctly African and Caribbean components, and the *son cubano* as somehow foreign and proper both created this sublimated, mediated, phantasmatic blackness that through movement, transition, aural and oral exchange with the Caribbean becomes simultaneously proper and other, foreign and Mexican.

"Pero que bonito y sabroso": The Sounds of Orphanhood

Pero qué bonito y sabroso bailan el mambo las mexicanas. Mueven la cintura y los hombros igualito que las cubanas. Con un sentido del ritmo, para bailar y gozar, que hasta parece que estoy en la Habana, cuando bailando veo una mexicana.

—Beny Moré, "Bonito y sabroso" (1950)

Whether they be shipwreck narratives, "cubanos," or just plain anomalies, blackness in México has become a phantasmatic reality. Unknown, orphaned, but ineluctably felt, black Mexicans constitute a sensory "aftertaste" to be enjoyed but also defamed. With the exception of Toña la Negra and la Negra Graciana, who are just that—exceptional—the main black protagonists in Mexican cultural production (whether as characters or producers) continue to languish in an uncertain anonymity. However, the emerging consciousness on behalf of Afro-Mexicans and academics involved in the recognition of the "third root" is quickly changing this reality.

As witnessed in many of the representations of mulatas we have examined in previous chapters, the trope of unknown origins forms a critical element in the construction of the mulata subjectivity. The nation's resolution to maintain the invisibility of their African past through the exceptionalization of its mulato figures is part of this narrative of disappearance: Carmelo, the phantasmatic dance partner in *Danzón* who escaped Julia at every turn, serves as leitmotif that initiates and ends the film; la Negra Graciana whose musicianship "a la antigüita" ironically locates her at the center of one of México's most beloved musical genres; and of course, the towering figure of Toña la Negra, whose paradoxical sultry voice and matriarchal presence constitutes her as the quintessential Mexican diva, despite her claim to blackness.

This same trope continues to circulate, weaving its way in and out of the aural fabric that entwines the black presence with Mexican music. The lost Afromestizo universe that begat "the Chuchumbé" and the *son jarocho* as a musical form testifies to this because there is a fundamental ambiguity surrounding the origin of the Chuchumbé; its arrival with Cuban sailors may just be one of the many myths regarding mulato-inspired musical forms. The effect of this proto-*son* throughout the viceroyalty points to the connection the authorities made early on between Afro-Mexicans and vice, while its origin in Veracruz or Cuba would explain the "exotic" elements of this nefarious song. The ambivalence with regards to the authenticity of certain instruments in the *son jarocho* also speaks to a sense of vague origins, as some claim the *quijada* and *marimbol* are essentials instruments, while still others maintain that *son jarocho* is never complete without a harp. The debated percussive "rasgueado" of the *jarana* or the African-inspired "punteado" of the harp also speak to this disputed, but indubitable, presence. The persistence of oral poetry (also an essential part of indigenous and Iberian cultural forms) as a vital, lived practice and the spontaneity necessitated by the call-and-response of the *jarocho* poet is also testament to this long tradition in plural worlds. Finally, the ardent integration of *danzón* and *son cubano*, and the perseverance of the former for the last one hundred and thirty years, winding its way back to its place of origin through the reinsemination into Cuban culture, speaks to the immanence of Afro-Mexican culture in México.

The trope of blackness in Mexican arts is marked by these constant disappearing acts and sudden emergences, however, the sonic and visual flickers of Africanness belie these supposed cloudy origins as part of a magical and mythical past. The black voice—with its multiple textures and myriad articulations—has remained in myth, legend, film, and sound. Indeed, music is one of the nation-state's most prized assets; it registers a claim to cultural "authenticity" and is a source of national pride. Toña la Negra's music, sound, voice, and figure reflect, almost metonymically, a region deeply marked by racial, social, and cultural heterogeneity. This region is a product of the violence, conquest, movement, and polyphony that results when diverse peoples come together. The *jarochos* (whether they be boorish "half-breeds," wild pigs, or stick-wielding militiamen) today exhibit a pride in their origins, music, and culture, which besides European, is strongly African and Amerindian. However, the case of the African is also mitigated through yet another middle passage: that which passed through the Caribbean in order to land on Veracruz.

Conclusion

To Be Expressed Otherwise

From May until August 2015, the Vincent Price Museum in East Los Angeles hosted a superb exhibition titled "Soldadera" by internationally renowned performance and video artist Nao Bustamante. The multimedia exhibition imagined, through what the Chicana artist calls a "speculative reenactment," the soldadera's participation in the Mexican Revolution. Thoroughly mesmerizing, haunting, and dreamlike, at the same time it is tactile, concrete, and physical. The exhibition featured several pieces that mix archival footage and photography with Bustamante's revisionary imagistic work and material craft. She blurs the boundaries between archive and invention, rending and weaving these women's stories tightly together through the symbol of a yellow, bullet-hugging Kevlar Edwardian dress. Filling the exhibition hall, the cinematic installation was a five-minute loop of a mostly black-and-white film, projected onto a 16' × 9' screen. The video transposed reenactments of soldaderas wearing yellow Kevlar dresses onto archival footage in order to create Bustamante's rendition of the chapter dedicated to the soldadera from the unfinished film *Qué Viva México!* (1931), by Russian filmmaker Sergei Eisenstein. Unfortunately, he was unable to complete it because the project ran out of money and he was forced to leave México before production on this segment could begin. The soldadera's important role in the Revolution was first visually imagined by an avant garde Russian filmmaker, only to be completed eighty-six years later by a Chicana performance artist from the San Joaquin Valley.

At the center of the room was a series of yellow dresses, bulky and prissy, thoroughly unfit for the battleground of war. Bustamante consulted the revolutionary photographs at the UC Riverside Special Collections Library, and was struck in particular by one portrait that featured a battalion of female participants in late-Edwardian dresses. So different from the images we are accustomed to seeing of the soldadera, so striking for its incongruity, this photograph became the inspiration for the series of military vestments she would design. The dresses, "Tierra y Libertad–Kevlar˚ 2945," are crafted as bulletproof gowns that would withstand the piercing gunshots of the Winchester 30-30 rifle, the preferred weapon of the revolutionary insurgents. Kevlar (designed by a female chemist) is a synthetic material woven so tightly that it is five times stronger than steel; however, after a single penetration it begins to unravel. Body armor the soldaderas never had (if only their *rebozos* could have been lined with this stuff), it is a speculative tribute to the thousands of nameless, denigrated women who were killed on the battlefield, raped or maimed, and left unrecognized. In the words of Hannah Manshel, "Nao Bustamante's Kevlar dresses are, in a way, garments protected by unraveling [. . .] the dresses perform a kind of vulnerability about thinness and thickness—a kind of vulnerability that cannot go to pieces. When hit by a bullet—or, when cut by an artist's scissors—the fabric wears thin; unravels to protect the body inside" ("Soldadera: The Unraveling of a Kevlar Dress," May 28, 2015). The display includes several of the dresses, but only one lies in a glass box (a sleeping beauty), pierced with the slugs of an original Winchester 30-30. The remaining dresses will also eventually be fired on, and, in this way, it is an ongoing performance that will continue to record and violate the imagined and invented bodies of these nameless women. Phantasmatic violence that continues to pierce, that withstands time and its punctuating deformations, ephemeral and yet ineluctably felt.

Hidden at the back of the exhibition hall was an understated piece called "Chac Mool," perhaps the most complex component of the entire "Soldadera" exhibition. It is a remake of a Mesoamerican statue that features a reclining figure whose head faces forward ninety degrees, whose abdomen usually houses a bowl for sacrificial items, and who is often associated with Tlaloc, the Aztec god of rain and fertility. An almost incredible reenactment, to see it the spectator is forced to peer through an antique viewfinder (whose large circular form reminds us of Tlaloc's prominent eyes) in order to observe a small screen that loops twelve minutes of Leandra Becerra Lumbreras on her bed. Lumbreras was the oldest person alive at the time (although Guinness refused to put her in the record because she lost her birth certificate forty years prior), and the last surviving soldadera of the Mexican Revolution. At 127 years of age, she reclined on her perch of pillows piled on a makeshift bed—a living Chac Mool—who a month later, was to leave the earth, having outlived all of her children and many of her grandchildren. She finally told her story through the persistent tapping of an unknown rhythm, her communicatory gesture revealing her engagement in the Revolution for the first time in public, and for the last time in private, to the team Nao Bustamente

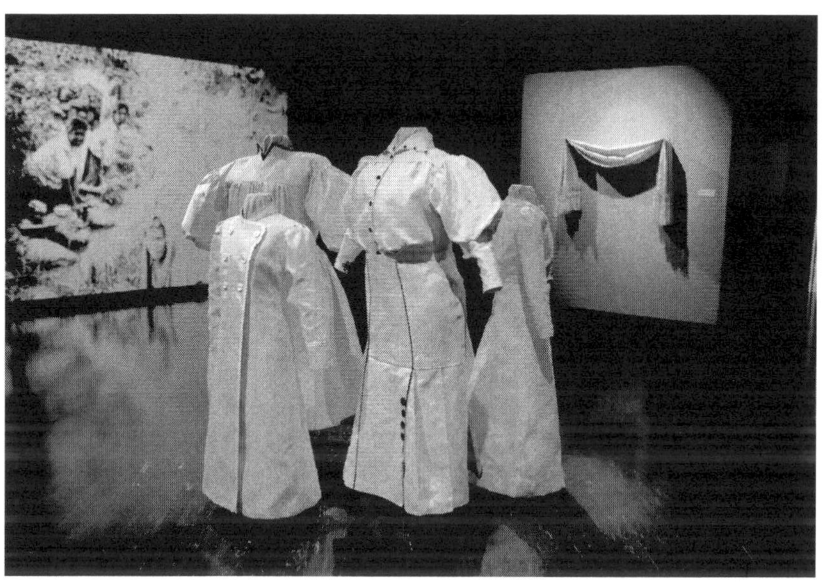

FIGURE C.1. Foreground: Installation of "Kevlar Fighting Costumes." Left Background: "Soldadera" film installation. Right background: "Kevlar rebozo."

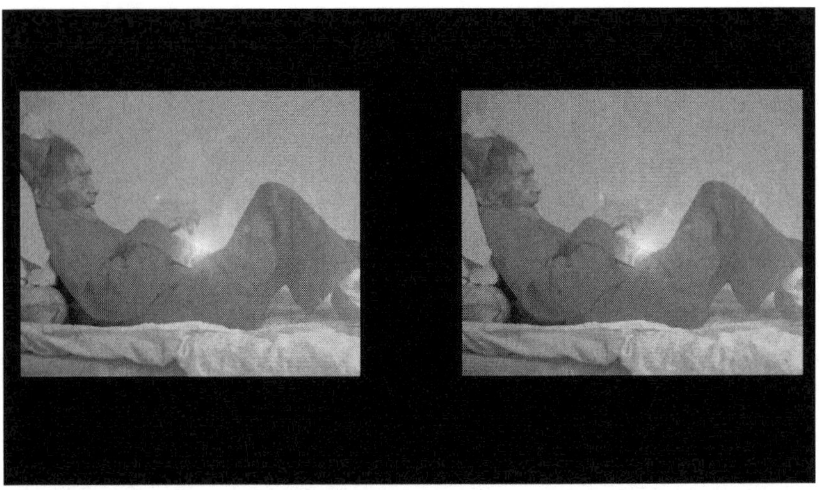

Figure C.2. "Installation piece 'Chac-Mool.' Video still of Leandra Becerra Lumbreras drumming."

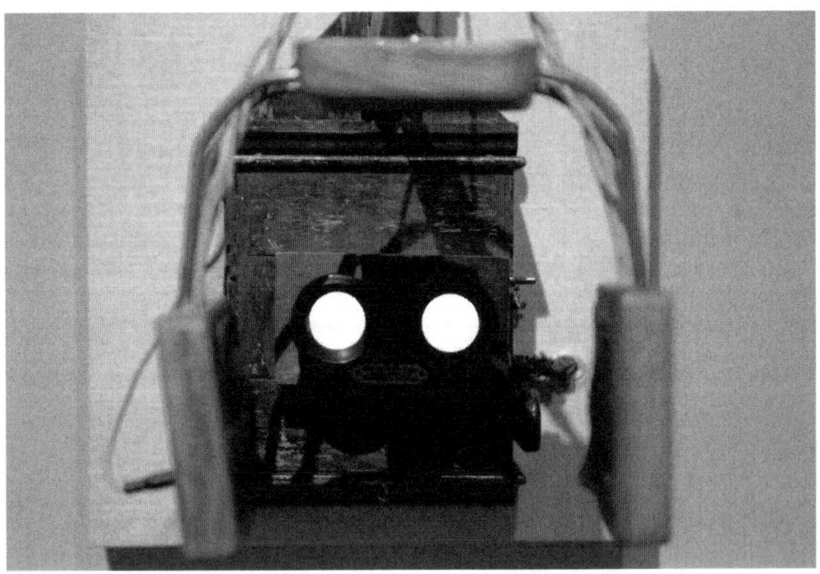

Figure C.3. "Chac-Mool contraption." The viewfinder exhibits video loop of Leandra Becerra Lumbreras drumming.

gathered in their quest to meet the last living soldadera. It took over a hundred years—she waited patiently—but her body spoke, and she was heard. Artist Moises Medina, who accompanied Bustamente's crew, attests that "[v]ery little was vocalized. But much was said" ("Soldadera, The Tiny Things They Carried," June 12, 2015).

Becerra Lumbreras was one of the few who fought for her communal land grant and withstood the chiding of others as she demanded her revolutionary pension: "[S]he lined up with other men demanding that she too receive compensation in the form of land for her military service. Men pushed her while woman berated her but she held steadfast, vocally insisting that she had bled, fought, and mothered children of the revolution" (Medina 2015). The cleverness of this installation is the paradoxical analogy Bustamante draws between Lumbreras and the Chac Mool. The Chac Mool is a Mesoamerican statue whose role is not clearly understood, who lays in an almost semi-supine position (except that he rests on his forearms), reclined, vulnerable and yet active, located outside of the sacred temples but not part of them, spread throughout the diverse indigenous world across time and space, associated with fertility, but upon whose belly rested the bowl for the sacrificial victims (or reverential items, no one knows for sure), an icon that was misnamed by the person who discovered it. Not unlike the soldadera, the name stuck. Jennifer Doyle, the curator of the exhibition, explains the work: "Our intention, as artist and curator, is to invite the viewer of the exhibition [. . .] to consider the possibilities of speculative, even utopian thinking as not a retreat from the here-and-now, but as a deep engagement with how we might imagine the here-and-now differently" ("Nao Bustamante's Soldaderas, Real and Imagined," May 14, 2015). The women in this book may have frayed stories, occupy semi-supine positions, hover in the shadows between maternal instinct and macho valor, blackness and whiteness, respectability and audacity. Like Becerra Lumbreras, they have outlived and questioned their very abjection in the art they have inspired, in the stories that are told or tapped with their fingers, and in the case of Becerra Lumbreras, in the very life she refused to leave behind as a supercentenarian.

Whether as sultry mulata witches, abject cucarachas, or stoic Indians, all of the personages I consider have been *figured* and simultaneously *disfigured* by the tropological forms their representations have taken. Yet through (dis)figuration in the arts, the important presence of these people has been indirectly inserted into Mexican history and culture where historiography and political rhetoric have remained silent. Hayden White contends that "[d]iscourse is the genre in which the effort to earn this right of expression, with full credit to the possibility that things might be expressed otherwise, is preeminent" (2). Despite being metonymically congealed in rigid caricatures and deformed stereotypes, discourse, in all of its forms, has allowed for the possibility of their presence to be "expressed otherwise" because troping is the "soul" of discourse. An attentive reader, spectator, or listener can conversely find in these (dis)figurings multiple possibilities: to see, hear, and feel the extraordinary contributions they have made to Mexican culture and history.

The abundance of marginalized figures in national culture is not a new phenomenon. We might recall Diego Velasquez's obsession with the street urchins and the subaltern subjects to whom he would continually turn in seventeenth-century Spain. We might also remember the nineteenth-century European obsession with the figure of the prostitute and the bucolic peasant class, whose influence can be found in the twentieth-century Mexican revolutionary novel. Even in Nahua poetry and art, the figure of the prostitute emerges time and again. These marginalized figures have no doubt been seminal to the history of all nations despite their anonymity, reflecting a sort of abstracted age-old disenfranchisement that nonetheless becomes the inspirational material for art. However, our figures have made historically *specific* contributions to the Mexican nation's culture and identity that have been mostly disappeared.

There has been a longstanding cliché in Latin *América* that states that "modernity" coexists with the stone age, where you are as likely to see a giant prehistoric-sized butterfly an hour away from a skyscraper, where people conduct business as they would on Wall Street coexist with those who believe in witches, do not enjoy electricity, lock their doors or travel outside of their villages. How can the domains of the aesthetic reach and interact with a public as diverse as this? The political and historical possibilities of art do not restrict themselves to the instrumentalist guise of raising awareness or enlightening consciousness (even if they pretend to effect just that), nor is art mere delectable artifice; it exists somewhere in-between as slippery words, images, and sounds that make their presence into historical fields and imaginaries, that constitute alternatives, although not always consciously. Indeed, the cliché is not totally wrong: the multiple domains of the aesthetic reflect these diverse realities in a way that official discourse attempts not to. It intervenes, slips in and out, twists and turns and, as suggested by Rancière, not necessarily by intention. The spectator is important because she too contributes to the production and consumption of art, poetry, song, and storytelling, and thus, creates knowledge. The "West" and its concomitant imposition of sameness would have us believe in an epistemic and cultural amnesia where indigenous and African knowledge died with the conquest and slavery. The iterative excess of these embodied tropes in addition to the plasticity and longevity of the aesthetic realm, I maintain, prove otherwise. Its permanence but permeability, its movement throughout the ages, its resurrection, recycling—even in its most debased and parodic forms—presents us with knowledge, with disruptions or tears, with slippery forms that present possibilities.

The soldaderas were not just pathetic, dutiful camp followers; they rescripted traditional gender roles, and in their performative language created a radical space where women and men often fought side by side and maintained fluid sexual relations. Michel De Certeau's tropological notion of a " 'residing rhetoric' ('*rhétorique habitante*')" has inspired my reading of the social impact of the soldadera's appropriation of place (100). These women enunciated their own "residing rhetoric" by appropriating the public places and spaces that were previously unfit for the interventions of women. The paradoxical veiling of these women through the lack of an official title in conjunction with the superfluity and ambiguity of unofficial names (adelita, cucaracha, galleta, valentina) speaks to the way their radical shifting of gender roles affected the construct of womanhood in the national imaginary. The vagaries of war would permit them this power, but when wartime exigencies diminished, so did the opening that allowed this monumental contribution. Through the creation of new roles, both in the domestic *place* and public *space*, and in the creation of a *scenario*, they in effect "revolutionized" the Revolution, simultaneously provoking a great anxiety for those beholden to normative gender conventions.

Mulatas reflect the violence of slavery, and their blind spot in history has subsequently blinded the Mexican nation to the way black female sexuality has been manipulated in order to disguise larger social "problems": racial, cultural, and epistemological miscegenation. In retrospect, these mulatas often take the blame for the vilified otherness that is present in the Mexican imaginary—the witches, temptresses, and Amazons—while neglecting the very real violence enacted on their bodies. Like the soldaderas, they too lack a proper title and are recognized by the sexual congress of slave and master that is literally mapped onto their bodies and the language that defines their identity. This sexual congress continues to utter an undeniable threat: the nation's "purest" members (including "noble" Indians) may be contaminated by the unnatural power of the mulata.

Africans and their descendants have been in México for at least five hundred years, as long as the first Europeans, yet have been relegated to a flickering, ambiguous past where they also hover in the shadows. Their voices have been heard in music, in the festivities of carnival all over México, in the style, tempo, and timbre of the multiple *sones* that each makes a claim to constituting "traditional" Mexican music. Yet, in contrast to the Caribbean that actively celebrates black heritage in music and folklore, often to the exclusion of all else, African descendants have never been explicitly recognized as contributors to the forging of this unique culture. They are so deeply embedded in Mexican culture that the apparent lack of a sizeable physical presence, occasioned by the insistence on phenotype, allows for the larger nation to forget and exclaim at the curiosity of the singular figures who emerge almost *sui generis*. Thus there is no apparent contradiction when superlative mulata figures such as la Mulata de Córdoba, la Negra Angustias, la Negra Graciana, and Toña la Negra emerge to take center-stage. Nor is the nation uncomfortable with figures such as Vicente Guerrero, the independence hero and second president of the Republic, who, in his attempt to effect racial and class parity by eliminating the racial taxonomies in the national census, unwittingly opened the door for Afro-Mexicans to be disappeared two hundred years later. Because of racial and economic intermarriages, blacks quickly integrated into colonial society and were no longer archived in the registries, becoming absorbed by the *castas*. In a society that is keenly aware of color, they were no longer documented by this standard and thus, in an ironic twist, many today neglect that Vicente Guerrero himself was an Afro-Mexican.

As the original inhabitants of these lands, indigenous societies in México are not just ancient people that contributed strange-sounding toponyms and exotic dishes to the national culture. They possess and exercise specific forms of knowledge that are not manifested solely through the interesting atavisms that, in the rhetoric of an all-inclusive mestizaje, are celebrated by *criollos* as a curious throwback to an ancient time long since past. They are not primitive forms of a more modern or advanced concept of personhood in Mexican society. Rather than belonging to the romanticized past to which the nation's patriarchs and ideologues have relegated them, they still speak their languages, practice their life forms, and continue to develop as communities that are part of a vital present, a divergent modernity they are crafting on their own terms.

In *Divergent Modernities* (2001), Julio Ramos makes a fascinating argument regarding the title of the essay "Nuestra América" by Cuban poet José Martí, arguably one of the most important essays about Latin American culture and identity. Ramos claims that "nosotros," the subject pronoun from which the possessive pronoun "nuestra" comes, already points to the "others" within, as "nos" refers to the collective "I" and "otros" means others. Therefore, the very title of Martí's essay highlights his preoccupation with including those whom he feels have contributed most to the construction of Latin American identity and culture, but who have been left out due to the Europeanizing discourse of creole intellectuals. As illumined by Ramos, "Nuestra América" is at once a personal, ambivalent, and paradoxical term. It creates a place for the others inside while highlighting their exclusion. *América* is a place that is quite different from other parts of what has been considered the hegemonic "West." Therefore, the fact that these often flat and disfigured characters are simultaneously mobile and fluid does not incur contradiction. Indigenous people, mestizos, and Afro-Mexicans have been inhabiting multiple worlds, engaged in what José Rabasa has called "plural-world dwelling." The form of dwelling was not simply what was thought to be a "syncretic" jumble, where names, ruins, and culinary traditions remain, but the ultimate epistemic power was dictated by and for the "West." Rabasa reminds us that in fact this is not true. Indigenous systems of thought not only persist, they have also inflected non-indigenous culture of mestizos and Euro-Americans. African culture and thought has also become part of the system of knowledge that exists in *América*, as blacks have been in *América* as long as Europeans have, if not longer.[1] The realm of the aesthetic exists in a context where the participant is as important as the artist; lest we forget that the Nahua codices required embodiment in order to be interpreted, as the *tlacuilo*[2] did not write in a cell, but rather, wrote for the priest who would read and "perform" his work, for the audience that would participate by watching, but also interpreting. Similarly, the balladeer (like the Wixárika weavers) who performs for his/her community, is informed by the immediate social, cultural, and political milieu.

What then, is this Mexican community, or *pueblo* (the people)? In *Amor perdido*, Carlos Monsiváis makes a beautifully candid statement when he reminds us that the Mexican Revolution, in all its glory and disillusionment, was put into place by the *pueblo*, and that this Revolution will continue as long as there is still a *pueblo* to speak of: "Vámonos al monte, éntrale a la bola y sépanlo bien pinches méndigos: sólo hay pueblo mientras hay revoluciones y (1910–1917) las revoluciones duran el día entero, el año entero, el tiempo que duran y la revolufia es la mezcla orgánica de situaciones culminantes y vida cotidiana" [Let's take to the mountains, join the Revolution and let it be known you dumb jerks: there is only a pueblo while there are revolutions and (1910–1917) revolutions last the whole day, or whole year, or the time they need to last and this Revolution is an organic mixture of culminating situations and daily life] (22). Although he refers to a specific Revolution—the culture of Revolution brought on by the infamous insurrection of 1910—he wants us to understand that there is only a *pueblo* while there is revolution, and it is in these revolutions (small and large) that the community simultaneously coheres and disrupts its identity (both as heroes or *pinches méndigos*). This *pueblo* is not monolithic; indeed, it is composed of all different kinds of people, life ways, histories, bodies and *saberes*. The practice of daily life, the organic mixture of quotidian ritual and the praxis of culture, even in the midst of its creation, points to the constant revolutions that happen when diverse people come together in the wake of violent events. Whether these events are slavery, invasions, revolts against tyranny, spiritual violence, the unjust appropriation of ancestral land, or gender aggression, the practice of living these events—of living rupture and continuity—generates this sense of *pueblo* even when the *pueblo* itself is far from homogenous.

Not unlike Juan Rulfo's watershed novel, *Pedro Páramo* (1955), the whispers and murmurs of *el pueblo* seek redress but also reveal new and disruptive life forms. This canonical Mexican novel operates almost as an allegory of México's nobodies because the sounds of the *pueblo* are all filtered and interpreted through the experience of a melancholic, avaricious cacique whose ill-gotten gains damn the town *in perpetuum*. But despite the iron-fisted dominance of the town's cacique whose name constitutes the title of the novel, the story is moved by the whispers and murmurs of the nobodies in the background. Indeed, the power of trope to condition the way in which people and events are represented has been instrumental to understanding the official narratives that have surrounded many of these unsung figures. While often blurry in the foreground, they are strident, even powerful, in the background.

This notion of *pueblo* serves as a metaphor to think about the multifarious engagements of our figures—indigenous peoples, soldaderas, mulatas, and blacks—in Mexican history that, through heroic intervention or the practice of everyday life, helped to forge what we consider to be Mexican culture. Art, in all of its diverse media and forms, reflects these revolutions that last "a day, a year, or the time they need to last." Art and popular culture can intervene, although not always evenly, where history leaves off; at least this has been the case with México's nobodies.

Notes

Introduction

1. All translations in this book are mine unless indicated otherwise.

2. *Son jaliciense* is a Mexican musical genre from the state of Jalisco that produces much of the mariachi repertoire. Not surprisingly, some controversy surrounds the origins and theme of this *son*. While some insist that this *son* is dedicated to the train that traveled toward Zapotlán uphill crossing the "Cuesta de Sayula," I would just as easily point to the second stanza as evidence that it is in honor of a black woman: "Cuando me traes a mi negra / que la quiero ver aquí / Con su rebozo de seda / que le traje de Tepíc." Or, perhaps, it honors both the train and the *mulata*.

3. From this point forward I will no longer italicize this word.

4. Henceforth, I will use the Spanish orthography of the word mulata without italics in order to distinguish it from the English word, mulatta, which is charged with its own history of race and subjectivity. Furthermore, because I study the figuring of the mulata in México (and the Caribbean) and compare it with that of the "tragic mulatta" in the United States, this orthographic distinction will help to make these comparisons clear.

5. Latin for "discourse" as Hayden White reminds us in *Tropics of Discourse*. The Oxford dictionary (1982) informs that it means to roam or wander.

6. In his book, *Without History*, José Rabasa explains that indigenous people have been subjected to an historical erasure by European epistemes, existing as expressed by Christopher Columbus, "without culture and without creed." But rather than insist on its negativity, its absence, "without history" operates as an amphibology that can countermand the teleological impulses of Western discourses that place indigenous people outside of, and in opposition to, "modernity." Instead, Rabasa claims these discourses can be manipulated into a language and practice crafted on indigenous terms that avoid this aporetic status (3). This concept can likewise be useful for comprehending how soldaderas and Afro-Mexicans were agents of military, cultural and gender change, operating outside of official history while they fill in the background that, paradoxically, ushers in "modernity."

7. Malinche, also referred to as Doña María or Malinalli, was the consort and translator of Hernán Cortés. Malinalli, later pejoratively known as "la Malinche," is an

extremely important figure in Mexican history, especially for the identity of the Mexican woman. As the assistant to Cortés, her skill and intelligence were invaluable to him. She provided great military and diplomatic services as her companionship seemed to guarantee his success. However talented she may have been, she is not considered a *soldadera*, *capitana* or *conquistadora*. Her infamy remains as "La Chingada:" the whore who bore the first of a bastard race. Not unlike the biblical Eve whose deceit got humanity expelled from paradisiacal Eden, she became the mythical bane of the Mexican people who have exclusively linked her "traitorous" behavior with the fall of the Mexica Empire. The blame for the Conquest is placed on her mythified figure, while the role of the other groups who fought with Cortés against the Mexicas has been in general downplayed.

8. I have omitted far too many important studies to list them here, but the scholarship has been prolific and broad.

9. The PRI (Partido Revolucionario Institucional) lost its first elections after 71 years to the right-wing political party PAN (Partido Acción Nacional) during the period of 2000–2012, after which it regained power with the election of Enrique Peña Nieto.

10. I will explain these terms more precisely later, but *tlacuepa* is a Náhuatl phrase that means "the turning or twisting of words." *Olin* in Náhuatl means movement but also refers to a Nahua deity, and comes from the verb "olini." It is an intransitive verb that describes the kind of movement that takes place during an earthquake, or when a house settles (John Sullivan, personal communication). In turn, *tlalticpac* is defined by Louise Burkhart as not "on earth," but "on the point or summit of earth" (*The Slippery Earth* 58).

11. Fray Alonso de Molina's *Vocabulario en Lengua: Castellana/Mexicana/Mexicana/Castellana* was written during 1555–1571, and is considered one of the definitive dictionaries of Náhuatl from the early colonial period.

12. This is the definition according to the 22nd edition of the *Real Academia Española*.

13. Many post-structuralists, such as Jacques Derrida, have theorized at length on the undecidablity of language. Derrida's famous neologism "différance" maintains that language is in a constant state of deferment; words can only be defined through the constant appeal to other words in an "endless chain of signification." I will not enter into this debate as I engage the meaning of the word "translation" in English, Spanish, and Náhuatl, and not theories of language or translation. My argument stems from the fact that the very nature of the word in Náhuatl already renders the possibility of translation tenuous, while the direct translation in English or Spanish suggests a transparency in signification.

14. In their respective dictionaries, Frances Karttunen and Rémi Simeón spell *olin* with only one "l." I will follow this orthographic preference.

15. Similarly, critic Nestor García Canclini might call these emancipated spectators "co-producers."

16. Even though women are often associated with the task of weaving, men are also talented weavers. In the Zapotec town of Teotitlán del Valle, for example, entire households are dedicated to working as textile artisans in different capacities. Weaving is taught at an early age, but to varying degrees and levels of competencies. Oftentimes, women will card and dye the wool with cochineal in order to continue with their more traditional domestic duties such as food preparation while older boys and men will frequently perform the more laborious work on the loom.

17. According to the same chart compiled by Aguirre Beltrán, there were 15,000 Europeans, 10,000 Africans, 3,676, 281 indigenous people and 624,461 Afromestizos, 704,245 Indomestizos and 1,092,367 Euromestizos (234).

Chapter 1

1. A shawl worn by Mexican women of all classes. However, it is associated with female indigenous apparel.

2. María Félix, often referred to as "La Doña" (a reverential term that implies the boss), is one of the most iconic actresses of Mexican cinema's Golden Age, appearing in almost fifty films. She is renowned for embodying a tough, spirited leading lady and has played various versions of soldaderas in *La Cucaracha*, *La Valentina*, *Enamorada*, *La Generala*, *Juana Gallo* among many other films about the Mexican Revolution.

3. *Saber* literally translates to "knowledge." I will often employ the Spanish word because it can be used as a both a verb, "to know" or "to taste like," as well as a noun, as in "knowledge." It better encompasses, in my opinion, the idea of a divergent, subaltern knowledge because of these multiple possibilities.

4. A *molcajete* is a kind of mortar and pestle made from vesicular basalt that is common for grinding food.

5. This phrase translates as "They missed the train." However, it borrows from a common idiomatic expression that figuratively implies that one lost out on a chance or opportunity.

6. My translation.

7. The difference between place and space has been traditionally understood as a distinction between the particular and universal, between a specific location and a generalized locale marked by forward-facing movement. John Agnew informs that this has largely been translated into an understanding that "[p]lace is the setting for social rootedness and landscape continuity" while "[l]ocation/space represents the transcending of the past by overcoming the rootedness of social relations and landscape in place through mobility and the increased similarity of everyday life from place to place" ("Space and Place" 319).

8. There has long been the contention among many scholars that the participation of women in the military can be dated back to pre-Columbian figures of the Mexica war goddesses Coyolxauhqui (daughter of Coatlicue) and Chihuacóatl (Snake Woman, and the warlike manifestation of Coatlicue). Elizabeth Salas reminds us of other earlier war goddesses: Yaocihuatl (Enemy Woman) of the ancient Toci tribe; the ancient war deity Itzpapálotl (Obsidian Knife Butterfly) of the Chichimecas; the Toltec's (who were the cultural predecessors of the Mexicas) queen Xóchitl (ca. AD 1116) who created a female battalion that she led into battle, losing her life in the process (3). The presence of these warlike deities, as well as archeological evidence, suggests that female warriors played active roles in the defense of their polities. It also underscores that many ancient indigenous civilizations were centered on the power of females as sources of reproduction and military strength. We have only to read the *Cantares mexicanos*, among many other texts, to see how females are invested with military power through the many hymns that honor "our mother" of war and death. As the power of Mexica

empire consolidated and the imperative for war increased, it is hypothesized that they consequently tried to reduce the importance of the female war goddesses by creating male war gods who were stronger and more dominant. Because the Earth Mother/War goddess stories were manipulated in order to strip them of their power, the mythology surrounding these ancient goddesses changed. These cult figures became transformed into monstrosities, as Chihuacóatl was later depicted with blood dripping from her shark-toothed mouth, eventually becoming the basis for the legend of *La Llorona*, as is evidenced in *Visión de los Vencidos* [The Broken Spears] (4). These new interpretations were manifestations of the need to accommodate the growing patriarchy and reflected themselves in the roles played by the Mexica women. While women were forbidden to be chiefs or bear arms in war, a new role emerged. The *mociuaquetzque* (valiant woman) replaced the warrior, and although not allowed to bear arms, went into battle as a neutral coach. If she died in battle, she was honored and even guaranteed a place in "the heaven reserved for warriors" (Salas 7). Later, ill-fated Mexica women became *auianimes* (pleasure girls) who worked to satisfy the personal and sexual needs of the Mexica warriors, thus providing an incentive to good warriors not to marry. Although they were held in a rather hostile disdain by society, their importance grew as the level of warfare did. Eventually they became accepted and were "officially recognized and valued as members of society" and were later transformed into *mociuaquetzques* in the battlefield (9). Far from their mythical past, Mexica women as predecessors of the soldadera ultimately served the military by "bearing sons to become fighters and daughters to become wives, mothers, or sexual companions to warriors" (10). Although symbolic homage was paid to the war goddesses, the active participation of women in fighting decreased dramatically.

9. According to Elena Poniatowska in *Las Soldaderas*, this word originates from Aragonés, the language once spoken in the region of Aragón, Spain (20).

10. In the war for Mexican Independence from the Spanish, women participated as soldaderas, conspirators, soldiers, journalists, intellectuals, financiers, and arms smugglers. As the wars of 1810 commenced, many women were enlisted to help provide food for the soldiers because there were no commissaries. Women became soldaderas for both sides, while many joined the *chusmas* (which were the mobs of the army insurgents). The participation of women was so influential to the anti-royalist cause that more draconian punishment was enacted as it was perceived that their agency had become a formidable threat. A royalist judge declared that women were "one of the greatest evils we have had from the beginning of this war for on account of their sex they were the instrument of seducing all classes of persons" (Salas 27). He refers mainly to their role as seductresses to the independence cause, but clearly in all respects they disrupted the political realm. Gertrudis Bocanegra was an important female leader, as was Antonia Nava de Catalán, known as "La Generala."

11. Salas draws this information from interviews conducted by Esther R. Pérez, James Kallas, and Nina Kallas with Mexican veterans who had migrated to California, *Those Years of the Revolution, 1910–1920, Authentic Bilingual Life Experiences as Told by Veterans of the War*.

12. The history of middle- and upper-class women is much more complete. The work of Jocelyn Olcott, Shirlene Soto, and Ana Macías are compelling historical narratives.

13. My translation.

Chapter 2

1. Translations of "La Adelita" and "Marijuana, la soldadera" are by Guillermo E. Hernández in the album *The Mexican Revolution* by Arhoolie Records, 1996.

2. The first textbook I read on Mexican history from Pre-Colombian times to the present had three-quarters of a page on these women.

3. Some theorists in rhetoric do not identify a substantive difference between the two.

4. The term "Adelita" has also been appropriated by Chicana activists as emblems of Chicana power. It was also deployed as part of the imagery of the United Farmworkers Movement in California.

5. The "Adelita Complex" is a term I borrowed from Norma Cantú, who, according to Elizabeth Salas, coined it at a Chicano Studies Conference in 1984 in reference to the academic propensity to subordinate issues specific to Chicanas to the larger issues within Chicano studies (117).

6. Translation by Guillermo E. Hernández.

7. Besides innumerable Mexican musicians of all genres, "Adelita" has been covered by Nat King Cole, British rockabilly bands such as Carlos and the Bandidos, and has loosely inspired music by the American Gothic Country band O'Death and the Sambarock band Trío Mocotó.

8. The name given to Villa's troops.

9. Translations of "La Adelita" are by María Herrera-Sobek in her monograph *The Mexican Corrido* (1990).

10. This is found in his landmark 1937 article, "Romance y corrido," published in *Crisol*.

11. Some ballads more closely resemble the *décima*, which is a ten-line stanza that is also octosyllabic. The "bola suriana," in turn, has a somewhat rigid structure that differs significantly from what are considered "traditional" corridos.

12. A rivalry exists between México and its Central American neighbors in part because the latter contain considerable indigenous communities, which some Mexican elites consider a sign of backwardness and lack of development. Furthermore, similar to the immigration dynamic that exists between México and the United States, México is the recipient of many of the immigrants and economic refugees from Central America that try to traverse its borders in order to arrive to the United States.

13. This broadside, which was also quoted in the introduction, is Document 41 taken from the collection of Catalina Giménez in *Asi cantaban la Revolución*.

14. My translation.

15. All translations of *Los de abajo* (*The Underdogs*) are by Sergio Waisman in his 2008 edition.

16. In Waisman's translation, he refers to "La Pintada" as "War Paint." In other parts of this chapter I translate it as "The Painted One."

17. *Costumbrismo* is a literary and artistic technique that evolved out of realism. It focused on reproducing picturesque scenes and the minute details from everyday life. It began in Spain in the nineteenth century, but became very popular throughout Latin America.

18. The "tienda de raya" was the store on the estate where the peasants were forced (at the risk of losing their meager lands and possessions) to purchase goods at

exorbitant prices, thus incurring huge debts that could be passed on to their children. This institution was detested by the rural *campesinos*.

19. Niggli worked in the 1950s as a stable writer for Metro-Goldwyn-Mayer by contributing love stories and comedic lines to such films as *Seven Brides for Seven Brothers*, and in 1953 she co-wrote the screenplay for *Sombrero*, the adaptation of her acclaimed novel *Mexican Village* (16).

20. Arrizón highlights what she considers to be the problematic nature of the production of the play *Soldadera*: Anglo-American students in the Department of Dramatic Arts played the roles of the main characters, with Niggli as the only Latina actress in the part of María. Additionally, she critiques the colorful, folkloric set as purposefully designed to elicit a sense of primitivist wonder (99).

21. Niggli concludes the 1938 edition of *Mexican Folk Plays* with two fascinating "Appendices": one "On Mexican Costume" and another "On Spanish Pronunciation." In these appendices, she offers a primer on Mexican history, dress, and language, which ironically, are intended to dispel U.S. stereotypes of Mexican culture as well as provide the proper context for the staging of her plays. Needless to say, she indulges—and perpetuates—her own prejudices in the process. For example, she begins the appendix on Mexican costume in a sarcastic tone that teases Americans for their florid imaginations regarding Hispanic women: "There are two general conceptions in the United States of the Mexican woman's costume: 1. That she wears a high comb, a lace shawl draped over it, a ruffled skirt, a rose in her hair and a dagger in her garter. 2. That she wears a glittering, bespangled red and green skirt, a white blouse, a rose in her hair and a dagger in her garter" (213). She quickly informs the reader that this costume is a "romantic dream," long since disappeared from México, and constitutes the dress typical of Spanish—not Mexican—women. Shortly after her rebuke of this stereotype, the modern reader might wince upon her description of "Aztecan" dress: "The Aztecans, although a cultured race, possessed enough barbaric traits to love brilliant colors and many ornaments. When gathered before their temples they looked like a field of flaming tropical colors" (219).

22. These are traditional genres of the corrido that refer to the "last goodbyes" of an epic hero or local figure. A classic example of this genre would be "Las mañanitas de Benjamín Argumedo." The last goodbye or goodnight genre is also common in Anglo and Anglo-American popular balladry.

23. Later we will see the partial appropriation of this sub-trope combined with that of la Cucaracha and the servile, racialized peasant in the eyewitness account of John Reed about a soldadera named Elizabetta.

Chapter 3

1. Neither John Mraz nor Elena Poniawtoska comment with any specificity on the origin of this image. Shirlene Soto claims its author is unknown while the Casasola family claims it as his. The Fototeca of the INAH identifies it as part of the Casasola collection.

2. "Vieja" literally translates to old lady, but in this context is a pejorative, albeit humorous, term used to refer to female companions, either as girlfriends or wives.

3. This phrase is taken from the novel, *Hasta no verte Jesús, mío* by Elena Poniatowska and means "So happy flying around in the guts of the vultures."

4. A scavenging bird of prey (also referred to as "aura") found in México and other parts of Latin America.

5. Other peoples, cultures, and religions in parts of India, Tibet, and China subscribe to this form of ritualized burial. For example, the Parsis of India, followers of the Zoroastrian tradition who migrated from greater Iran to the regions of India called Gujarat and Sindh in the eighth century believe that "the elements of earth and fire should never be contaminated by the impurities of human flesh, and as a result, burial and cremation are unacceptable. The Parsis, therefore, 'bury' their dead in the sky" (Malcolm Tait, "Towers of Silence," 4). The Tower of Silence, the name given to the raised circular structure where the undressed bodies of the dead are left, has concentric circles designated for men, women, and children. Usually within a few hours the vultures will have devoured the flesh leaving only the bones, which then are dried, and purified by the sun. These practices are becoming difficult to continue due to the fact that chemicals used to feed livestock have decimated the vulture population in India. I am not suggesting Jesusa's ideas of death are drawn from the beliefs of the Parsis, only that these ideas exist in other parts of the world. Poniatowska, in her rendering of Jesusa, may or may not have been influenced by this when choosing to construct her narrative. Certainly, the *zopilotes* in México were a threat to those wounded and dead soldiers not yet recovered from the open battlefield, and were a familiar sight anywhere there was carnage. However, for a traditional Mexican Catholic it would be sinful not to be buried in holy ground, making Jesusa's volition to be excarnated by vultures suggestive of competing spiritual beliefs and cosmologies.

6. Translates to "Young Nellie and her dead."

7. All translations of *Cartucho* are by Doris Meyer and Irene Mathews in their 1988 English edition.

8. A colloquialism, which literally means a "ball," that refers to the Revolution.

9. This term refers to the state of being a mulatto, or mulattohood. I shall retain this word in Spanish as it speaks more specifically to questions of racial identity in Latin America than the word in English.

10. Some sources dated it as 1910, others to 1915; it is now dated by the Fototeca (INAH) to 1913.

11. During the Mexican Revolution of 1910 as well as other insurrections it was not uncommon for soldaderas who actively engaged in military combat, whether as official or non-official members of military units, to cross-dress and abandon their female-gendered attire.

12. Cesare Lombroso, considered the father of criminal anthropology, claimed to have made a scientific discovery in the study of criminology: the born criminal. He identified certain innate characteristics that would determine a person's likelihood for criminal behavior, and in this study, a woman's propensity to commit a crime. In 1893, he wrote *Criminal Woman, the Prostitute, and the Normal Woman* with Guglielmo Ferrero. In this treatise he claims that: "In general, the moral physiognomy of the born female criminal is close to that of the male. The atavistic diminution of secondary sexual characteristics which shows up in the anthropology of the subject appears again in the psychology of the female offender, who is excessively erotic, weak in maternal feelings,

inclined to dissipation, and both astute and audacious. She dominates weaker people, sometimes through suggestion, sometimes through force. Her love of violent exercise, her vices, and even her clothing increase her resemblance to a man. These virile traits are often joined by the worst qualities of woman: her passion for revenge, her cunning, cruelty, love of finery, and dishonesty, which can combine to form a type of extraordinary wickedness . . . However, when muscular strength and intellectual power come together in the same individual, we have a female criminal of an indeed terrible type" (192).

13. There is a robust bibliography that has taken up the problem of the fraught relationship between testimony, informant, and writer in the case of Poniatowska's text. Undoubtedly an important issue, I do not have the time to examine it here, but rather, will center my analysis on Jesusa's interpretations of death.

14. Lydiette Carrión, "Mujeres en la 'guerra' de Michoacán," *El Universal* (January 24, 2014).

15. "Over 100 Mexican Women Take Up Arms To Defend Community In Xaltianguis," *Huff Post Latino Voices* (August 20, 2013).

Chapter 4

1. See Herman L. Bennett's book, *Africans in Colonial México*, for a fascinating account of blacks in México City.

2. As mentioned in the introduction, I will use the Spanish orthography of the word mulata without italics in order to distinguish it from the English word, mulatta, which is charged with its own history of racialized subjectivity.

3. As mentioned in the previous chapter, *mulatez* is the state, or condition, of being mulato, but refers to all the social, political, and ontological issues that are bound up with a mixed-race subjectivity and its application to identity. "Mulattohood" in English does not encapsulate the complexity of this term nor its sociohistorical implications for the Caribbean, Brazil, or México.

4. We can find the sexualized mulata trope in the poetry of Puerto Rican Luis Palés Matos, *Tuntún de pasa y grifería*, Nicolás Guillén, *Motivos de son*, the short stories of Lydia Cabrera *Cuentos negros*, and any number of classical or contemporary Caribbean writers, not to mention popular musical genres such as *bolero*, *salsa*, *merengue*, *bachata*, and of course *reggaetón*.

5. As explained earlier, *saberes* literally translates to "knowledges." While these terms may literally mean the same thing, I will employ the Spanish word because it can be used as a both a verb, "to know" or "to taste like," as well as a noun, as in "knowledge." Furthermore, it better encompasses, in my opinion, the idea of a divergent, subaltern knowledge because of these multiple possibilities.

6. See "Participación de los africanos en el desarrollo del Guanajuato colonial," in *Presencia africana en México* by María Guevara Sanguinés.

7. See "La gran negritud en Michoacán, época colonial" by María Guadalupe Chávez Carbajal.

8. See Brígido Redondo's article, "Negritud en Campeche: De la Conquista a nuestros días."

9. See Juan Carlos Reyes's article, "Negros y afromestizos en Colima, siglos XVI–XIX."

10. See "Historia de la población negra en Tabasco" by Juan Andrade Torres.

11. María Luisa Herrera Casasús examines runaway Africans as well as the role of blacks in the military in "Raíces africanas en la población de Tamaulipas."

12. Chapter 6 will further elaborate on the Afro-mestizo origins of the "son jarocho" as a musical genre in addition to "La bamba" as one of the first *sones* to emerge from New Spain.

13. According to Gonzalo Aguirre Beltrán, castizo is the product of the union between a Spaniard and a mestiza (176).

14. *Casta* refers to mixed-race people of African, Amerindian, and European origin in New Spain who were bound to a racial caste system based largely on phenotype. This system strictly determined their social, economic, legal, and political importance and opportunities.

15. Aguirre Beltrán also states, in the "Colección Marrauri Montaño," that a "torna atrás" is the product of a Spaniard and an "albina," which in turn, is the product of a Spaniard and a mulata (176).

16. The product of a Spaniard and a "torna atrás" (176).

17. Susan Migden Socolow provides an excellent discussion of the experiences of slave, mulata, and native women in her text, *The Women of Colonial Latin America* (2000). She informs that affronts to Christian decency stimulated the regulation of the dress of black and mulata women as there were concerns regarding "nudity" and moral decay. The application of Christian values to racial "inferiors" seems to coincide with Bennett's argument regarding the emergent creole consciousness that was a product of the invocation of a Christian identity among blacks and mulatos (141–42).

18. In "La leyenda de la Tatuana," a story that is supposed to be based upon Mayan myth, Asturias writes of a slave who escapes her punishment by drawing a ship on the wall.

19. The screenplay by Xavier Villaurritia and the film version starring Toña la Negra will be discussed in more detail in the following chapter on the figure of the mulata in Mexican Golden Age film. The cinema adapts the myth to a more traditional tragic mulatta narrative and derives little of the storyline from the local legend. The importance of the figure of Toña la Negra in interpreting these kinds of roles will be developed in the last chapter.

20. This word literally means "quality" but refers to one's social position in colonial society. The predominant factors that determined this were skin color, clothing, occupation, personal relationships, cultural practices, and *limpieza de sangre*, and excluded African, mixed-race, mestizo, and casta members (Bristol 2).

21. In the case of the Port city of Veracruz, it has also been associated with infirmity due to the diseases produced by the swamps that surround it. A foreign visitor once wrote that the Port of Veracruz was like a walled cemetery.

22. This symphony premiered in in the United States and was performed by Boston Symphony Orchestra. Chávez was extremely popular in the U.S., frequently performing in New York and delivering lectures at Harvard University during the period of 1958–1959 as a Charles Eliot Norton professor.

23. Chávez blamed the stagnancy of opera in México on the private opera companies, and in particular, the Ópera Nacional A.C. managed by Ernesto Quezada because they were beholden to a conservative, Eurocentric clientele. Companies such

as these could not support experimental or Mexican-authored opera featuring Mexican performers because they depended on generating revenue through ticket sales (Saavedra 4).

24. A CD recording of the opera performed by the Orquesta Sinfónica Carlos Chávez, directed by Juan Carlos Lomónaco and produced by Marisa Canales, was recorded and released in 2005 by Conaculta.

25. The music written by Agustín Lara for the singer Toña la Negra (which will be discussed in chapter 6) likewise performs a racialization of the popular performer's voice by incorporating tropical ambient sounds and musical motifs that riff off of what is interpreted by the songwriter as a coastal black culture.

26. Previous operas, such as Aniceto Ortega's *Guatemotzín* (1871) and Ricardo Castro's *Atzimba* (1900), resurrected indigenous icons such as Cuauhtémoc (the last Aztec emperor). De la Madrid develops a fascinating argument regarding the place and musical innovation of these operas, as critics have often considered them exoticist works that appropriated Mexican legends in a completely European musical idiom. *Atzimba* was performed for the first time in 1900, but when revived in 1928 (and again in 1935) was eschewed as lamentably *indianista*, indebted to the European tradition, and according to Carlos González Peña, not reflective of Mexican "spiritual lifestyle" and "idiosyncracy" (quoted in Madrid, 141). *Indianismo* was an aesthetic tendency in Latin America born of European romanticism that, in an effort to find a national icon, problematically idealized indigenous culture in the arts by relying on notions such as the "noble savage."

27. This citation was taken from *La ópera mexicana* by Gabriela de la Vega (2002). Mauricio Magdaleno was a socialist playwright who wrote *Emiliano Zapata*, among other plays inspired by social justice.

28. Laura Lewis, in *Hall of Mirrors*, informs that "Yuman" (I read the word as "Yumara") refers to the name of an indigenous group from Baja California (232). It is probably a reference to the Cocopah people, speakers of Yuman, who inhabited what is today Baja California, Sonora, California, and Arizona. Neither Lewis nor I can identify the meaning of "Achula."

29. AGN, Inq vol 525, exp 48, 1691. All citations from this case are from the AGN (Archivo General de la Nación) or the National Archives in México City. This quotation was written in a subsequent document two years later, but is located in the same file.

30. See Hernando Ruiz de Alarcón's spectacular account of indigenous witchcraft in colonial Guerrero, *Treatise on the Heathen Superstitions That Today Live Among the Indians Native to This New Spain* written in 1629.

31. Drawing on Solange Alberro and Julio Caro Baroja, Joan Bristol hypothesizes that it was this supposed closeness to nature and barbarism that granted them a magical "instinct" in the minds of elites (3).

32. *Sombra* literally means "shadow" or "shade" but refers to a vital energy or ancestor that inhabits the earth after death or during sleep.

33. Recently arrived or African-born slaves.

34. Gonzalo Aguirre Beltrán discusses the case of Lucas Olola, an African from Biafra who became a *curandero* and demi-god for the Huastecas of the Pánuco province. Beltrán describes the celebration of the Huastec god, Paya, who is revered in a small jar or pitcher filled with flowers and feathers, not unlike the veneration paid to the ancestor

who inhabits the *prenda*. In the colonial document, Olola is described as participating wholly in this ceremony, dressed entirely in Huastecan attire and speaking in their language, while the ritual elements of the ceremony including song, dance, and emotion are strictly indigenous. However, the single mutation to the ceremony is when Olola incorporates the god Paya (not an orisha) through mystical possession, something practiced in African religions but not indigenous ones. This group of Huastecs admired Olola for his healing abilities, and this case is an excellent example of the metaphysical and spiritual intermingling of indigenous groups and Africans (*Medicina y magia* 65–67).

35. A practitioner of the Afro-Cuban religion "Palo," also called "Regla de Congo or Ochá."

36. In another part of *El monte*, Cabrera describes the process by which a *brujo* [witchdoctor], or palero, invokes the spirit of a deceased person to "work" for him in almost a transactional language. The palero writes the deceased person's name on a piece of paper, and if the practitioner is illiterate, the palero pronounces the name of the summoned spirit loudly and clearly: "The *brujo* writes on a piece of paper the first and last name of the deceased, and with some coins,—the price of the transaction; because the dead practically sells himself to the *brujo*—places it in the bottom of the cauldron; if he doesn't know how to write, then in that case it is sufficient to speak the name loudly and clearly" (My translation, 122). Here we see how the technology of writing clearly makes its way from medieval Europe into Afro-Cuban practices.

37. This phrase refers to the inquisitor's assessment of Antonia de Soto's mental state as simple-minded.

38. Gonzalo Aguirre Beltrán also shares this opinion, as he claims the sheer number of auto-denunciations in the Inquisition records by people of mixed-race (both mulatos and mestizos) is testament to this "internal [spiritual] conflict" (*Medicina y magia* 76).

39. AGN, Inq vol 525, exp 48, 1691.

Chapter 5

1. This article is part of the compilation by Luz Montiel, *Presencia africana en México*. In 2016, almost twenty years after this article was first published, the signage at the entrance of the town of Coyolillo now explicitly welcomes visitors to an Afromestizo community. Furthermore, some prominent community members I met with identify as Afro-descendants.

2. These terms are deployed to refer to people with dark skin and have differing racial connotations.

3. The previous chapter examined the operatic version written by Villaurrutia, Agustin Lazo, and Pablo Moncayo.

4. "Rumbera" is the name given to the showgirls who performed in a film genre often referred to as "cabareteras" that emerged during México's Golden Age of filmmaking. Beginning in the 1930s and reaching their apex in the 1940s and 1950s, these films usually took place in tropical locales or cabarets and featured exotic song and dance sequences showcasing the vedettes who came to be known as the *rumberas*. While the plotlines were often secondary and at best predictable, these films were wildly successful but produced a backlash from conservative Mexicans—especially women.

5. In *Soldaderas,* Elizabeth Salas discusses the various female military leaders in the Mexican Revolution of 1910 and provides information regarding the "real" Angustias.

6. The Instituto Nacional Indigenista (INI) was originally conceived of by President Lázaro Cardenas in 1940 and formally put into operation by President Miguel Alemán in 1948. Initially it was designed under the progressive principles of bilingual education and land redistribution according to traditional indigenous customs but was quickly repurposed into an institute that espoused an assimilationist plan to integrate indigenous communities into a hegemonic Spanish-speaking mestizo society. For an interesting discussion on the assimilation of indigenous groups and their representation in the arts, see Analisa Taylor's *Indigeneity in the Mexican Cultural Imagination: Thresholds of Belonging* (2009).

7. See Vaughn, "México in the Context."

8. This refers to the policies of hypodescent in the United States that determined racial identifications and according to which a person with any African heritage would be considered black. This became legally institutionalized in the twentieth century with the Racial Equity Act of 1924 and affected one's social mobility and freedom to marry.

9. José Vasconcelos's philosophical treatise, *La raza cósmica* (1925), includes blacks as part of the "cosmic race"; however, their contributions are eclipsed by his discussion of the Spanish and indigenous elements, while the Asian component is acknowledged in nothing less than problematic terms.

10. A folk healer or witchdoctor.

11. María Félix plays a haughty aristocrat who becomes a ferocious military leader in the film *La Generala* (1971). Akin to *La Negra Angustias*, this film features a graphic scene where the protagonist castrates her antagonist. This act of violence ultimately leads to her demise.

12. *Moreno* means dark-skinned person and is often used euphemistically to refer to mulatos and blacks, but also can refer to any dark-skinned person.

13. As an anthropologist, Francisco Rojas González would surely have been familiar with this fact as he performed fieldwork and contributed to many ethnographic books about indigenous communities throughout México, including the Costa Chica, a region known for its Afro-Mexican population.

14. The innkeeper's race is not explicit in the book or film, but given the postrevolutionary rhetoric that insists on the notion of a cosmic race, he is most likely a mestizo.

15. My translation from the original Spanish.

16. It is important to note that although the PRI, or the Partido Revolucionario Institucional (Institutional Revolutionary Party) ruled México with an iron-fist for seven decades since 1929, at the time the novel was written in 1944 the party was not called the PRI yet, but rather, the PRM (Partido de la Revolución Mexicana), having been changed by Lázaro Cárdenas in 1938 from the PNR (Partido Nacional Revolucionario). It was renamed PRI in 1946 by President Manuel Ávila Camacho when the military section was eliminated. After a lapse of twelve years the PRI was voted back into presidential power in 2012 with Enrique Peña Nieto.

17. The film *La Mulata de Córdoba* directed by Adolfo Fernández Bustamante premiered in 1945 three years earlier. The screenplay of *Angelitos negros* was inspired by Fanny Hurst's novel *Imitation of Life*, which was made into two different North American films.

18. A *comadre* is a term that describes the godmother of one's child. It can also refer to more informal relationships among friends and neighbors.

19. The *Reconquista*, which began in the eighth century and ended in 1492, marks the historical period that spans eight centuries when Christian kingdoms attempted to reconquer the parts of the Iberian Peninsula that had been taken over by the Islamic kingdoms known as *Al-Andalus*.

20. Marga López was actually born in Argentina and acquired Mexican nationality.

21. *Teatro bufo* is a Cuban brand of musical theater which is usually comedic and was popular throughout the nineteenth century.

22. Blackface has not ceased to operate in popular cultural mediums. In 2011 local TV out of Miami has continued to feature Cuban comedians in blackface, with skits such as "Madrina María y su conexión espiritual" simulating a Cuban *santera* (priestess of Santería). This appeared on TN3, América Teve on November 11, 2011.

23. Race-relations in Cuba are still tense, as evidenced by the removal of the well-known intellectual Roberto Zurbano from his post as director of the Fondo Editorial for Casa de las Américas because of an op-ed piece he wrote for the *New York Times* on March 23, 2013, denouncing the perseverance of racism in Cuba.

Chapter 6

1. Quoted in Rafael Figueroa, *Toña la Negra*, 18.

2. This is a concept I borrow from Licia Fiol-Matta in her article about the figure of Lucecita Benítez in Puerto Rican music. In this superb essay, she theorizes the power of the voice as it relates to the complex relationship between the audience and the artist: "The thinking voice is an event that can be apprehended through but is not restricted to music performance. It exceeds notation, musicianship, and fandom, although it partakes of them all. No artist owns the thinking voice; it cannot be marshaled at will or silenced when inconvenient. Its aim is not to dazzle or enthrall, although it may do so [. . .] Her vocal phenomenon may be regarded as an unwitting outmaneuvering of celebrity culture whereby something resistant, the thinking in the voice, points to, as Jean-Luc Nancy writes, 'participation, sharing, or contagion' versus the 'imaginary capture' of the visual, which has dictated the terms of the artist's critical and popular reception" (1092–93).

3. Veracruzano refers to a resident of the state of Veracruz in the Gulf Coast of México. The Port of Veracruz was one of the first points of entry during the colonial period and a key point of transit for the Spanish galleons.

4. There is a debate among scholars in the field of Afro-Mexican studies with regard to the appropriateness of the term "Afromestizo." Scholars such as Ted

Vinson and Bobbie Vaughn eschew this term as a subordination of the contributions of black Mexicans to the problematic rhetoric of an all-inclusive mestizaje. Although I agree this is often the case, I will continue to employ this term to describe the music and cultural production of Africans and African-descended people in Veracruz because many people—scholars, musicians, and ordinary citizens—employ this term to describe themselves. Despite the very fraught and manipulated history of mestizaje as national discourse, the musical culture of Veracruz reflects not only an African and mulato imaginary and cultural context, but also one marked by indigenous and mestizo culture and cosmology. Many early Afro-Mexicans integrated with the native people, and it was precisely this racial mixing that led to their identification as "jarochos;" it is this confluence of diverse cultures that created what many still refer to as Afromestizo music. Even though important scholars such as Christina Sue have uncovered the problematic nature of race-identification in the Port of Veracruz, attributing the deferral of blackness to internalized racism and the rhetoric of mestizaje, other members of this community positively see themselves as Afromestizos, such as Edgar Cano in the interview for *Callaloo*.

5. "Gran Caribe" (Greater Caribbean) refers to a pan-Caribbeanist concept that considers the vital sociocultural and geopolitical convergences and intersections as part of a larger Caribbean consciousness that reach across the Caribbean basin. A concept that developed over time but came into being as an institutional entity in 1994, "el Gran Caribe" encompasses "all of the islands including the Bahamas, and the entire littoral including Mexico, the whole of Central America, Panama, Colombia, Venezuela, Guyana, Suriname and French Guiana" (Norman Girvan 2–4).

6. The Real Academia Española is the dictionary of the Royal Academy in Spain, and will henceforth be referred to as RAE.

7. See the RAE.

8. For more information on the Afro-Mexican military participation, see Vinson's book *Bearing Arms for His Majesty: The Free-Colored Militia in Colonial México* (2001). This book offers a rich discussion of African and *mulato* participation in the Mexican colonial military.

9. The historian José Luis Melgarejo Vivanco, in his book *Los Jarochos* maintains that this definition is most appropriate, claiming that early colonial militiamen were only armed with sticks (47).

10. Anthropologist Arturo Warman Gryj and historian Irene Vásquez documented the following regions as areas of the different *son*-types: (1) the tierra caliente (hotlands) of Guerrero; (2) the tierra caliente of Michoacán; (3) Jalisco, both lowlands and highlands, and (4) the isthmus of Tehuantepec; (5) the Huasteca, including Tamaulipas, San Luís Potosí, Veracruz, Hidalgo, and Puebla and, finally; (6) the coastal plain of Veracruz. Each of these regions developed and evolved its own *son* tradition, with a distinct musical style, repertory and instrumentation (47).

11. This definition is taken from the RAE and all translations from this source are mine.

12. A *zapateado* is a percussive dance with complex rhythms executed by the feet on a wooden platform.

13. *Coplas* literally means couplets but refers to rhymed verse. *Coplillas* are short verses and *letrillas*, comes from *letras*, which means verses (or lyrics) as well. Rendered in the diminutive it means short verses.

14. The popularity of this *son* has persevered throughout these long centuries, as this song is still preserved as a vital part of the *son jarocho* repertoire. One of the more popular contemporary groups of *soneros* who are revitalizing the *son jarocho* tradition took Chuchumbé as the name of their band.

15. This statement was taken from the documentary *Son Jarocho: Sensualidad compartida* by director Francisco Viveros Domínguez in 2006. It means, "The *son* has a first and last name: Veracruz, México."

16. *Son jarocho* in Veracruz proper is simply known as "son" or "sones de la tierra."

17. A jitanjáfora is a semantic invention that is used in poetry as a device that simulates something else, such as a sound in nature or an imagined language.

18. My translation from the original Spanish. These are all variants of music from southern Spain that fall within the genre of flamenco or are related to it.

19. The word "fandango" which is often rendered as "huapango" is supposed to come from Náhuatl, meaning "sobre la tarima" or "on top of the wooden platform." Composer and musician Baqueiro Foster contends that this word originates from the Náhuatl word "cuahpanco" which derives from the word "cuahitl" (wood), "ipan" (on it, on top of) and "co" (place). He also suggests that this word could very well refer to music that comes from native "huastecas" who live along the border of the river "pango," in which case it would mean "huastecas" from the river "pango" (174).

20. My translation from the original.

21. On July 13, 2013, I attended a *fandango* in Los Ángeles hosted by a local group from East Los Ángeles called Cambalache. Besides the performance, there was a *zapateado* workshop and local musicians showed up with their own instruments to improvise after the official "performance." They claim that there are *fandangos* taking place all over Los Ángeles and throughout California.

22. This festival in honor of the Virgin of the Candelaria occurs all over Latin America and is generally celebrated the first fortnight in February.

23. Jaraneros are musicians of the jarana; trovadores are singers and musicians; decimeros are balladeers; and repentistas are poets who write extemporaneously.

24. In the Encuentro Jaranero held in August 2012, popular groups from Los Angeles performed, such as Quetzal, Las Cafeteras, Conjunto Jardín, Son Real, Conjunto Xi, Juan Parroquín, Los Alebrijes en Vuelo, Los Tremendos del Sur, Violeta Quintero y su Grupo, and Eastside Café Son Jarocho Students, in addition to over a half dozen others.

25. Even the popular Japanese ska band Yum! Yum! ORANGE has covered it.

26. Ramos, in his insightful article "Descarga acústica" from *Papel Máquina* also critiques the insistent focus by some critics on polyrhythm and syncopation—opposing it to European-derived melody—as a musical sign of a felicitous *mulatez*: "Entonces, digamos, para resumir la crítica del fonocentrismo caribeñista: la oposición esencializada entre el ritmo y la melodía reinscribe un estereotipo de origen europeo que merece más atención crítica. Pareciera que el estereotipo—el fetichismo del ritmo—condensa una lógica suplementaria del discurso caribeñista contemporáneo, heredera seguramente de aquellos influyentes experimentos de los poetas negristas y de los modernistas brasileños, esencializadores de la síntesis 'mulata'" (70).

27. This was the rhythm employed by Pablo Moncayo in his operatic rendition of *La Mulata de Córdoba* discussed in chapter 4.

28. Graciana Silva died in July 2013 at the age of 74 in the Port of Veracruz.

29. Andrés Huesca (an Afro-descendant himself) is a famous *sonero* who reformed the *son* by incorporating a bigger harp, the *arpa michoacana* for purely cinematographic reasons. While he was working on the film *Allá en el rancho grande* (1936) he decided to use this harp so that he would appear more impressive in the film. The larger physical presence and louder sound also impressed fellow harpists, who likewise exchanged the smaller diatonic *arpa jarocha* for this one. The large harp made the *son* catchier, allowing for the *son jarocho* to compete with the *son jaliciense* and the *música ranchera*.

30. My translation from original Spanish.

31. Statement made by la Negra Graciana on March 8, 2002.

32. Jesús Flores y Escalante, in his exhaustive book on the *danzón*, claims it arrived in 1868 (a decade before Faílde would coin it "danzón") on the steam ships Angola and Dahomey from the Elder-Dempster shipping company as part of the triangulated route of Cuba-Yucatán-Veracruz that also brought Cuban dissidents and musicians looking for a better living (*Salón México* 1).

33. Flores y Escalante remarks that early on *danzones* were written by Mexican composers, such as "Hijas de Jalapa" with two distinct musical scores written by the Jalapeño Daniel Rodríguez in 1899, and as early as 1872 the pre-Faílde "Danzones Veracruzanos" were composed by the Cuban Enrique Guerrero while living in Veracruz (55). In Yucatán and in México City, Luis Arcaraz (Abuelo) wrote *danzones* between 1889 and 1931, such as "Salón Rojo," and "Las Calles de la ciudad" while the famous Mexican composer Juventino Rosas wrote "Flores de Romana" for piano in 1893 (81–82).

34. By 1905 orchestras in México were already called "danzoneras" to distinguish them from other musical groups, breaking from the Cuban name of "charanga" or "orquesta típica."

35. These men are seminal figures in Cuban Independence movement.

36. See Bernardo García Díaz's article, "La migración cubana a Veracruz 1870–1910" in *La Habana/Veracruz/ Veracruz/La Habana* (2002) for a solid discussion of the Cuban migration to the Sotavento region of Veracruz.

37 My translation from the original Spanish.

38. Ibid.

39. In 2007 the "Parque Zamora" was filled with hundreds of people from all over Veracruz and the rest of the country who arrived to listen and dance to the famous orchestra, Danzonera la Playa. Residents from the capital came to appreciate the *jarocho*—and for some, more authentic—interpretation of the *danzón*.

40. Memo Salamanca, from Tlacotalpan, is an important figure in the history of Mexican *son cubano*, and *mambo* particularly, as well as Toño Barcelata, who directed La Sonora Veracruz while playing the trumpet. Early on, they began playing Cuban *son* with a distinctive Veracruz flavor, and Toño Barcelata began composing his own music while continuing to play traditional Cuban songs, producing over forty records. La Sonora Veracruz has been one of the preferred bands to accompany Cuban and Puerto Rican singers on their tours of México.

41. My translation from original Spanish.

42. This particular conga is specific to carnival music in Veracruz, and as with other congas is usually played at the end of a set or performance.

43. Since the mid- to late-1970s, Brazilian *samba* and *batucadas* (drum groups) have also been included. These *samba* groups emerged from the popular barrio of La Huaca (the birthplace of Toña la Negra) at the impulse of Brazilian Sugar Machado who created the group Tradiciones de Brasil and has since become one of the emblematic elements of the parade, although the more traditional residents and participants lament the introduction of Brazilian music as a commercialization or deterioration of what they consider the "orthodox" musical forms of carnival, such as *son cubano* and *rumba*. Nonetheless, today the young people seem to enjoy the introduction of Brazilian music and culture as well as the proximity they perceive in the relationship between Brazilian culture and that of Veracruz.

44. This statement was made by the director of the Instituto Veracruzano de Cultura (IVEC), Rafael Arias Hernández. It means, "Veracruz, fortunately, is and will always be the Caribbean."

45. Past conferences have included a forum called "Experiencias y Vivencias" which consisted of panel discussions and workshops on religion, magic, and spiritual practices.

46. My translation from original Spanish.

47. This is one of the most folkloric neighborhoods in Veracruz.

48. This poem, written by Venezuelan poet and politician Andrés Eloy Blanco, was posthumously published in *La Juanbimbada* (1959) and made famous by the musical adaption sung by Mexican artist Pedro Infante.

49. In spite of her fame, very little is known about her life due to her inclination for privacy, and her famous songwriter's (Agustín Lara) propensity for mythomania. Myriad rumors—some so itcrated that they have practically come to constitute hard truth—have enveloped her life in myth.

50. Figueroa maintains that the family patriarch, Severo Peregrino, emigrated from Port au Prince, Haiti in the nineteenth century in "Rumberos y Jarochos" (388). I have read no other accounts that make this claim.

51. Figueroa provides another version where at a performance at the club El Retiro in México City, she met Emilio Azcárraga and Enrique Contel, the owner and manager of the influential radio station XEW, who, admiring her voice and seeing her potential, offered her a job and encouraged her to change her name (*Toña la Negra* 27).

52. "Peregrino" is Toña la Negra's surname, which was associated with a successful family dynasty of Mexican musicians from Veracruz. Hence, "La Peregrino" roughly translates to "Ms. Peregrino."

53. He was infamous as a mytho- and megalomaniac, inventing dozens of versions of the same episode.

54. This poem was analyzed in chapter 4.

55. My translation from original Spanish.

56. A term coined by Roger Bartra in *The Cage of Melancholy* (1992) which discusses the importance of the mother/whore dialectic in Mexican society whereby women are expected to be at once passionate lovers and consoling, virginal saints. The impossibility of reconciling these contradictory expectations that regulate female

behavior result in the following neologism: "Chingada" (meaning "fucked women" and of course referring to Malintzín, Cortés's consort and mother of the "first" mestizo child) and "Lupe" (the Virgin of Guadalupe, the patron saint of the Americas).

57. In his book *Toña la Negra*, Rafael Figueroa cites the following critique of Toña from a series of articles in the Mexican magazine, *México al día*, published in April, 1933. The author of the article sternly compares her to Rita Montaner, inciting a bitter rivalry between the two: "Acostumbrados al estilo seco, demasiado serio y sin movimiento de Toña "La Negra," el público se vio de pronto sorprendido con este, para él, nuevo estilo de la canción criolla que nos ha mostrado Rita Montaner, más alegre, más movido, con más vida. (. . .) Ante ella Toña 'La Negra' no tiene más recurso que el milagro de su voz" [Accustomed to the dry, overly serious and motionless style of Toña la Negra, the audience was suddenly surprised with this new, lively style of the creole song that has been shown to us by Rita Montaner; happier, more energetic, more lively (. . .) Next to her Toña la Negra has no other recourse but the miracle of her voice] (46).

58. Toña la Negra, *Lamento Cubano* (Tumbao Cuban Clasics, 2004). This song and the first two-thirds of the music from this album were recorded in 1958 with the *conjunto* of Pablo Peregrino. The rest of the music was recorded between 1950 and 1953 with other orchestras, such as that those led by Rafael de Paz, Chamaco Domínguez, Avelino Muñoz, and Juan García Esquivel.

Conclusion

1. Some scholars have instigated heated debate by claiming that Africans arrived to México even before the Spanish. See Ivan Van Sertima's *They Came Before Columbus*.

2. An indigenous scribe.

Bibliography

Aburto Castillo, Raúl. *San Juan de Ulúa: Historia de una fortaleza*. Veracruz: Editorial Galaxie, n.d.

Aceves, Ricardo Romero. *La mujer en la historia de México*. México, D.F.: Costa-Amic Editores, 1982.

Acosta, Abraham. *Thresholds of Illiteracy: Theory, Latin America, and the Crisis of Resistance*. New York: Fordham UP, 2014.

Addis, Elisabetta. *Women Soldiers*. Ed. Valeria E. Russo and Lorenza Sebesta. New York: St. Martin's Press, 1994.

Agnew, John A. "Space and Place." *The Sage Handbook of Geographical Knowledge*. Ed. John A. Agnew and David N. Livingstone. Los Angeles; London: SAGE, 2011. 316–330.

Aguilar Mora, Jorge. Prologue. *Cartucho: relatos de la lucha en el norte de México*. Nellie Campobello. México: Ediciones Era, 2000.

———. *Una muerte justa, sencilla, eterna*. México: Ediciones Era, 1990.

Aguirre Beltrán, Gonzalo. *Obra Antropológica XVI El negro esclavo en Nueva España*. México: Fondo de Cultura Economica, 1994.

———. *Medicina Y Magia: El Proceso de Aculturación en la Estructura Colonial*. México: Instituto Nacional Indigenista, 1963.

———. *Cuijila, esbozo etnográfico de un pueblo negro*. Illus. de Alberto Beltrán. México: Fondo de Cultura Económica, 1958.

———. *La población negra de México*. México, D.F.: Ediciones Fuente cultural, 1946.

Alatorre Mendieta, Angeles. *Revista de la Universidad de México*, 28.3 (1973), 15–21.

Andrade Torres, Juan. "Historia de la población negra de Tabasco." *Presencia africana en México*. Ed. Luz Martínez Montiel. México: Consejo Nacional para la Cultura y las Artes, 1997. 423–60.

Andrews, George R. *Afro-Latin America, 1800–2000*. Oxford: Oxford UP, 2004.

Ankersmit, F. R. *History and Tropology*. Berkeley and Los Angeles, CA: U of California P, 1994.

Aparicio, Frances R. *Listening to Salsa: Gender, Latin Popular Music, and Puerto Rican Cultures*. Hanover, NH; London: UP of New England for Wesleyan UP, 1998.

Arias Hernández, Rafael. *Fiesta Internacional Afrocaribeño Veracruz*. Veracruz: Instituto Veracruzano de Cultura, 1997.

Archivo General de la Nación. "Denunziazion que contra si hizo Antonia de Soto Mulata esclava de Francisco Noriega." Inq. Vol. 525, exp. 48, 1691.

Aristotle. *Poetics*. Cambridge, MA: Harvard UP, 1999.

Arrizón, Alicia. *Queering Mestizaje: Transculturation and Performance*. Ann Arbor: U of Michigan P, 2006.

———. "Soldaderas" and the Staging of the Mexican Revolution." *TDR* 42.1 (1998): 90–112.

Azuela, Mariano. *Los de abajo*. 1915. 2a ed. México: Fondo de Cultura Economica, 2002.

———. *The Underdogs: A Novel of the Mexican Revolution*. Trans. Sergio Waisman. New York, NY: Penguin Classics, 2008.

Barthes, Roland. *Camera Lucida*. Trans. Richard Howard. USA: Farrar, Straus and Giroux, Inc., 1981

Bartra, Eli. "How Black Is La Negra Angustias?" *Third Text* 26.3 (2012): 275–83.

———. "El género en el cine de la revolución mexicana." *Casa del tiempo*, México: UNAM, 1999.

Bartra, Roger. *Mexican Transition: Politics, Culture and Democracy in the Twenty-First Century*. Cathays, Cardiff, GBR: U of Wales P, 2013. ProQuest ebrary. Web. Oct. 1, 2015.

———. *La sangre y la tinta. Ensayos sobre la condición postmexicana*, México: Océano, 1999.

———. *The Cage of Melancholy: Identity and Metamorphosis in the Mexican Character*. New Brunswick, NJ: Rutgers UP, 1992.

Beckles, Hilary. *Centering Woman: Gender Discourses in Caribbean Slave Society*. Kingston, Jamaica: Ian Randle Publishers; Princeton, NJ: M. Wiener; Oxford, UK: James Currey Ltd., 1999.

Bennett, Herman. *Colonial Blackness: A History of Afro-Mexico*. Bloomington: Indiana UP, 2009.

———. *Africans in Colonial Mexico*. Bloomington: Indiana UP, 2005.

Bergson, Henri. *The Creative Mind*. New York: Greenwood Press, 1968.

Berkin, Carol R., and Clara M. Lovett, eds. *Women, War and Revolution*. New York: Homes and Meier Publishers, Inc., 1980.

Blanco Borelli, Melissa. "'¿Y ahora qué vas a hacer mulata?': Hip Coreographies in the Mexican *Cabaretera* film *Mulata*." *Women & Performance: A Journal of Feminist Theory* 18.3 (2008): 215–33. Web. Nov. 1, 2013.

Blázquez Domínguez, Carmen. *Breve historia de Veracruz*. México: Colegio de México, Fideicomiso Historia de las Américas: Fondo de Cultura Económica, 2000.

Boone Elizabeth, Hill. *Stories in Red and Black*. Austin: U of Texas P, 2000.

Boone, Elizabeth H., and Walter Mignolo. *Writing Without Words: Alternative Literacies in Mesoamerica and the Andes*. Durham, NC: Duke UP, 1994.

Bost, Suzanne. *Mulattas and Mestizas*. Athens, Georgia: U of Georgia P, 2003.

Boundas, Ed. *Deleuze and Philosophy*. Edinburgh: Edinburgh UP, 2006.

Boyd, Lola Elizabeth. *Emiliano Zapata: En las letras y el folklore mexicano*. Ediciones José Porrúa Turrua: Madrid, 1979.

Bristol, Joan Cameron. *Christians, Blasphemers, and Witches: Afro-Mexican Ritual Practice in the Seventeenth Century*. Albuquerque: U of New Mexico P, 2007.

———. "From Curing to Witchcraft: Afro-Mexicans and the Mediation of Authority." *Journal of Colonialism & Colonial History* 7.1 (2006). Web.

Brooks, Peter. *The Melodramatic Imagination*. 1976. New Haven, CT: Yale UP, 1995.

Burkhart, Louise M. *The Slippery Earth: Nahua-Christian Moral Dialogue in Sixteenth-Century Mexico*. Tucson: U of Arizona P, 1989.

Buscaglia-Salgado, José F. *Undoing Empire: Race and Nation in the Mulatto Caribbean*. Minneapolis: U of Minnesota P, 2003.

Camín, Héctor Aguilar, and Lorenzo Meyer. *In the Shadow of the Mexican Revolution: Contemporary Mexican History, 1910–1989*. Austin: U of Texas P, 1993.

Campobello, Nellie. *Mis libros*. Chihuahua: *Secretaria de Educación y Cultura*, 2004.

———. *Cartucho: Relatos de la lucha en el norte de México*. México, D.F.: Ediciones Era, 2000.

Campos, Arturo, and Juan G. Partida. "Cumple Cherán 4 años de autogobierno, sin partidos." *La Jornada*, Apr. 20, 2015. Web. Jul. 2015.

Cano, Gabriela. "Unconcealable Realities of Desire: Amelio Robles (Transgender) Masculinity in the Mexican Revolution." *Sex in Revolution: Gender, Politics, and Power in Modern Mexico*. Ed. Jocelyn Olcott, Mary Kay Vaughan, and Gabriela Cano. Durham NC: Duke UP, 2006.

Carpentier, Alejo. *La música En Cuba*. La Habana, Cuba: Letras Cubanas, 2004.

Carrión, Lydiette. "Mujeres en la '*guerra*' de Michoacán." *El Universal* [México City, D. F] Jan. 24, 2014. Web. 7 Mar. 2014.

Carroll, Patrick. "Black Aliens and Black Natives in New Spain's Indigenous Communities." *Black Mexico: Race and Society from Colonial to Modern Times*. Ed. Ben Vinson and Matthew Restall. Albuquerque: U of New Mexico P, 2009.

———. *Blacks in Colonial Veracruz*. Austin: U of Texas P, 1991.

Casasola, Gustavo. *Historia Gráfica De La Revolución, 1900–1954* [varies]. México, D. F: Archivo Casasola, 1950.

Castillo, Debra A. *Easy Women*. Minnesota: U of Minnesota P, 1998.

Castillo Failde, Osvaldo. *Miguel Failde, creador musical del danzon*. Habana: Oficina del Historiador de la Ciudad, Editora del Consejo Nacional de Cultura, 1964.

Chávez Carbajal, María Guadalupe. "La gran negritud en Michoacán, época colonial." *Presencia africana en México*. Ed. Luz Martinez Montiel. México: Consejo Nacional para la Cultura y las Artes, 1997. 79–145.

Clifford, James. *Routes*. Cambridge, MA: Harvard UP, 1997.

Coffey, Mary L. *How Revolutionary Art Became Official Culture. Murals, Museums and the Mexican State*. Durham, NC: Duke UP, 2012.

Crespo, Francisco J. "The Globalization of Cuban Music through Mexican Film." *Musical Cultures of Latin America: Global Effects, Past and Present: Proceedings of an International Conference, University of California, Los Angeles, May 28–30, 1999*. Ed. Steven J. Loza and Jack Bishop. Los Angeles: Dept. of Ethnomusicology and Systematic Musicology, University of California, Los Angeles, 2003. 225–31.

Cruz Carretero, Sagrario, Alfredo Martínez Maranto, and Angélica Santiago Silva. *El Carnaval en Yanga*. Serie Ollin 2. México: Consejo Nacional para la Cultura y las Artes, 1990.

Cypess, Sandra Messinger. *La Malinche in Mexican Literature*. Austin: U of Texas P, 1991.

Dabove, Juan Pablo, and Carlos Jáuregui, eds. *Heterotropías: narrativas de identidad y alteridad latinamericana*. Pittsburgh, PA: Biblioteca de América, 2003.

De Certeau, Michel. *The Practice of Everday Life*. Los Angeles, CA: U of California P, 1984.

"Dedica Cuba IV Festival de Danzón Habana a la ciudad de Guadalajara." *El Universal*: México, D.F. March 9, 2007. Web. <http://www.eluniversal.com.mx/notas/411371.html>

Deeds, Susan M. "Subverting the Social Order: Gender, Power, and Magic in Nueva Vizcaya." *Choice, Persuasion, and Coercion: Social Control on Spain's North American Frontiers*. Ed. Jesús F. Teja, and Ross Frank. Albuquerque: U of New Mexico P, 2005. 95–119.

De la Peña, Ernesto, and María Cristina Gabriela de la Vega y Vega, eds. *La ópera mexicana*. México City: Joaquín Porrúa Editores, 2003.

Delgadillo, Theresa. "Singing Angelitos Negros: African Diaspora Meets Mestizaje in the Americas." *American Quarterly*, 58.2 (2006): 407–30.

Delgado Calderón, Alfredo. *Historia, cultura e identidad en el sotavento*. México, D.F.: Culturas Populares de México, 2004.

Delgado-P., Guillermo, "Bordering Indigeneities: Two Notes on Decolonization and Sp/l/ace." *Indigenous Research Center of the Americas*. Dec. 14, 2009. Web. Nov. 16, 2013. <http://irca.ucdavis.edu/2009/12/borderingindigeneities-two-notes-on-decolonization-and-splace/#_ftn1)>

Deleuze, Gilles. *Bergsonism*. New York: Zone Books, 1988.

———. *Francis Bacon: The Logic of Sensation*. Minneapolis: U of Minnesota P, 2003.

———. *A Thousand Plateaus Capitalism and Schizophrenia*. Minneapolis: U of Minnesota P, 1987.

Derrida, Jacques. *The Gift of Death*. Chicago: U of Chicago P, 1996.

Díaz Balsera, Viviana. "Nombres Que Conservan El Mundo: Los Nahualtocaitl y El Tratado Sobre Idolatrías De Hernando Ruiz De Alarcón." *Colonial Latin American Review* 16.2 (2007): 159–78.

Díaz-Sanchez, Micaela, and Alexandro D. Hernandez. "The Son Jarocho as Afro-Mexican Resistance Music." *Journal of Pan African Studies* 6.1 (2013): 187–209.

Diccionario de la lengua española. 22nd ed. Madrid: Real Academia Española, 2001.

Doyle, Jennifer. "Nao Bustamante's Soldaderas, Real and Imagined." *Artbound*: KCET Los Angeles, May 14, 2015. Web. Aug. 8, 2015.

Duvalier, Armando. "Romance y corrido." *Crisol, revista mensual publicada por el Bloque de Obreros Intelectuales de México*, XV (1937), 16.

Edgerton, Robert B. *Warrior Women: The Amazons of Dahomey and the Nature of War*. Boulder, CO: Westview Press, 2000.

Eidsheim, Nina. "Synthesizing Race: Towards an Analysis of the Performativity of Timbre." *Revista Transcultural de Música Transcultural Music Review* 13 (2009): Article 9. Dec. 30, 2009. Web.

Elam, Jr., Harry, and Kennell Jackson, eds. *Black Cultural Traffic*. Ann Arbor: U of Michigan P, 2005.

El cuento veracruzano: Antología. Comp. Luís Leal. Veracruz: Colección Águila o Sol, 1966.

El rostro colectivo de la Nación Mexicana. Eds. Chávez Carbajal, María Guadalupe. Morelia, México: Universidad Michoacana de San Nicolás de Hidalgo, Instituto de Investigaciones Históricas, 1997.

Farquharson, Mary. "El son jarocho como la iguana, se niega a morir." *México Desconocido* 230 (1996): 35–41.

Figueroa Hernández, Rafael. *Toña la Negra*. Xalapa, Veracruz: Gobierno de Estado de Veracruz, 2012.

———. *Viva La Cuenca: Décimas*. Tlacotalpan, Veracruz: Fiestas de la Candelaria, 2006.

———. *Rutilo Parroquín*. Xalapa, Veracruz: Reproscan, 2005.

———. *Los veracruzanísimos Pregoneros del Recuerdo*. Xalapa, Veracruz: Reproscan, 2005.

———. *Julio del Razo*. ConClave: México, 2003.

———. *Son Jarocho: Guía Histórico-Musical*. PACM y S: México, 2002.

———. "Rumberos y jarochos." *La Habana Veracruz/ Veracruz/La Habana*. Ed. Bernardo García Díaz and Sergio Guerra Vilaboy. Veracruz, México City, D.F.: Universidad Veracruzana; Havana, Cuba: Universidad de La Habana, 2002. 383–400.

Figueroa Torres, Carolina. *Señores, Vengo a Contarles: La Revolución Mexicana a través de sus corridos*. México, D.F.: Secretaria de Gobernación, Instituto Nacional de Estudios Históricos de la Revolución Mexicana, 1995.

Fiol-Matta, Licia. "The Thinking Voice: When Listening Trumps Celebrity." *PMLA: Publications of the Modern Language Association of America* 126.4 (2011): 1092–1101.

Flores y Escalante, Jesús. *Salón México: Historia documental y gráfica del danzón en México*. México, D.F.: Asociación Mexicana de Estudios Fonográficos, A. C., 1993.

Flores Martos, Juan Antonio. *Portales de múcara: Una etnografía del puerto de Veracruz*. Xalapa,Veracruz, México: Universidad Veracruzana, 2004.

Forty, George. *They Also Served: A Pictorial Anthology of Camp Followers through the Ages*. Speldhurst: Midas Books, 1979.

Frías, Heriberto. *Tomochic*. 1893. México: Porrúa, 1968.

Furst, Jill. *Natural History of the Soul in Ancient Mexico*. New Haven, CT: Yale UP, 1995.

Gamboa, Federico. *Santa*. 1903. México: Editorial Grijalbo, 1979.

García Díaz, Bernardo. "La migración cubana a Veracruz 1870–1910." *La Habana Veracruz/Veracruz/La Habana*. Ed. Bernardo García Díaz and Sergio Guerra Vilaboy. Veracruz, México: Universidad Veracruzana; Havana, Cuba: Universidad de La Habana, 2002. 297–320.

García Díaz, Bernardo, and Sergio Guerra Vilaboy, eds. *La Habana Veracruz/Veracruz La Habana*. Veracruz, México: Universidad Veracruzana; Havana, Cuba: Universidad de La Habana, 2002.

García Riera, Emilio. *El cine mexicano*. México: Ediciones Era, 1963.

Garibay, Angel María. *Poesía indígena*. Universidad Autónoma de México: México, D.F., 1940.

Geliz, Ricardo Chica. *Cuando las negras de Chambacú se querían parecer a María Félix. Cine, cultura popular y educación en Cartagena 1936–1957*. Cartagena de Indias: Editorial Universitaria, 2015.

Giménez, Catalina H. *Así cantaban la revolución*. México: Grijalbo, 1991.

Girvan, Norman. "El Gran Caribe." *CaribSeek Kaleidoscope*. 1–9. June 4, 2002. Web. Nov. 15, 2013.

Githiora, Chege J. *Afro-Mexicans: Discourse of Race and Identity on the African Diaspora*. Trenton, NJ: Africa World Press, 2008.

Gonzalez, Anita. *Afro-Mexico: Dancing between Myth and Reality*. 1st ed. Austin: U of Texas P, 2010.

González de la Parra, Manuel. *Luces de raíz negra*. Spain: Fondo Nacional para la Cultura y las Artes, Universidad Veracruzana, 2004.

González Echevarría, Roberto. "Literatura, baile y béisbol." *Jornada Dominical*. México, March 26, 1995.

González, María R. *Imagen de la prostituta en la novela mexicana contemporánea*. Madrid: Editorial Pliegos, 1996.

Grito del Norte/La Chicana. "Our Unknown Revolucionarias." N.p. June 5, 1971, sec. 4B. Print.

Guadarrama Olivera, Horacio. "Los carnavales del puerto de Veracruz." *La Habana Veracruz/Veracruz La Habana*. Ed. Bernardo García Díaz and Sergio Guerra Vilaboy. Veracruz, México: Universidad Veracruzana; Havana, Cuba: Universidad de La Habana, 2002. 469–94.

Guevara Sanguinés, María. "Participación de los africanos en el desarrollo del Guanajuato colonial." *Presencia africana en México*. Ed. Luz Martinez Montiel. México: Consejo Nacional para la Cultura y las Artes, 1997. 133–83.

Gutierrez, Laura G. *Performing Mexicanidad: Vendidas Y Cabareteras on the Transnational Stage*. Austin: U of Texas P, 2010.

Hallen, Barry, and Olubi J. Sodipo. *Knowledge, Belief and Witchcraft: Analytic Experiments in African Philosophy*. Redwood City, CA: Stanford UP, 1997.

Hallward, Peter. "Staging Equality: Rancière's theatrocracy and the Limits of Anarchic Equality." Ed. Gabriel Rockhill and Philip Watts. *Jacques Rancière: History, Politics, Aesthetics*. Durham, NC: Duke UP, 2009. 140–47.

Hartman, Saidiya. *Scenes of Subjection*. New York: Oxford UP, 1997.

Harvey, David. "From Space to Place and Back Again." *Mapping the Futures Local Cultures, Global Change*. Ed. Jon Bird, Barry Curtis, Tim Putnam, George Robertson, and Lisa Tickner. London: Routledge, 1993. 2–29.

Hernández Cuevas, Marco Polo. *Carnaval in Mexico*. México: Plaza y Valdés, 2005.

———. *African Mexicans and the Discourse on Modern Nation*. Lanham, MD: UP of America, 2004.

Herrera Casasús, María Luisa. "Raíces africanas en la población de Tamaulipas." *Presencia africana en México*. Ed. Luz Martinez Montiel. México: Consejo Nacional para la Cultura y las Artes, 1997. 463–521.

Herrera-Sobek, María. *The Mexican Corrido: A Feminist Analysis*. Bloomington: Indiana UP, 1990.

Hershfield, Joanne. "Race and Ethnicity in the Classical Cinema." *Mexico's Cinema: A Century of Film and Filmmakers*. Ed. Joanne Hershfield, and David R. Maciel. Wilmington, DE: Scholarly Resources, 1999.

Irwin McKee, Robert. *Mexican Masculinities*. Minneapolis: U of Minnesota P, 2003.

Jones, Anne Goodwyn, and Susan V. Donaldson, eds. *Haunted Bodies: Gender and Southern Texts*. Charlottesville: UP of Virginia, 1997.

Jorgensen, Beth E. *Documents in Crisis: Nonfiction Literatures in Twentieth-Century Mexico*. Albany: State U of New York P, 2011.

Karttunen, Frances. *An Analytical Dictionary of Nahuatl*. Austin: U of Texas P, 1983.

Katzew, Ilona. *Casta Painting: Images of Race in Eighteenth-Century Mexico*. New Haven, CT: Yale UP, 2004.

Kohl, Randall. *Ecos de La bamba: Una historia etnomusicóloga sobre el son jarocho del centro-sur de Veracruz, 1946–1959*. Diss. Universidad Veracruzana: Xalapa, Ver. México, 2004.

Kusch, Rodolfo, Walter Mignolo, Maria Lugones, and Joshua M. Price. *Indigenous and Popular Thinking in América*. Durham, NC: Duke UP, 2010.

Laclau, Ernesto, and Chantal Mouffe. *Hegemony and Socialist Strategy*. London: Verso, 2001.

Lakoff, George, and Mark Johnson. *Philosophy in the Flesh: The Embodied Mind and its Challenge to Western Thought*. New York: Basic Books, 1999.

———. "The contemporary theory of metaphor." *Metaphor and Thought*. Ed. Andrew Ortony. Cambridge, MA: Cambridge UP, 1993.

———. *Metaphors We Live By*. Chicago: U of Chicago P, 1980.

Lane, Jill. *Blackface Cuba, 1840–1895*. Philadelphia: U of Pennsylvania P, 2005.

"Las Adelitas." [Canción Vals (Corrido)] Lyrics by José G. Mathus and Music by Alberto P. Holguín. México, D.F.: Archivo General de la Nación, 1951.

Las Mujeres en la Revolución Mexicana 1884–1920. 2nd ed. INEHRM and Instituto de Investigaciones Legislativas de la H. Cámara de Diputados. México, D.F., 1999.

Lau, Ana, and Carmen Ramos. *Mujeres y Revolución*. México, D.F.: Instituto Nacional de Estudios Históricos de la Revolución Mexicana, 1993.

Leon Portilla, Miguel. *La filosofía nahuatl: Estudiada en sus fuentes, con un nuevo apéndice*. 8a ed. México: Universidad Nacional Autónoma de México, 1997.

Lewis, Laura A. *Chocolate and Corn Flour: History, Race, and Place in the Making of Black Mexico*. Durham, NC: Duke UP, 2012.

———. "From Sodomy to Superstition: The Active Pathic and Bodily Transgressions in New Spain." *Ethnohistory* 54.1 (2007): 129–57.

———. *Hall of Mirrors: Power, Witchcraft, and Caste in Colonial Mexico*. Durham,NC: Duke UP, 2003.

Linhard, Tabea A. *Fearless Women in the Mexican Revolution and the Spanish Civil War*. Columbia, MO: U of Missouri P, 2005.

Lombroso, Cesare. *Criminal Woman, the Prostitute, and the Normal Woman*. 1893. Trans. and ed. Nicole Hahn Rafter and Mary Gibson. Durham, NC: Duke UP, 2004.

Lomnitz-Adler, Claudio. *Idea de la muerte en México*. México, D.F.: Fondo de Cultura Económica, 2006.

———. *Deep Mexico, Silent Mexico: An Anthropology of Nationalism*. Minneapolis: U of Minnesota P, 2001.

López Alcantara, Alvaro. "Negros y afromestizos del puerto de Veracraz. Impresiones de lo popular durante los siglos XVII y XVIII." *La Habana Veracruz/ Veracruz/ La Habana*. Ed. Bernardo García Díaz and Sergio Guerra Vilaboy. Veracruz, México: Universidad Veracruzana; Havana, Cuba: Universidad de La Habana, 2002. 175–91.

López Austin, Alfredo. *Tamoanchan y Tlalocan*. Fondo de Cultura Económico: México, 1994.

————. *The Human Body and Ideology. Vol. I.* Trans. by Thelma Ortiz de Montellando, and Bernard Ortiz de Montellano. Salt Lake City: U of Utah P, 1988.

López, Silvia L. "Beyond the Visible, the Audible and the Sayable: Rethinking Aesthetic Modernity in Latin America." *Parallax*, 20.4, (2014): 93–302.

Lorenzo Camacho, Bernardo. *Leyendas y vivencias de Veracruz.* Veracruz: self-published, n.d.

Lozano, Pepe. "Embracing the African Presence in Mexico." *Peoples Weekly World Newspaper.* Feb. 23, 2006. 16:44. Web. <http://www.pww.org/article/article view/8650/1/142/>.

Lund, Joshua. *The Mestizo State: Reading Race in Modern Mexico.* Minneapolis: U of Minnesota P, 2012.

————. *The Impure Imagination: Toward a Critical Hybridity in Latin American Writing.* Minneapolis: U of Minnesota P, 2006. Print.

Macías, Anna. *Against All Odds.* Westport, CT: Greenwood Press, 1982.

Madrid, Alejandro L. *Sounds of The Modern Nation: Music, Culture, and Ideas in Post-Revolutionary Mexico.* Philadelphia: Temple UP, 2008.

Madrid, Alejandro L., and Robin D. Moore. *Danzón: Circum-caribbean Dialogues in Music and Dance,* New York: Oxford UP, 2013.

Maffie. James. *Aztec Philosophy: Understanding a World in Motion.* Boulder, CO: UP of Colorado, 2014.

————. "Aztec Philosophy." *Internet Encyclopedia of Philosophy.* ISSN 2161-0002. Nov. 11, 2012. <http://www.iep.utm.edu/aztec/>

————. " 'In the End, We Have the Gatling Gun, and They Have Not': Future Prospects of Indigenous Knowledges." *Futures* 41 (2009) 53–65. July 19, 2008. Web.

Manshel, Hannah. "Soldadera: The Unraveling of a Kevlar Dress." *Artbound*: KCET Los Angeles, May 28, 2015. Web. Aug. 8, 2015.

Manuel, Peter. *Creolizing Contradance in the Caribbean.* Philadelphia: Temple UP, 2009.

Markman, Peter T., and Roberta H. Markman. *Masks of the Spirit: Image and Metaphor in Mesoamerica.* Berkeley: U of California P, 1989.

Martínez, Elizabeth C. *Josefina Niggli, Mexican American Writer: A Critical Biography.* Albuquerque: U of New Mexico P, 2007.

Martínez-Echazábal, Lourdes. *Para una semiótica de la mulatez.* Madrid: Editorial Porrúa Turanzas, 1990.

Martínez Maranto, Alfredo. "Dios pinta como quiere: Identidad y cultura en un pueblo afromestizo en Veracruz." Ed. Luz Martinez Montiel. *Presencia africana en México.* México: Consejo Nacional para la Cultura y las Artes, 1997. 525–70.

Marcos, Silvia. "The Borders Within: The Indigenous Women's Movement and Feminism in Mexico." *Dialogue and Difference: Feminisms Challenge Globalization.* Ed. Marguerite Waller and Silvia Marcos. Palgrave Macmillan: New York, 2005.

Marcos, Subcomandante. *Our Word is our Weapon.* New York: Seven Stories Press, 2001.

McDowell, John H. *Poetry and Violence: The Ballad Tradition of Mexico's Costa Chica.* Urbana: U of Illinois P, 2000.

————. "The Mexican Corrido: Formula and Theme in a Ballad Tradition." *Journal of American Folklore.* 85.337 (1972): 205–20.

Medina, Moises. "Soldadera: The Tiny Things They Carried." *Artbound*: KCET Los Angeles, June 12, 2015. Web. Aug. 8, 2015.

Melgarejo Vivanco, José Luis. *Los Jarochos*. Xalapa, Veracruz: Editora del Gobierno de Veracruz, 1979.

Mello, Renato, and Diane Miliotes, eds. *José Clemente Orozco in the United States, 1927–1934*. Trustees of Dartmouth College, Hanover, NH: W. W. Norton, 2002.

Menchaca, Martha. *Recovering History, Constructing Race the Indian, Black, and White Roots of Mexican Americans*. Austin: U of Texas P, 2001.

Mendoza, Vicente. *El corrido de la Revolución Mexicana*. Universidad Autónoma de México: México, 1990.

———. *El corrido mexicano*. México: Fondo de Cultura Económica, 1976.

Mexican Border Ballads and Other Lore. Ed. Mody Boatright. Denton, TX: U of North Texas P, 2000.

Meyer, Michael, and William Sherman. *The Course of Mexican History*. 5th ed. New York: Oxford UP, 1995.

Miller, Marilyn G. " 'The Soul Has No Color' but the Skin Does: *Angelitos negros* and the Use of Blackface on the Mexican Silver Screen, ca. 1950." *Global Soundtracks: Worlds of Film Music*. Ed. Mark Slobin. Middletown, CT: Wesleyan UP, 2008.

———. *Rise and Fall of the Cosmic Race: The Cult of Mestizaje in Latin America*. Austin: U of Texas P, 2004.

Miliotes, Diane. *José Guadalupe Posada and the Mexican Broadside*. New Haven, CT: Yale UP, 2006.

Miranda, Ricardo. *Ecos, Alientos y Sonidos: Ensayos Sobre Musica Mexicana*. Xalapa, Veracruz: Universidad Veracruzana; Fondo de Cultura Económica, 2001.

Moedano Navarro, Gabriel, and Emma Pérez Rocha. *Aportaciones a la investigación de archivos del México colonial a la bibliohemerografía afromexicanista*. México, D.F.: Instituto Nacional de Antropologia e Historia, 1992.

Molina, Fray Alonso de. *Vocabulario en Lengua: Castellana/Mexicana/Mexicana/Castellana. 1555–1571*. 5th ed. Ed. Miguel León Portilla. México: Porrúa, 2004.

Moncayo, José Pablo. *La Mulata de Córdoba: Ópera en un acto*. México: Ediciones Mexicanas de Música, 1979.

Monsiváis, Carlos. *Amor perdido*. México: Ediciones Era, 2000.

Montaldo, Graciela. "Dialogues in Theory: Emancipation and Emancipatory Acts." *Parallax*, 20:4 (2014): 334–44.

Montiel, Luz María, ed. *Presencia africana en México*. México, D.F.: Consejo Nacional para la Cultura y las Artes, 1995.

Mora, Carl J. *Mexican Cinema: Reflections of a Society, 1896–2004*. 3rd ed. Jefferson, NC: McFarland & Co., 2005.

Mora, Sergio. *Cinemachismo: Masculinities and Sexuality in Mexican Film*. Austin: U of Texas P, 2006.

———. *Una muerte sencilla, justa, eterna*. México: Ediciones Era, 1990.

Morton, Patricia. *Discovering the Women in Slavery*. Athens: U of Georgia P, 1996.

Moya Palencia, Mario. *Madre África: Presencia del África negra en el México y el Veracruz antiguos*. Xalapa, Veracruz: Universidad Veracruzana, 2003.

Mraz, John. *Photographing the Mexican Revolution: Commitments, Testimonies, Icons*. Austin: U of Texas P, 2012.

———. *Hechos sobre los rieles: una historía de los ferrocarrileros mexicanos.* [Puebla, Mexico]: Universidad Autonoma de Puebla; [Santa Cruz, Calif.]: Division of Social Sciences, University of California, Santa Cruz, [1988].

Muñoz, Kim Anne Carter. "Huapangueros Reclaiming Son Huasteco in Trans-Local Festivals: Youth, Women and Nahua Musicians." ProQuest Dissertations Publishing, 2013.

Muñoz, Rafael F. "Agua." *20 Cuentos de la Revolución.* México: Factoría Ediciones, 2000.

Muñoz Ramírez, Gloria. *El fuego y la palabra.* City Lights Books: San Francisco, 2008.

"Negros de México piden reconocimiento." *La Jornada.* n.p, June 24, 2007. Web. Oct. 10, 2015.

Nietzsche, Friedrich. *Untimely Meditations.* "On the Uses and Disadvantages of History for Life." Trans. R. J. Hollingdale. 1874. Cambridge UP: Great Britain, 1983.

Niggli, Josephina. *Soldadera. Mexican Folk Plays.* Chapel Hill: U of North Carolina P, 1938.

Ocampo, María Luisa. *El corrido de Juan Saavedra,* 1929. *Perfil y muestra del teatro de la Revolución mexicana.* Ed. Comp. Marcela del Río Reyes. México: Fondo de Cultura Económica, 1997. 314–34.

Ochoa, T. R. "Prendas-Ngangas-Enquisos: Turbulence and the Influence of the Dead in Cuban-Kongo Material Culture." *Cultural Anthropology: Journal of the Society for Cultural Anthropology* 25.3 (2010): 387–420.

Ochoa Serrano, Alvaro. "Mariacumbeche, Mestizo Charros, and Mariacheros." *Musical Cultures of Latin America: Global Effects, Past and Present: Proceedings of an International Conference, University of California, Los Angeles, May 28–30, 1999.* Ed. Steven J. Loza and Jack Bishop. 2003. 35–39.

Olcott, Jocelyn. *Revolutionary Women in Postrevolutionary Mexico.* Durham, NC: Duke UP, 2005.

Old Roots in New Lands: Historical and Anthropological Perspectives on Black Experiences in the Americas. Westport, CT: Greenwood Press, 1977.

Orchard, William, and Yolanda Padilla. "Introducing Josefina Niggi." *The Plays of Josefina Niggli: Recovered Landmarks of Latino Literature.* Madison: U of Wisconsin P, 2007.

Palmer, Colin. *Blacks in Mexico.* Cambridge, MA; London: Harvard UP, 1976.

Palou, Pedro Angel. *El fracaso mestizo.* México: Grupo Planeta Editorial Planeta Mexicana, 2014.

Paredes, Américo, ed. "The Mexican Corrido: Its Rise and Fall." *Folklore and Culture on the Texas-Mexican Border.* Austin, TX: Center for Mexican American Studies, 1993.

———. "The Ancestry of Mexico's Corridos: A Matter of Definitions." *Journal of American Folklore.* 76.301 (1963): 231–35.

———. *"With his pistol in his hand,"* A Border Ballad and Its Hero. 1958. Austin: U of Texas P, 1996.

Parra, Max. "Memoria y guerra en 'Cartucho' de Nellie Campobello." *Revista de Crítica Literaria Latinoamericana,* 24.47 (1998): 167–86.

Paz, Octavio. *El Laberinto De La Soledad.* México: Fondo de Cultura Económica, 1959.

Peñalosa, Joaquín Antonio. *Flor y canto de poesía guadalupana*. México, D.F.: Editorial Jus, 1984.

Peralta, Saúl Chávez. *Emiliano Zapata: Crisol de la Revolución Mexicana*. México, D.F.: Editorial Renacimiento, 1972.

Pérez Fernández, Rolando Antonio. "El son jarocho como expresión musical afromestiza." *Musical Cultures of Latin America: Global Effects, Past and Present: Proceedings of an International Conference, University of California, Los Angeles, May 28–30, 1999*. Ed. Steven J. Loza and Jack Bishop. Los Angeles: Dept. of Ethnomusicology and Systematic Musicology, University of California, Los Angeles, 2003. 39–56.

———. *La música afromestiza mexicana*. Xalapa, Veracruz: Universidad Veracruzana, 1990.

Pescatello, Ann M., ed. *The African in Latin America*. New York: Alfred A. Knopf, 1975.

Phillips, Wendy. "Representations of the Black Body in Mexican Visual Art: Evidence of an African Historical Presence or a Cultural Myth?" *Journal of Black Studies* 39.5 (2009): 761–85. Web. May 10, 2015.

Poniatowska, Elena. *Las Soldaderas*. México: Ediciones Era, 1999.

———. *Hasta no verte, Jesús mío*. México, D.F.: Editorial Planeta DeAgostini, 2003 [1969].

Quintero Rivera, Ángel. *Cuerpo y cultura: las músicas mulatas y la subversión del baile*. Madrid: Iberoamericana, 2009.

———. *¡Salsa, sabor y control!: sociología de la música "tropical."* México: Siglo Veintiuno Editores, 2005.

Quiroz Malca, Haydee. *El carnaval en México: abanico de culturas*. México: Consejo Nacional para la Cultura y las Artes, Dirección General de Culturas Populares e Indigenas, 2002.

Rabasa, José. *Without History: Subaltern Studies, the Zapatista Insurgency, and the Specter of History*. Pittsburgh, PA: U of Pittsburgh P, 2010.

———. "Revolutionary Spiritualities in Chiapas Today: Immanent History and the Comparative Frame in Subaltern Studies." *Race, Coloniality, and Social Transformation*. Ed. Jerome Branche and Elizabeth Monasterios. Gainesville: U of Florida P, 2008. 160–203.

———. *Franciscans and Dominicans Under the Gaze of a Tlacuilo: Plural-World Dwelling in an Indian Pictorial Text*. Morrison Library Inaugural Address Series: University of California, Berkeley, 1988.

Raimon, Eve Allegra. *The Tragic Mulatta Revisited: Race and Nationalism in Nineteenth-Century Antislavery Fiction*. New Brunswick, NJ: Rutgers UP, 2004.

Ramos, Julio. "Descarga acústica." *Papel Máquina: Revista de Cultura* 2.4 (2010): 49–80.

———. *Divergent Modernities: Culture and Politics in 19th Century Latin America*. Durham, NC: Duke UP, 2001.

Ramos, Marisela Jimenez. "'I Am Not the Mulata De Córdoba': The Cultural Meaning of Blackness in Nineteenth-Century Mexico." *Journal of Pan African Studies* 6.1 (2013): 90–109.

Ramsay, Paulette A. "History, Violence and Self-Glorification in Afro-Mexican Corridos from Costa Chica De Guerrero." *Bulletin of Latin American Research* 23.4 (2004): 446–64.

Rancière, Jacques. *The Emancipated Spectator*. London: Verso, 2009.

———. *The Politics of Aesthetics: The Distribution of the Sensible*. London: Continuum, 2004.

Rebolledo Kloques, Octavio. *El marimbol: Orígenes y presencia en México y en el mundo*. Xalapa, Veracruz: Universidad Veracruzana, 2005.

Redondo, Brígido. "Negritud en Campeche. De la Conquista a nuestros días." *Presencia africana en México*. Ed. Luz Martinez Montiel. México: Consejo Nacional para la Cultura y las Artes, 1997. 337–419.

Reed, John. *Insurgent Mexico*. 1914. New York, USA: Penguin Books, 1983.

Reff, Daniel T. "The 'Predicament of Culture' and Spanish Missionary Accounts of the Tepehuan and Pueblo Revolts." *Ethnohistory* 42 (1995): 63–90.

Reyes, Juan Carlos. "Negros y afromestizos en Colima, siglos XVI–XIX." *Presencia africana en México*. Ed. Luz Martinez Montiel. México: Consejo Nacional para la Cultura y las Artes, 1997. 259–333.

Riva Palacio, Vicente, and Juan de Dios Peza. *Tradiciones y leyendas mexicanas*. New York: Thomas Nelson and Sons, 1927.

Robinson, Cedric, and Luz Cabral. "The Mulatta on Film: From Hollywood to the Mexican Revolution." *Race & Class* 45.2 (2003):1–20.

Rodríguez, Domínguez E. *Iconografía Del Danzón*. Habana, Cuba: n.p., 1967.

Rodríguez, Eugene, ed. "Introduction." *Soneros Jarochos*. Mono Blanco. Arhoolie Records, 1990.

Rojas González, Francisco. *La negra Angustias*. México, D.F.: E.D.I.A.P.S.A., 1944.

Romo, Marta. "Y las soldaderas? Tomasa García toma la palabra." *Fem*, (1979): 12–14.

Rosenthal, Debra. *Race Mixture in Nineteenth-Century U.S. and Spanish American Fictions. Gender, Culture and Nation Building*. Chapel Hill; NC; London: U of North Carolina P, 2004.

Ross, John. *¡Zapatistas!: Making Another World Possible: Chronicles of Resistance, 2000–2006*. New York: Nation Books, 2006.

Rout, Leslie. *The African Experience in Spanish America*. Cambridge, MA: Cambridge UP, 1976.

Rowell, Charles H., and Marcus D Jones. "Edgar Cano." *Callaloo* 29.2 (2006): 515–22.

Ruiz, Ramon Eduardo. *The Great Rebellion Mexico, 1905–1924*. 1st ed. New York: Norton, 1980.

Rulfo, Juan. *Pedro Páramo*. México, D.F.: Fondo de Cultura Económica, 1986.

Salas, Elizabeth. *Soldaderas in the Mexican Military: Myth and History*. Austin: U of Texas P, 1990.

Sánchez, Sonia. "V Festival Internacional Danzón Habana 2008." *Cubarte*: La Habana. Web. Mar. 15, 2008. <http://www.cubarte.cu/global/loader.php?cat=actualidad& cont=showitem.php&id=45650&tabla=articulo&seccion=Titulares&tipo=Noticia>

Sánchez Prado, Ignacio M. "The Limitations of the Sensible: Reading Rancière in Mexico's Failed Transition." *Parallax* 20.4 (2014): 372–83.

———. *Naciones Intelectuales: Las Fundaciones de la Modernidad Literaria Mexicana, 1917–1959*. West Lafayette, IN: Purdue UP, 2009.

Saavedra. Leonor. "Staging the Nation: Race, Religion, and History in Mexican Opera of the 1940s." *The Opera Quarterly* 23.1 (2008):1–21.

Sandstrom, Alan R. *Corn Is Our Blood: Culture and Ethnic Identity in a Contemporary Aztec Indian Village.* Norman: U of Oklahoma P, 1991.

Schaefer, Claudia. *Textured Lives: Women, Art and Representation in Modern Mexico.* Tucson: U of Arizona P, 1992.

Schaefer, Stacy B. *To Think with a Good Heart: Wixárika Women, Weavers, and Shamans.* Salt Lake City: U of Utah P, 2002.

Seed, Patricia. *To Love, Honor, and Obey in Colonial Mexico: Conflicts Over Marriage Choice, 1574–1821.* Redwood City, CA: Stanford UP, 1988.

Serrano, Francisco. "La mulata de Córdoba." *Cuentos de espantos y aparecidos.* Ed. Verónica Uribe. Brazil: Editora Ática, 1984.

Sevilla, Amparo. *Los templos del buen bailar.* México, D.F.: CONACULTA, 2003.

Sheehy, Daniel Edward. *The "Son Jarocho": The History, Style, and Repertory of a Changing Mexican Musical Tradition.* Diss. University of California Los Angeles: UMI, 1979. ATT 7921454.

Simeón, Rémi. *Diccionario de la lengua Náhuatl o Mexicana.* México, D.F.: Siglo Veintiuno, 2007.

Simmons, Merle. "The Ancestry of Mexico's Corridos." *Journal of American Folklore* 76.299 (1963): 1–15.

Sjogren, Britta. *Into the Vortex: Female Voice and Paradox in Film.* Urbana: U of Illinois P, 2006.

Socolow, Susan. *The Women of Colonial Latin America.* London: Cambridge UP, 2000.

Sontag, Susan. *On Photography.* New York: Picador [Macmillan], 1977.

Soto, Shirlene. *Emergence of the Modern Mexican Woman.* Denver, CO: Arden Press, Inc., 1990.

Styles, Ruth. "Fashion for Revolutionaries! The Incredible Story of how the Colourful Rebozo Scarf Changed the Course of Mexican History." *MailOnline.* May 28, 2014. Web. Dec. 7, 2014. < http://www.dailymail.co.uk/femail/article-2640556/ The-incredible-story-colourful-rebozo-scarf-changed-course-Mexican-history. html#ixzz3KtFTkfUc>

Sue, Christina A. *Land of the Cosmic Race: Race Mixture, Racism, and Blackness in Mexico.* New York: Oxford UP, 2013.

Sullivan, Thelma D. "Tlazolteotl-Izcuina: The Great Spinner and Weaver." *The Art and Iconography of Late Post-Classic Central Mexico.* Ed. Elizabeth Hill Boone. Washington, DC: Dumbarton Oaks, 1982. 7–36.

Tait, Malcolm. "Towers of Silence." *The Ecologist* 10 (2004): 14. *ProQuest.* Web. Nov. 28, 2014.

Tamayo, Rodríguez C, and Acosta F. Ramos. *Barbarito Diez, El Rey Del Danzón: Textos De Los Coloquios 2005–2007 Correspondientes Al Festival De Música Popular Barbarito Diez.* Las Tunas: Editorial Sanlope, 2008.

Tarica, Estelle. *The Inner Life of Mestizo Nationalism.* Minneapolis: U of Minnesota P, 2008.

Tavanti, Marco. *Las Abejas: Pacifist Resistance and Syncretic Identities in a Globalizing Chiapas.* New York: Routledge, 2003.

Taylor, Diana. *The Archive and the Repertoire.* Durham, NC: London: Duke UP, 2003.

Tuñon Pablos, Julia. *Mujeres en México: una história olvidada*. México, D.F.: Planeta, 1987.

Turner, John Kenneth. *Barbarous Mexico*. Chicago, IL: C. Kerr & Co., 1911.

Urquijo-Ruiz, Rita. *Wild Tongues: Transnational Mexican Popular Culture*. Austin: U of Texas P, 2012.

Varela, Jesse. "Toña la Negra—cantante de México—TT: Tona la Negra—TA: singer from Mexico." *Latin Beat Magazine*. February 2, 2001. <http://findarticles.com/p/articles/mi_m0FXV/is_1_11/ai_73324264>

Vasquez, Irene A. "The Longue Duree of Africans in Mexico: the Historiography of Racialization, Acculturation, and Afro-Mexican Subjectivity." *The Journal of African American History* 95.2 (2010): 183+. *U.S. History in Context*. Web. Sept. 7, 2015.

Vázquez Santa Ana, Higinio. *Canciones, cantares y corridos mexicanos: Coleccionados y comentados*. México, D.F.: Imp. León Sánchez, 1926.

Vaughn, Bobby. "Mexico in the Context of the Transatlantic Slave Trade." *Diálogo*. <http://condor.depaul.edu/~dialogo/back_issues/issue_5/mexico_slave_trade.>

Velasco Toro, José, and Felix Báez-Jorge, eds. *Ensayos sobre la cultura de Veracruz*. Xalapa, Veracruz: Universidad Veracruzana, 2000.

Villarreal, Andrés. "Stratification by Skin Color in Contemporary Mexico." *American Sociological Review* 75.5 (2010): 652–679. Web. May 10, 2015.

Villegas de Magnón, Leonor. *The Rebel*. Ed. Clara Lomas. Houston, TX: Arte Público Press, 1994.

Vincent, Theodore G. *The Legacy of Vicente Guerrero: Mexico's First Black Indian President*. Gainesville, FL: UP of Florida, 2001.

Vinson, Ben, and Bobby Vaughn. *Afroméxico*. México: Fondo de Cultura Económica, 2004.

Wade, Peter. *Race and Ethnicity in Latin America*. London: Pluto Press, 2010.

Weltman-Cisneros, Talia. "Cimarronaje Cultural: Towards A Counter-Cartography of Blackness and Belonging in Mexico." *Journal of Pan African Studies* 6.1 (2013): 125–39.

White, Hayden. *Tropics of Discourse: Essays in Cultural Criticism*. Baltimore: John Hopkins UP, 1978.

———. *The Content of Form: Narrative Discourse and Historical Representation*. Baltimore: John Hopkins UP, 1987.

Wiegman, Robyn. *American Anatomies: Theorizing Race and Gender*. Durham, NC: Duke UP, 1995.

Williams, Gareth. *The Mexican Exception: Sovereignty, Police, and Democracy*. New York: Palgrave Macmillan, 2011.

Winifield Capitaine, Fernando. Comp. *Esclavos en el Archivo Notorial de Xalapa, Veracruz. 1668–1699*. Veracruz, México: Universidad Veracruzana, 1984.

Womack, John. *Zapata and the Mexican Revolution*. New York: Knopf, 1969.

Wood, Warner W. *Made in Mexico: Zapotec Weavers and the Global Ethnic Art Market*. Bloomington: Indiana UP, 2008.

———. "Flexible Production, Households, and Fieldwork: Multisited Zapotec Weavers in the Era of Late Capitalism." *Ethnology* 39. 2 (Spring, 2000): 133–48.

"Yanga, Mata Clara and Nearby Villages: Africa in Contemporary Mexico/Yanga, Mata Clara y Pueblos Cercanos: Africa En México Contemporánea." *Callaloo: A Journal of African Diaspora Arts and Letters* 31.1 (2008): 1–11.

Zackodnick, Teresa. *The Mulatta and the Politics of Race.* Jackson: UP of Mississippi, 2004.

Discography

Kuhn D'Flon, Enrique. *Yanga.* Luzam, 2001.

La negra Graciana. *En vivo desde el Théâtre de la Ville, Paris.* Corasón, 1999.

———. *Sones Jarochos con el Trío Silva.* Corasón, 1994.

Los Negritos. *Los Negritos.* Comosuena, n.d.

The Mexican Revolution: Corridos. "Adelita." "Marijuana, la soldadera." "Valentina." "General Emiliano Zapata Fusilamiento de General Argumedo." Recordings between 1904 and 1974. Ed. Guillermo Hernández. Arhoolie Records, 1996.

Mono Blanco. *Soneros Jarochos.* Arhoolie, 2006.

Toña La Negra. "El Cascabel." *Lamento Cubano.* Perf. Conjunto de Pablo Peregrino, Avelino Muñoz. Orq. Rafael de Paz, Chamaco Domínguez, Juan García. Comp. Tumbao Cuban Classics, 2004.

———. *Cenizas.* Orfeon, n.d.

———. *Colección Bolero.* Orfeon, 2001.

———. *La Sensación Jarocha.* Warner Music Latina, 2002.

———. *20 Éxitos.* BMG, 1995.

Filmography

Aventurera. Dir. Alberto Gout. Estudios Churubusco, 1949.

Angelitos negros. Dir. Joselito Rodríguez, Producciones Rodriguez Hermanos, 1948/1969.

Danzón. Dir. María Novaro. Tabasco Films; Televisión Española (TVE), 1991.

Enamorada. Dir. Emilio Fernández. Panamericana Films, 1946.

Flor silvestre. Dir. Emilio Fernández. Films Mundiales, 1943.

Konga Roja. Dir. Alejandro Galindo. Producciones Raúl de Anda, 1938.

La Cucaracha. Dir. Ismael Rodríguez. Quality Films, 1958.

La mujer del puerto. Dir. Arcady Boytler and Rafael J. Sevilla. Eurindia Filks, 1933.

La Mulata de Córdoba. Dir. Adolfo Fernández Bustamante. Films Mundiales, 1945.

La negra Angustias. Dir. Matilde Landeta. Estudios Churubusco, 1949.

La raíz olvidada. Dir. Rafael Rebollar; Screenplay by Antonio Noyola and Beatriz García. Baltimore, MD: Las Américas Film Network, 2001.

La ruta del son. Dir. Leticia Arriaga Stransky, n.d.

La soldadera. 1966. Dir. José Bolaños. Producciones Marte. Excalibur Media Group, 2004.

La Valentina. 1938. Dir. Martín de Lucenay. Atlántida Films. Distrimax, 2004.

Negro es mi color. 1951. Dir. Tito Davison. Filmex. Pegassus Films, 2010.

Pancho Villa y Valentina. Dir. Ismael Rodríguez. Películas Rodríguez, 1960.

¡Qué Viva México! Dir. Sergei Eisenstein. Mosfilm Production, 1931/1979.

Ramona: Mujer, Indígena, Rebelde. . . . Dir. José Luís Contreras, María Carmen Ortiz. Colectivo Perfil Urbano A. C., 2006.

Salón México. Dir. Emilio Fernández. Clasa Films Mundiales, 1949.

Santa. Dir. Luís G. Paredo. Edicciones Camus, 1918.

Son Jarocho. Dir. Francisco Viveros Domínguez. Producciones OMSA, 2006.

Index

abnegación (erasure of self), 4, 6–7, 9, 21, 56–60
Acuña y Rossetti, Elisa, 62
"La Adelita," 79, 81–91, 105–109, 116, 119
  "Adelita" character in *Soldadera* (Niggli), 106–113
  Adelita complex and, 83–91, 287n5
  "La Adelita" *corrido*, 32, 83–91
  Cucaracha/Adelita dichotomy, 3–4, 11, 21–22, 29–30, 40, 71, 92–93, 95, 118–119, 121
  emergence of, 71, 82– 84
  nature of tropes, 81–83
  other names for "adelitas," 84, 89
aesthetic, 17–24
  aesthetic reciprocity, 17–19
  contradictions of popular sensorium, 21–22
  "distribution of the sensible" (Rancière), 18–20
  significance of, 17–18
  weaving metaphor, 22–24, 284n16
Afro-Caribbean rhythms, 2, 217, 257–263. *See also* Toña la Negra
Afro-Cubans, 3, 4–5, 185, 223–224, 241–249. *See also* Veracruz
Afro-Mexicans. See also *mulatas* (women of African and Spanish ancestry); slavery; Toña la Negra; Veracruz

"The African Presence in México: From Yanga to the Present" exhibit, various locations (2006–2011), 139
Angelitos negros (film), 31, 187, 205–212, 213, 215, 216, 223
authoritarianism of México, 20
blackface/blackbody and, 191, 203, 206, 208–209, 215–218, 222, 226, 263, 295n22
caricatures of, 4–5, 22
Christianity and, 151–152, 157–158
creole consciousness and, 149–153, 206
geographic distribution of, 149–150
history in México, 16, 149–153, 251–253, 279–280
invisibility in Mexican history, 2–3, 148–153, 185, 204–205, 209–212, 219, 223–224, 271–272, 279–280
La Mulata de Córdoba (film), 31, 154, 185–187, 213, 218–222, 226
La negra Angustias (film), 31, 187, 188–192, 202–204, 207, 213, 221–222
La negra Angustias (Rojas González), 31, 64, 141, 187, 189–205
Negro es mi color (film), 31, 187, 212–218, 220, 221, 223
plural-world dwelling by, 167–173, 177–178, 180
population size, 30, 147–149, 150

Afro-Mexicans *(continued)*
  Carmen Robles, *soldadera,* iv, xi, xii,
    21, 138–142, 188–189
  Graciana Silva (La Negra Graciana),
    242–243, 271–272
  as *soldaderas,* 30, 116, 138–141
  terms for, 185
  "third root" of México, 251–253
  unknown origins of, 185, 223–224,
    271–272
  urban concentration of, 150–152, 218
  as "visitors," 16
  witchcraft and, 153–164, 172–183
Against All Odds (Macías), 59–60, 189
AGN (Archivo General de la Nación,
    Mexico City), 31, 90, 165–166, 231
Agnew, John A., 52–53, 80, 285n7
agon, 23
"Agua" (Muñoz), 103–104
Aguascalientes Convention, 19
Aguilar Mora, Jorge, 128–129, 135,
    136
El águila y la serpiente (Luís Guzmán),
    189
Aguirre Beltrán, Gonzálo, 30, 148,
    175–177, 228, 285n17, 292–293n34
Aguirre, María, 63
Alarcón, Ruiz de, 166
Alberro, Solange, 154–155, 292n31
Alcántara López, Álvaro, 231
Alemán, Miguel, 230, 294n6
Alfonso Castillo, Luís, 229
Amaro, Joaquín, 65
Amazon trope, 91, 190, 192, 193–198,
    279
American Anatomies (Wiegman), 7–9
Amigas del Pueblo, 62
Amor perdido (Monsiváis), 58, 93, 99,
    281
amulets, 160, 176, 178–180
Ángeles, Felipe, 89–90
Angelitos negros (Caignet), 205
Angelitos negros (film), 31, 187,
    205–212, 213, 215, 216, 223
Aparicio, Francés R., 255–256, 257, 268
Appadurai, Arjun, 14

Archive and the Repertoire, The (Taylor),
    50–51
Archivo General de la Nación (AGN,
    Mexico City), 31, 90, 165–166, 231
Arcocha, Joseph de, 180–182
Arévalo, Pepe, 225
Argumedo, Benjamín, 89–90, 107, 112,
    135–136
Arias Hernández, Rafael, 251, 252
Aristotle, 1
Armendáriz, Pedro, 259
Arrizón, Alicia, 105
Asturias, Miguel Ángel, 154
asyndeton, 55–56
Aventurera (film), 258, 259
Ayotzinapa, 20
Aztec Philosophy (Maffie), 11–12
Azuela, Mariano, 6, 39, 93–96, 98–101,
    107, 123, 131, 189, 203

"La Bamba" (song), 32, 150, 230, 238
Bañuelos, Hermanos, 79
Barba, Meche, 259
Barragán, Miguel, 91
Barthes, Roland, 37–38, 40, 68
  on *punctum,* 71–74
Bartra, Eli, 191, 203
Bartra, Roger, 4, 24, 267, 299–300n56
Becerra Lumbreras, Leandra, 274–277
Benítez, Lucecita, 268
Bennett, Herman, 30, 151, 158, 177
Bernal Jiménez, Miguel, 163
Bernardo Couto, José, 154
Birth of a Nation (film), 192
blackface/blackbody, 191, 203, 206,
    208–209, 215–218, 222, 226, 263,
    295n22
Blackface Cuba, 1840–1895 (Lane), 217
black magic, 172–183
Black Mexicans. *See* Afro-Mexicans
Blacks in Colonial Veracruz (Carroll),
    149–152
Blanco Borelli, Melissa, 186
Bolaños, José, 47–48, 101, 117, 118
bolero, 32, 198, 225, 228, 254, 256, 270
Bórquez, Josefina, 116, 122

Brecht, Bertolt, 97
Bristol, Joan Cameron, 154, 158,
    159–160, 172, 176
Brooks, Peter, 207–208
Brown Berets, 91
Bufo Habanero, 217, 245, 248
Burkhart, Louise M., 15–16, 284n10
Buscaglia-Salgado, José F., 239
Bustamante, Nao, 76, 91, 273–277

Caballero, Fernán, 92
Los Caballeros Templarios, 143–144
cabaretera (cabaret girl) films, 217, 222,
    258–260, 263, 293n4
Cabral, Luz, 190–192, 193, 204–205
Cabrera, Lydia, 178–179
Las Cafeteras, 238, 242
Cage of Melancholy, The (R. Bartra), 4,
    267, 299–300n6
Caignet, Félix B., 205
Calderón, Antonio, 158
call-and-response, 235, 240, 272
A calzón amarrado (Serrano), 68
Camera Lucida (Barthes), 37–38
campesinos, 5, 6, 288
Campobello, Nellie, 30, 73, 105, 113,
    116
    and death, 127–138, 141–142
    as literary figure, 116, 127–138
Cano, Edgar, 227, 267
Cano, Gabriela, 64, 112
canto responsorial (call-and-response),
    235, 240, 272
Cantú, Norma, 91, 287n5
Cárdenas, Tomás, 158, 172
Carillo, Julián, 161
Carlota (Sandi), 162
Carlota, Emperatriz, 163
carnival, 248–251, 259
Caro Baroja, Julio, 154–155
Carolina Playmakers (Chapel Hill), 104,
    105
Carpentier, Alejo, 231, 244–245
Carranza, Venustiano, 37, 62–63, 65,
    85, 120
Carroll, Patrick, 149–152, 170

Cartagena, Colombia, 27
Cartucho (Campobello), 113, 116,
    127–138
    "Nacha Ceniceros," 73–74, 130–131,
    138
Casasola, Agustín Victor, xii, 9, 21, 30,
    37, 39, 40, 138–139, 141, 142, 188
Casasola, Gustavo, 40, 188–189
"El cascabel" (song), 270
castas, 152, 280, 291n14
Castellanos, Rosario, 191
Castillo, Debra A., 4, 13, 50, 66, 68,
    70–71, 94–95, 110, 143
castizos, 151, 152, 291n13
Catholic Church. *See also* Christianity;
    Inquisition
    "El Chuchumbé" (song) and, 32,
    231–235, 260, 272
    conversion of African slaves to
    Christians, 151–152
Cecilia Valdés (Villaverde), 215
Ceniceros, Nacha, 130–131, 138
chachachá, 244
Chac Mool, 274–277
Chávez, Carlos, 154, 161–162, 164
Chica Geliz, Ricardo, 27
Chicano/a activists, 91, 113, 143–144,
    287n4
"La Chingada," 283–284n7, 299–300n56
"Chingadalupe" (Bartra), 4, 267,
    299–300n56
Los Chinos Ramírez, 245
Christianity. *See also* Inquisition
    Afro-Mexicans and, 151–152,
    157–158
    La Mulata de Córdoba and, 174
    slavery and, 151–152, 157–158
    Antonia de Soto and, 171, 174–183
"El Chuchumbé" (song), 32, 231–235,
    260, 272
Cinemachismo (S. Mora), 4
Clifford, James, 14, 28, 41–42, 45, 50,
    54, 126
Codex Telleriano-Remensis, 167–168
Colonial Blackness (Bennett), 30
comadre, 206, 295n18

Comedia Mexicana, 96–97
El corrido de Juan Saavedra (Ocampo),
    96–98, 100–101, 107
Corro Lara, Julio César, 237
Cortés, Hernán, 148, 150, 283–284n7
costumbrismo, 287n17
creole consciousness, 149–153, 206
Creolizing Contradance in the Caribbean
    (Manuel), 244
Crespo, Francisco J., 257, 260
Cruz, Celia, 252–253
*Cuando las negras de Chambacú se
    querían parecer a María Félix*
    (Chica Geliz), 27
Cuauhtémoc, 26, 62, 163
Cuba. *See* Afro-Cubans
La Cucaracha (film), 94–98, 118, 198,
    203, 285n2
Cucaracha/Adelita dichotomy
    in *corridos,* 29–30, 92–93, 106–107
    nature of, 3–4, 11, 21–22, 40, 71, 95
    in Niggli, 106–112
    in Reed, 118–119, 121
"La Cucaracha"/"The Cockroach,"
    1–3, 29–30, 32, 39, 81–82,
    88–90, 92–93, 106, 116. *See also*
    Cucaracha/Adelita dichotomy
    nature of tropes, 81–83
    peasant scavenger trope, 98–102,
    122–127
    "La Pintada" and, 93–98
El cuento Veracruzano (Leal, Comp.),
    154
curanderismo, 173
Curiel, Gonzalo, 254

danza habanera, 245
danzas, 230
danzón, 32, 228, 243–249, 251, 252,
    271, 272
Danzón (film), 243–244, 271–272
Danzonera Veracruz, 245
death
    and Nellie Campobello, 127–138,
    141–142
    in "El Chuchumbé" (song), 233–234

and "Elizabetta" (*Insurgent Mexico,*
    Reed), 117–118, 141–142
and "Jesusa" (*Hasta no verte, Jesús
    mío,* Poniatowska), 124–127,
    141–142, 289n5
and melancholic *mestizaje,* 24–25
Nahua views of, 125–127
De Certeau, Michel, 10, 43–45, 47,
    51–52, 54, 56, 120–121, 136, 279
Deeds, Susan M., 168, 169, 171, 176,
    181–183
Deep Mexico, Silent Mexico (Lomnitz-
    Adler), 9
Deleuze, Gilles, 16, 18
Delgadillo, Theresa, 206, 209
Delgado Calderón, Alfredo, 236
Delgado-P., Guillermo, 47, 53
Del Río, Dolores, 95, 118
Derrida, Jacques, 136, 284n13
Díaz Balsera, Viviana, 166–167, 173
Díaz regime, 62, 63–64
Dios Peza, Juan de, 155
"distribution of the sensible" (Rancière),
    18–20
Divergent Modernities (J. Ramos), 280
Dorotea (slave), 172
Dow, James W., 173
Doyle, Jennifer, 277
Dromundo, Baltasar, 85
drug cartels, 143–144
Duvalier, Armando, 89

Earth Mother/War goddess, 285–286n8
Easy Women (Castillo), 4, 66, 68
Edsheim, Nina, 265, 266
Eguía, Francisco, 150
Eisenstein, Sergei, 117, 273
Elena (Hernández Moncada), 162–163
"Elizabetta" (*Insurgent Mexico,* Reed),
    47, 73, 81–82, 100, 116, 117–122,
    288n23
Eloy Blanco, Andrés, 205–206, 254, 256
Emancipated Spectator, The (Rancière),
    17, 22
*Emergence of the Modern Mexican
    Woman* (Soto), 63

Enamorada (film), 203, 285n2
"Enamorada" (song), 256
"Encuentro de Jaraneros"/"The
    Encounter of the Jaraneros"
    (event), 237
"Encuentro Jaranero" (California), 238
Escobar, María Luisa, 63
Esperanza Iris Theater, 256
Espinosa Barrera, María de la Luz (La
    Coronela de Yautepec), 189
La Estanzuela, 237

Faílde, Miguel, 244
fandango, 236–238, 241, 297n19, 297n21
Farquharson, Mary, 237–238, 242
Farrera, Remedios, 189–191
*Fearless Women in the Mexican
    Revolution and the Spanish Civil
    War* (Linhard), 7, 85, 86
Félix, María ("La Doña"), 18, 27, 39,
    94–96, 118–119, 198, 203, 285n2,
    294n11
female agency, 108, 110, 143–144,
    197–198, 221–222
Earth Mother/War goddess, 285–286n8
soldaderas and, 57, 66–71, 73–74,
    84–88, 93–98, 117–127, 138–144
Fernández Bustamante, Adolfo, 154,
    185–187, 218–219
Fernández, Emilio, 95, 248
Ferrero, Guglielmo, 140
Festival Cómo suena la clava (Xalapa),
    249–250
Festival Danzón Habana, 247
Festival de la Candelaria, 237
Festival de Son Montuno (Veracruz),
    249–251
Figueroa Hernández, Rafael, 231, 236,
    245, 249–250, 252, 256, 264–265
film. *See* Golden Age of Mexican
    cinema
Fiol-Matta, Licia, 225, 268–269, 295n2
Flores, Pedro, 254
Flores y Escalante, Jesús, 245, 248,
    298nn32–33
Flor Silvestre (film), 203

food shortages
    of 1624, 170
    of 1692, 170
    of 1915, 93
Fototeca, Mexican Institute for
    Anthropology and History, 21, 89,
    139, 140, 188–189
Francisco Villa y la "Adelita"
    (Dromundo), 85
Franco, Jean, 4
French Revolution, 102
Furst, Jill, 125, 126, 177

Galindo, Blas, 1, 154
Galindo, Hermila, 62–63
Gamboa, Federico, 68, 96, 259
Garay, Sindo, 254
García Canclini, Nestor, 284n15
García Diaz, Bernardo, 241–242, 246
García Riera, Emilio, 206, 222–223
García, Tomasa, 85–86
Garrido, Juan, 2
Gatica, Valentina, 89
General Archives of the Nation (Mexico
    City), 31, 90, 165–166, 231
Gift of Death, The (Derrida), 136
Giménez, Catalina H., 87
Golden Age of Mexican cinema, 27,
    185–224, 257, 285n2
    Angelitos negros (film), 31, 187,
        205–212, 213, 215, 216, 223
    La Mulata de Córdoba (film), 31, 154,
        185–187, 213, 218–222, 225–226
    La negra Angustias (film), 31, 187,
        188–192, 202–204, 207, 213,
        221–222
    Negro es mi color (film), 31, 187,
        212–218, 220, 221, 223
Golpazos, Juana, 166, 167, 176, 183
Gómez de Avellaneda, Gertrudis, 191,
    220
González Echevarría, Roberto, 246–247
Gran Caribe, 252
Griffith, D. W., 192
"Las Guadalupanas," 102–113
Guatarri, Felix, 18

Guatemotzín, 163
Guerra, Jorge, 39
Guerrero, Julio, 59–60
Guerrero, Vicente, 152, 205, 280
Guiú, Emilia, 206
Gutiérrez de Mendoza, Juana, 62
Gutierrez, Laura G., 4, 26
Gutmann, Matthew, 5

hacienda system, 97, 101
Hall of Mirrors (Lewis), 5
Hallward, Peter, 19
Hartman, Saidiya, 197, 198, 209–211, 263
Harvey, David, 52
Hasta no verte, Jesús mío (Poniatowska), 64, 84, 113, 116, 122–127
Hechos sobre los rieles (Mraz), 42
Hegemony and Socialist Strategy (Laclau and Mouffe), 14
Hernández, Gerónimo, 40–41
Hernández Moncada, Eduardo, 162–163
Hernández, Rafael, 254
heroic *corridos*, 92–93
Herrera-Sobek, María, 86–87, 89, 92–93, 105
Hershfield, Joanne, 208
Hijas de Cuauhtémoc, 62
Historia Gráfica De La Revolución, 1900–1954 (G. Casasola), 40, 188
Historia Tolteca-Chichimeca, 49–50
Holguín, Alberto P., 90
huapango, 162, 270, 297n19
Huastecan Náhuatl, 23, 284n13, 284nn10–11, 297n19
    inamic ("complementary opposites"), 23
    olin ("deified movement"), 10, 15, 27, 28, 32, 45, 47, 80, 124, 127, 284n10, 284n14
    tlacuepa (turning or twisting of words), 10, 11–12, 15, 16–17, 27, 284n10
    tlalticpac ("on point or summit of earth, Náhuatl), 10, 15–16, 17, 27, 284n10

Huesca, Andrés, 242, 298n29
Humo en los ojos (film), 259, 269
hypermasculinity, 4, 5

inamic ("complementary opposites," Náhuatl), 23
Independence Movement (1810), 2, 58–59
Indians. *See* indigenous people
indigenismo, 25
indigenous people. *See also* Huastecan Náhuatl
    Nellie Campobello and, 133–135
    cult of *mestizaje*, 24–25
    current mobilization of, 143
    "Elizabetta" (*Insurgent Mexico*, Reed), 47, 73, 81–82, 100, 116, 117–122, 288n23
    feminization of, 5
    linguistic assimilation of, 190
    paternalism and, 22, 182
    plural-world dwelling by, 167–173, 177–178, 180, 182
    Pueblo revolt (1680), 168–169
    Tepehuan uprising (1616–1620), 168–169, 173–174
    weaving metaphor, 22–24
Infante, Pedro, 206
Inner Life of Mestizo Nationalism, The (Tarica), 25
Inquisition, 30–31
    "Chuchumbé," 32, 231–235, 260, 272
    "La Mulata de Córdoba" legend and, 153–164
    Antonia de Soto and, 139–140, 149, 160, 164–169, 171, 172, 174–183, 223, 234–235
    witchcraft and, 153–164, 172–183
Instituto Nacional de Bellas Artes (INBA), 162
Instituto Nacional Indigenista (INI), 190, 294n6
Insurgent Mexico (Reed), 113
    "Elizabetta," 47, 73, 81–82, 100, 116, 117–122
"International Afro-Caribbean Festival" (Veracruz), 251–252

Into the Vortex (Sjogren), 267–268
Irwin McKee, Robert, 4, 5, 6
IVEC (Institute of Culture of Veracruz), 248, 251–252, 257

"El Jarabe gatuno," 231, 235
jarana (instrument), 235, 236, 240, 272, 297
jarocho, 32, 227–229, 256–257
Los Jarochos (Melgarejo Vivanco), 296n9
"Jesusa" (*Hasta no verte, Jesús mío,* Poniatowska), 64, 84, 113, 116, 122–127, 289n5
Jiménez y Muro, Dolores, 62
Johnson, Mark, 13–14
Jones, Marcus D., 227
José Clemente Orozco in the United States, 1927–1934 (Mello and Miliotes, eds.), 99
Juana (slave), 172
Junco, Tito, 259
Junco, Victor, 218

Karttunen, Frances, 284n14
Klein, Cecilia, 23
Koch, Frederick, 104
Konga Roja (film), 225–226, 258, 259

El Laberinto De La Soledad/Labyrinth of Solitude (Paz), 4
Laclau, Ernesto, 14
Lakoff, George, 13–14
Lamento Cubano (album), 256, 270, 300n58
"Lamento jarocho" (song), 256, 260–263
Landeta, Matilde, 141, 188–192, 202–204, 221
Land of the Cosmic Race (Sue), 25–26, 252
Lane, Jill, 217
Lara, Agustín, 249, 254–269, 292n25
Lazo, Agustín, 154, 157, 159–161
League of Decency in México, 248, 263
Leal, Luis, 154
Lewis, Laura A., 5, 160, 170–171, 177, 181

Leyendas de Guatemala (Ángel Asturias), 154
Lille, Pedro de, 256
Linhard, Tabea A., 7, 85, 86, 106, 108, 109–110, 128–131, 134
Llerenas, Eduardo, 243
Lola Casanova (Rojas González), 189, 204
Lombroso, Cesare, 140, 198, 289–290n12
Lomnitz-Adler, Claudio, 9, 24
London Museum of Textiles, "Made in Mexico: The Rebozo in Art" (2014), 76–77
López Austin, Alfredo, 15, 176–177
López, Marga, 217
Los de abajo/The Underdogs (Azuela), 6, 39, 93–94, 98–101, 189, 203
Loyola Fernández, José, 247
Lucio, Juana, 63
Luís Guzmán, Martín, 129, 142, 189
Lund, Joshua, 24

Maceo, Antonio, 245–246
Macías, Anna, 59–61, 66, 189
Macías, José, 249
Madame Butterfly (Puccini), 157
Madero, Francisco, 62
Madero, Sara, 65
Madrid, Alejandro L., 161–162
Maffie, James, 10, 11–12, 23
Magdaleno, Mauricio, 163–164
Mail Online (Styles), 76
malinalli, 12, 23
La Malinche, 4, 70, 95, 148, 283–284n7
Mallarmé, Stéphane, 18
mambo, 244, 298n40
"mammy" trope, 7, 206, 213, 215, 222
Manichean polarization, 126, 207
Manshel, Hannah, 274
Manuel, Peter, 244, 246
"Marijuana, la soldadera" (song), 79
marimbol, 241
Martí, José, 206, 245–246, 280
Martínez Baños, Roberto, 70
Martínez de Castrejón, Sebastiana, 172
Martínez-Echazábal, Lourdes, 239
Martínez Maranto, Alfredo, 185

"La Mulata de Córdoba" legend, 3–4, 30–31, 149, 153–164, 166, 171–172, 174–175, 183, 186, 192, 193, 218, 219, 221, 234–235, 262, 280

mulataje, 239, 262. *See also* Buscaglia-Salgado, José F.

mulata mesmerism, 153–164, 219–220

mulatas (women of African and Spanish ancestry). *See also* Afro-Mexicans; Soto, Antonia de; Toña la Negra
defined, 2, 144, 148
as emblem of otherness, 2, 154–156, 186, 279
invisibility in Mexican history, 14, 148–149
La Malinche, 4, 70, 95, 148, 283–284n7
orphanhood trope and, 14, 148–149, 156–157, 271–272
plural-world dwelling by, 167–173
revolutionary *mulatez* and, 138–144
self-abnegation and, 4, 6–7, 9, 21
sexuality and, 149, 153, 156–158, 159–160, 161, 174–176, 192–198, 213–215, 290n4

Munguía, Enrique, 99

Muñoz, Rafael F., 80, 103–104, 109–110

Murray, Nathaniel, 178

museum exhibits
"The African Presence in México: From Yanga to the Present," various locations (2006–2011), 139
"Made in Mexico: The Rebozo in Art," London Museum of Textiles (2014), 76–77
"Soldadera," Vincent Price Museum (2015), 76, 91, 273–277

músicas mulatas (Quintero), 32, 234, 239–241, 259–260, 265–267, 270

música tropical, 30–32, 210, 228, 234, 235, 238–239, 248, 250

myth of objectivism (Lakoff and Johnson), 14

"Nacha Ceniceros" (*Cartucho,* Campobello), 73–74, 130–131, 138

Naciones Intelectuales (Sánchez Prado), 5–6

Náhuatl. *See* Huastecan Náhuatl

National Archives of the Nation (Mexico City), 31, 90, 165–166, 231, 292

National Indigenous Institute (INI), 190, 294n6

National Symphony Orchestra, 161

Natives. *See* indigenous people

Natural History of the Soul in Ancient Mexico (Furst), 125

Navar, Isabelle, 91

La Negra (The Black Woman). *See* Toña la Negra

La negra Angustias (film), 31, 187, 188–192, 202–204, 207, 213, 221–222

La negra Angustias (Rojas González), 31, 64, 140–141, 187, 189–205

"La Negra Concepción" (song), 256–257

La Negra Graciana, 241, 242–243, 271–272

Los Negritos, 237

Negro es mi color (film), 31, 187, 212–218, 220, 221, 223

Neri, Margarita, 63–64

Niggli, Josephina, 64, 73, 80–81, 101, 104–113, 126, 134

nobody/nobodiness
hope for, 28
of *soldaderas,* 57
as term, 8–9

"Noche criolla" (song), 262–263

Noriega, Francisco de, 166

Novaro, María, 248–249

"Nuestra América" (Martí), 28, 206, 280

Nueva Era (newspaper), 40

objectivism myth (Lakoff and Johnson), 13–14

Obregón, 65

Ocampo, María Luisa, 73, 96–98, 100–101, 107, 126

Ochoa, Todd Ramón, 179–180

October Revolution (Russia), 117

Olcott, Jocelyn, 4, 6–7

olin ("deified movement," Náhuatl), 10, 15, 27, 28, 32, 45, 47, 80, 81, 124, 127, 284n10, 284n14

Olola, Lucas, 292–293n34

"Oración Caribe" (song), 262–263

Orchard, William, 104–105, 108, 110

Orozco, José Clemente, 98–99, 101

Orozco, Pasqual, 41

orphanhood trope, 2–4, 14, 148–149, 156–157, 185, 223–224, 271–272

Other/otherness, 2, 4, 6–9, 120, 154–156, 186, 267, 279

Pacheco, Severiano, 245–246

Padilla, Yolanda, 104–105, 108, 110

Palancares, Jesusa (*Hasta no verte, Jesús mío*, Poniatowska), 64, 84, 113, 116, 122–127

palenques (fortified runaway slave colonies), 150

Palo, 167, 179, 183, 293n35

pardos, 228

Paredes, Américo, 89

Parra, Max, 131, 132–133

patronymics, 8, 21, 92–93, 95, 107, 144, 218–219

Paz, Octavio, 4, 24

Pedro Páramo (Rulfo), 281–282

Peña Nieto, Enrique, 284n9, 294n16

Pennington, Campbell W., 169–170, 182

Peregrino Álvarez, María Antonia del Carmen, 249, 253. *See also* Toña la Negra

Peregrino, Pablo, 270

Pérez Fernández, Rolando Antonio, 240–241

performative "scenario" (Taylor), 29, 41–42, 50–51, 54

Performing Mexicanidad (Gutierrez), 4, 26

peyote, 175–176

Photographing the Mexican Revolution (Mraz), 40–41, 188

Pinal, Silvia, 118

Piñeiro, Ignacio, 254

"La Pintada" (Azuela), 96, 98, 99, 123, 203

"La Pintada/The Painted One," 39, 93–98, 101, 198

"Píntame angelitos negros"/"Paint Me Little Black Angels" (Eloy Blanco), 205–206, 254, 256, 299n48

Pitalúa, Carlos, 249

La Placita Olvera, 238

Plays of Josefina Niggli, The (Orchard and Padilla, eds.), 104–105, 108, 110

Plotting Women (Franco), 4

La población negra de México (Aguirre Beltrán), 148, 228

Poetics (Aristotle), 1

Politics of Aesthetics, The (Rancière), 17, 88

polycentric epistemology (Maffie), 10

Ponce, Manuel, 161

Poniatowska, Elena, 30, 37, 38–39, 40, 46–47, 50, 57, 68, 74, 84, 85, 91, 113, 116, 121, 122–127, 129

Pons, María Antonieta, 258, 259

Porfirian regime, 5, 62, 66, 162, 233, 245

Posada, Guadalupe, 233

Practice of Everyday Life, The (De Certeau), 43–45, 120

Pregoneros del Recuerdo, 249

prendas-ngangas-enquisos, 177–180

Promoter, Cirilo, 238

prostitution
mulatas and, 156
soldaderas and, 66–71, 73–74, 93, 285–286n8

Puccini, Giacomo, 157

punctum (Barthes), 71–74

¡Qué Viva México! (film), 117, 273

Quintero Rivera, Ángel, 32, 234, 238, 239, 241–242, 259, 263–267, 270

Quiroga, Vasco de, 163

Rabasa, José, 4, 10, 20–21, 53, 167–168, 280–281, 283n6

Race and Ethnicity in Latin America (Wade), 25
Raimon, Eve Allegra, 187
La raíz olvidada (film), 243
rajada (tear), 24
Ramirez, Estela, 62
Ramírez, Valentina, 88, 89
Ramos, Julio, 239, 280
Rancière, Jacques, 10, 16–20, 22, 23, 88, 278
   Eurocentrism in, 18–20
rape
   and Campobello, 133–134
   and Niggli, 107–108
   and Rojas González, 194–198
   and *soldaderas*, 61–62, 107–108, 110, 116, 274
La raza cósmica (Vasconelos), 251
Real Academia Española, 228, 229
The Rebel/La rebelde (Villegas de Magnón), 84
Rebolledo Kloques, Octavio, 241
rebozos, of *soldaderas*, 38–39, 41, 56, 74–77, 96, 99, 101, 143, 274, 275, 285n1
Reconquista, 216, 295n19
Red Cross, 62
Reed, John, 30, 47, 73, 100, 113, 116, 117–122, 288n23
Reff, Daniel T., 169, 173
Regeneración y Concordancia, 62
Regis Theater, 96–97
Rentería, Matías de, 165–167, 169, 171, 174, 175, 178–179
El Retiro, 254
Revolutionary Women in Postrevolutionary Mexico (Olcott), 4
Río, Antonio del, 85
Rioarmante, Antonio del, 84
Rio Reyes, Marcela del, 97
Rise and Fall of the Cosmic Race (Miller), 24–25
Riva Palacio, Vicente, 155–156, 160–161, 262
Rivas Mercado, Antonieta, 96–97

Rivera, Bernardo, 256
Rivera, Diego, 97, 98–99
Robinson, Cedric, 190–192, 193, 204–205
Robles, Amelio (transgender), x, 63–64, 112, 141, 142, 303
Robles Carmen (Colonel), iv, xi, xii, 21, 138–142, 188–189
Rodríguez, Eugene, 230, 247
Rodríguez, Ismael, 95
Rodríguez, Joselito, 205–212
Rojas González, Francisco, 31, 64, 140–141, 189–205, 294n13
Rojo, María, 243–244
Romo, Marta, 85
Rosillo Heredia, Eduardo, 246
Routes (Clifford), 14, 50
Rowell, Charles H., 26, 227
Rulfo, Juan, 281–282
rumbera (showgirl) films, 185–186, 222, 225–226, 257, 258, 259, 293n4

Saavedra, Leonora, 157, 162
saber (knowledge), 41, 116–117, 136, 141, 144, 149, 160, 281, 285n3, 290n5
Salamanca, Memo, 298n40
Salas, Elizabeth, 59, 64, 65, 84–86, 91, 92, 190, 285–286n8, 287n5
Saldívar, Gabriel, 230
Salón México (film), 248
Salón México (Veracruz club), 248
salsa, 234, 270
¡Salsa, sabor y control! (Quintero Rivera), 234
Sánchez Prado, Ignacio M., 5–6, 19–20
Sánchez, Sonia, 247
Sandi, Louis, 162
La sangre y la tinta (R. Bartra), 24
San Miguel de las Bocas, 169
Santa (film), 259
Santa (Gamboa), 68, 96, 259
Scenes of Subjection (Hartman), 197, 263
Schaefer, Claudia, 59, 143
Schaefer, Stacy B., 22–23

Scott, Rebecca, 179
Serdán, Carmen, 58, 62
Serrano, Francisco, 147
Serrano, Irma, 68
shamans, 173
Sheehy, Daniel Edward, 230, 231, 240
Silva, Graciana (La Negra Graciana),
    241, 242–243, 271–272
Simeón, Rémi, 284n14
Sinfonia India (Chávez), 162, 291n22
Siquisirí, 237, 242
Sjogren, Britta, 267–268
slavery. *See also* Afro-Mexicans
    abolition in México, 152
    Christianity and, 151–152
    history in New Spain, 150–153, 231
    palenques (fortified runaway slave
      colonies), 150
    "tragic mulatta" trope, 31, 187, 191–
      198, 202, 203, 206–207, 211–214,
      218, 220–221, 239, 257, 283n4
    urban concentration in México,
      150–152, 218
Slippery Earth, The (Burkhart), 15–16
slippery word, 10, 15–16, 28, 122, 144,
    278
Socolow, Susan, 153, 291n17
La soldadera (film), 47–48, 101, 117,
    118
Soldadera (Niggli), 64, 73, 80–81,
    104–113, 288n20
soldaderas, 37–77
    Afro-Mexican, 30, 116, 138–141
    contradictions of image, 2–11, 13,
      39–41, 59–61, 67–71
    cross-dressing by, 9, 21, 63, 88, 96,
      138–141, 142, 289n11
    La Cucaracha (film), 94–98, 118, 198,
      203, 285n2
    female agency and, 57, 66–71, 73–74,
      84–88, 93–98, 117–127, 138–144
    habitus in motion, 41–56, 74
    importance of, 2, 3–4, 13, 14–15,
      28–29, 39–40, 56–60, 64, 286n10
    invisibility in Mexican history, 2–4,
      65–66

Los de abajo/The Underdogs (Azuela),
    6, 39, 93–94, 98–101, 189, 203
    "macho" valiance of, 6–7, 9, 61–64,
      74, 84–88, 285–286n8
    middle- and upper-class women and,
      62–63, 65, 70–71, 80, 93, 95–96,
      127–138
    modern examples of, 65, 143–144
    museum exhibits featuring, 76–77,
      273–277
    mythification of, 58–61, 68–69
    La negra Angustias (film), 31, 187,
      188–192, 202–204, 207, 213,
      221–222
    La negra Angustias (Rojas González),
      31, 64, 140–141, 187, 189–190,
      193–205
    other names for, 84
    "place" and "space" for, 47, 51–56, 80,
      112, 279, 285n7
    prostitution and, 66–71, 73–74, 93,
      285–286n8
    punctum (Barthes) and, 71–74
    qualities attributed to, 8–9
    rape and, 61–62, 107–108, 110, 116,
      274
    rebozos of, 38–39, 41, 56, 74–77, 96,
      99, 101, 143, 274, 275, 285n1
    removal from Mexican army, 22, 65
    Amelio Robles (transgender), x,
      63–64, 112, 141, 142, 303
    Carmen Robles (Colonel), iv, xi, xii,
      21, 138–142, 188–189
    self-abnegation and, 4, 6–7, 9, 21,
      56–60
    as term, 2, 59, 65, 81–83
    trains and, 16, 29, 38, 41–49, 41–56,
      67, 72, 76–77, 77, 79–80, 86, 112,
      189
"Las soldaderas" (Orozco mural), 101,
    102
Las Soldaderas (Poniatowska), 37, 39, 84
Son Clave de Oro, 249, 254
Son Cuba de Marianao, 249
son cubano, 32, 228, 243–249, 269–271,
    272, 298n40, 299n43

Son de la Negra, 1, 3
"El son de la negra"/"The Son of the
    Black Woman" (Galindo), 1
sones, 229–235
   defining, 229–230
   as metaphor, 230–231
   regional differences, 296n10
son jaliciense, 3, 283n2
son jarocho, 30, 150, 157, 162, 186, 219,
    228–231, 235–243, 297n16
   African origins, 238–242
   improvisation in, 240–241
   instrumentation, 235–236, 240, 241,
    242–243, 272
   jarana (instrument), 235, 236, 240,
    272, 297
   La Negra Graciana (Graciana Silva)
    and, 241, 242–243, 271–272
   son cubano and, 32, 269–271, 272
   Toña la Negra and, 256–257, 269–271
Son Jarocho (film), 237, 297n15
Sontag, Susan, 40
Soto Angli, Edilberto, 70
Soto, Antonia de, 31, 139–140, 149, 160,
    164–169, 171, 172, 174–183, 192,
    223, 234–235
Soto, Shirlene, 62–64, 89, 120
Sounds of The Modern Nation (Madrid),
    161–162
Spivak, Gayatri, 109
Stanford, E. Thomas, 240
Styles, Ruth, 76
Sue, Christina A., 25–26
Sullivan, Thelma D., 23
supernumerary role, 4, 16, 19, 27, 222
synecdoche, 54–55, 83, 131, 135, 136

Tarica, Estelle, 25
Tata Vasco (Bernal Jiménez), 163
Taylor, Diana, 10, 29, 41–42, 50–51, 54,
    74–75, 124
teatro bufo, 217, 295n21
Teatro Principal de Veracruz, 245–246
Ten Days That Shook the World (Reed),
    117
Tenochtitlan, 49–50

teotl, 23
Tepehuan of Chihuahua, The, 169
Textured Lives (C. Schaefer), 59, 143
"thinking voice" (Fiol-Matta), 225,
    268–269, 295n2
tlacuepa ("turning or twisting of words,"
    Náhuatl), 10, 11–12, 15, 16–17, 27,
    284n10
tlalticpac ("on point or summit of earth,
    Náhuatl), 10, 15–16, 17, 27, 284n10
Toboso, 182
Tomás de Guadalajara, 171
tonadillas, 230, 235, 238
Toña la Negra, 2, 9, 32, 243, 252–272,
    280
   background, 249, 253–254, 299nn51–
    52
   and Caribbeanity, 225–228, 257–263
   Humo en los ojos (film), 259, 269
   as *jarocha* sensation, 256–257,
    269–271
   Konga Roja (film), 225–226, 258, 259
   Agustín Lara and, 249, 254–269,
    292n25
   La mujer del puerto (film), 259
   La mujer que yo amé (film), 266
   La Mulata de Córdoba (film), 31, 154,
    185–187, 213, 218–222, 225–226
   in performing blackness, 253–256
   and racialization of sound and voice,
    257, 262, 263–269
   recordings, 256, 259, 260–263, 270,
    300n58
   Santa (film), 259
   as "thinking voice" (Fiol-Matta), 225,
    268–269, 295n2
Toscano, Salvador, 39
tragedy, 207–208, 211, 218
Tragic Mulatta Revisited, The (Raimon),
    187
"tragic mulatta" trope, 31, 187, 191–198,
    202, 203, 206–207, 211–214, 218,
    220–221, 239, 257, 283n4
Trejo de Zepeda, Patricia, 70
Treviño, Guillermo, 42, 43
Trío González, 79, 83

tropes, 81–83, 277–279. *See also* "La
    Adelita"; "La Cucaracha"/"The
    Cockroach"
  Chac Mool, 274–277
  "Las Guadalupanas," 102–113
  irony in, 82
  metaphor in, 82–83
  metonymy in, 83, 84, 91, 121,
    141–142, 143, 277–278
  nature of, 12, 54, 81, 113, 142–143
  synecdoche in, 54–55, 83, 131, 135,
    136
Tropics of Discourse (White), 10, 12, 54,
    81–82
Trotacalles (film), 203–204
Tuñon Pablos, Julia, 61, 68
Turandot (Puccini), 157
twisting and turning (concept), 10,
    11–16, 18, 22, 28, 284n10. See also
    tlacuepa ("turning or twisting of
    words," Náhuatl)

United Farmworkers Movement, 91,
    287n4
United States
  citizenship of blacks and women, 7–8
  Mexican inferiority complex and, 65,
    112
  racial attitudes of, 26
  "tragic mulatta" trope, 31, 187,
    191–198, 203, 206–207, 211–214,
    218, 220–221, 239, 257, 283n4
University of California at Berkeley,
    Empowering Women of Color
    Conference (2005), 91
University of California at Riverside
    Special Collections Library,
    273–274
Urfé, José, 244
Urquijo-Ruiz, Rita, 4
Usigli, Rodolfo, 105
Uzcanga-Peregrino, Trio, 254

Valens, Richie, 32, 230, 236
"La Valentina," 24, 29, 89–90, 97–98
Vanegas Arroyo, Antonio, 93

Varela, Jesse, 256
Vargas Dulché, Yolanda, 5
Vargas, Pedro, 263
Vasconcelos, José, 251, 294n9
Vaughn, Bobby, 223, 238, 241
Velasquez, Diego, 278
Vélez, Guadalupe, 61–62
Veracruz, 235–238. *See also* Toña la
    Negra
  Afro-Cubans in, 243–249
  Afro-Mexican culture in, 25–27, 32,
    185, 223–224
  carnival, 248–251, 259
  "La Mulata de Córdoba" legend, 3–4,
    30–31, 149, 153–164, 166, 171–172,
    174–175, 183, 186, 192, 193, 218,
    219, 221, 234–235, 262, 280
  regional festivals, 249–251
"Veracruz" (song), 262–263
Veracruz Institute of Culture (IVEC),
    248, 251–252, 257
"Vereda tropical" (song), 262–263
"Victoria" ("Agua," Muñoz), 103, 104,
    109–110, 112
Villa, Francisco "Pancho," 19, 20–21, 37,
    62, 85, 89–90, 117, 128, 130
Villarreal, Teresa, 62
Villasana López, María, 61
Villaurrutia, Xavier, 154, 156, 157,
    159–161, 185–187, 218, 221
Villaverde, Cirilio, 215
Villegas de Magnón, Leonor, 65, 84–85,
    105, 127
Vincent Price Museum (East Los
    Angeles), "Soldadera" exhibit
    (2015), 76, 91, 273–277
Virgin of Guadalupe, 2, 4, 102–113,
    206, 215
virgin/whore dichotomy, 2–4, 267
Viveros Domínguez, Francisco, 237,
    297n15
*Vocabulario en Lengua: Castellana/
    Mexicana* (Molina), 284n11
voting rights, 143

Wade, Peter, 25

weaving metaphor, 22–24, 284n16
White Cross, 62, 65, 84
White, Hayden, 10, 12, 13–14, 15, 16,
    54, 81–82, 113, 142–143, 277–278
"White Water Lilly, The" (Mallarmé), 18
Wiegman, Robyn, 7–9, 194
Wild Tongues (Urquijo-Ruiz), 4
Williams, Gareth, 19–20, 68–69
witchcraft, 153–164, 172–183
Without History (Rabasa), 283n6
Wixárika (Huichol) communities,
    weaving in, 22–24

Women of Colonial Latin America, The
    (Socolow), 153, 291n17

Yanga (formerly San Lorenzo de los
    Negros), 26, 139, 150
Yanga, Gaspar, 26, 150

Zapata, Emiliano, 20–21, 37, 62, 89–90,
    98, 112–113
zapateado, 230, 235, 236, 237, 251, 296n12
Zapatismo, 3, 20, 28, 62, 64, 201, 204
Zapatista uprising (1994), 25